Letters from the Country
OMNIBUS

Letters from the Country
OMNIBUS

Marsha Boulton

McArthur & Company

First printed in Canada by McArthur & Company, 2001.

Copyright © Marsha Boulton, 2001.

Canadian Cataloguing in Publication Data

  Boulton, Marsha
    Letters from the country omnibus

  Contents: Letters from the country – More letters from the country – Letters from across the country
  ISBN 1-55278-196-8

  1. Farm life – Ontario – Anecdotes. I. Title.

  S522.C3B683 2001   630'.9713   C2001-930111-1

Composition and Design by *Michael P. Callaghan*
Typeset at *Moons of Jupiter* (Toronto)
Interior Author Photograph by *John Reeves*
Cover Design by Tania Craan
Printed in Canada by *Transcontinental Printing*

McArthur & Company
322 King Street West, Suite 402
Toronto, ON, M5V 1J2

The publisher would like to acknowledge the financial support of the Government of Canada through the Book Publishing Industry Development Program (BPIDP) for our publishing activities. The publisher further wishes to acknowledge the financial support of the Ontario Arts Council for our publishing program.

10 9 8 7 6 5 4 3 2 1

This book is dedicated to the loving memory of Alexander "Sandy" Ross — journalist and editor, who encouraged me to write about "stupid sheep tricks" and the vagaries of rural life.

Table of Contents

❧❧❧❧❧❧❧❧❧❧❧

SPRING

SUMMER

FALL

WINTER

Foreword and Acknowledgements

Confession: When I traded my high heels for Wellington boots and moved to the country some 20 years ago, I had no idea what I was doing. The closest I had ever been to a sheep was the Pure Wool tag on a sweater. In fact, I only decided to raise sheep because they looked small enough for me to handle and they only have front teeth on their lower jaw, so they couldn't bite me.

I had been working at *Maclean's*, Canada's national news magazine, where I edited the "People" section and wrote what might best be described as informed gossip. My job involved interviewing celebrities, actors, writers, musicians, poets and politicians. I had cocktails with Sophia Loren and lunch with Cary Grant. Willie Nelson once invited me on-stage with him to sing "Mommas Don't Let Your Babies Grow Up to Be Cowboys," and Cab Calloway offered me a sip of gin from his private stash. I never stood in line at film festivals. If I saw a sign in a night club that said VIPs only, I scooted right in. Plus, the magazine gave me a clothing allowance.

Most mortals would be happy with that, but I felt that I was missing something. It was like a mystical void that refused to reveal itself under fluorescent lights.

I knew how to order a limousine, but I had never seen anything be born. My eggs came in cartons and my chicken was vacuum sealed. Appearances meant more to me than the weather. Half the time I didn't even know what the weather was like because I was sitting in an office cubicle talking on the telephone. The closest I ever came to an agricultural experience was attending the opening night of the Royal Agricultural Winter Fair. When I watched *Green Acres* on television, I identified with Eva Gabor. And counting sheep never occurred to me when I wanted to go to sleep.

So, my move from the city to the country was not a festering dream waiting to be fulfilled. It was a spur of the moment thing; a case of extreme impulse buying. One morning, I was visting friends in the country. By that afternoon, I was in the real estate agent's clutches, signing a mortgage on a yellow-brick Victorian farmhouse and 100 acres of unfenced land somewhere in southwestern Ontario. I knew that it took two hours to get there from Toronto, but I had been meaning to learn to drive anyway. Had I thought too long about the commitment I was making and the huge lifestyle changes it entailed, I might never have embarked on the great adventure.

I have learned a few things in the decades I have spent on the farm. I have learned that dinner is what is served at lunchtime and supper is what you eat at dinnertime. Lunch is a sort of snack that the "ladies" serve when the euchre game ends or the dance is over.

And one thing I know for certain is that my farm will never be mine. I could write BOULTON FARM on the barn in 10-foot high letters, but nobody will ever call it "the Boulton place." No, my farm will always be "the Noonan Place." This despite that fact that no Noonan has trod the land for three generations and those who first settled the land are all ecologically integrated in the pioneer cemetery two farms away from mine. But I don't mind that anymore. It teaches you respect for the past. Ultimately, it is what we, as farmers, do with the land that makes our imprint on the future.

It has been a pleasure writing stories that are basically true about people, animals and events that are basically real. However, as a consequence, you start to gain a certain notoriety in the absolutely real community you live in. For instance, I was attending a luncheon on the day that I learned my first book of rural stories had been shortlisted for the Stephen Leacock Medal for Humour. Nothing fancy. The Board of Directors of the local history society had discovered there was money left over from the sale of a family history book I had helped them edit and they decided a good dinner was the way to spend some of it. I was congratulated vaguely over dessert. Then one Board member raised her chin and asked: "So, if you win will you be on TV?"

As it happened, I did and I was and, occasionally I still am. Many channel changes later, people still stop me on the street to say, "I saw you on TV."

So, I would like to take this opportunity to thank all of the people who have removed themselves long enough from the television to actually to read my stories. I am always pleased when farmers tell me that my stories put them to sleep at night. Knowing how hard farm families work and the stresses they are under, it is a great compliment to be granted any moment of their time.

No one person makes a book happen, but much of the credit must go my publisher of long-standing, Kim McArthur. When I first submitted my rural stories to her, they stood in sheepish contrast to my alternate writing persona, the very same Marsha Boulton who writes wildly entertaining Canadian historical anecdotes in a series of books (and a thick omnibus, like this one) titled *Just A Minute!* However, as luck would have it, Kim's grandfather had been a veterinarian and some of her fondest childhood memories involved accompanying him to various barns where she was awed by such things as the birth of a foal. So thanks to the legacy of Dr. William Drennan, we were off and running. The team at McArthur & Company is a jolly lot of professionals who are a pleasure to work and party with.

I am also grateful to the community of neighbours who have unwittingly contributed to this book. From them, I learned that humour is the observation of an unprejudiced heart. No one has tried to tar and feather me. In fact, a few have taken to calling me and saying, "Marsha, I think I have a story for our new book that you're working on." In addition, listeners to the CBC Radio program *Fresh Air* have assured me there is a universality to many of the experiences I have shared, such as the ritual slaughter of rural mailboxes that happens every spring.

Over the years, my friend, the great Canadian photographer John Reeves, has done a terrific job of capturing the joy I feel when I am with my animals. Urbane as he is, John also has an uncanny ability to correctly guess the weight of live pigs, something that has stayed with him since his boyhood days on the farm.

My Mother was a farm girl, so she understands what it is that drew me to this place. Dad was horrified when he first arrived at the farm and saw the sheep. His English father had owned a wool mill and much of his youth was spent hovering near stinking raw sheep fleeces. He has accepted my choice and learned to enjoy watching wool on the hoof. Most of all, Dad is fond of Wally the Wonder Dog, my lovable English bull terrier who is a clown in a dog suit and a disaster when it comes to herding sheep.

Finally, it takes a special sort of man to survive life with "the crazy lady who raises sheep." I am blessed to have found that man in Stephen Williams, affectionately known as "Moose-cat."

Marsha Boulton
Mount Forest, Ontario

Spring

SOLD ON NIRVANA

When people ask me why I traded city life for life in the country, I always feel that I should have some reasoned and well-thought-out explanation. Instead, I blame it all on a real estate agent who caught me in a romantic moment and played on that vision until I signed on the dotted line.

In years of talking to urban transplants much like myself, I find that I am not alone. The real estate agent I am referring to has become something of a legend.

We call him "the Boss Hog," because in some ways he resembles the portly character who once appeared on a really bad, Cracker-Jack-box of a television series called *The Dukes of Hazzard*. Our Boss Hog also has that streak of unctuousness that seems to flow naturally from the personality of all really good salespeople.

Just like the funeral director who can fit you to a casket while you are still standing, the Boss Hog can figure out what sort of gem of a property you really need in that instant when you pause before the pictures displayed in his Main Street office window. Somehow he manages to cajole shy people — street-proofed people and people who check their children's Halloween apples for razor-blades — to jump into his big shiny Buick and go for a ride. Something about him makes strangers believe that he can lead them to nirvana, and that it is just around the corner.

There are, of course, tricks to the trade. Some back roads look better than others. If the Boss Hog is trying to sell a country lot to someone who wants to build their dream cabin in a sylvan glade, he won't take them past the gravel pit down the road. No, he will drive along a winding wooded concession, where other log cabins are barely visible through the cedar trees and the silence is only broken by the chatter of pheasants in the bush.

If you are looking for a property that has a stream running through it, he will drive you along a route that has a seemingly endless number of bridges that all pass over a bubbling brook.

Perhaps, he will stop to point out a secret trout hole where the river curls around the roots of willow trees. This works best in the early spring when the banks are gushing with clear cold water, or in the fall after the mosquitoes and black flies have gone to rest.

It seems water has a great appeal to most people who are thinking of country life, but not every property actually has a river running through it.

That is no problem for the Boss Hog.

"You're better off starting from scratch," he will say. And from then on the words to watch for are: "This one has an ideal pond site."

Virtually everyone he sells a property to believes that an underground Amazon of water is flowing just beneath the surface of their land, waiting to be tapped and transformed into a picture-perfect, spring-fed pond.

The Boss Hog never takes you past the places where muddy holes in the ground have been waiting for years for water to fill them. But he can recommend a dowser who is so proficient at finding water with a witching rod that he can locate the indoor plumbing in any house without even asking for directions.

There are always lots of properties on the market in the country. But if the Boss Hog has his way, you might be led to think that Eden is almost all sold-out.

I have friends who bought a glorious old stone farmhouse several years ago with every intention of making it a permanent residence. They poured a ton of money into reconstructing the gingerbread trim, creating the perfect wrap-around porch and landscaping with a riot of wild flowers to complement the whole shebang. Things change, and their jobs have since overtaken the dream. They make it out to the country for a few weeks each summer, and at Christmastime the whole family comes up to do the Currier and Ives stuff, but otherwise the place is vacant.

It came as quite a surprise when the urban owners showed up one weekend unexpectedly to enjoy the autumn leaves. There, on the front lawn, was a large real estate sign from the Boss Hog's emporium and across it was a big red "SOLD" sticker. Naturally, the Boss Hog had a simple explanation — just a mistake someone in the office made. The sign disappeared into his trunk, along with a bunch of others.

That is another trick of the trade.

Once you are trapped in that Buick, the "SOLD" signs seem to be everywhere, all of them the product of the Boss Hog. By the time you get to the dilapidated old place that needs a new roof and some severe work done on the septic system, the Boss Hog has you in his crosshairs believing that it may just be the last place on earth that is ever going to come up for grabs.

"There aren't many of these beauties left," he will say, pointing out the hardwood floor underneath the linoleum and scraping the painted banister to show you the cherry wood underneath layers of aged paint.

Anyone will tell you that if you buy an older home there is bound to be some renovation, restoration and re-decorating involved. The Boss Hog can make it sound like an adventure. All of a sudden you feel like Martha Stewart. Visions of frilly country curtains and flower-box herb gardens dance in your head. The bleak, fly-specked wallpaper in every room becomes a blank canvas upon which you will sponge paint and appliqué yourself into heaven on earth. Every dark space with a roof over its head seems to be a perfect candidate for a skylight. There is no end to the possibilities.

Next thing you know, you are signing on the dotted line and the "SOLD" sign becomes a reality.

Buying the rural dream and living it turn out to be two separate realities, but true to the Boss Hog's word, it is an adventure.

I am actually glad I took the drive in the big old Buick all those years ago. One of these days, I expect I will get around to finding the underground river beneath my perfect pond site. Every few years, I pull up some ancient linoleum and finish a few more feet of hardwood floor to a gleaming polish. There is plenty of time to shape nirvana to my liking. Who needs another leaky skylight?

At least with the Boss Hog watching, I will know when I have achieved perfection.

One day, I will come home unexpectedly and find a "SOLD" sign at the end of the lane. The Boss Hog will tell me it was planted in error, but I will know that all of my effort has finally elevated me to "country gem" status.

In the meantime, I think I'll just enjoy the endless possibilities that have no explanation.

MAILBOX MURDERS

Here in the country we still have mailboxes, and on my rural route the mailman, Len, is an expert at deciphering illegible handwriting on envelopes addressed to me. If I put insufficient postage on a letter or parcel, I will often find a note from Len advising me that he paid the extra few cents, and the next day I leave the change in the mailbox for him to pick up. With thanks. Now that is service.

You get attached to your mailbox. It becomes a sort of signpost for directions. In blinding rain or snow, the old mailbox is a faithful and familiar marker.

It's a pleasant walk to my mailbox — a kind of Zen stroll with plenty of time to pause and examine the buds on the trees for signs of spring. And around this time of year there is a particular excitement to fetching the mail, because seed orders are arriving. Every box contains wonderful surprises that looked good in the catalogues during a January blizzard.

So when your mailbox is murdered, it's upsetting. It is also a sure sign of spring.

A few days ago, I found my mailbox lying like a slain thing at the side of the road. Mine was not the only mailbox slaughtered in the night. Mailbox murders tend to be cluster killings.

I have had half a dozen mailboxes cut down in the prime of their lives. At first I used to replace them with those cutesy mailboxes with birds on them or the ones that are shaped like barns and cost 50 bucks. But finally I got smart. At local auctions, I stocked up on well-worn mailboxes in need of a coat of paint.

Pretty mailboxes are primo targets. The ones with a few dents and a bit of rust tend to survive longer. I know one retired farmer who spent an entire winter crafting a Chinese pagoda-shaped mailbox out of Popsicle sticks. It lasted for two days and the remains were never found.

I have sort of resigned myself to the concept of losing a mailbox every spring. But when my neighbour Cheryl's mailbox went down, she organized a midnight posse. Now we call her Sheriff Cheryl.

Although mailbox killers generally strike only one area per year, Cheryl was not going to stand for having her new mailbox destroyed. She patrolled the concession half the night waiting for the return of the midnight whackers. And, surprise, return they did.

All we learned for her efforts was that the vandals drove "a big black car with tail fins." Does this mean we have to be on the lookout for Batman and Robin? It would be fairly ridiculous to ask the police to stand guard at rural mailboxes all night long, so I called the cop shop to find out what we could do to protect our mailboxes without becoming vigilantes. The sergeant in charge of mailbox decapitation told me what I already knew — that it happens every spring.

He said great stuff like, "something in the male nature makes them want to do this sort of stuff in the spring — it could be a coming-of-age ritual or a hormone problem. Our civilization has reached the point that they know they cannot pillage and rape so they take out their aggression on mailboxes." So much for the good news.

His most memorable investigation of box bashing occurred when an entire concession of mailboxes was severed and the boxes were all dumped off on the church's front lawn. Only one mailbox on the concession was untouched. "You don't have to be a dumb cop to figure that one out," he advised.

According to the officer, there isn't much anyone can do to protect a defenceless mailbox.

You could build a stone cairn around the post and weld iron bars around the box, but all that does is present a challenge. Hooligans have been known to use their vehicles as battering rams in such cases. One of my neighbours tried installing a battery-operated burglar alarm. It was activated every time the mailbox was opened. This got to be a bit of a pain in the ear, especially for Len the mailman.

The police officer's fantasy solution was to have neighbours organize a sort of group protection plan. In his "to serve and protect" dream, neighbours would link their mailboxes electronically and stock them with small explosive devices. When a mailbox was molested, the electronic device would send a signal to the next mailbox in the chain causing it to blow up approximately 37 seconds later, thereby terrifying the perpetrators. Nice concept.

I applied a rubber mallet to pound out the major dents in my old blue mailbox. Four-inch screws secured it to the post. Then one day I found it crunched on its side with a mortal crease in the metal — another victim of violence. But this time, I took it personally. Inside the scarred remnants of the mailbox, someone had left a funeral parlour advertisement and an empty beer bottle. This was most disconcerting.

The pattern continued and I lost two more well-aged mailboxes to the beer-bottle basher. None of my neighbours suffered similar attacks. I began to spend more and more time checking the box throughout the day, and inspecting the roadway for walkers, bicyclists and slow-moving vehicles. I had a feeling that some cowardly evil was out to get me through my mailbox. Paranoia? Perhaps, but just because you live in a place where it is actually possible to stop and smell the roses, it doesn't mean that you can drop your guard.

My neighbours agreed that the singular nature of the attack on my box and the signature beer bottle was becoming serially suspicious. Cheryl and her husband Jim came up with the solution, courtesy of a piece of two-by-four. They mounted a plastic mailbox on a wooden box that fits neatly over the mailbox post.

Every day, I transport the box to its post before Len comes, and I pick it up when I know he has delivered. The effect gives me great pleasure. My mailbox is delivered from an evil that is too gutless to attack in broad daylight. And I enjoy two walks to the mailbox every day, taking time to stop along the way.

AWAY IN A MANGER

Pregnant sheep seem to think that they have a lot to complain about. All I hear are grunts and groans from the time I arrive at the barn in the morning to the last barn rounds before bed. Sheep are not mean by nature, but they sure get cranky in the homestretch to lambing.

I can appreciate that they might have mood swings. After all, I'm sure I'd be less than perky if I were carrying twins or triplets and looked like an inflated marshmallow ready to burst. The gestation period for sheep averages out to between 148 and 152 days. The first 100 days are a breeze, but in the last trimester, the lambs start growing — and growing. My library of "how to be a shepherd" books yields the useful advice that as much as 70 percent of the growth of unborn lambs takes place in the last six weeks. Now that's a growth spurt.

The ewes seem to expand on a daily basis. Their sides bulge and the udders that were barely visible two months ago now swell in preparation for milk production. The sheep do not kick up their heels anymore. They sort of shuffle around. If they are in a hurry, they just shuffle faster.

Ewes that used to listen for my footsteps in the barnyard and line up smartly for their grain are now slow to even bother getting up when they see me. They haven't lost their appetites, however. With all of that growing going on, they need extra grain —whole grains only, if you please. I add soya meal for a protein boost and a lick of molasses to make it tasty. This is washed down with so much fresh water that sometimes I swear they should be floating. Ewes with a due date drink four times as much water as usual.

Their hay is only the finest. It should smell as sweet as a summer day and look green enough to take into the house and dress with vinaigrette. Only then is it good enough for my ladies. Since they do not have a lot of room in their four-stage ruminant stomach with all those lambs taking up space, the issue of quality is critical. An old shepherd once told me that he could share his secret of a lifetime with sheep in six words.

"Feed them and feed them well," was all he said.

For all the tender loving care I give, all I get are long lazy sighs. When I scatter their bedding, they lounge uncomfortably looking for all the world as though they expect fluffed pillows instead of simple straw. When they choose to lie down it can take several minutes. First there is the drop to the front knees, followed by a grunt. Then somewhere between gravity and willpower, the hind legs fold and the ewe adjusts the configuration of legs, udder and lambs until she is satisfied.

The demands just never stop. One wants her head scratched; another casts me a baleful glance when I laugh aloud at the antics of a chicken. Some of them enjoy a sliver of apple; others spit it out. There is plenty of attitude. Dominant ewes stake out their territory. They will accept certain of the flock as their neighbours, but nudge away those they do not like. Some ewes snore a bit more loudly than others. Some of them are subject to explosive flatulence.

The older ones know what is going on. They know that this is their time to be pampered. They know that I will forgive every last woolly one of them for being so demanding. Someday soon, I'll be holding a newborn lamb, and that makes all the grunts and groans worthwhile.

LETTING THE AIR OUT

As an urbanite, all I knew about chickens was that I liked to eat them and they were a source of eggs. Much has been learned about the vagaries, species and confounding behaviours of poultry since then, but for me it all started with the "capon."

For years, I had seen the word "capon" used in fancy restaurants where it appeared as a high-priced "breast of" item — usually roasted or grilled — and always "succulent." At city supermarkets, the capon in the poultry section was presented as a meaty chunk of a bird, slightly smaller than a turkey, but always a chunk of change more than common chicken. Add the words "free-range" to capon and the price went even higher. Since my farm seemed to be nothing but free-ranging space, I figured I could make a killing growing capons for my city friends.

Sometime in March, I picked up the list of what sort of chicks were available at the local Co-Op farm supply store. All manner of fowl were itemized — everything from goslings to pheasants. At the bottom of the list, there were capons. They were more expensive, but then by the time they were delivered they would be three weeks old, as opposed to the day-old varieties of most other chicks. Since all of my chicken books said that mortality would be highest in the first few weeks of chick-raising, I figured the added price of buying fully started capons would be worth it. I ordered fifty capons. The hatchery was notified.

By the time "Chick Day" came, I had everything set up according to the book. Heat lamps were strategically placed above the wood shavings in a well-ventilated pen that I had personally disinfected. The chick waterers were slightly raised so that the chicks could not foul them with their fowl droppings. There were long rows of aluminum feeders specially designed to allow only the chicks' heads to get at the food. I even installed a paper towel rack beside the doorway to the pen, lest I needed to wipe anything untoward from my hands.

Chick Day turned out to be a noisy affair. Lining the store alleyways there were corrugated boxes full of peeping, chirping and squawking new life forms. Four boxes had my name on them.

One by one, I unloaded the capons at the barn. They were bigger than the day-old chicks that were on display beside the coffee machine at the Co-Op, but they still had a lot of growing to do. I dunked each tiny yellow beak into the water so that they got the idea right from the start.

Within a few hours they had fed and watered themselves, soiled their fresh wood shavings and settled down to sleep under their cosy heat lamps. I breathed a sigh of relief and went to bed.

The next morning I hurried to the chick pen to see how my partially feathered charges had managed the night. Some were startled to see me scooping food into their troughs, others looked up and ran around in circles. A few just lay there like cantaloupes on the vine.

They looked like cantaloupes, too. While the others were taut packages of feathered wings and downy underbellies, the cantaloupe capons were positively bloated. I knew they were supposed to grow quickly, but this was ridiculous. I picked one up and it felt like yesterday's balloon from a bridal shower. I ran for the phone.

"They're blowing up," the woman at the hatchery told me. "You've got to let the air out."

"Hello," I said, holding the phone in one hand, examining the chick in my other hand as though it was a live grenade. "What do you mean 'blowing up'?"

Patiently, the voice on the other end of the line explained that capons are just male chickens, simple roosters, that have gone through a small surgical process that removes or prevents the manufacture of testosterone. Thus the "caponized" bird grows to adulthood with the frame of a male and the breast meat of a female. In the meantime, air is sometimes drawn into the surgical site, causing the birds to "puff up."

I was told to take a sterilized hypodermic needle and re-puncture the small healing scar area that I would find on the underside of each afflicted chick. This was to be followed by squeezing. "You just squeeze until you've let the air out," the hatchery woman said, as casually as though she was telling me to pour salt on a red wine stain and then vacuum. "Excuse me," I exhaled.

"Well you don't want them to blow up, do you?" came the response.

At this point, I was too early in my career as a farmer to have learned anything about giving animals injections. And I had no idea where I was going to purchase a hypodermic needle in a small rural town without being labelled a junkie.

I called my doctor's office and asked the receptionist to have him call me as soon as possible on an urgent matter of an extremely personal nature involving life or death. He called right away.

"Tom," I whispered into the receiver, "I need a hypodermic needle or my chickens will blow up."

Dr. Tom is a man known for his calm and kindly bedside manner. Even in a crisis situation, his demeanour is such that you have the feeling that just touching the sleeve of his white gown will make everything all right.

"Tell me about it from the beginning," he said.

When I was done, I imagined him holding his head at his desk and chastising himself for not detecting this obvious insanity during a routine check-up.

"Look Marsha," he said. "Just go into the store where you got the chickens and ask them for what you need. It is perfectly legal, trust me. Sterilize the needle with alcohol each time, and make as small an entry as possible without probing into the muscle tissue. Call me if you have any problems."

Okeedokie, I said to myself, and I headed for town.

As casually as possible, I approached the counter where a young fellow with the body structure of a Hereford calf was serving customers.

"I would like a hypodermic needle," I announced.

"You want disposables? What gauge? And do you need a syringe?" he asked as though selling hypodermics was an everyday occurrence.

"Disposables are fine," I blurted. "Small, very small."

"Well, is it for a calf or a pig, or what?" he asked.

By this time our conversation had attracted the attention of waiting customers. I leaned across the counter and quietly said, "It's for my capons. They're blowing up."

Even the stoic Mennonite farmer standing behind me burst out laughing. Red-faced, I left the store with a little brown bag and complete instructions on assembling the device.

Back at the barn, a couple of the chicks had expanded to near volleyball size. I laid out my tools on an upturned grain bucket, wondering all the while what St. Francis of Assisi, the patron saint of animals, would have to say about this schmozzle.

The first one was the scariest. I propped the little fellow on his back against a towel and looked for the troublesome scab site. Then ever so gently I nudged the tip of the needle into the little brown scab.

Nothing happened. There was no sound. The bird did not flinch. I do not know what I was expecting, but this sure was not it.

I picked up the little capon and cradled both puffy sides of him, squeezing him softly with my eyes closed tight. Then I felt a slight breeze on my cheek.

It was working! A slow but steady stream of air was flowing from the tiny hole. My capon was deflating.

It took about five minutes to let all of the air out. I completed the job by spraying the wound site with Bactine and releasing the "patient." He cocked his head and casually trotted off to the feed trough.

I let the air out of a dozen capons that day. All of them lived.

When I was ready to market the capons, customers lined up for the androgynous birds. In accordance with their dubious beginnings, I sold each capon at an inflated price.

FLY WARS

I guess there are some questions that just cannot be answered. For example: "Where do all the flies come from?"

As soon as the sun starts to warm my window panes, flies seem to emerge fully grown to crowd onto the window ledge and buzz away at the outside world where they belong. Who are these flies, and why do they think they should live inside my house?

These are not smart flies. They don't even try to fly away when I come at them with the swatter. And swat as I may, an hour later still more dastardly flies will be buzzing away on the ledge.

I make no claims about being a great housekeeper, but I certainly do not deliberately leave fly food lying around my house. Yet the flies are not starving to death. I don't put out a water bowl for them. So why don't they just dry up or leave?

Granted, I do not live in a hermetically sealed environment. Dogs are always begging to go outside and I am always traipsing out to the barn. I can accept that a couple of flies might slip in occasionally, but that does not explain the hordes of flies on the window ledge in the guest bedroom.

I have tried just about every flying insect killer on the market. The most effective types seem to be those that are used in milking parlours, but considering some of the precautions on the labels I've had to think twice. When a product recommends that a space should be ventilated for 30 minutes after spraying before a half ton cow is allowed back in the room, it makes me wonder how long a person of my body weight has to stay outside.

My grandmother used to hang flypaper in her old farmhouse.

When all the aunts and uncles and nieces and nephews came to visit and the house was bulging at the seams, I'd get to sleep on the kitchen couch next to the woodstove. It was fun, until the morning sun shone through the windows and activated the sleeping flies.

I would wake up to their steady tormented buzzing from the flypaper. I would listen to their little fly screams, and pray for the rooster to start crowing so that everyone would wake up and save me from the chamber of flypaper horrors.

So I will not have flypaper in my house. I tried it in the barn once, but I forgot to tell the banty hen who flew into it while escaping from a dog. Removing flypaper from a frantic chicken is no fun.

I have been told that flies can somehow weasel their way through the smallest gap in old wooden window frames. So I thought about replacing the windows. A friend recently tried this, and I called to find out whether or not it had worked. It hadn't.

The next theory is that flies can weasel their way through old bricks and mortar and underneath shingles. However, the prospect of new windows, new roofing and new walls is utterly unrealistic.

Of course, I could always move. I have a friend who lives in an elegant apartment 21 floors above a busy Toronto intersection. There are no flies up there. The windows do not open. There is no breeze scented with the fresh smell of the earth awakening to a new season. Instead of flies droning, the background sounds consist of sirens and honking horns. Somehow I think putting up with a few flies is a less stressful option.

The fat and furry flies of spring will disappear shortly, to be replaced by the wily and more manageable flies of summer. In the meantime, I will wage war on the many-eyed insects with my faithful vacuum cleaner. I will try not to hear their death buzz as they are sucked into oblivion, and I will show no mercy when I stuff the vacuum nozzle with a rag soaked in bug killer to dissuade any fly escape artists.

In the quiet of the evening, when the lights are out and the flies are dreaming little fly dreams, the spring breeze will rustle through the buds on the lilac bushes. No wonder the flies like it here.

THE RICHEST DOG IN CANADA

One nice thing about being a shepherd is that you are never stuck with providing a boring answer to the ubiquitous urban question, "And what do you do?" Most city people have never met a shepherd. Before I became one, I had never met a shepherd. So after the initial shock of hearing something totally different, some form of discussion is bound to ensue. And that is how the richest dog in Canada came to live with me.

Years ago I was attending one of those mammoth charity affairs orchestrated by the ladies-who-lunch. The theme of the day seemed to be "the lady with the biggest hat wins." Even the people serving lunch wore doilies in their hair. A girlfriend's mother had cajoled me into doing some writing and fund-raising for what was a very good cause. The "free" lunch was my reward. Hatless, I sat where I was told and tried to blend in with the crowd.

There were seven other women at the table and collectively I would estimate that their hat bill could have made a significant dent in the national deficit. They talked amongst themselves about far-flung vacations and hat-hunting expeditions, until a gracious table-mate turned and asked me the ubiquitous question.

A torrent of queries followed about sheep and what it was like to raise sheep and where one acquires the best lamb chops. When the luncheon ended, I was enthused by the prospect of signing up a few new freezer lamb customers. My girlfriend's mother told me that from her head-table position she thought our group seemed to be having the best time in the room.

'"We talked about sheep," I told her.

"Just the thing we need," bubbled my hostess. "Something different."

A few weeks later, one of the women called me at the farm. Her name was Shirley, and I remembered her joking about renting a sheep to trim her lawn. At the time she was married to newspaper potentate Conrad Black, so I suggested a *bête noire* would be appropriate. But Shirley was not calling to rent a sheep. She wanted to arrange an adoption.

The adoptee was a six-month-old Shetland sheepdog, which had been purchased on something of a whim for their children. However, transatlantic travel plans and the general failure of the puppy to adapt to an elite lifestyle had rendered it "a problem." Also, the pup had taken to relieving itself in the master's shoes.

City people often live under the fantastical notion that the kindly farmer always has room for another dog, but so few bother to ask. When they have an unwanted puppy, they drive out into the country and drop the animal off near the end of a laneway for the kindly, anonymous farmer to "find." If it does not wander into traffic, or starve, or become fodder for a hawk, the poor animal is most likely to end up running with other abandoned, wild pets and harassing livestock. Then the kindly farmer ends up having to get out the varmint gun.

If it does not become a dog dumping ground, "the farm" is also often perceived as doggy heaven by people who don't want to live on a farm themselves. I still remember the day my suburban parents told me that our boisterous, wild-hearted mongrel, Bingo, had gone to live on a farm where he could run and be happy. The same six-year-old school chum who shattered the myth of Santa Claus for me told me that Bingo had actually bought the farm on the bumper of a delivery truck. I forgave my parents that betrayal. I still prefer to think Bingo is frisking around a farmyard somewhere.

So when Shirley asked me to take the dog, I recognized her plaintive cry for honourable closure and her good manners.

"One dog's a companion," says the wit and wisdom of my neighbour Elmer. "Two dogs make idiots of each other, and three dogs make an idiot of their owner."

I already had two dogs. Not exactly what you would call "farm dogs," either. My big red Bullmastiff, Mingus, lived in terror of sheep after being rammed as a puppy. Diva, the slightly wrinkled Chinese Shar-Pei, still thought that groundhogs wanted to be her friend. Idiotically, I thought a bona fide Shetland sheepdog would render some sanity to the kennel.

In a burst of originality, Shirley had named the puppy Sheltie. She was a tricolour bread box of a dog, with a white mane, a white tip on her tail and a pointy nose. I picked her up at a mansion. Shirley and the butler put her into a dog travelling crate, along with her yellow blanket.

"She's shy and she doesn't like big shoes," Shirley told me.

The little dog stayed in her crate for a solid week. She would only venture out of it when I put it on the porch. Then she would skitter out and do her business before rushing back to the comfort of her blanket. She would only take her food and water in total privacy. The other dogs would peek in the crate at her, but she would not come out and play.

Like people, animals that are thrust into unfamiliar situations need time to adjust. Before I tried to saddle my youngest horse, I spent two years getting her used to the idea of standing to be groomed and picking up her feet to be cleaned and trotting in a circle on a long lead. Cows do not automatically line up to have milking machines fastened to their udders. It is all a matter of routine and trust.

Gradually, Sheltie and I became friends. She liked to be cuddled and stroked and tummy-rubbed, but only when we were alone. No sharing with the other dogs. She would not play with their "toys," and she hid her squeaky toy under her blanket after each session.

Getting her out and about was another thing. She was a dainty dog and the notion of sheep sniffing her did not sit well. Her herding instincts came into play with the goose gaggle. All it took was a touch of praise, and Sheltie took it upon herself to ensure that the geese stayed behind their fence and feared to stray anywhere near the house or the garden.

I grew to love the eccentric, timid creature. Sheltie and Shar-Pei made great sport of each other, racing around the yard and sniffing out groundhog holes. They made perfect idiots of each other, until exhaustion set in and I would find them snoozing next to the cedars beside a patch of pansies. When the much-loved Mingus met his maker courtesy of a speeding cement truck, Sheltie was a comfort and she seemed to understand my pain.

As sensitive as she was to me, Sheltie had little concern for others. She had a most irritating bark that she would let rip with when anyone came to visit. The only way to shut her up was to confine her to the crate, where she huddled quietly, waiting for the intruders to go away. Any male guests with big shoes had to tread lightly around her. She could urinate on a shoe faster than any dog I have ever seen.

Although the Blacks would later divorce (Shirley would change her name to Joanna and Conrad would wed my former *Maclean's* magazine colleague, Barbara Amiel), they were still married when I met them at a Christmas party one year. When they inquired after Sheltie, I sensed they had felt a certain failure with the puppy, and there was some relief in knowing that she had indeed found happiness.

Privately, their young son came to me and asked if Sheltie was *really* living on my farm. It took me back to my childhood and the times when I had wanted to confront my own parents about the true whereabouts of poor Bingo, but never had. It was great to look a little boy in the eye and tell him, "Yes, your puppy is on a farm and she's having the time of her life."

JUST THE FACTS

I might have been as green as a corn sprout when I came to the farm, but I had a lot of ideas. After all, I had managed to purchase a one-hundred-acre farm without any fencing. There was no barn, just one little shed built near a swamp and a rickety old chicken coop close to the house. As a farm, the whole thing was not much more than an idea.

While disentangling myself from urban life, I spent weekends in the country studying books and creating game plans. I asked the government for information, and huge envelopes started arriving. Each one contained some sort of single-page, agricultural fact sheet. Page by page, the mystery of farming was revealed.

When I was ready to get down to it, I called in a government specialist to review my plan. This procedure was *pro forma* according to fact sheet 96.

A nice man came to the door and shuffled his feet when I asked him to come in. On the kitchen table I had a pile of books about sheep and a rough map of the farm and where I thought things should go. A look of panic crossed his face, but it eased when my companion, the Moose, came through the door. Moose is a large, genial fellow. They shook hands and nodded in a manly way. Then Moose left the room.

Panic reconfigured on the specialist's face when I explained that the farm was *my* operation. The Moose would continue working in the city until such time as the bounty of the farm provided a living. According to fact sheet 33, this might take five years, unless I fast-tracked the sheep according to Accelerated Breeding Plan B in fact sheet 56, which was my Plan A.

We started out by examining land-base strategies. The specialist suggested sharecropping the hay and grain fields. Details of this procedure were spelled out in fact sheet 16. Since I had no machinery for planting or harvesting or much of anything really, it made sense. Besides, fact sheet 82 indicated that I would need to have a storage area for machinery and a well-lit area for making repairs, but that would have to wait until I had a barn.

I was not surprised when my barn plan passed muster with the specialist. It was taken directly from fact sheet 65 — "Loose Housing For Sheep." My only modification was an annotation along the front wall for a gallery that would contain various posters, needlepoints and other forms of art depicting sheep. Fact sheet 21 said that a barn should be designed to make the farmer comfortable, as well as the livestock. A variety of visual images in the barn would brighten my day. I was halfway through a needlepoint of grazing sheep.

When it came to fencing, the specialist seemed quite impressed by my combination of materials. Fact sheet 43 said flexibility was key to farming. The hard lines on my map indicated page-wire fence, the dotted lines were for electric fencing to divide pastures, and the ziggy lines were for picturesque cedar rail fencing near the house.

Fence posts could be cut from the forest, which counted as Woodlot Management according to fact sheet 79. The short-stop on Moose's baseball team would do the job. He was also an experienced tree-cutter. After reading fact sheet 80 about safety in the bush, bringing in an expert seemed prudent.

Fact sheet 52 talked about admitting your limitations, so I admitted that I would also be hiring someone to install the fences. I had not known who to hire until Irving, the handyman who washed the second-storey windows on the house, told me that he knew a guy who had a tractor and a fence puller. His name was Bo and he was a retired circus clown, but Irving said he was good at straight lines. I also had a backhoe operator lined up to dig the post holes because the ground was Class 6 soil — in other words, solid rock.

By this time we had downed two pots of tea and barely a word had been spoken about sheep. In accordance with the general instruction on "Planning Your Sheep Operation," I presented my flow chart. Based on a fifty-fifty ratio of female to male lambs at one and a half lambs per ewe on a breeding cycle of three lambings over thirty-two months I estimated that my core group of twenty ewes would multiply to a flock of 175 within five years. I knew that was optimistic, but fact sheet 104 said a positive attitude was a prerequisite to farming.

Then I waited for advice.

"Do you have a wheelbarrow?" the specialist asked.

I told him I did — a fine, big, blue one.

"Good," he said. "Fill it up with money and you can start farming."

Almost twenty years later, the clown-built fence is still standing and the needlepoint on the barn wall always gives me great pleasure. There are fewer sheep to feed now than there were after the first five years, but there is also less land to sharecrop since the stony ground became a gravel pit. Although it is not a full-time job, the wood-lot is now managed by Moose. He says it will be ready to harvest when we are ready to retire. We call it the RRSP forest.

Oh yes, I still have the blue wheelbarrow. I could not have farmed without it. Every time I have a new idea, I ask myself, "Will that be one wheelbarrow full or two?"

There really should be a fact sheet about that.

A MIDWIFE'S TALE

For the record, there is nothing sweeter than a baby lamb.

Sure a snuffling, oinky, pink baby piglet has a certain charm. And a newborn calf with liquid brown and trusting eyes can melt the hardest heart. But a lamb — now that's something special.

Lambs are snugly. You can hold them like puppies. You can pet them like kittens. If their mother trusts you, they will fall asleep in your arms like a baby.

The heart-tugging beauty of lambs is never more apparent than during that critical period when the shepherd is also a midwife. It is a time of constant watching and worrying. Rounds of the barn must be made every couple of hours — day and night. The effort is wearying, but the result is holding new life. I wouldn't miss it for the world.

A shepherd knows when a ewe is intending to give birth because sheep tend to dig a sort of nest before they have their lambs. It is the oddest thing. The ewe will go off into a corner and begin to paw in one section of the straw, all the while making a guttural baaing sound that seems to come from deep in her chest.

Then the water bags appear.

It scared the living daylights out of me the first time that I saw one of my sheep digging madly in the straw with what looked like a liquid-filled balloon hanging out of her backside. Fearing a crisis was occurring on my first time out of the gate as a sheep midwife, I placed a panic-stricken midnight phone call to an experienced shepherd.

"Did they teach you nothing at that university?" he asked. Then I heard him snicker to his wife: "The girl's so daft that she doesn't even know about water bags." I left the phone red-faced, with instructions to get back to the barn and watch.

That was 15 years and hundreds of births ago, but everything about the process still strikes me with wonder.

Most sheep are quite capable of delivering their lambs all by themselves. All I have to do is daub the lambs' navels with iodine to prevent infection and watch to see that they find the food source. The ewe licks her newborn lambs and prods them to their feet, from whence they toddle in the general direction of the faucet of life.

You can always tell when a lamb has found mother's milk because its tail wiggles like a happy puppy's. That first milk, the colostrum, is crucial to the lamb's survival. It is thick and rich, loaded with vitamin A and protein and all sorts of antibodies to protect the newborn from bacterial infections. When the lamb has figured out the food source and had its fill, I get out my clipboard and attend to the administrative duties of the shepherd. This includes identifying the lamb by placing a numbered metal tag in its ear, noting the sex, the birth weight, the number born and the mother's tattoo number. Once everything is duly noted and going nicely, the lamb family moves into a private pen where they can spend "quality" time getting to know each other for a week or so.

Twins are a common occurrence in sheep and they are the goal of most breeding programs. Triplet lambs are a bonus. I have even had a few sets of quadruplets. Nature is full of surprises.

When I have to help deliver lambs, it is usually a multiple birth. Lambs should ease into life front feet first, but there are always lambs that are determined to be born backwards, sideways or in some odd combination of legs and head. This is hot, soapy water time for the shepherd midwife.

Untangling lambs and repositioning them gets to be up-to-the-elbow-in-sheep-work. It is slow and patient work — gentle work that requires enormous trust between the midwife and the ewe.

In a way, it's like being an intimate Lamaze coach for someone who does not speak your language, but I expect that the ewe can understand from my tone of voice that I'm helping her. We are a team.

Once the first lamb is delivered, the ewe's spirits rise and so do the shepherd's. But there is no time for awe — the lamb's nostrils have to be cleared immediately to ensure that that first breath of life jump-starts the little critter and tells it "yep, I'm born." If the ewe is tired, it's up to the midwife to towel-dry the lamb, stimulating it to stand up and seize the day. A nice bucket of warm water flavoured with molasses can usually perk up the old mom, and a cup of soothing tea does wonders for the shepherd.

Birthing can take hours, or it can be over in a matter of minutes. I have seen older ewes deliver two fine big lambs with natural grace and then stand up and deliver a third one as though they were spitting out a watermelon seed. First-time mothers sometimes fret and panic, but once their lambs are born the mothering instinct takes over. In fact, sometimes a hugely pregnant ewe is so anxious to have a lamb that she just cannot wait for her own to come and tries to steal another newborn away from its mother. In other cases, the act of one ewe giving birth seems to inspire others and the next thing the shepherd knows, the stage is set for a marathon of midwifery. Life is never boring in the sheep maternity ward. I had a five-year-old visitor who summed up the process nicely — "totally awesome."

It doesn't take long for day-old lambs to start butting heads and dancing backward at the sight of their shadows. Ewes that once needed me will stomp their hooves in protest if I dare intrude into their space.

But every once in a while, I will be allowed to hold a woolly baby and marvel, as we do with all newborn things, at the perfection of little ears, innocent eyes and tiny, tubby tummies. And that's why there is nothing sweeter to me than a baby lamb.

MURPHY'S LOBSTERS

I'm thinking about putting steel toes on my hip waders when fishing season opens — just in case Murphy is right about the lobsters.

You see, as I was quietly quaffing a cold one next to the pool table at the Mount Royal Hotel and Tavern in Mount Forest, I heard that lobsters are invading our river beds.

It all started with Mike Murphy. Mike is a character you couldn't invent — for some reason we call him Murph the Smurf. When he was a town councillor, he was affectionately known as Mr. Graft. Legend has it that Murph's expenses were right up there with the Mayor's. We're talking a little over $800, including a bottle of white wine he ordered for the table at the Good Roads Convention. That was front page news.

Mount Forest is like a lot of small rural towns. Industry comes and goes. Subdivisions pop up where there once were rolling fields. Local business groups form in order to "Put the town on the map." But the local news still runs to police reports that don't name the people who were arrested and social notes about who visited whom on the weekend. Hard news can be hard to find.

Still, Murphy has a way of hitting the front page quite frequently. For instance, a few years ago he decided to stop in to see a friend. He happened to be flying a small airplane at the time. When he tried to land it on a ploughed field, there were headlines.

His biggest headlines came when he decided to go over Murphy's Dam in a barrel. The dam is located close to town, and the drop is about ten feet. Murph has a special affection for the dam because it was named after one of his relatives, and he keeps his eye on it.

So one fine day, Murphy went out and had a special steel-rimmed, padded barrel made. He sealed himself in it wearing nothing but a motorcycle helmet for protection.

About 100 people stood on the bridge and watched as Murphy sort of clunked over the dam, landing with a bit of a thud because the water level was kind of low. Murphy was knocked out, but otherwise okay. There were big headlines, and quite a few letters to the editor about the wisdom of allowing town councillors to go over dams in barrels.

That year the town council even considered passing a bylaw restricting the citizenry from going over the dam in barrels. Murphy, however, remains convinced that going over the dam in a barrel could put the town on the map, just like Niagara Falls.

Murphy now works for a local waste disposal company. In a previous incarnation, he says he was a mercenary soldier. In fact, he claims to have been one of two mercenaries who participated in a covert activity some years ago in the Dominican Republic. I seem to have missed that war.

Because Murphy is a great storyteller, it's natural to listen to his tales. Occasionally, he will tell some outlandish story and follow it up with irrefutable evidence. This gives him credibility for another six stories.

Murph was still in my credibility zone when he came into the Mount Royal and announced that the lobsters were running in the Saugeen River. He was cussing and stewing because one of his buddies had just been picked up by the "nature narcs" (conservation officers) for catching lobsters out of season.

According to Murph, lobsters from the East Coast found their way into the St. Lawrence River system many years ago. Gradually, they have been moving into the rivers. They are not monster lobsters because adapting to fresh water has limited their growth to about a pound or a pound and a half. Naturally, he explained, the government was keeping a lid on this because the population was so small and they didn't want any commercial trapping taking place too soon.

Murphy promised to bring me a lobster.

The next day I called the Ministry of Natural Resources. It gave the nature narc on the other end of the line a good laugh. The only new species that had been found in the Saugeen River recently was a lost otter. The biggest crayfish he had seen was five inches long.

While I sat at the pub waiting for Murphy to bring me my lobster, I mentioned the tale to some of the boys. This drew great guffaws, and my gullibility has since become legendary. Apparently Murphy had been telling lobster stories out of school since time began. A lot of mention was made about the stress of the bump on the head he took going over the falls.

"Did he ever tell you about going parachuting when he was a kid?" asked Black Jack the bartender. "He was about seven years old and he got an umbrella and went up to the third floor attic of his house and jumped out the window with the umbrella open."

Everyone except me remembered that one, and great debate ensued over whether Murph had broken one or two legs.

Just then Murphy walked in.

He didn't have my lobster. Instead, he explained that he had not visited his traps at the dam that day because he had been mending his parachute.

SISTERHOOD CAN BE CHAOS

When the sheep begin to have their lambs, the chaos theory of farming kicks in. That is to say that no matter how much experience a shepherd has — no matter how well prepared, or attentive — something unpredictable is bound to happen.

There is the medical kit to think about. All sorts of little things to stock. Mineral oil to remedy constipated lambs and Pepto Bismal for little fellows with diarrhea. There are plastic paddles with shoelaces tied to them that are intended for use on ewes who suffer from gynaecological prolapses. I tried this out once and immediately called the vet. Still, there they are in the medical kit like a reminder from a David Cronenberg horror film of what happens when things get worse.

I also have a margarine tub filled with Epsom salts to use as a warm wash over tender udders. Sometimes I use it on my own weary fingers when I make a cup of tea in the middle of lambing — dipping my digits in the margarine tub filled with soft warm water with one hand

and sipping a cuppa Earl Grey in the other. I have Handi-Wipes, in the kit along with rubbing alcohol, Band-Aids for me, just in case, and iodine to daub on the lambs' umbilical cords to prevent infection.

The kit is stocked with elixirs and medicines that I hardly ever have to use. There are usually a few orange-flavoured cough drops thrown in. I use them on myself or I give them to a ewe who is bored waiting to deliver her lambs.

Diversions are also an important part of birthing.

The sheep all know my little medical kit. Many of them have been butting their heads against it since they were lambs. It is a battered yellow plastic lunch-box type-thing that a child once gave me. On the side of it is the lettering "Dr. U. Be Well."

I carried the kit into the barn last week in the middle of a chill but calm night. It had been four hours since the last barn rounds, and the sandman was still in my eyes. When sheep start to have their lambs, there is no particular time or reason. They do it in the dark, or at dawn or in the middle of Sunday brunch. When one does it, another is sure to follow — or it may be days until a whole slew decide to try for a simul-birthing at supper time.

What I found this night were two sister ewes Franny and Zooey — in full birthing pre-performance. They are three-year-olds, both big husky girls with the same long crimp to their wool. If you removed their yellow ear tags, it would be hard to tell them apart without checking their tattoos. They walk alike, they baa alike and they both chew their cud in a clockwise motion. I checked my breeding records and, sure enough, they both had romantic interludes with the ram on the same October day.

It followed that they would both decide to have their lambs in the same corner of the barn at the same time.

Head to head, I found them pawing diligently at the straw, turning in circles to arrive back at the same spot. Franny was the first one to lie down and begin pushing, arching her head backward to the sky and groaning great sheep groans. All the while her sister pawed at the straw around her and made the same sort of guttural sounds an Inuit throat singer would make if imitating a pregnant sheep.

There was great excitement when a large glob of lamb slid easily from Franny. Both ewes had licked it clean before I could get anywhere close. That was when noticed that Zooey was taking a proprietary interest in Franny's baby.

The lamb did not mind the attention at all. In no time, the little guy was on its soft hooves wobbling around and looking for some milk. Franny tried to nose it in her direction, but Zooey was right there as well, offering to feed a newborn that was not hers. Then Franny gave another great groan and sat down like a giant dog. She curled over on her side to give birth to another lamb.

This was just the opportunity Zooey needed. While Franny was busy doing her sheep Lamaze breathing, Zooey was cuddling and cooing over her sister's lamb, fairly inviting the newborn critter to file for adoption papers.

Franny delivered her second lamb without a problem. A fine big ram lamb with a tip of white on the end of his tail. Both ewes were on him like a flash, nuzzling and licking and making quiet eh-eh-eh sounds to let him know that mother was near. Or rather mothers.

I went off to get fresh straw and a portable pen to put them into. By the time I got back Franny and Zooey were contentedly nursing one lamb apiece — as though sharing udders and lambs was a natural act of sisterhood. Zooey seemed to have completely forgotten that she was still in labour. In fact, she seemed relieved to have avoided the whole contraction and pushing routine. Without the pain, she had the gain.

Sisterhood is powerful. When I had the pen set up for Franny and her two lambs, I discovered how powerful it is. I took the lamb Franny was nursing and backed into the pen with it while she followed, baaing with great concern. Once installed, she finally realized that something was missing — her other lamb. Whatever horror a ewe can reflect in her face was written on poor Franny's when she saw her other lamb nuzzling his Aunt Zooey's bountiful udder.

I tried to approach Zooey casually, using a handful of grain to divert her attention from the abduction I was planning.

Scooping the lamb, I made a dash for the pen and plopped it in beside Franny. That is when Zooey butted me a good one in the backside, sending my toque flying into Franny's pen where it landed squarely over the face of the lamb with the white-tipped tail. I leaped into the pen, as much for safety as to retrieve my cap.

Franny did not mind me being there, she busied herself with sniffing both lambs — first one, then the other and back again. Sheep do not count much past two or three. Outside the pen an irate and frantic Zooey circled like a bull after blood. Long baleful baas whined out of her. She was so caught up she did not even seem to notice that she had passed a water-bag the size of a grapefruit.

Then suddenly she flopped into the straw, arched her nose to the sky and groaned. A few minutes later she had her own lamb to lick and coo over. Then another, and another.

Sisterhood can also be productive.

After a week or so of togetherness, Franny and Zooey and their lambs will be turned in with a pen of lambs and mothers who have bonded with each other sufficiently to know who belongs to whom. With triplets to care for, Zooey is too busy with her own brood to contemplate lamb-napping her sister's twins.

There is nothing in my medical kit that deals with maternal instinct. It cannot be injected, prevented or prompted. It just happens as naturally in a sheep barn as it does in a maternity ward.

I have two more sister sheep who are waiting to have their lambs. But one has big old floppy ears and the other has pointy ears that twitch like propellers. One chews clockwise, the other chews counterclockwise. I do not think they even like each other much.

But if I find them both pawing in the straw together, readying to deliver their lambs at the same time — nothing will surprise me about the chaotic sisterhood of sheep.

RABIES AND RELATIONSHIPS

I guess it might be difficult for a city person to understand the relationship between rabies, travelling salesmen and Jehovah's Witnesses. In the country, I live with all these scourges and in my experience they share a curious bond.

I had a case of rabies on the farm a few years ago, and frankly, I'd prefer to see a Fullerbrush man any day.

One of my cows, Lindy the Limousin, was just not looking right when she should have been starting to look quite pregnant. I put Lindy into a private pen and watched her closely. At first, I thought the isolation made her lonely because she started mooing constantly and pacing like a restless child on a rainy day.

She would not eat grain, even when I tried feeding her by hand. I brushed her and gave her the cow equivalent of a massage. I talked to her and took her temperature. Nothing was working and Lindy was running a bit of a fever. By the time the vet arrived the following day, it was evident that something was very wrong with Lindy.

She was behaving like an animal possessed. Tossing her horns around wildly and charging at the wall of the barn like a Hemingway nightmare.

She was not the cow I knew lying peacefully under an apple tree, snoring as only a cow can and waking only when an apple knocked her on the head. She was a demon. The federal government descended after the vet pronounced the dreaded word "rabies."

Lindy had to be destroyed. Henry the Chicken Farmer, from whom I had purchased Lindy as a calf, arrived in his big diesel four-by-four with a .30.06-calibre rifle. He felled her with one bullet. Any innocence I had left went when Lindy went down. My neighbour buried her with his back hoe and the government took her brain away for analysis. The horror of it sank in and I cried on the slush and mud grave of my beautiful cow.

Of course, I had to have rabies shots. Rabies is a terrifying disease which spreads through the saliva of infected animals, and I'd been thrusting my battered and chafed farm hands under Lindy's drizzling muzzle trying to get her to eat. The shots weren't bad. Five in the arm and I was virtually guaranteed not to froth at the mouth. However, as the news spread through the neighbourhood, I had to endure story after story about the days not so long ago when rabies shots were given in the stomach and the cure was often as deadly as the disease. A few old-timers even recalled the days before the vaccine when a person stricken with rabies was simply led off into the woods, tied to a tree and left to die in screaming insanity.

It got fairly depressing.

My farm was quarantined for 90 days. The dog had to be tied up even though he had been vaccinated. It turned into three months of fear, because the federal vet warned me that, if any other animal on the farm developed symptoms, I could be forced to destroy the whole works. When a horse so much as yawned, I worried.

In its own way, however, there was a lot of peace in those three months. Almost no one came to visit. City friends had no desire to visit a "rabid farm" and even my neighbours were reluctant to drop over for a cup of tea.

The only people who did drop by unannounced and uninvited were travelling salesmen and Jehovah's Witnesses, both of whom seem to share a mission that glues them to a doorstep and translates polite words like "no thanks, I already have some" into an invitation for further discussion. After a few undesired interruptions to refuse pamphlets, cleaning agents, subscriptions and salvation, I remembered the rabies.

I've been using it for years now and it works like a charm.

I greet the uninvited with a cheerful and welcoming smile. Then, just as they prepare to step inside, I feel obliged to inform them that the farm is under quarantine for rabies. The effect is quite dramatic. They vanish. And I bless poor Lindy as they hightail it down the lane.

THE KINDERGARTEN DUCKS

People are always trying to give you stuff when you live in the country. When you first move, country people try to fob off their old junk on you. I had one neighbour who had been collecting old wooden doors for no apparent reason. When he found out I had sheep, he brought over a wagonload for me to use as pen dividers. He just dumped them off and left, as though (1) I needed the doors and (2) I knew what to do with them.

My city friends seem to think that my farm is a retirement home for any pets they do not want, or cannot take care of anymore. I have had everything from a Siamese cat that ate its owner's tropical fish to a hundred-pound Japanese husky that grew up in a beauty salon. Both animals were terrified of sheep. They got used to it. I like to think that their twilight years were heaven on earth.

Then there are the kindergarten ducks.

I have a friend who works with a class of urban pre-schoolers. Last spring, she thought it would be a great learning experience to hatch a bunch of eggs at Easter.

She got some duck eggs and an incubator, I know not where, and the kids observed the whole hatching phenomenon.

Great concept.

The problem is that baby ducks grow at a furious pace. So, within several weeks my friend had a bunch of quackers that had doubled in size, and the kids had bonded to their duckies. It took a whole morning for their teacher to explain that growing ducks belong on farms and ponds, not in school.

Apparently the school's janitorial staff grew insistent. After a frantic late night call, I agreed to take the kindergarten ducks.

I picked up the gaggle and put them in a cardboard box. All I could see were fluffs of yellow down through the diamond-shaped holes the kids had fashioned to give them breathing space. They quacked every time we came to a stop. Really quacked big time in rush hour traffic out of the city. I tried talking to calm them down, but they preferred a motherly "quack." You get some strange looks at stoplights when other drivers spot you quacking at a cardboard box.

At the farm, a dozen handfuls of quacking fluff waddled dutifully into their pen. I put out their duck food and gave them a vat of water, but that was not enough. These ducklings had been socialized. They wanted to follow me around while I did my chores.

Twelve ducklings do nothing but eat and do what comes naturally. I gave them a little duck house to live in and a plastic swimming pool to play in. All summer long I plucked leafy greens from the garden for them to nibble and they made a great game out of eating every insect that came their way.

They demanded "quality time," quacking away as though I understood just what they were saying. All of this because from the time they came out of their eggs, they became used to the idea that anything larger than them and roughly shaped like a human being would say "quack, quack, quack" to them and give them food.

They liked to be sprayed with the garden hose. They discovered where the nozzle end of the hose was and if I did not turn it on they would poke it with their orange beaks and quack at me as though I were a bad parent.

Now they are grown ducks. They quack a lot louder, and they do what comes naturally in larger amounts. They ate all of the leftover tomatoes from the garden and then they started gobbling corn.

I am a shepherd, not a duckherd. From my point of view as a farm businesswoman, the only future these fine, well-fed waterfowl had was as duck à l'orange.

Then I got the letter from Haley.

"Dear Farmer," she wrote, "I am in Grade One now. How are the ducks? My favourite was Boinker. He said boink instead of quack."

The letter ended with, "I hope Boinker is happy. I love him. Please give him some lettuce." Attached was a picture that approximated a large child holding out her hand to a small yellow creature wearing orange shoes.

What was I supposed to do? What sort of heartless duck foster mother would fire back a letter saying, "Boinker doesn't boink any more and he should be golden brown after two hours at 350 degrees"?

I went to the duck house and called out, "Boinker, come here!"

All of the ducks waddled happily toward me, and I knew I did not have the heart to pluck one feather from any duck that had been to kindergarten.

Let it not be said that old shepherds cannot learn new tricks. A neighbour who raises waterfowl has advised me on how to winterize my duck house.

I even learned how to tell the difference between boy and girl ducks. You do this by turning the duck upside down and gently poking around. Males, who are called drakes, will ultimately raise their drakehood in a rather flimsy display of masculinity.

Now all four of my drakes have blue bands on their duck ankles, so we do not have to go through that undignified procedure again. In the spring, I will divvy up the girlfriends. Building nest boxes can be a winter project.

Then my teacher friend can fire up the incubator and introduce a new batch of kids to the miracle of life. But those little quackers will not be coming back to my farm. I have that one figured out already.

A young couple down the road have just bought a few acres with a little pond and they want to have some ducklings. They are thrilled that at least one of them might say "Boink."

I wrote back to Haley.

"Boinker is fine. His feathers are white. He's learned how to quack like the other ducks, but he still comes if you call him Boinker. Your love helped make him a fine and happy duck. Thanks for letting me look after him.

PS. How did you know that he was a boy duck?"

HOLD THE KITTY LITTER—
THE CAT CAME BACK

You really have to hand it to my old cat Webster. He's 12 years old and still purring like a kitten, even though he has surely used up more than his share of the proverbial nine lives.

Webster is a barn cat. He started out life living in town, but when he decided to make a habit of destroying curtains and toppling knick-knacks while his owners were at work, he came to live with me.

The sheep loved him instantly. He is pure black, and when the ewes first saw him they assumed he was a lamb. He lives with them now. Sometimes he even sleeps on top of one of the old girls.

Barn cats have to work for their keep. Webster gets his scoop of feed and minds his business. He hunts constantly, patiently and methodically and since I do not see many mice, he must be doing a good job. Webster has even been known to hunt rabbits and young groundhogs.

When he rubs up against your leg and purrs, it is hard to imagine that he has the heart of a killer. Although his tom-catting career was surgically ended many years ago, Webster has an uncanny knack for getting into brawls — usually with species other than cats. He has been pecked by geese, sprayed by skunks, butted by lambs and chased by foals. His early penchant for rubbing against other creatures resulted in a crook at the end of his tail, caused by a calf kick.

Today he doesn't have much of a tail. One winter he decided to abandon his straw bed in the barn and snuggle up under the hood of the pick-up truck. He has always been a sound sleeper, so I guess he slept right through the usual morning commotion of barking and baaing and crowing. When I started the truck, the fan belt devoured all but two inches of his tail.

Webster has never had much luck with vehicles.

At last count, he had been struck or rolled over four times. Nothing serious has happened to him, and he tends to hide himself away while his bruises mend, only to emerge with a slightly tilted gait.

He disappeared for almost a month after being shot clear through by an arrow. Apparently, some young fool had spotted the Web hunting in a pasture and decided to take aim with a practice arrow on what would be considered "an impossible shot."

It seems anything is possible where Webster is concerned, however, and the flimsy projectile whipped right through him, much to the surprise of the errant Robin Hood. Webster ambled up the lane with the arrow still in him and stood on the front porch looking mildly confused.

I immediately went into paramedic paroxysms. When he saw me coming for him with the traditional blanket used to contain him on trips to the veterinarian, Webster loped off into the bush, with the arrow intact.

I could not track him and, of course, assumed the worst after a few days. Almost a month later, the cat came back — without the arrow. The entry and exit arrow marks were fully healed and Webster was looking for a dish of milk.

Webster has developed a measured dignity over the years. Even the dogs tend to respect his position as senior statesman in the barnyard. Although he still hunts, he has learned to be discriminating. The other day I found him snoozing on a bale of straw just above a banty hen who had just hatched ten peeping chicks. Webster paid them no mind whatsoever.

Occasionally, I will find him looking weary. But just as I prepare to think about making up a bed for him in the house and tending him indoors during his twilight years, he will roll over on his back purring and then snap to attention, careering across the yard to chase some vagabond chipmunk up the old maple tree.

Webbie's place is in the barn, or stalking the evening pastures or sitting on a fencepost in the moonlight. He is not a kitty-litter kind of guy, and he never will be as long as he has one life left in him.

HAPPY TRAILS,
"SADDLE PARDNER"

When I heard the news that the King of the Cowboys, Roy Rogers, had died, I took it hard.

The first letter that I ever wrote to anyone was to Roy Rogers.

I was five years old and I had been a Roy Rogers fan from the first moment that the black and white television flickered to life in the suburban living room where I grew up in the fifties.

Those were the days when television was a kind of a miracle and watching anything on it was a special event. I would spend half an hour just getting dressed to watch *The Roy Rogers Show*. It was the polite thing to do. (Heck, the lady who lived next door used to say "excuse me" to her television whenever she left the room.)

I wore a white straw cowboy hat, strapped firmly under my chin with an elastic of sorts. And I tied a plaid kerchief at my neck above a red-checkered western shirt that had silver buttons shaped like horseshoes. They didn't make designer blue jeans for kids in those days, so I wore regular blue pants that my mother made into regulation cowboy chaps by adding a strip of leather fringe down the side.

My cowboy boots might have looked like plain old puddle jumpers, but they had tinfoil covering the toes. Around my waist I wore a holster with two plastic six-shooters capable of delivering a payload of water in any direction for about three feet.

Before the show started, my parents would move my rocking horse in front of the TV screen. It was a pink rocking horse that bounced on springs, but while I watched Roy Rogers it was transformed into a golden stallion who would rear at my will and gallop after any bad guys that dared stray into the living room.

Six-guns might blaze, but I don't remember seeing any blood or ever being afraid that the good guys wouldn't win. In fact, the only thing I remember ever being mortally wounded on *The Roy Rogers Show* were the rubber tires on Nellybelle, Roy's ranch jeep. And that was just fine with me because the Old West wasn't about jeeps, it was about horses and chuckwagons and herding cows named doggies. It was Cole Porter for goodness sakes, and Roy singing: "Oh give me land, lots of land, Under starry skies above, Don't fence me in . . ."

In all of the years that I spent watching the adventures of Roy Rogers and Dale Evans on the Double R-Bar Ranch, it never occurred to me that they were both older than my parents. It never occurred to me that they were a childless couple living in the middle of a post-war baby boom. Dale ran a diner, but the only help Roy ever gave her seemed to involve testing her pies. And even though they always rode happily into the sunset together, Roy saved his kisses for Trigger. Weird, but it helped me to establish some priorities.

For instance, after watching *The Roy Rogers Show*, I never wanted to be a cowgirl because it was obvious that cowboys got the best horses.

The Lone Ranger had Silver.

The Cisco Kid had Diabolo.

Gene Autry had Champion, and Hopalong Cassidy had Topper — but surely the best horse was Trigger.

Girls usually rode nameless brown horses. Sure Dale's little buckskin gelding Buttermilk was a nice horse, but nothing compared to Trigger who could run like the wind and untie knots with his teeth.

So when Nestle's Quick announced a contest that involved kids writing in with the name for a palomino pony that was the spitting miniature of Trigger — I was there. The kid with the best name would win the pony.

I remember wracking my brain for days. It was all I could think about. My mother read the rules and told me that the contest was only open to American kids, but I was sure that couldn't be true.

Roy Rogers would never deny his Canadian "pardners."

As long as we took good care of animals, and treated other kids and old people right, we were all "saddle pals" according to the Code of the West.

It took me two days to write the letter. Painstaking writing, just to keep all of the letters between the lines I had drawn with my ruler.

When I was done, I gave it to my mother to mail. And I waited. I waited for months and months. But I never got a reply.

Around that time, I gave up on cowboys and contests.

Years later, when I was a teenager, we were on a family trip in California. Crossing a scrubby wasteland where the tumbleweed was real, we came to a kind of middle-class oasis known as Apple Valley — home of Roy Rogers and Dale Evans and their museum.

We stopped.

America is full of kitsch disguised as museums, and this was no exception. It had everything from Dale's square-dance dresses, encased in glass, to every saddle Roy ever sat in and every guitar "The Singing Cowboy" ever held.

But the shrine was surely the critters — or at least their preciously preserved remains.

Poised against a painted western panorama there was Bullet the Wonder Dog — Roy and Dale's faithful German Shepherd — standing next to Dale's horse, Buttermilk, still as plain as plain, despite his red saddle and trimmings.

The *pièce de résistance* was Trigger — the real Trigger — the half-thoroughbred palomino foaled in 1933 and originally named Golden Cloud — The Smartest Horse in the West — Roy's co-star in more that 180 television show and movies — the horse he fell in love with in 1939 and bought for the princely sum of $2,500 with his own money when the studio wouldn't pony up the dough.

Trigger was mounted in that famous rearing pose of his, wearing his black and silver parade saddle with the solid silver saddle horn that would have given any cowboy pause on a hot day.

He looked frozen. He looked so real that he was unreal. He certainly did not look anything like a 33-year-old horse, which is what he was when he died in 1965. For crying out loud, when I was watching *The Roy Rogers Show,* Trigger was old enough to be my father. And just seeing him there, breathless but forever golden, made me want to cry out loud. Further back in the exhibit, Trigger Jr. — no relation — was stuffed. I looked around, but there was no sign of the Nestle's Quick pony.

The museum had everything and anything you ever wanted to know about Roy and Dale and their private lives, their marriages, their children, their tragedies and their Christianity. They were human. Roy wasn't even really Roy — he was Leonard Franklin Slye, born in Cincinnati and raised in Duck Run, Ohio. He'd never been a real cowboy.

On the way out, there was the inevitable souvenir shop, filled with postcards and paper weights, cowboy hats and string neckties. Something about the whole experience disturbed me terribly. Right beside the cash register there was a wicker basket filled with cellophane-wrapped, fossilized Trigger droppings. For sale.

I left without any souvenir. The museum folks said Roy and Dale often stopped by the museum, but it just wasn't our lucky day. Besides, I don't know what I would have said to a hero who didn't have the good manners to write a letter back to a little "pardner."

Decades afterward, I still harboured a childish hurt in my heart over Roy Rogers and my failed entry in the Nestle's Quick contest.

Then, last summer, my mother visited the farm and brought with her one of those inevitable bags full of "stuff" that mothers always show up with. Stuff she has been "keeping for you" for years. Stuff she finds while cleaning out a drawer that she's cleaned out 20 times before.

One of the things she brought me was the letter that I wrote to Roy Rogers. She never did mail it.

Dear Mr. Rogers, I had written:

I know the Quick contest is only in America, but I was thinking — I'm a great lover of ponies and horses. So couldn't I enter the contest? If I could I would name the pony: Goldy, Sunburst or Gift of Gold, which I like best of all.

Yours truly,

Marsha Boulton,

a Canadian pardner.

Of course, I couldn't blame my mother for not sending the letter. And I could only blame myself for my lack of imagination. The letter wouldn't have gone to Roy anyway. Some contest droid in Milwaukee or Des Moines would have chucked it in the garbage along with all of the other Canadian posts.

But seeing the letter, with one silver horseshoe-shaped button still carefully glued to the corner, brought back all my wonderful memories of those rocking horse days of childhood when the Old West-That-Never-Was came into my living room and the guy with the best horse and the whitest hat always won the day.

There was always a happy ending. Then, the forever young Roy Rogers would smile that squinty-eyed smile of his and say something like "May the Good Lord take a likin' to you."

And he and Dale and Buttermilk and Trigger would ride off into the sunset.

Happy Trails, Roy. 'Til we meet again.

THE GREAT SQUIRREL DIASPORA

Squirrels do not always live in trees. Given half a chance they are perfectly happy to live indoors. They tend to prefer heights, however, which makes attics ideal. Once they set up house, it can be very difficult to evict them, and the sound of little feet scampering overhead multiplies awfully quickly.

A plague of red squirrels invaded my friend Barbara's garage. Since the garage is attached to the house, invasion of the attic was imminent. Food sources were battened down. The dog slept in the garage as a warning to fur-bearing rodents. But at night Barbara could hear them scampering along the rooftop, frolicking in the eaves-troughs, looking for any easy access. Soon they were chit-tering happily somewhere in the attic.

Barbara is a gentle soul. She could not bring herself to poison the squirrels, especially not after finding a nest of hairless ruddy babies squeaking helplessly in a ceiling crawl space. To her, every red squirrel was as endearing as Beatrix Potter's Squirrel Nutkin. She waited until they were big enough to leave the drey — as squirrel nests are called — and then she brought out the humane trap.

One litter of squirrel babies proved to be just the tip of the red-tailed iceberg in the attic. Every day, Barbara would find one or two new squirrels in the trap. To lure them she used everything from peanut butter to marshmallows to pine nuts. Once trapped, they were transferred to a wire pen in the barn where they devoted themselves to trying to escape. When that failed, they decided to propagate.

The harvest of the squirrels went on for weeks. Just when she thought it had to be over, Barbara would hear the sound of little feet racing across the roof in the moonlight. She had a dream about laughing squirrels and woke up wondering if it had been a dream.

Adolescent squirrels joined adult squirrels and aged squirrels in the barn. When Barbara spotted one particularly plump-looking squirrel gathering materials for a nest, she decided enough squirrels was enough. The squirrel pen was loaded into the back of the truck and she drove them two townships away before letting them loose in a field next to a woodlot. Knowing Barbara, she probably left a bag of nuts with them, just to get them started.

"It is over, done. They are gone. They are free at last," she crowed cleverly.

The way of the world and the way of squirrels being what they are, Barbara was not the only person relocating squirrels hither and yon. In fact, the very day Barbara told me about the great squirrel diaspora, another friend called with a squirrelly tale.

This time squirrels had squatted in Brian's granary. They were bold and thieving squirrels. He tried everything from cats to the anti-terrorist tactic of playing Guns N' Roses at full blast. The squirrels were immovable. Even more disturbing, they seemed to thrive on Heavy Metal. So he trapped them.

Then he took them to a woodlot two townships away and let them go.

Next spring I expect that Brian's Axl Rose-loving nut-busters will be knocking about in Barbara's attic, and Barbara's Squirrel Nutkins will be building condominiums in Brian's granary.

So far, I have not experienced the challenges of living with squirrels. I am lucky. I live three townships away from Brian and Barbara.

TIGGER, TIGGER, BURNING BRIGHT...

How do you tell a baby lamb that his mother does not love him? It is not because he is stupid, or ugly or poorly tempered. It is not because his high-pitched baa wakes the roosters in the dead of night. Neither his small size, nor his silly habit of hopping in the air and landing squarely on four hooves has anything to do with motherly rejection. So, how do you tell a lamb that his mother just has no love to give him?

The problem is that you cannot explain anything to a feisty, hungry lamb that does not know anything about life, let alone love. You just have to find it a new mother, or become one yourself.

I sat in wonder while a big old ewe I call Wilma delivered her lambs. She was huge and I was expecting a big set of twins or triplets from her. Sure enough, the first two lambs were a healthy size. They were on their feet looking for milk when Wilma sank down again and produced a triplet. I watched and put down some more bedding.

The biggest of the lambs was suckling when Wilma rolled her eyes and plunked her behind down like a sitting dog. She arched back, pointed her nose to the sky and I could see there was another lamb coming! I jumped into the pen just in time to towel off its head, clear its mouth and wipe its little nose. Wilma just looked at it and turned her attention to the trio that were sucking impatiently on her droopy ears.

The fourth lamb was much smaller. While the others tipped the scales at a meaningful 9 or 10 pounds, the little guy was half their size. Curled up, you could fit him in a catcher's mitt. He was thirsty from the start, and he wasted no time finding his way to the faucet of life. Poor old Wilma was just beginning to realize the dimension of her production. By the time all of the lambs had enjoyed that crucial first supper, the line-up started forming again.

I guess that's when Wilma put her foot down.

She has always been a good and gracious mother, but her patience (and apparently her reservoir) stopped at three lambs. So every time the little guy tried to belly up to the bar, she butted him away with her nose. He was determined. That is how he earned his nickname, "Tigger."

I suspected this was going to happen. All morning I kept waiting for another ewe to go into labour. If that happened, I could rush Tigger to her side and begin adoption proceedings. Sheep identify their lambs by smell rather than sight. So, in theory, I could rub Tig next to a fresh-born lamb to help him take on its peculiar scent. And I always keep a jug of Royal Copenhagen men's cologne in my medicine chest. Rubbing that olfactory nightmare on a ewe's nose and dousing all of her lambs with it leaves her totally at a loss to sort the poseur from the progeny.

The perfect candidate for foster motherhood was a young ewe who was not overtly tubby. I thought she might have a single lamb and cleave to the tiny Tigger without any problems. Wrong. She had triplets. Of course, by this time I had doused her nose and the lamb with Royal Copenhagen. I sat Tigger down beside me on a bale of straw where we could contemplate the meaning of life and formulate a new game plan. It's hard to think clearly when you smell like a Danish pimp.

The bottle is always my last resort — the one with the lamb nipple, I mean. Tigger was ready to try anything. Nothing is as good as mother's milk, but powdered commercial preparations with names such as "Lambmo" are potable substitutes. Tigger was soon packing back a warm one every few hours. His birth mother allowed him to sleep with his siblings, but an undrawn line remained between him and her precious udder.

Bottle lambs are precious and precocious. Every shepherd should have one because it makes you truly appreciate the value of a good milk-producing ewe. From the moment the lamb tastes milk through that plastic nipple, it is imprinted. The bottle is "King" and the bottle holder is "mother." The first time around this is an endearing experience, but after tending a few bottle lambs it becomes an all-too-time-consuming experience and an exercise of last resort.

Normal lambs do not socialize with the shepherd. They live in their own woollen world and consort with each other. A bottle-fed lamb, however, is like a demanding child. If Tigger did not get his bottle as soon as I entered the barn, he would let out a cry that could crack an egg. If he wanted more, he would suck at my kneecaps while I was trying to feed and water the rest of the barn. He quickly mastered the art of escaping from any enclosure and thought nothing of toddling along with me and the dogs to fetch the mail. He found a hole in the barn wall that the cats used as an access route and he started showing up on the front porch to cadge more milk. Or maybe just to see what "mom" was up to. He liked to have his chin rubbed, and he liked to be held and burped.

Shepherds are susceptible to projecting themselves onto their bottle babies. Psychiatrists could probably come up with some fancy "syndrome" for it. A woman friend of mine was so touched by her orphan lamb that she took it into her home. Darling little Cricket would wake her in bed each day by bouncing on her pillow. Darling little Cricket was subjected to paper training. Cricket took over the passenger seat of the pickup truck and on long journeys they made regular pitstops for bottles and other Cricket business. Cricket on a leash was a model of good behaviour. Her "mother" went so far as to enter the spoiled "baby" in an amateur dog obedience class. To the chagrin of the fourth place Beagle, Cricket took third prize.

By the time my Tigger reached 30 pounds, he was too big to be jumping on my lap, and he was beyond the stage of needing a burp. His bottle grew at the same rate that he did, and soon he was sucking it dry from a holder on the wall. I started catching him poking his head into the hay and discovering the joys of solid food. When I stopped bringing bottles altogether, he pushed me around like a ruffled teenager, and he gave his best shriekish baa. Two weeks later, he was not even interested in a chin rub.

The problem with lambs is that they grow into sheep. Love cannot conquer all.

IT'S A WONDERFUL DOG'S LIFE

Traditionally, farm dogs bark when strangers come up the laneway. The dogs can be any breed, but usually they are a mixture of a few designed to be loyal to their masters. They chase the odd cat or groundhog, but little kids can pull their tails without fear. Farm dogs eat kibble and table scraps. They do not whine, and they only howl when they have a marauding raccoon up a tree. Good sheep-herding dogs can work a flock tidily into the barn or shift them from one field to another with a combination of quiet precision and bursts of speed. They work for a living.

I have never had a good sheep-herding dog, and the only living my various dogs have made has been the veterinarian's. Still, most of the dogs who have lived on the farm at least bore some farm dog traits.

The Bullmastiff Mingus was the namesake of legendary jazz bass player Charlie Mingus who was as massive as his instrument. Dog Mingus was also massive. From a breadbox of a puppy he grew to develop a head the size of a 4H calf's and the body to go with it. His bark could shake a coon out of a tree.

The Ming was a lovable character. He was the kind of dog who inspired men in groups to offer him a beer. Brave-hearted two-year-olds thought he was an over-sized stuffed toy to be tweaked and mutilated. And he did tricks. Watching him sit up and beg was akin to watching an elephant rise on its haunches. Hold two fingers in front of his nose and he would bark. The dog snored louder than a tugboat fog horn.

But Mingus was a collar-slipping kind of dog. He took to wandering, and nothing from love to surgery, from discipline to electric fence could stop him. He was going to play with the dog one-tenth his size who lived next door no matter what. I would see him halfway across the field, and run at top speed, hurdling the electric fence, to chase him and call him back. He would stop momentarily, shake his great head, spew some muzzle juice and lope off.

When I went to pick him up, I would often find him happily chewing chicken bones that the little dog was allowed to eat. Thus horrified, I would then have to hoist the huge dog one half at a time into the pickup truck. The day he decided to spare me the effort and walk home along the sideroad was the day a cement truck hit him. I still miss everything about him, except his bad breath.

Other dogs have come and gone. Stella, an Akita, who was raised by a hairdresser and lived most of her life on the twenty-eighth floor of an apartment building, never fully adapted to the farm. She would bark at the bird feeder but ignore an oil truck coming up the lane.

Sheltie, a Shetland Sheepdog I adopted from the family of newspaper potentate Conrad Black, spent most of her waking hours barking at anything that moved. Together, they formed one semi-cohesive farm dog. Both dogs lived on the farm until they died and their memory is as bonded to the land as their graves. Still, there is always some psychic gap to raising dogs you did not start with as puppies, some youthful experience unshared that will always remain unknown. Where, for example, did Stella develop a fear of hockey pucks? Why did Sheltie like to urinate in men's shoes?

My next dog was going to be a puppy. I discounted the possibility of ever having a dog that did a day of work in its life, so I deliberately sought out a breed that interested me from an aesthetic point of view. I chose a knee-high wrinkly breed, a relatively rare breed and an offensively overpriced canine: the Chinese Shar-Pei. At the breeder's, the puppy came close to picking herself out of the litter by tumbling out of a squirming pile of wrinkled siblings to have a look at me. She licked my ankles. Her tongue matched the colour of her coat — jet black.

Diva Dog's name sprang automatically, since she was a born prima donna with a faultlessly assured attitude. Her wrinkles made her a daily photo opportunity, but gradually she grew to fit her skin. With the exception of her ears and a few lines on her forehead, the final dog emerged as a compaction of solid muscle.

"Kinda dog is that?" farmers would ask. "Looks like a pit bull with a pig's tail."

A long-winded explanation would follow, delineating the distinctions between Shar-Peis and pit bulls and

Staffordshire Bull Terriers and any other breed. Finally, I gave up trying to make a case for a wrinkle dog that had no wrinkles.

"Marsha ironed her when she was little," became Moose's stock response. End of story.

Diva's bark is appropriate and loud. She chases groundhogs with a passion and digs so far into their holes that I think she might well end up back in China. Early on, when a nesting goose grabbed her loose puppy skin, she learned to give a wide berth to anything wearing feathers. After almost a decade, she still twirls like a top and spins ludicrously around the yard. Among her tricks is the art of lying perfectly still and, instead of shaking paws, she gives "five," slapping her catlike paw across my palm. Overall, she is one of the happiest animals I have ever known.

It is her relationship with lambs that is most curious. During lambing time, Diva will not leave the barn. From outside the pen, she watches constantly. Baby lambs who toddle near the fence are greeted with loving licks.

One morning I arrived at the barn to find two newborn lambs already dried and suckling. While I cursed myself for not being there sooner, Diva bounced frantically outside of the pen. When all was fed and done and I tried to leave the barn, the dog circled around me in ever tightening circles, herding me back.

Then I heard a sleepy little baa. Tucked next to a feeder almost out of sight, there was a triplet lamb, probably the first born and the first to eat. He was just waking up after that first snooze of life with a full tummy and a warm place to sleep. With two lambs demanding her attention, the ewe had apparently forgotten about this self-sufficient fellow.

I let Diva into the pen and she ran to the lamb. While I got the iodine for its navel, Diva fussed with the lamb, nudging him to his feet just like a miniature, mothering ewe. When we presented the foundling to its mother, she stamped her hooves at Diva with as much physical anger as a sheep can muster and took over. I closed the gate and the dog whined. Not a sheepdog, perhaps, but certainly a friend of sheep.

A traditional farm dog Diva will never be. She is unlikely to learn that I am not thrilled by the gift of a dead skunk on the front lawn. Nor do I appreciate spending Sunday afternoon at the vet's office while porcupine quills are wrested from her muzzle. But when she lays with her back legs splayed and her head flattened against the grass, snoozing beside the lilies-of-the valley and barking at her dreams, it's a wonderful dog's life.

PAVLOV'S SHEEP

Flexibility is key to surviving in the country. Years ago, asthma forced my veterinarian to give up his farm animal clientele, as well as his own flock of sheep. He became a federal meat inspector, with a small practice for dogs and cats on the side just because he loves animals. When his wife Pat and her nurse friend, Jan, opened a specialty butcher shop and delicatessen, Dr. Ron became their parttime butcher and sausage maker. His smoked sausages are the absolute best, and — coincidentally — his partner in sausage making is Jan's husband, Norm, who is a firefighter. It has all evolved quite naturally. However, when you are hosting a barbecue get-together, guests tend to pause when you explain that a vet and a fireman made the smoked sausage that they are so enthusiastic about.

People who start farming from scratch, and have a dream that they will make a living at it, have to be flexible enough to appreciate that simply not losing money may be a more realistic goal. Subsidization is often a necessity. This can take many forms from finding a job in a nearby town, to driving a school bus or inventing a home-based business. If you have a spare room and a decent recipe for muffins, the next thing you know you have a bed and breakfast. Farmers should not have to work double-time to make a living, but we do. When all is said and done, it boils down to the lifestyle.

I know a retired farmer who makes more money playing the pork bellies futures market than he ever did actually raising pork bellies. But he still keeps a miniature Vietnamese pot-bellied pig in the backyard of his tidy house in town. Every spring he "just happens" to stop by my barn to look at the newborn lambs, before he heads off down the road to check on the neighbour's calf crop.

Writing is an easy occupation to combine with farming, although it shares the same sporadic income pattern and rush to deadlines as market gardening and lambing seasons. Also, it has an invisible element. Advances in computer technology and electronic information retrieval allow a writer to function virtually anywhere in the world. Often it is just a question of convincing an editor that an article from a Rural Route address has the same cachet as one that comes from Downtown. In terms of journalism, a telephone interview is a telephone interview, no matter what area code it comes from.

One of the first things I added to my barn was a telephone. While working away — whether collecting eggs, stacking hay or grooming a horse — I leap at the sound of the telephone, bounding over gates and lunging up alleyways to make the connection.

At first, the sheep ignored this flurry of activity. But after a month or so, they developed a stomach-centred telephone response. They baa mercilessly when the phone rings.

Sheep are basically stomachs covered with wool. As ruminants, they have four stomachs, each of which seems to need to have something to do. Unless they are sleeping, sheep are constantly engaged in some action related to eating or chewing.

Commands such as "Cease and desist!" or variations thereof have no effect on sheep. To shut them up, I keep a pail of grain beside the phone and toss the contents in their trough before I say "hello."

The effect of this is Pavlovian. Even a wrong number earns the sheep an added treat. Sometimes I have as many as two calls in an hour and I forget to replenish the grain bucket. The second call is always one of some importance.

On one such occasion, an editor of a fledgling fashion magazine was calling. The sheep were relentless and I could not hear a word she was saying. When I called her back from the house, my apologetic explanation seemed to relieve her.

"Oh, I'm glad it was just sheep," she said. "I was afraid you had very unusual children."

Another time, I was desperately trying to get an interview with the chairman of a stock exchange. The story had the scent of scandal, so I was not the only journalist trying to obtain such an interview. While the distinguished gentleman declined my request, the sheep baaed willfully in the background.

"Are those sheep?" I heard him ask, while I strained the phone cord to reach around the corner for a scoop of grain to silence the lot of them.

"Yes, sir," I responded as professionally as a person could while balancing over a grain trough and flinging oats at caterwauling ruminants.

"What kind, might I ask? I grew up on a farm, you know."

While the sheep chewed, we chatted about farm life — his and mine. Gradually we came back to the topic of business, which became an interview.

As it turned out, I got the "scoop" — and so did the sheep.

THE MOTHER GOOSE WARS

Geese know no mistress.

At the best of times, they are bound to peck the hand that feeds them. In the spring, when they begin laying their eggs and tending their nests, they become commandos and straying too close sets off the mother of all goose wars.

Geese in a defensive mode are not attractive. Their necks crane and flatten out like feathered vipers. They wave their heads, weaving from side to side in a goosey rendition of the evil eye. One step too close can elicit a hissing volley. It is a long expulsion of goose breath that is made even more intimidating by the waggling of their dreaded goose tongues, which are peppered with spiked ridges. When they feel threatened, they attack with their wings spread and peck at any appendage within the grasp of their hardened beaks.

My geese are of the Toulouse variety. They are big grey birds about as tall as a regulation-sized three-year-old. A group of geese form a gaggle, and that is about what they sound like as they waddle around honking and yakking away to each other.

I have heard that the Chinese once kept geese to ward off intruders and it certainly seems possible. Mine function as barnyard doorbells. Any vehicle that ventures up the lane is heralded with honks and hisses from the goose collective.

You can say "goose" to just about anyone who grew up on a farm and a tale will unravel about an old gander that loved to torment children with hissing flights of fancy and toe-pecking antics. The fact is, my buddy Loggie contends he would have never made it beyond the third grade if it had not been for the old grey goose chasing him down the lane and on to the school bus.

My unruly gaggle are the descendants of a trio who escaped the annual harvest five years ago. They were just too fast and feisty for me to capture. They have been multiplying ever since.

Goose mating is an awfully noisy, rambunctious affair. They mate in freezing rain. They mate in snowstorms. They mate at dawn or in the afternoon. But usually they mate around midnight.

From all of the honking and hissing and running around they do, I don't think you would call this activity an act committed out of love. At first, I thought they were just trying to keep warm. Unfortunately, they make the same sort of commotion when a fox ventures too close. It has caused me to make a rush to the barnyard more than once.

And there I'd find them, coy as teenagers caught necking on a sofa. Some calmly smoothing their feathers and others swaying their necks. They would even honk at me as if to say, "Yeah so nothing's happening here, lady. What's the beef? Chill out."

They have a goose house, but they prefer to winter in the snowbanks along the fence line where they can keep an eye on me. In their purely belligerent and self-reliant tradition, they totally ignore the nesting boxes I built for them. This year, four of them are nesting on top of the manure pile. Two are cleverly hiding out in the straw loft and the rest have planted their nests squarely in the middle of the barnyard gateway. One young goose is so befuddled by this egg-laying business that she simply deposits them in the middle of the laneway and runs away.

A nest of eggs is called a clutch. Being clutched by a goose is what you risk when you try removing eggs. Early in the spring, I gambled my digits to gather fresh eggs that would have otherwise suffered from frost damage. One goose egg makes a fine omelette and I had a couple of double-yolk goose eggs that scrambled into brunch for four.

The geese have been sitting on their nests for weeks now. Every few hours they go through a strange ritual of examining their eggs and rolling them around with their beaks and their feet to ensure an even and constant heat. The nests are lined with downy feathers that they have plucked from their own breasts. When they take an occasional stroll, the eggs are prudently covered with down and straw. As I wander around checking on lambs and repairing fences, I can hear the constant, low-level, one-way chattering they maintain with their eggs. I imagine them saying: "Never trust the blonde human. Always hiss at her and bite her if you can." Those would seem to be typical goose training instructions.

When the first gosling hatches, it triggers a maternal frenzy of honking and fretting and rolling of eggs. Such a fuss over an awkward ball of fluff with tiny orange-webbed feet that are the buttery texture of fine suede.

Inevitably, one over-anxious goose will abandon her own nest to sit next to the real mother, who hides the gosling under her wings and pecks angrily at the intruder.

I checked with my neighbour, Scotty, who has been raising web-footed creatures ever since he gave up truck driving many years ago, and apparently the phenomenon of abandoning a nest in favour of surrogate motherhood is not uncommon. There is no ready fix. Other less fickle geese will adopt the abandoned eggs, although placing them in new nests may require the protection of welding gloves and a construction helmet.

Once all of the goslings have hatched, the geese will lead their flopping and stumbling babies to the pond. Great displays of honking and flapping will defend them from curious lambs and warn the wild ducks to keep their distance.

Soon the goslings will be cruising the water, practising their goose-breath hissing at the frogs and giving the evil eye to the turtles.

I guess there are some things you have to be a Mother Goose to love.

SOMETHING IN THE AIR

March can come in like a lion or not, as it pleases, but one thing I can be certain of — on my farm March will go out with me smelling like a lamb.

When the barn is full of sheep who are either giving birth or tending newborns, there just doesn't seem to be any way to avoid contaminating whatever environment I inhabit with some barnyard scent. It might be something as minor as a barn mitt left in the truck, or a barn sock in the laundry hamper, but there is always something sheepish lingering in the air, no matter how hard I try.

I know that I am not the only farmer effused with the scent of the workplace. Many times I have picked up the whiff of a barn in the aisles of rural supermarkets. We who spend time in barns always seem to think that we can just run in quickly, grab what we need and leave before anyone notices.

One winter, I rode all the way to the "Big Smoke" in a bus that reeked of chicken manure. The offender was a clean-cut fellow whose only mistake was wearing his distinctly well-worn barn boots in a public conveyance. No one on the bus said a word. We just wrapped ourselves tightly in our coats and opened all the windows. Stoic or stupid, you be the judge.

People who have lived on farms or know farmers learn to accept occasional olfactory pungency. Males of the species are particularly prone to not even noticing. Wives, mothers, and lovers of farmers, all have the same mantra: "You can't wear that, it's been in the barn." But sometimes, it just can't be helped.

So, I thought it would be pardonable for me take an emergency run into the Co-Op farm supply store during a break in March lambing. In and out, nobody gets hurt.

Of course, I ran into Mrs. Hayward at the door. She is as legitimate a farm woman as I have ever met. In fact, she sold me my first sheep. The Hayward children were off to university and she was dispersing her flock. I didn't have a clue what I was looking for, but Mrs. Hayward helped me sort the ewes and find some "good uns." She never patronized me and she has always been there when I needed advice.

"Still got the sheep?" she asked, as we entered the store. It is the same question she asks every time we meet, and the most pleased of smiles crosses her face when I tell her that I do.

Not that I had to say a word on this particular day. I was wearing my full barn suit, and the strip of lipstick I had swiped across my mouth in the parking lot was no camouflage at all. I stank of the lambing shed. Even worse, I reeked of iodine, which was why I was at the Co-Op in the first place.

When we hooked up again at the cash register, I felt compelled to explain.

"Lambing time," I said, and her big smile radiated over me like the winter sun. Lambing season had always been Mrs. Hayward's favourite.

"Big ewe butted me sideways when I was trying to clean the lamb's navel. So I expect I smell like a sheep and more," I explained, plunking a fresh bottle of iodine beside the cash register.

Mrs. Hayward nodded, seeing the iron-red iodine stain across the snowsuit and no doubt inhaling enough of its fumes to purify her sinuses for several months.

"Don't let it bother you," she said. "Father Hayward's in the calving barn so I've been taking care of the pigs for a month. Can't smell anything but pigs these days."

My senses had been so self-centred that I had failed to even notice what was definitely a piggery stench.

"You can't let farming get in the way of living," Mrs. Hayward said, in the common-sense way that she says all things. She was at the Co-Op picking up some sort of pig tonic for pregnant sows.

I guess I looked fairly beaten, between the iodine, the bruise blossoming on my thigh from the ewe's butt, and the endless rounds at all hours of the day and night in the lambing barn.

"Nobody who really works on a farm looks like they just came from the beauty parlour," Mrs. Hayward offered.

I tried to remember the last time I had been to a beauty parlour and I must have looked more dejected than when we started talking. So Mrs. Hayward decided to tell me her "most mucked-up experience of all time."

Years earlier, she had been caught out in the barn late on the afternoon that one of her daughters was bringing home a likely prospect for matrimony. And not a farm boy to boot, rather an urban sort of the likeable, open-minded variety.

The whole Hayward family was assembling for supper, anticipating an announcement. Mrs. Hayward had done her usual best, planning and preparing a superb meal, including her famous homemade bread which is made from grains that are grown and ground on the farm.

At the mere mention of Mrs. Hayward's bread I became a salivating mess covered in iodine.

But that was not the end of the story.

Instead of abandoning her chores and joyfully greeting the daughter and meeting her beau, Mrs. Hayward decided she could not leave the barn before penning a loose cow with a young calf. An easy enough thing to do, she thought.

"I was just scooting them in when a darned seagull flew through the barn and scared the cow," she explained. Seagulls in the barn was one I hadn't heard before, but in the autumn, when the crops are being harvested, flocks of the avid scavengers accumulate in the fields. This one had apparently become disoriented.

The protective cow was so flustered that she charged the gate just as Mrs. Hayward was closing it. The latch shut, but the force of the cow sent Mrs. Hayward flying across the alley into the manure gully.

"I went sliding through all that muck for I don't know how far before I stopped," she said, holding her face and brushing her hands over her chest in remembrance.

Covered in dung, Mrs. Hayward slunk to the house and entered the basement through the cold-cellar door leading to the laundry room. She tore off her sodden barn clothes, scrubbing her face and other exposed bits in the laundry tub. Then, clad only in a yellow bath towel she retrieved from the clothes dryer, Mrs. Hayward quietly snuck up the basement stairs.

Father Hayward and the boys had returned from the fields. She could hear them laughing in the porch mud room. It was only a matter of time before her daughter began the introductions, giving Mrs. Hayward just the chance she needed to tiptoe across the kitchen and up the staircase to the comfort of a warm shower and fresh clothes.

She was halfway there, when she tripped on the cat.

"The towel was the first thing to go," she said shaking her head. "Everyone ran into the kitchen and there I was, hanging onto the counter, stark naked. My daughter was handing me the towel when I saw the diamond on her finger.

"What could I do? I stuck out my hand and welcomed the poor boy to the family. You can imagine what he said in the speech to the bride," Mrs. Hayward snorted, slapping the air with her hands.

There we were — two women stinking to high heaven, doubled over giggling in a public place in the middle of the day without an apparent care in the world.

"Can I ring this up now?" said the clerk, and we both straightened into a straighter mode.

I drove back to the farm with the truck windows open, imagining the fumes trailing after me in a purple cloud. Mrs. Hayward probably did the same thing. Neither of us would have missed our trip to town for something so insignificant as worry about the smell of our workplace.

JUST SAY NO TO PORCUPINES

Drugs are serious business. Addiction is serious business. But somehow I never expected that any of the animals on my farm would develop a habit. The truth is that one of my horses seems to have a craving for tranquilizers.

Her name is Karma. She is a half-thoroughbred, four-year-old golden palomino, and she is the first horse I have raised from a foal.

She was born just outside my living room window. Her mother, Lady, was let loose in the yard before she foaled because she seemed to want to be close to me. She liked to look through the window and watch TV.

I had the vet on call for the birth. Neighbours who raise horses were quizzed thoroughly about equine midwifery procedures and birthing complications. Ultimately, one June morning there was a little horse running around the garden with Lady.

Karma was a wondrous spindly-legged thing. Once she had figured out her food source and gotten her footing, she rested. I found her lying flat out amid a patch of purple lupins, resting in the morning sun while her mother grazed nonchalantly nearby. At first, I breathed softly in her nostrils. Then I rubbed her all over from her ears to her tail. We have been good friends ever since.

It's hard for me to accept her as a drug addict. She only seems to get the craving in June, but it has happened every year for the past four years. I think we can safely say an unhealthy pattern is emerging.

Karma gets her drugs by sniffing porcupines.

She had her first taste of tranquilizers when she was a yearling and decided to investigate a spiny woodland creature. Unfortunately, she used her nose. Now you can't just tell a horse to stand still while you get out the pliers and pull the porcupine quills. The vet suggested we sedate Karma for the duration, and the drugs took effect pretty fast. First Karma's lower lip became loose and quivery. Then her ears lopped off both sides of her head like a pack mule. Her eyelids drooped like Tammy Faye Bakker's on a bad day, and her long white tail folded like a mop between her legs.

When her front knees bowed, the vet and I helped rumple her to the ground, where she stretched out and began to snore. I whispered comforting thoughts to her about carrots and apples, while the vet snipped and plucked. The whole process took about an hour, by which time Karma was ready to rejoin the land of the living but was far from "straight." In fact, she spent the next quill-less 48 hours hobbling around staring at fenceposts and contemplating blades of grass like a refugee from a party at Timothy Leary's.

Altogether, the horse was a model of mellow.

The first time it happened I could accept her porcupine nuzzling as a mistake made out of curiosity. The second time, I accepted it as the error of a half-ton animal fuelled by a two-pound brain. But since it has happened regularly every June for the past four years, I'm beginning to see it as a larger problem.

Fact is, I swear she sniffs porcupines because she knows that, for all the aggravation they cause her, she gets drugs that make her feel a weirdness she can't get from straight oats and hay.

Perhaps it is time I had a Betty Ford-style confrontation with Karma and the porcupine family. Or maybe I should just call out a porcupine posse and lock Karma up in the orchard for a year or two.

There aren't any "say no" brochures about dealing with four-legged tranquillizer addicts who only strike in June with porcupine accomplices. I guess I'll have to try "tough love" while Karma goes cold turkey next June.

LEAPING LIZARDS,
IT'S JUMPING SHEEP

Sheep are natural-born jumpers. Like Ian Millar and Big Ben, they soar over obstacles with a rectitude that can be breathtaking.

Sometimes I think sheep jumping should be an Olympic event. Our great Canadian lumping sheep would have a terrific advantage over the free-ranging Australian sheep who barely ever see a fence. Of course, we would have to watch out for the British jumping sheep. Goodness knows, they might find the genetic marker for jumping over tall buildings in a single bound and clone a whole team of high-flying Dollys.

I am not kidding when I say that sheep can really jump. By the time they are three months old most lambs could easily clear the heads of most five-year-olds. It is only up from there.

And they don't just jump. They spring, almost as though they have rubber bands in their knees. It actually begins when lambs are two or three days old. Wobbly woollen bundles start bobbing around their mothers like pop-up pool balls on the ricochet. They do this for no apparent reason other than the sheer joy of it.

When they are grown, jumping sheep are a problem. Sometimes the only way to contain them in their field is with a strand or two of electric fencing. A tingle of that on their tummies as they ease over a fence is a sure cure. Even in winter, when the electric fence is turned off, sheep maintain a healthy respect for it. They do not know it is unplugged.

This year, however, my electrified strand took a beating. I discovered one whole section of it coiled and crumpled near the barn. For all I know it could have been dragged there by a low-flying goose.

I kept intending to restring the ruse, but other springtime chores got in the way and most of the ewes were either giving birth in the barn or too pregnant to jump anyway.

This leaves the ram. And the ram loves to jump. He jumps without fear, and he jumps without reason which is one of the reasons that he is called Rambo. Once he jumped off a storey-high wagon of hay in a spine-tingling display of stupidity. Instead of ending up squashed in the yard, he landed upright, gave himself a shake and jumped the fence back into the field.

So when old Rambo finally noticed that there was no voltage impediment to jumping over one section of the fence, he just had to try it. I discovered this one morning when I opened the front door to let the dog out. There was the ram, calmly grazing on sunflower seeds that he had knocked out of the front porch bird feeder.

Well, I would have none of that. I dashed for my boots and the only tool I thought suitable — my broom. Thus armed, I attempted to bully Rambo off the porch. I poked him. I called him names that would make Sylvester Stallone himself blush. Then I tried irritating him into compliance. I swept his nose.

But those sunflower seeds had an irresistible allure. When he finally finished eating them, the ram looked up at me as though asking for seconds.

So I gave him a whack on the rump, solid enough that it would penetrate through his winter wool. Then I stood down on the steps and waited for him to take me seriously.

Inspired, or perhaps just stunned by my unshepherdly violence, the ram drew himself to his full and noble height. Next thing I knew, he was headed for me. Barrel-housing across the porch with his head down, he threw himself across the steps. With both hands, I raised the broom defensively in front of me.

The last thing I heard was the crack of the broom handle breaking.

Rambo struck me with full force. I came to in a puddle of wet grass about six feet from where I had been standing, still clutching the remnants of my broom. My eyeglasses were neatly scattered around me — in four pieces.

Bruised, blurry-eyed, and feeling more than a tad vanquished, I crawled back to the porch. The ram was nowhere to be seen. I finally found him in the backyard where he was butting at another bird feeder and nibbling on fallen niger seed. When that was gone, he did the logical thing and jumped back into the field. But I knew he would be back.

That afternoon, I spent an hour or so rewiring my fenceline. The sheep gave passing notice to my labours. Only the horses seem to marvel at the fact that I can touch materials that otherwise electrify them.

In the barn, the spring lambs bounce around as though they are tethered to bungee cords. Their ears flop and their tails jiggle when they hit the ground. They butt their heads together and then jump backwards. They fly through the air and kick up their heels.

It is all quite endearing, but one day they will be full-blown jumping sheep.

After all, they are their father's children.

A FINE DAY
FOR WASHING PALOMINOS

The thing about mud on a farm is that it devours the soul. After the dark days of winter, when the sun finally shines for extended periods, if you look down instead of up, much of what you see is mud. People talk about it. Children wear it on their boots and backsides. Trudging through it, animals draw the sound of sucking ooze with each hoof displacement.

Farmers become cranky when they cannot move machinery onto the land and begin their seeding. They end up talking amongst themselves, stewing and chewing and wringing their hats in coffee shops. At home, even the busiest kitchen linoleum pattern cannot hide the dried streaks of mud that inevitably find their way indoors. Dogs smell of barnyard muck. Chickens roost on slim metal gates to avoid the stuff, and cats balance on cedar fence-lines like tightrope walkers to make their way to higher and drier hunting grounds.

In such an environment it is impossible to feel clean, yet cleaning seems to be the response that heals and motivates. Windows get washed. Porches are swept. Lawnmowers are scrubbed free of last year's dried grass and emollients smoothed over their plastic places creating an illusion of newness. At hardware stores, little metal brushes that can scrape the grease from hidden places in barbecues enjoy brisk sales.

The first warm windy day of spring finds clotheslines fluttering with alternating strands of shorts and halter tops removed from mothballs and snowsuits and long underwear being prepared for mothballs. At the town laundromat, Mennonite men in workboots line up at the industrial-strength washing machines loading horse blankets that have grown stiff with winter sweat and shedding hair. While the mud is upon the land, the ritual rug-beating of spring becomes its panacea.

I have found myself caught up in this phenomenon and I always wonder why hope seems to spring eternal from hot sudsy water and air drying. On the other hand, when you live with mud for about a month out of every year, the idea of paying to attend a spa where dipping in the stuff is *de rigueur* simply does not compute.

Fortunately, sheep stay away from mud. Lambs will not go near the stuff. This is one of the few innate signs of intelligence that sheep display. Horses, on the other hand, do not seem to differentiate between mud, manure and green pastures. They will lie down in anything, which is particularly distressing when they are of a pale hue.

My horses are palominos — "designer equines" some would say. Their bloodlines are a mixture of American

Saddlebred, Thoroughbred and Quarter Horse, with a dollop of Arabian in there somewhere to provide a fine perk to their ears and some distance between their dark eyes. A mother and daughter team, they have yet to earn a cent toward their upkeep. I call them riding horses but to anyone wrestling with the red ink of farming they are little more than pasture decorations, otherwise known as "hayburners." Still, old Lady, the mother, and her fully mature daughter, Karma, gladden my heart with their coats of gold fringed with white manes and tails. They are the kind of horses that the good guys got to ride in old Western movies, and the feminist cowperson in me strikes a blow for all women when I put them under saddle and gallop into the sunset.

But mud destroys any mindset of palomino mythology. Spring bedraggles both of them. Their shaggy winter coats come off in handfuls of hairballs, leaving them as patchy shades of yellow mixed with whatever muck they have come up against. So I do the only thing that seems to trigger positive endorphin activity in the mud-swamped brain of spring — I wash them.

There is always one spring day when the temperature soars beyond whatever lie the weekend weather person has perpetrated. It is the day that fragile tomato transplants begin taking firm root. It is the day when the fragrance of lilac blossoms mingles with the smell of cars being waxed. And that makes it a fine day for washing palominos.

You basically wash a horse from the top down. I spray the whole working area and follow that with gobs of livestock shampoo. Lady goes first and Karma follows.

Neither one is the least bit reticent, until it comes to spraying their bellies. I dress for the event in tatters of clothes that never need to see mothballs again. Standing on an old fruit box in the sun, rubbing a smelly old horse might not be everyone's ideal of spring cleaning, but it works for me.

Horse washing takes a good half a day. At the end of it, the horses gleam. Tangle-free, platinum blonde manes and tails float with any breeze. Blackened hooves look ready to tap-dance. The horse washer, however, is generally a soggy mess of half-dried lather matted with horse hair.

When the horses are freed in their pasture, it is like a scene from a picture book. They trot smartly with their heads aloft, snorting and flaunting their fair complexions to the whisper of grass. Sometimes their muzzles meet. Then their heads shake away in a flurry of stiff-legged bucking that ends in a canter glide to the far fenceline and back. Pulling up stock-still, they look poised, collected and ready for their close-up.

It is best to leave them in that instant of wonder and beauty. Somewhere in the pasture there is a swale. Lady and Karma know the spot well. To them it is a panacea that oozes an invitation to lie down and roll. Kicking at clouds, they let their souls wallow in the last mud of spring. As rituals go, it must be a lot more fun than rug-beating.

WALLY COMES
HOME TO ROOST

Moose and I had been talking about getting another dog as a companion to the aging yet elegant Shar-Pei, Diva, who had lost her friend the Bullmastiff, Mingus, in an accident involving a cement truck. Moose had been devastated by that loss and swore that he would never raise another dog unless he knew it was "indestructible."

Then, I had the dream. In it, I saw Moose walking down the laneway with a miniature rhinoceros on a leash. I saw him throwing a soccer ball to the leather-plated, miniature rhinoceros and watched the little horned thing leap into the air to butt it. The wee rhino wagged its tail happily and Moose caressed its stumpy horn. It was a thoroughly satisfying dream.

A few days later, I was cajoled into watching *Hockey Night in Canada*, even though frost had not yet even threatened the garden. At some point in the broadcast, legendary curmudgeon broadcaster Don Cherry was shown cavorting with his dog Blue, a white English Bull Terrier.

I was transfixed, watching the sturdy knee-high dog leaping in the air and demonstrating all sorts of manly affection to his master. I held the image of the dog's head — its huge Roman nose, those varmint-like triangular eyes, a body made out of solid muscle — and over that I superimposed a horn. Bingo! Found: a mini rhino in canine form.

Two weeks later, we were in the home of a breeder looking at a pen filled with four-week-old puppies.

There were five in the litter. Three white females with a variety of trimmings such as stripes of red on their ears and black patches on one eye. But I knew that farm life dictated that a white dog would be a high-maintenance item. One male puppy was a soft shade of chocolate brown mixed with white. And then there was a chunk of a pup with four white feet, a blaze on his face and a brindle coat, shades of brown, striped with orange — a baby rhino-tiger.

He was about the size of a beanie baby and just as floppy. When he leapt to the side of the pen in response to Moose's beckoning finger and fell backward in a perfect reverse somersault, that pup became "the one."

We passed the breeder's interview, a question-and-answer period that is akin to facing a parole board hearing. We promised to love, honour and teach the dog to obey. We learned that this life form, whose eyes were barely open, came from a long line of carefully bred champions. His pure white, milk-filled mother eyed us suspiciously, while his brindle father trotted handsomely in his outdoor run. Pictures of his grandparents and pedigrees of his great-grandparents elevated the puppy in the pen to a form of doggy royalty.

We pledged fences, the finest food and quality time. Then we wrote a big cheque. Moose muttered something about having to give the dog a car on his sixteenth birthday.

Reluctantly, we left the puppy with his litter mates for a few more weeks. At home we prepared a house for him, collected a stack of newspapers for eventualities and pondered the virtues of several puppy schools. Mostly, we debated the subject of names.

In the popular culture, Bull Terriers have had names like Spuds (the Budweiser beer dog) and Bodger (the aged hero of Sheila Burney's lost-dog saga *The Longest Journey*.)

American Army General George Patton had a white Bull Terrier named Willie, who travelled with his master throughout World War II. There was even a legendary Bull Terrier named Patsy-Ann, who greeted ships at Juno in Alaska for many years.

Moose and I were like new parents, arguing the merits of every name from Anvil to Zydeco.

I finally retreated and decided to take my thoughts somewhere distinctly void of anything to do with puppies. I turned to poetry, grabbing from the shelves *The Collected Poems of Wallace Stevens*. On page nine, in a poem called "The Snow Man," I found the place my thoughts needed to be.

Stevens wrote:

One must have a mind of winter
To regard the frost and the boughs
Of the pine-trees crusted with snow

When I reminded the Moose of those lines from his favourite poet, the deed was done. I called the breeder and told her that the puppy would be named "Wallace Stevens."

On his "dog home," as we called the plastic and metal box otherwise known variously as a "cage" or a "crate," we inscribed the word "Wally."

What a difference two weeks make in one so young. Little Wally had almost doubled in size. We swooped the pooch into a blue blanket and cuddled him all the way to the car. From the back seat, Diva the Divine observed the squirm-some thing with the waggly tail and promptly went to sleep.

At the farm, Wally sat on the front lawn trying to comprehend what had just happened to him. Diva made it patently clear that she was neither his mother nor an udder.

A huge white rooster, Foghorn Leghorn, had the run of the farm. When he saw the small brown and white "thing" on the grass, the bird ran toward "it," sending Wally into a jumping, leaping, yelping spin toward the safety of the front porch, where I was watching from a big wicker chair.

We went out together to meet the creature. I lay down on the grass, leading Wally to smother me with licks until he climbed my back and began tearing at my T-shirt. Foghorn approached and I looked up at him from the vantage of a puppy.

The old bird's feet looked like something George Lucas devised for a *Star Wars* epic. Three huge, gnarled toes with spiked toenails were topped by scaled, leathery yellow skin leading to a ball-bearing knee joint.

The rooster's eyes were black, his pupils dilated in an amber orb. Flanges of blood red flesh dribbled beneath a bone-hard beak that arched like a sickle underneath a crowning comb as jagged as the back of a stegosaur.

Then the feathers around Foghorn's neck puffed out at the sides as he drew his head back, thrusting his chest forward and raising his wings like an evil angel. Foghorn closed his eyes for an instant, and I realized that Wally had inveigled himself underneath my chin for protection from the fearsome warrior before him. The scissored beak opened, the neck drew back and the crow that emerged was so ear-splitting that I imagined it cracking the well-built clouds above his ghastly visage.

Wally shot out from under my arms. He raced around a cedar tree and tore a path through a ribbon of pansies. He stopped. Then he bolted again, hopping over my ankles, around and under my chin before I could even move. After spinning circles through my herb garden, a slightly oregano-scented handful of puppy flopped at Foghorn Leghorn's feet, gazing at the rooster as though it was some sort of icon.

Moose was standing at the kitchen door, taking in the scene. I started laughing, but he warned me against it.

"You must not laugh at Wally, you must laugh with him," he said in all seriousness.

Wally stirred, leaning far back into his haunches and mustered a mighty "yip." We laughed and Foghorn turned on the gnarly excuse that passes for a rooster's heel.

Before we introduced the puppy to his new home, Wally and Moose took a stroll down the lane. It was like watching a dream grow younger, a big man walking his future mini-rhino. Indestructible.

SHEAR DELIGHT

I have bathed four times. I have shampooed my hair six times. My skin is anointed with French perfume and my hands are softer than a Bay Street lawyer's. But I still smell a bit like a sheep.

Yesterday we sheared the flock. For hours and hours I was tackling wool on the hoof, trimming sheep feet and tying fleeces into puffy packages for the market. It is dirty work, and this year it was even more difficult because the ewes are hugely pregnant. Stripped of their wool they look as though they've swallowed bowling balls.

My shearer, Judy, is a five-foot dynamo and she loves sheep. Judy would like to be reincarnated as a sheep. She raises sheep, her brother raises sheep and her father raised sheep. She married a cattle man. Now he raises sheep too.

You can tell Judy has generations of shepherding in her background because she calls ewes "Yos," which is the old-time way of talking about sheep.

Judy hauls her shearing stuff around in the back of a pickup truck that serves many purposes. When she goes to sheep shows, Judy will often take the sheep she's showing in the truck, along with her shears and grooming stand, a few bales of hay and her sleeping bag. Her truck becomes a sort of combination barnyard motel and beauty parlour.

When Judy arrived, I had all of the ewes penned in the barn ready for the first de-fleecing. Unfortunately, sheep don't just line up quietly to be sheared. They have to be caught, wrestled to the ground and set into an upright seated position for Judy to do her work.

After a certain number of years, I have developed a technique that I find works better than my first few shearing adventures, which featured a lot of flying through the air and missing the sheep.

I set my sights on one sheep in the bunch and move slowly toward her. No distraction can deter me once I have set my goal. This is an old trick I learned by watching sheep dogs.

Talking softly, moving slowly with my beady eyes on the chosen sheep, I get close enough to grapple her under the chin with one hand and grab her stubby tail with the other. This can get messy.

With the front and back of the sheep in my control, I can sometimes propel the sheep to the shearing area, but most often the sheep drags me around for a while until we end up there by luck.

Sheep cannot be trained to lie down, roll over and sit up. "Tipping the ewe" as it is called, involves a number of techniques which are prevalent at Wrestlemania events. For instance, if you twist the ewe's head in the direction you want her to fall she inevitably will. But that neck wrenching stuff makes me feel like an unlicensed chiropractor and I cannot bear the bone-cracking nature of it.

You can also try tripping the sheep, but this is tricky because a sheep has four feet while the tripper only has two feet.

This year, Judy and I performed a team effort. Both of us stood on one side of the sheep and we co-ordinated our efforts to grab one opposite leg and gently roll the sheep over in consideration of their delicate condition.

Thus prone, I propped the ewes into a sitting position for Judy to shear.

Judy shears in great long curves down the sides and back of the sheep, trimming around the sheep's cheeks and neck with great delicacy. It is a real art. When she is done, the bald ewe scampers off and the whole fleece lies in one piece on the shearing tarpaulin.

My sheep are Suffolks — the black-faced models. Their wool is not the finest. I think it ends up being used in carpets. Each ewe produces six to eight pounds of wool, and after shearing costs I figure that I earn about 20 cents per sheep in wool sales.

You really have to be a few bricks short of a load to be a shepherd.

The fleeces are bundled and wrapped with twine. It's not like folding a sheet because, of course, each fleece is shaped like a flattened-out sheep. The belly wool is tucked into the middle and the leg wool is tucked under that and then you make four folds to get it sort of rounded out and tie it up like a present.

The joy of folding fleece is in the touch. Sheep produce lanolin in their wool. The stuff you pay for in fancy skin creams oozes from the fresh-sheared wool. It stinks like a sheep, however, when you handle it from the source.

Bruised, battered and desperately in need of a lower back massage, I bade Judy goodbye as she charged off to denude her next flock.

Before the first of many bouts with bubble bath, I went to the barn to check on the girls and assure them that this enforced air conditioning of their bodies was in their best interest.

In the far corner, I found two future candidates for shearing — newborn twin lambs on wobbly legs, nursing at their mother's side. Never was bald so beautiful to me.

THE BARN DUCK IN LUST

It is Spring and the barn duck is in love. It is not a seasoned, mature love, but rather the unchained lust of a duck that does not know he is a duck. The barn duck is in love with a barred rock hen, but I fear his passion will be unrequited, because the old hen has been around the barn long enough to know that she is not a duck.

The barn duck is an odd one. I call him Groucho, because he runs slouched forward, with his wings folded tight and his little orange feet going a mile a minute. Although he is primarily black, a few arches of white above his eyes give him the look of the infamous Marx Brother and I could well imagine a cartoonist drawing him with one of Groucho's trademark cigars.

Much smaller than the big white Emden ducks and the gentle Mallards, he also walks upright like a penguin or a man for that matter. Although he has wings, he cannot fly. He just runs faster than anything on two webbed feet.

Groucho is an Indian Runner duck. I hatched him two years ago. In fact, he was forming in the incubator when a fox killed his parents and all of his kin.

Indian Runners are a helpless kind of duck. I have seen geese actually face off with a fox, waving their strong wings fearlessly and wagging their ugly spiked goose-tongues. Even fat geese and ducks can usually raise themselves into the air long enough to find some safety. But Indian Runners can only run; otherwise they are quite literally, sitting ducks.

In fact, I acquired my original gang of Indian Runners because they run. My neighbours, Scotty and Sarah McComb, raise all sorts of fowl, but they never eat them. Their birds are destined for the show ring or other fowl-fanciers' farms. When Scotty showed me their big flock of Indian Runners, a huge grin swept his face.

"Useless as sticks," he laughed. "But watch 'em run."

Sure enough he rattled his grain pail and hollered, "Here Duck, Here Duck," and the whole colourful lot of them came quacking over the hill into the yard. Running like upright maniacs.

There is something absurdly joyful about running ducks. That is what Scotty said he liked about them. And so did I, until the fox came and started plucking them one by one. The ducks that ran like men could not outrun a fox. They were not happy when I penned them up, but even then, the fox found a way.

When little Groucho hatched, I vowed that he would always stay within my sight, or within the barn.

Because he is singularly odd, Groucho cannot stay in the same pen as the other ducks. They pick on him, probably as much for his irritating quack as for his differences. I figure he is better off loose in the barn, where he can roam freely and accompany me as I do my chores, quacking at will when the barn door closes.

Consequently, the only other birds Groucho sees are Guinea fowl and chickens. For the longest time, he hung out with a black and white Polish rooster. Polish chickens are another thing I have collected simply because of their looks. They have huge tufts of feathers on their heads, like great fluffy crowns. My Polish rooster's head is so fine and full that the feathers sometimes obliterate his vision, which may be the reason that he accepted Groucho as his buddy. At night they sleep together, the Indian Runner duck and his visually challenged Polish friend.

Groucho's love affair with the barred rock hen started a few weeks ago. She was quietly sitting on her nest making the clucking sounds that go with producing an egg. I watched the little duck scramble up on a bale of hay beside her. He looked down at the hen, quacked furiously and pounced. Apparently ducks do not believe in foreplay.

The hen was beside herself. Before this, she had simply ignored the duck the way all of the chickens did. Now he was astride her trying to grab the back of her neck with his tough duck beak — and she was in the middle of passing an egg.

This breach of etiquette did not elude the Polish rooster, who heard the commotion and tried to figure out where it was coming from. Before he could scoot the feathers from his eyes, three other hens were pecking away at Groucho. The duck finally surrendered to their will.

Now I have to watch Groucho every day. When I start doing chores, he waddles at my feet, quacking at lambs and just quacking in general. As we get close to the chicken pen, he starts stomping his little webbed feet. Weaving back and forth, anxiously.

I have to be quick. If the pen door stays open one second too long, the duck runs straight past me into what he perceives is his personal harem. The mere sight of the lusty duck sends the chickens flying for the rafters, clucking and letting out long chicken growls.

Groucho just stands there. A duck at centre stage. Looking up, flapping his useless wings and quacking.

One of these days — soon — I will have to head over to Scotty and Sarah's and find Groucho a suitable mate. I can put up with another barn duck. The chickens will be pleased to go back to laying their eggs in peace. And maybe Groucho will not be so grouchy if he finds a true love who walks upright and loves to run, and looks a lot like him.

LET'S GET READY TO GAMBOL

The annual ritual of putting the sheep to pasture has begun.

When I opened the barnyard gate the ewes rushed forward in delight. They have been begging for green pastures since the first sprigs of clover began fluttering in the breeze.

The lambs followed their mothers in a clump. Timorous at first, they were wary of the larger world outside of the barn. Then one bold little ram took a charge across the pasture before stopping dead to look around. The others followed him, just like little sheep, and soon the whole lamb crop was a gamboling mass.

Lambs do gambol. It is the perfect word to describe the dancing kind of gallop-cum-foxtrot that they perform when they are playful. Sometimes you would swear they had springs on their tiny hooves because they tend to bounce in leaps and bounds.

After nibbling at sweet grass and poking their noses around in a sand pile created by groundhogs, the lambs set about determining the perimeters of their grand new environment.

This is where good fencing comes into play. On my farm, the first pasture new lambs find themselves in is one bounded in part by several strands of sturdy electrified wire. It is something no one can prepare them to avoid, and their discovery of it is always — well — quite shocking.

The great Canadian thinker Marshall McLuhan determined that "The medium is the message." Although he was defining the impact of electronic communication in the Global Village, his vision certainly applies concretely to the true nature of electric fencing.

Sheep can be quite stupid about many things, but when it comes to recognizing the consequences of breaching a charged fence wire, they quickly become mental giants with awesome retentive power.

I have had cattle who would not think twice about trying to go through a brick wall just to get to the other side, but they would halt warily at the sight of a single silver strand of wire. One particularly belligerent Hereford cow, who seemed to feel that going through fences was her purpose in life, met her match when she touched her nose to a wire and found herself doing a bovine tango that would have made any Brazilian dance company proud.

On a personal level, I can tell you that I learned how to break dance, slam dance and fandango simultaneously the first time I "tested" the fence by mistake. The voltage is not strong enough to do any damage, but the shock is definitely enough to create an indelible impression.

I could set a bowl of barbecued hamburgers just inside the electric fence and my dogs might drool and fuss, but they would not be led into temptation. Such is the power of shock therapy.

Electric fencing has been a boon to me because it is lightweight and easy to use for temporary pasture divisions. A single strand of it strategically placed on permanent wire fences and old cedar rail fences helps to prevent the animals from straining their heads over or through the fences.

Years ago, I installed a strand of electric wire above a page wire fence, but I never did get around to hooking it up to a power source. Today, that fence remains pristine simply because the animals have not been willing to bet on what is a live wire and what is not.

Nothing is infallible when it comes to sheep and fencing, but for the time being the borders appear to be secure.

The lambs are contentedly grazing with their mothers. When they tire of eating they form little play groups and tear around the field at full tilt, pulling up to a skidding stop at the fenceline. Month-old ram lambs square off to butt heads together and aggressive ewe lambs bully their younger sisters. On a mound of old hay they play king-of-the-castle, galloping to the top and awaiting challengers.

The real gamboling has just begun. Even the old ewes are prone to kick up their heels now and then from the pure pleasure of being in the wide open spaces. From my kitchen window I can watch the band of lambs chasing killdeers and dancing backwards as puffs of wind blow the heads off a few dandelions.

When the sun is shining and the grass is lush, a shepherd can savour the moment. There really is restorative power in knowing that your flock can lie down in green pastures.

CHICKEN SOUP
FOR THE CHICKEN'S SOUL

Of all farm animals, the lowly chicken is the least likely of creatures to draw its caretaker into the sort of personal bond that can develop between a goatherd and a favourite nanny, or a swineherd and a lovable old boar.

The words "chicken" and "personality" are seldom seen in close proximity. However, occasionally one bird will rise above the rest and display a willful temperament that distinguishes it from the others. Such can be said of certain roosters who will crow back at you when you feel like crowing yourself.

Of course, this is the sort of behaviour one keeps to oneself. It can be highly humiliating to have a neighbour drop by and catch you out in the barn crowing with the roosters. I know this to be true.

Chickens tend to be helpless creatures, viewed largely as economic units and raised in confined situations designed to maximize production. Those of us who cast monetary considerations to the wind, and pamper our chickens with things such as leg room and natural light, generally suffer some unexpected consequences.

One summer I raised 100 chicks from day-olds to six-week-olds, which is adolescence in terms of chickens. At that stage, I allowed them to range freely in the field behind their coop, where they could forage for bugs and greenery to supplement their grain-fed diet.

Moose and I felt confident enough to leave them alone one sunny afternoon when we went off to an auction in search of 50-cent lots of nuts and bolts and other treasures. While we were gone, storm clouds gathered squarely over the farm, suddenly depositing what must have been a wall of water.

On our return, we galloped across the muddy field to the coop and found the range full of sodden chickens lying like saturated feather pillows in the mud. Instead of retreating to their straw-dry coop, the young idiots had stayed out in the rain. Worse, they had apparently tried to swallow the deluge.

From the tense, skyward projection of certain of their legs, some of them were definitely past-tense chickens. But many were still gurgling.

Hauling them into the coop, Moose and I rubbed them with straw. Their eyes were vacant black holes; scrawny necks twisted back over clammy feathers glued to bony breasts. I was ready to give up when the Moose decided that what they needed was a stiff drink.

Separating Moose from his vodka is not something that occurs every day. I am not even allowed to sip a martini, it having been determined years ago that such rocket fuel is "too spicy" for my delicate constitution. But in this life-or-death situation, Moose became the soul of generosity. While I tended the sputtering flock, he fetched the freezer-cold Stolichnaya.

Finding the vodka was no problem, but the eye-dropper eluded him. Instead, Moose brought with him the smallest spoon he could find — the slightly tarnished, sterling silver baby spoon my godmother gave me.

I cradled one of the birds, forcing its beak ajar, and Moose carefully measured a tiny quantity of spirits into the spoon. We didn't hear the creature gulp, but its eyes did flash wide open as the refined Russian potato mash slid down its gullet. The chicken began jerking weakly, cocking its head and blinking. When we set the pathetic thing back onto the straw, it stayed upright.

"It works," exclaimed Moose. "If chickens had lips, he'd be smacking them."

And so it went.

Two hours and twenty-six ounces later, the doused and soused survivors were back to preening and clucking as though nothing had happened.

For the longest time, I thought that Moose and I might be alone in the invocation of extreme measures involving alcohol and chickens. But as in everything associated with farming, once the story is out, someone else has already been there.

For Sandy, a genteel chicken-keep who lives at Farmer's Walk farm in the Hockley Valley north of Toronto, it all started with a rooster named Clarence.

Clarence was a barred-rock cockerel in the bloom of youth when he arrived at Sandy's henhouse with his mate Mabel in tow. The henhouse was heaven on earth to

Clarence. Sandy called it "The University Women's Club," much to the dismay of her upstanding aunt who had been a member of the real thing.

Clarence slept beside Mabel faithfully every night but came the dawn and he was up and crowing, ready to make his amorous rounds. Sandy noted the wear and tear on the hens, particularly her favourite, a plump red-feathered bird named Henny Penny.

"Henny Penny went tits up one day because Clarence wore her out," Sandy told me. Thereafter, she determined that: "Roosters should not live with hens." With that pronouncement, Sandy was halfway up the poultry learning curve.

A crisis arose one day when she found Clarence leaning against the side of the henhouse looking decidedly unwell.

By then, Sandy knew that a sick chicken in the morning would be a dead chicken by noon. Panicked, she called Anson, her neighbourhood chicken expert, and he arrived with his wife's baby thermometer to check Clarence's vital signs. The message, according to the mercury, was that Clarence was almost a broiler.

Although the stockpot was the obvious solution to Clarence's dilemma, Sandy refused to accept the prognosis without pursuing all options. While Anson watched in wonderment, she bundled Clarence into her car and took him to the veterinarian.

The vet took one look at Clarence and promptly declared that she was not a chicken vet. However, Sandy was adamant. In the examining room, Clarence was once again subjected to the indignity of the thermometer. The formal diagnosis was that Clarence was "a very sick bird." The vet gave him a shot of antibiotics and provided a small jug of medicine which was to be administered with an eyedropper.

Thirty-seven dollars later, Sandy and Clarence were free to leave.

Back at Farmer's Walk, Sandy struggled to treat the squirming rooster. She secured Clarence under her arm and held his rubbery wattles to immobilize him. After three tries, she got the eyedropper into Clarence's beak.

Then disaster struck. Clarence shook his head abruptly and swallowed the tip of the eyedropper in the process.

Horrified, Sandy again bundled the rooster into the car and sped back to the vet's.

After Sandy explained the circumstance, the vet examined Clarence again and announced that retrieval of the foreign object would involve a surgical intervention approximating evisceration and a procedural fee of $150.

Since the initial curative investment of $37 was arguably ten times the market value of past-his-prime Clarence, Sandy decided to see if the old bird could get along with an eyedropper nib somewhere in the works.

Clarence lived out his days shaking his head frequently as if trying to dislodge something in his throat. His crow was more of a disjointed *ack ack ack* than *cock-a-doodle-do*. Otherwise, he thrived as the cock of Farmer's Walk.

The rooster was ill toward the end of his life, but Sandy eschewed the vet this time. Like Moose, she put her faith in the bottle. Accordingly, Sandy told me that

Clarence "became something of an alcoholic," but he did not appear to suffer.

Fortunately, Sandy's husband was an airline pilot who could avail himself of the miracle of duty-free shopping, as well as those perfectly chicken-sized airline booze mini-bottles. Thus, Clarence was able to consume the best whiskey money could buy as he made his gradual march to the great single-malt-maker in the sky.

Between Dr. Moose's Miracle Vodka Cure and Sandy's Whiskey Poultry Hospice, perhaps extreme measures involving poultry and alcohol are not as uncommon as I thought. Even the lowly, lipless chicken can benefit from an occasional cup of good cheer.

MOTHER'S DAY IN BLOOM

I grow a hillside full of daffodils for Mother's Day — but my Mother never gets them — someone else's does.

It all started about fifteen years ago when I temporarily lost fiscal sanity and bought a couple of hundred daffodil bulbs. One brisk fall day, I planted every last one of them on a hillside next to the forest, just beside the roadway at the end of the farm lane.

Visions of a miniature rolling meadow dotted with nodding trumpet heads of yellow filled me with anticipation all that winter. And, when the daffodils made their debut the following May, it made any memory of muddy April disappear. Every time I turned the truck up the lane it made me smile.

Over the next five years, I added clumps of lilies, tall poppies and iris to the hillside. Any flowering perennial that could be divided and transplanted from the garden beds around the farm house ended up finding a place on the hill. Some thrived, some faded away. Wild flowers added their own colour.

Every spring the daffodils grew in number. Left to their own devices they divided and conquered like a Dutch army. On Mother's Day, I had a big vase filled with daffodils in the house and when my Mother visited, she could leave with an armload of yellow flowers that we plucked from the wayside garden.

But about a decade ago something changed. When I went down the lane to pick the Mother's Day daffodils, they were gone. Every bloom had disappeared, leaving only the unfolded buds to provide a smattering of what once was, when they flowered a few days later. The hillside had been plucked like a chicken.

I was angry. I felt robbed and personally denuded. But there was nothing at all to be done. I still had batches of daffodils around the house. That was not the point. The flowering hillside had been a fantasy. To me it was like something out of A.A. Milne's Winnie the Pooh and Christopher Robin stories — "a warm and sunny spot" in the landscape; "that enchanted place on the top of the forest where a little boy and a bear will always be playing."

Then some ignoramus wrecked it all, on Mother's Day to boot.

Since then the Mother's Day flower theft has become an annual event.

One year, I put out a "No Trespassing" sign, but the wind blew it over and it looked fairly silly and mean-spirited to begin with.

My neighbours began noticing that the hillside of yellow joy only survived for a few days every spring. Some of them had their own fantasy of me living in a house filled with daffodils in vases in every room. When I told them the terrible truth, they started keeping watch over the roadway around Mother's Day, but no one ever saw the blooming bandit.

Suggestions poured in to accompany the solutions that fermented in my own fevered brain.

Leghold traps were out of the question, because small forest animals and deer sometimes crossed the hillside. Electric fencing would have been a nice solution, except it is far too visible to any daytime daffodil stalker, and you cannot clear-cut an entire hillside in the dark.

An older gentleman suggested incarcerating a pen of geese on the hillside to act as an early warning defence system. It seemed like a good idea, except all of my geese were sitting on eggs.

The one big goose I did manage to install in a makeshift chicken wire pen halfway down the laneway honked and screamed all night long. By dawn, he had beaten his way out of the pen with his powerful wings. That failure was heard all along the concession.

Someone suggested I try camping in the forest behind the hill overnight and catching the culprit yellow-handed. I even had the offer of a paint gun — the sort that crazed mercenary wannabes play with as a splatter-game sport. But I am not the sort who can curl up gracefully in a pup tent and sleeping bag when I have a comfortable bed within striking distance. And I just could not imagine myself rising from the hillside like a sleepy G.I. Jane and launching a missile of red paint on a crouched daffodil thief at dawn. I could, however, imagine missing my target and ending up with a hillside covered in red paint.

A child came up with the most inventive, noncombative solution. She suggested that I find a baby skunk to be a pet and keep it at a special skunkhouse on the hillside. Then the skunk could stink up any intruder and the flowers would live happily ever after. It was a charming idea, but I have never found a skunk to be that friendly. Better a hillside without flowers than a hillside filled with stink blossoms.

So I have resigned myself to enjoying the daffodils while they sway, oh so briefly, on the hillside. Five years ago, I began digging up bulbs and separating them, taking a few back to the farmhouse every year and planting them in the fenced orchard meadow just outside the kitchen.

Now it does not bother me when the daffodils disappear. I turn the truck up the lane on Mother's Day and sigh. But somewhere I imagine that there is a mother who is blessed with a bigger vase of flowers than she had ever hoped for. If she is a good mother, someday she will discover the personality defect in the off-centre offspring who gives her an ill-gotten gift and she will correct it.

In the meantime, there are plenty of daffodils in the orchard field for my Mother and I to pluck on Mother's Day, or any other May day that happens along.

And in the end, that is what it is all about.

Being with Mother.

WONDER WOMAN
IN WELLINGTON BOOTS

On a farm, you live closely with the tune and the turn of the seasons. Every spring is a reminder of springs past, but every year, when the first lavender lilac bursts from bud to flower, there is a refreshing newness to celebrate.

Spring is in the air these days. I know because the neighbouring pig farmer has been keeping his barn door open and every now and then I catch a powerful whiff.

With the bedroom window just slightly open, I awake to the sounds of the barnyard — the duelling of Banty rooster crows, and the ewes calling me to feed them while their restless lambs jiggle and jump at the gate, hoping for a romp in the field.

I was feeling quite in tune with the sensuality of the farm on a recent spring morning. The flock had been fed and I let them out to play in the sunshine. There's nothing quite like the happy chaos of lambs ripsnorting around the pasture, hellbent on nothing in particular, startled by their own shadows and flabbergasted by the sight of a groundhog scurrying for cover.

In the midst of this bucolic splendour, I decided to stroll to the hay shed to fetch a few bales of fine second-cut hay for the lambs. I pushed my blue wheelbarrow, and the old black barn cat, Webster, tagged along.

I could have driven the truck, but a walk with a purpose, that was what suited my mood.

The sheep must have been watching me because I heard them coming from a distance. Two bales were on the wheelbarrow and each member of the flock was determined to be the first to have a go at finding the best leafy bits. I was standing on a platform that is raised off the ground about four feet.

In that instant, for some inexplicable reason, I decided to defend the hay.

Hollering something pertinent, like "G'it, you bad sheep," I jumped off the platform.

In that midair moment, with my straw hat slipping sideways and the cat scurrying for cover, I thought to myself, "Just think girl, you've been doing this since you were 25."

I felt like Wonder Woman in Wellington boots.

Then I landed and heard a terrible crunch.

In that sickening moment, the blue sky opened up to me and, although I saw no clouds, I knew something painful was coming my way.

It seems my once-25-year-old bones, were no longer made for flights of fancy.

Lying beside the wheelbarrow, I waved my hat at the sheep and they stopped in their tracks. It hurt, as I knew it would, red pain in the right ankle. A few timorous lambs came forward to sniff me.

Suddenly alert, Wally, the non-sheep-herding bull terrier shot through the flock and bounded to my side, scattering lambs and licking my face with his doggy tongue, until I let out an anguished howl.

You lie there on the ground, feeling like a fool, and an old fool at that.

Of course, things must be done. Ice packs and x-rays, and "Sorry, I can't go horseback riding this Thursday."

But there's time for that, and time for stillness, especially when your left hand is planted in something that feels suspiciously like a well-aged mound of horse manure.

I spent the next ten days hobbling around with a tensor bandage supporting my swollen ankle. The good thing was that it was just a sprain. The bad thing was having to explain how it happened.

What I discovered is that the image of unstoppable youth stays with us despite the mirror's tale.

All I had to do was say, "I thought I was 25 and I jumped," and knowing looks spread across faces.

Stories flowed about childhoods spent swinging on ropes over haymows and leaping into rivers from railway trestles. They were all lithe memories from a time before knees knew how to creak. And everyone I talked to had tried in some way to recover the feeling later in life and found themselves foiled.

One poor man who had spent his youth climbing up the side of silos, told me he thought it would be a no-brainer when he decided to scale his three-storey television tower in an effort to correct a wayward antenna.

He was grappling with the mysteries of which way the wind blows channel 13 when he fell. Long before the body cast was removed, he decided to excise temptation by installing a satellite dish.

Then there was the story of someone's grandmother who insisted on picking pears well into her eighties.

Fuelled by her beverage of choice, granny mounted a stepladder and proceeded to go — quite literally — out on a limb.

She fell on a well-padded grandson who took the blame, although for the life of him he still can't figure out why. After that, grandma used her cane to whack pears out of the tree.

And a mature farm woman, whose sensible and practical wisdom I have often heeded, told me her own giddy tale about confronting a full-grown bull who was foraging in her garden.

"I don't know what I was thinking," she said. "I was just so mad. I picked up a pail and threw it at the darn bull."

In her day, she had been a passable basketball centre. She still remembers watching the arc of the pail before it slam-dunked the bull's backside.

"Best shot I ever made," she crowed. Fortunately, the startled bull charged the clothesline instead of her.

And it struck me how lucky we are to have the faultless memory of fearless youth, but how much wiser we would be to remember it rather than try to relive it.

I will remember that the next time I decide to jump anywhere on impulse. But I don't intend to become a worrywart.

I will continue to climb my metal paddock gate instead of unlocking it and going through the easy way.

I like the feeling of swinging my leg over the top of the gate.

When that gate was hung twenty years ago, it was the crowning glory that finished the job of fencing the sheep pasture. The scent of lilacs was in the air that day, too.

In the future, I guess I will have to storm the gate one rung at a time. But every time I manage to swing my leg over, I'll be saying to myself, "Just think, girl, you've been doing this since you were 25."

Summer

THE PICKLE SUMMER

There is an unwritten rule that when an urban person buys a quantity of land, they are bound to make a fool of themselves on at least one acre. The rest of the land may be well-planned for crops, or grazing, or tree-growing. It may be rented to a neighbour who knows what to do with the land. However, there is always that one little plot that seems to cry out willfully: "Do something crazy with me. Boldly go beyond where any normal farmer would dare."

So it is that virtually every urban-transplant farmer that I know has at least one horror story about a wayward experiment in trying to grow anything from asparagus to ginseng. Most often, these failures end up costing money, rather than making it. Most often, they are fuelled by an ambition to get rich quick.

In my case, it started with a little ad in a local paper. Something to the effect that you could earn up to $2,000 an acre growing pickle cucumbers. That sounded mighty fine. It was my first year on the farm and I was determined to make some money. A two-and-a-half acre field just behind the garden looked ripe for cash-crop pickling.

What I discovered is that you don't just grow the pickles, you also pick them and deliver them. And unless you are equipped with a pickle seeder on a tractor, you plant them by hand. I had a neighbour spread the field with sheep manure. It is rich in the nitrogen that pickle plants crave. It was ploughed and tilled and ready for planting.

Armed with my pickle grower's contract and $120 worth of pickle seed, I set out with hoe in hand to plant the rows. On weekends I had two helpers, a five-year-old and a nine-year-old. We planted from dawn till dusk. When you're planting a seed every four inches, two-and-a-half acres seems forever.

"I guess this must be what the slaves felt like," the nine-year-old commented during a mid-row break. The sun beat down and wind whipped dirt in our faces. When we were finished planting I bought the kids bicycles. I never saw them again.

I waited two weeks for the field to come to life. When the pickle plants started to grow, so did the weeds. I hoed and rototilled for days on end. When the pickles sprouted on the vines, I bought big burlap sacks at the feed mill to contain the bounty. Then I started picking.

Pickles can be mean and spiny critters. Especially the little ones, the ones that hide under leaves. But if you want to earn $2,000 an acre, it's those little pickles — the gherkin-size, no bigger than a baby's thumb — that make your fortune. Takes a lot of those suckers to fill one brown sack.

Every other day, I had to deliver my fresh-picked pickles to a sorting station near Teeswater, a half-hour drive away. I would start picking at 6 a.m. before loading my bounty into the old pickup truck at 4:30 and heading for the pickle depot. Rain or shine, it did not matter. Those gherkins could suck up rain drops and turn into full-blown cucumbers overnight.

I dreamed about pickles. Picking one whole row of perfect little gherkins was a fantasy. A whole row of eight-inch, slicing pickles was a nightmare.

My family thought I was nuts. Grandmother had once planted pickles, and all the aunts and uncles remembered the back-breaking work. Farm neighbours simply scrunched their foreheads and smiled. But with acres of nitrogen-powered pickles on the ground, there was nothing to do but pick.

The pickle depot opened at five p.m. I was never the first in line. Pickle people came in all shapes and sizes, just like their pickles. There were matrons in Buicks with pickles in their trunks. There were rusted out Volkswagens, barely more than roller-skates on wheels, with sacks full of pickles sagging out of the windows. Vans full of pickles, and pickup trucks full of pickles and kids and barking dogs. Four strapping teenage boys who were working their way through university on pickle money would pull up with a manure spreader chock full of pickles. The line of pickle-laden vehicles spread down the county road like a misplaced caravan from *The Grapes of Wrath*. While we waited our turn to unload, we shared pickle stories and worried about leafy mould.

None of us had figured a way to harvest the pickles mechanically. Stories circulated about motorized carts built low to the ground. A picker could lie belly-down, turn on the ignition and scoot through the rows picking from either side. No one ever saw the contraption, but we could all imagine it.

In a cavernous shed, the pickle-sorting machine clamoured and clacked for hours every night. It was a kind of triumph when you finally got to pour your pickle bags out onto the worn brown canvas that rolled and tossed the pickles to the pickle-grading slots. Two sisters kept a watchful eye for "bad uns," their short-nailed fingers grabbing wounded and distorted pickles as they bounced along the canvas. The littlest gherkins tumbled into big wicker baskets first, and the final Grade D cucumbers thudded at the end. Then thick-thighed farm boys hoisted the sorted pickles on a scale, shouting out weights and grades to the pickle accountant. Fixed, she sat at a maroon card table and tapped the information into an ancient adding machine in a never-ending pat-pat-pat, dwarfed by the rattling of the machinery and the rolling thunder of thousands of pickles.

When all of my pickles were counted, I would take the yellow weigh slip and tuck it into the glove compartment just like all of the other pickle people. No one ever showed their yellow slip. It was the big secret, but we all knew that not one of us was going to pocket $2,000 an acre.

I picked tons of pickles that summer. I picked pickles until my hands were green. I even smelled faintly like a pickle. When the pickle station closed in September, I still had hundreds of pickles in the field. Nobody wanted to buy my pickles. None of the neighbours wanted my pickles; they already had a few in the garden. My parents politely took two quart baskets. I gave away a few more thanks to a sign at the end of the lane. Before me sat a patch that could have garnished every restaurant plate in Toronto for two weeks, and they had no place to go.

So, I started canning. I ended up with five dozen quart jars of Aunt Marion's dill pickles before I finally quit. The cold cellar shelves groaned with the weight of pickles. I had dilled more pickles than a person could eat in three lifetimes. After that, anyone visiting the farm was not allowed to leave without taking at least one jar of dill pickles as a "memento." Customers who bought my freezer lamb and capons thought it was very sweet of me to include a jar of homemade pickles with their order. I gave dill pickles as Christmas gifts. I gave dill pickles as shower gifts. And I ate a lot of dill pickles.

The kicker arrived a few months after the frost had laid the leftover pickles and their vines to rest. A cheque in the mail came from my pickle boss. I savoured the feel of the envelope as I walked up the lane that autumn day, trudging past the pickle field where I had passed so many back-breaking days.

Even a cheque that realized the dream of $2,000 an acre would not have seemed enough. I knew exactly what the pickles had cost me, from the seed to the kids' bikes, to the burlap sacks, and the new tire for the old truck and the gas to keep it rolling. It was the most rude exercise in subtraction that I have ever done. All told, the whole effort earned me a total of $23.16. I did not tell anyone this sad state of affairs, because I knew that somewhere out there a joker was waiting to tell me that I was lucky that I did not lose money.

It has been nearly fifteen years since my "pickle summer," and I still cannot look at a jar of dill pickles without cringing. When I come to the cucumber page in a seed catalogue, I turn it quickly.

I guess everyone who moves to the country has to make their own mistakes. Mine was ambition founded in greed, which blinded me to those silly little words "up to" in small print before the bold-faced pickle fantasy of $2,000 an acre.

There is nothing wrong with boldly going where few farmers have dared to go. It is the boldest of individual farmers in this country who have given us some of its greatest wealth. Think of John and Allan McIntosh toiling to create that one special tree that grew the firmest, juiciest red apples they had ever encountered. Think of scientist Charles Saunders chewing his way through hundreds of kernels of wheat before discovering the grain that made Canada the breadbasket of the world.

But when you see a little advertisement in the local paper that promises $2,000 an acre for growing anything, think twice. It could land you in a real pickle.

CATCH A FALLING BALE

Haying can make you crazy. At the best of times, it is hot, sweaty work. At the worst of times, it is a rush against the rain.

The Moose and I did not know this when we signed up for our first haying. The neighbours said it was a communal activity and everyone helped everyone. So we showed up one promising July morning ready to learn how to bring in the hay.

It was going to be a scorcher of a day. I wore a halter top and shorts. Moose wore his bathing trunks and a big T-shirt with the arms cut off. We could work on our muscles and our suntans at the same time.

Before we set off on the hay wagon someone handed us gloves with the fingers cut off at the tips. They fit, sort of. We clapped our hands in delight and posed for the camera shot of our first hay day.

There was some discussion among the men about what sort of bales we would be hauling back. Apparently there were a number of settings on the baler that ranged from lightweight to heavyweight. The lightweight bales were called "ladies bales." Moose knew that I would have none of that and insisted that we could handle whatever was thrown at us.

"Done by noon," we shouted gaily, as we bounced down the lane on the wagon with a young lad who was going to supervise us.

The field was a good fifteen acres of what looked to be flat land. Cut hat lay in windrows that fluffed in the breeze under three puffs of cloud overhead. In the swamp beside the field, red-winged blackbirds made pitch with their high-sounding calls.

The bales of hay started shooting out of the hay binder with a certain regularity. I marvelled at the notion that some inventor has figured out a way to scoop dehydrated blades of grass out of the dirt and package them neatly with tied string, but no one has figured out how to automatically fold laundry as it comes out of the dryer. Bales kept coming. Soon all thoughts evaporated in a veil of sweat.

We had about twenty bales neatly stacked on top of each other when the teenager waved his arms and shouted for the tractor to stop. A quick course in hay stacking for idiots followed. We learned to place two bales sideways against one laid frontwards followed by two sideways, unless two frontwards were needed to end the row neatly. Overlaps of frontwards and lengthwise bales on the next layer "tied" the pile into some form of solid mass. The proximity of bales counted, otherwise you could find yourself wedged thigh-high in bales halfway lip the stack.

Somehow, we managed to load the whole wagon. Moose would not complain but my body ached. The only expanse of skin not covered with dirt or scrapes or sunburn was underneath my gloves. We returned to the barn in serious need of water, sustenance and body armour.

By this time, four clouds had collected overhead. Cows were lying down in the field, apparently a sure sign of rain to come. We were promptly transferred to a new wagon and handed a thermos of lemonade and a bag of baloney sandwiches.

While we gnawed and supped like hungry barn cats, the men fretted about the weather.

"Can you go any faster?" one asked the Moose. We immediately felt like slackers.

"She can't but I can," he responded. Inwardly, I thanked him, too tired to defend my Amazonian honour.

"Well, can you catch a bale?" came the next question.

"Sure, where do I catch it?" said the Moose, drawing himself to his full height with an enormous creak of his knees. I was proud of the big guy. This was his weekend away from the office. His time to revel in rural bliss. He could have been at home sampling the snap of fresh radishes from the garden and watching me arrange bouquets of peonies, but here he was slogging bales. We were farming.

The baler was adjusted. Long-sleeved cotton shirts and green work pants appeared and we strapped them, on. The lemonade jug was filled to the brim. We set out on a mission to fast-track some hay.

The tractor took off over the field with a bounce, and the bales started spewing out. The Moose grabbed them in mid-air and chucked them back toward me. He looked like an action hero on Ritalin.

We had half a wagon stacked when I noticed the pick-up trucks at the road edge. There were almost a dozen lining the edge of the field.

"Who's having an auction?" I wondered, but you do not have much time to think when bales are flying at you like giant spiked medicine balls. Frontwards, lengthwise, who cared about making a fancy pattern. I tied off at the end of each row and hoped for the best.

When the tractor finally stopped, Moose and I lay on top of the hay wagon, wordless, watching dark clouds drifting together. A raindrop hit my ankle and we scurried to the ground to latch onto the back of the wagon for the short ride back to the barn.

There were many trucks gathered in the yard. We rode the wagon straight into the barn, arriving just before the deluge. Pigeons cooed above the steady staccato on the metal roof.

In the doorway of the barn, a gaggle of hayers watched the rain beat down on the stubble in the fields.

"Catch a good bale, son," one older man said. Two others coughed in agreement.

"Never saw that done before," he added, blowing his nose. Then the whole mass of them started chuckling, shoulders moving up and down, backs bending to the knees. They laughed so hard that their baseball caps fell on the wooden-planked floor.

No one before or since has seen such a display of bale catching. Others have tried and failed. Somewhere between Samson and Babe the Blue Ox, the legend of the

Haying Moose was cast. When large round bales became the fashion, rumour had it that the Moose could roll a whole fieldful into the barn in a morning.

But that is just crazy hay talk. It took him almost all day.

ROY ROGERS AND ME

People move to the country for all kinds of reasons from altruism to economics to sanity, but when you get right down to it I think what swayed me was the notion that I could have a horse.

I was practically weaned watching *National Velvet*. My favourite childhood storybook was *Black Beauty*. And while my other little school friends talked about honourable career goals such as nursing or teaching, I wanted to be a cowboy.

The other kids may have known the names of the top scorers in the NHL, but I knew that the Cisco Kid's horse was named Diablo.

My mother took me horseback riding for the first time when I was five. We were on a family trip through the Tennessee hills and there just happened to be a stable at the roadside and it just happened to have a trail ride.

Mother was always game for adventure, so while my father leaned warily against an old rail fence, I found myself being hoisted aboard a large, broad palomino horse which was outfitted with a pony saddle to suit my size. I looked like a pea on an elephant, but I felt like Roy Rogers.

It turned out to be quite a trail ride. We went up a mountain, threading our way on a slender path that was edged by a substantial drop-off. Mother kept wanting to stop to check on me, but there simply was no place to stop and I was having a great time hanging onto the reins and chatting away with the trail guide who was riding behind me. Mother did not seem to understand that going up and down the mountain was what these horses did for a living.

Coming down the mountain was the best part of the ride because the horses had gravity on their side and the promise of a moment of privacy at their feed bucket once they got back to the barn.

My horse, old Thunder, trotted along quite smartly while I flopped in the saddle like a bean bag hanging on for dear life. That was the first time I felt the special communion that exists between horse and rider.

I spent the next ten years hooked on horses, and some of my happiest memories are of summers spent on horseback from dawn till dusk. I learned a lot about spirit and patience from those half-ton animals. Then I turned fifteen and discovered that boys were also animals.

Somewhere between the discovery of boys, the pursuit of education and the aspirations of a career, horses sidestepped out of my life. But when I saw this farm in a weak moment with a real estate agent, the one thing that clinched the sale was a small barn that looked just about the right size for a box stall.

Of course, I didn't want to be too obvious. So I bought some sheep, took courses at the University of Guelph, planted crops and learned the art of stacking a hay mow before I made my move.

All the ad said was "Palomino mare for sale." I just thought I would take a look. She was perfect.

I have loved many horses from my uncle's massive gentle Percherons to the roughest buckskin bronco with a mean streak, but when the palomino mare set off in a canter that rolled like a gentle wave I knew that I had found a truly significant other.

Lady is the kind of horse you can ride with a halter and a rope and turn just by shifting your weight. She will allow anyone to ride her. I can put a five-year-old on her bare back and count on her not to do anything foolish. If a grown idiot decides to handle her roughly, she will give him the ride of his life until he smartens up or finds himself tossed into the manure pile.

Her instincts about people are as unerring as her ability to find a hidden carrot in a back pocket.

My faithful steed is now sixteen years old. She still whinnies like a filly and prances like a showgirl. She has given me one daughter who is her spitting image, and together they roam the pastures making idiots out of each other. The young one is spoiled and she needs a lot of work, but old Lady is as dependable and smooth as the day I met her.

We do not hit the all-day trails as much now as we did in days gone by. Lady seems to prefer watching her daughter trot smartly in the exercise ring, but she is still game for fording a stream and corralling renegade sheep.

If she gives me another foal, she will have more than earned her hay.

Altruism and economics aside, there is a simple earthly comfort in greeting the day with a welcoming nuzzle from a golden horse. It does not guarantee sanity, but it does make some of the daily tribulations easier to accept.

All I have to do is fall prey to the lure of that gently swaying back and swing my leg up and grab a hunk of mane and — bingo! — I feel just like Roy Rogers again.

BUTTERFLIES ARE FREE

When Bruce bought the farm, he also bought all the bells and whistles, including a perfect little gentleman-farmer's tractor in shiny red with yellow-rimmed tires. Then he dressed the tractor up with every possible accessory — a tiny perfect plough, a tiny perfect harrow, a scaled-down seeder and a cute-as-a-button pull cart. Most of the time, however, Bruce just used his tractor as a large-scale lawn mower to trim the grounds surrounding his magnificent farmhouse.

He wasn't really farming, after all. A successful businessman, Bruce described the farm variously as "a good investment" or "a place where I can get away from it all," depending on whom he was talking to. But if you were to really pin Bruce down, the truth was that he always wanted to drive a tractor. Both of his wives had run off and left him for other men, but the bond between a man and his tractor was forever.

Bruce rented his farmland out to his neighbours, except for a four-acre plot running along the edge of his long lane way, which he mowed relentlessly every week-end.

He was cruising along on his tractor quite happily one spring day when it struck him that he really should put his fine accessories to work. Wife Number One would have told him they were taking up valuable space. Wife Number Two would have called them silly.

So he decided he would plough half of the laneway strip and prepare it for planting, just like a real farmer.

When he finished, Bruce was quite pleased with himself, although he noticed the plough had missed a few bits. Wives Number One and Two would have agreed he "screwed up, as usual."

Out of respect for the land, Bruce called up a neighbour who had a large tractor and plough and hired him to "take another pass" over the field.

During the week, looking dreamily out of his floor-to-ceiling office windows at the surreal city scape, Bruce contemplated the enterprise. *What would he plant?*

He considered everything from pumpkins to garlic, but all of it seemed like too much off-tractor work to maintain himself.

So he settled on wild flowers.

A gardening magazine called a plot of wild flowers "a butterfly meadow."

Wife Number One had been allergic to pollen and Wife Number Two hated bugs of any sort. Perfect! Bruce imagined himself riding his tractor through a cloud of winged creatures, past a field dotted with daisies and black-eyed susans and wild things no one even knew the name of.

He tried to hold that vision firmly in mind when Fred at the seed store told him that the bill for two acres' worth of wild flower seed came to $690.56. Bruce knew all too well what Wives One and Two would have said to that.

Although he always tried to get out of the city early on Fridays, on this particular Friday he did not quite make it.

Halfway there, he knew he would never make it to the seed store before closing time. He pulled off the road, pulled out his cellular phone and called Fred. He quickly explained that he wanted to start seeding first thing in the morning. Fred agreed to leave the seed on the back dock of the adjoining feed mill, with a tarpaulin over it in case it rained.

Bruce picked up the seed that evening around 10 p.m. It was the first "farm related outing" he had ever taken in the new pickup truck he bought to go with the tractor. A few clouds had gathered, but there hadn't been any rain. Bruce just hoped he wouldn't have to make two trips.

At what he assumed was the designated drop-off spot, Bruce was briefly confused. A single spotlight cast an otherworldly glow on the grain mill's deserted dock. Beside half a dozen large bags of grain marked "MARTIN," a small burlap sack lay under the blue tarp. It wasn't even half full, but Bruce's name was scrawled on the bag, just as the Martin name was scrawled in black felt pen on the bulging feed bags.

"Fred must have really thought it was going to rain hard," Bruce reasoned. "I guess he didn't want to take any chances with all that expensive seed. At least," he said to himself reassuringly, "I've got enough to get started first thing."

At dawn on Saturday morning, Bruce ate a hearty breakfast. Then he grabbed the seed sack and a rake and set off to get a jump-start on his planting.

The ground had been perfectly prepared, no bumps of dirt jutting out as he had left it. Not even any tufts of grass. Bruce reached in the bag and took out a handful of seeds. Some were round, some were flat, and some just looked like specks in his hand. Then he threw the seeds away from his body and ran the rake over their landing place until all he could see on the surface was dirt.

It was fun. So Bruce did it again and again, all the while thinking that this must have been the same method of planting the first farmers had employed.

When his heritage moment ended, Bruce had succeeded in planting a strip of wildflower seeds about ten feet wide across the top of the two-acre strip.

In preparation for the long day ahead, Bruce hitched the mini-seeder to the back of the tractor and pulled the rig into the yard so that he could pour the bags of wildflower seed directly from the tailgate of the truck into the seeder. Then he drove off to the seed store to pick up the bulk of his order.

Fred greeted him at the counter and presented the bill. Bruce filled out a cheque, furtively glancing now and again out at the dock, looking for a stack of burlap sacks with his name on them.

"You think I can make it in one trip?" he asked Fred.

"I figure you already did," said Fred, tucking the cheque into his cash box.

"We usually sell it by the ounce," Fred offered, with a shake of his head. "Don't know exactly how you'd seed two acres. Some of them wildflower seeds are so bitty they just look like flecks of dust to me."

Bells and whistles started going off in Bruce's brain. He looked at his invoice, now dutifully marked "PAID IN FULL."

The $690.56 Bruce had paid was for 13 pounds of wildflower seeds at $3.32 an ounce.

While he was at the seed store, Bruce also bought enough lawn seed to cover two acres, give or take a ten-foot strip across the top.

All summer long, very expensively fed butterflies fluttered amid the blossoms of the wild flowers.

On his shiny red tractor, Bruce mowed the grass around them.

He did not speak to anyone about the profusion of wild flowers, although his neighbours did remark on how well the new lawn seed had taken.

And, for the first time in his life, Bruce was happy that his wives had run off with other men.

You don't have to explain anything to your neighbours, or your tractor.

THE RITE TO THE SILENCE
OF THE LAMBS

As spring gives way to summer, I find myself wearing ear muffs. The time has come to wean the lambs from their mothers. Neither ewes nor lambs nor neighbours enjoy this process in animal husbandry.

When the lambs have reached a certain age and a certain size, they are simply too big to be butting up to their old mother and demanding milk. They have learned to eat grass, hay and grain. Instead of playing all day long, it is time for them to go about the serious business of growing up. This is often easier said than done.

It is a stressful time for all concerned, so I try to approach it methodically and prepare for all eventualities. What I would really like to do is complete the task and book into a motel in Rangoon until the screaming is over.

Separating ewes from their lambs is one trick. I herd them through a chute and divert their courses into one area for lamb containment and one for ewes. But there is always one clever lamb who has learned to jump straight in the air and bound over fence tops. And there is usually one young ewe who has figured out a way to turn herself around in the smallest of spaces in an attempt to return to her overgrown offspring.

I remove the ewes to a far paddock, but it is still close enough that they can hear the lambs' cries and bleat their own moans of separation. For the next few days, they will be fed last year's dry hay and given scant water. It may sound like a punishment, but it serves to help them stop producing milk in a process called "drying up."

In the barn the lambs cry like lost children. They nibble aimlessly at their fine alfalfa and ignore their molasses-scented grain. Some of them have louder baas than others, and there is always one little heartbreaker with a mournful soprano.

You cannot pat a lamb on the head and tell it everything is going to be all right. You cannot explain to a sad-faced ewe that her udder is not a punching bag, and she needs to get back into shape and get on with her life. You cannot reason with sheepish passion.

The screaming usually lasts for about 48 hours. Then the ewes go off to their pastures. The lambs settle into their barn and exercise paddock. And the shepherd gets a good night's sleep.

It is a sort of rite of passage. After they are weaned, the lambs seem to have lost their innocence. The young rams play tougher, and the young ewes become more docile. They are no longer "cute." They are eating machines. Over the next few weeks everything from their feed conversion and heredity will come under scrutiny to determine the "keepers" from the market lambs. This is a business, after all, and as much as I love my lambs, they are not pets. My farming neighbours understand that the few evenings of bawling is part of my operation, but less experienced folks could well imagine that I had opened a 24-hour sheep torture chamber.

At a shepherds' meeting a few years ago, the topic was "Animal Rights and Preparing for Activists." Perhaps we were ahead of our time, but one never knows when some vegetarian pop singer or ballerina or poet is going to announce to the world that shepherds are cruel and lamb chops are the consequence.

Indeed, it turned out that one shepherd had already been a victim of misunderstanding. A neighbour, who was a recent urban transplant, had heard the weaning of the lambs and decided it sounded more like a scene from *The Silence of the Lambs*.

Instead of inquiring politely about the well-being of the livestock, the neighbour called the Humane Society. You can imagine the outrage of the gentle shepherd when an inspector visited with the suspicious neighbour in tow.

I told this tale of woe to a friend who raises cattle and she laughed. Her farm is also a bed and breakfast, and most of her close neighbours are recent arrivals to the country who do not farm. She knew the cows and calves would raise a ruckus, so she had closed her farm for visitors while the weaning took its course. After the first gruesome night of choral mooing, she decided she should explain the situation to the neighbours and assure them that an end was in sight.

Her first stop was at the home of a young couple with a baby. The woman was weary-eyed, and my friend feared the worst.

No, she had not been bothered by cow sounds at night. She had been weaning her baby and he cried all night.

THE ORANGE DUMP TRUCK AND OTHER AUCTION NIGHTMARES

There is nothing like an auction for drama, entertainment, warm pop and organized confusion. Particularly if you want to buy something that you never thought you would ever feel a need to own. If your Tupperware collection is missing that one final element to reach completion, if you just can't own enough used waffle irons or if you are constantly in fear of running out of anything from pillowcases to jackhammers — a country auction is about as close to nirvana as you may ever come.

When I first moved to the country, every auction in my area seemed like a potential gold mine. People smart enough to be retiring from the business I was getting into were having auctions that served as a great repository both in terms of value and information.

At an auction you can ask questions about farm machinery that you have never seen before. More often than not, there will be someone leaning against it who can not only tell you what the contraption does, but also provide some insight on whether or not the particular model you are looking at can be serviced within a 50 kilometre radius. Sometimes you can also garner a mechanical and repair history of the implement in question, along with theories about its ability to ever function in the future.

Of course, you must be wary because disinformation can also form part of the auction mentality. Somehow items that were "in good working order" the day before a sale have a nasty habit of falling apart the day after a sale.

Also, the definition of "good working order" sometimes stretches the envelope of reality. A friend of mine bought a stone picker at an auction and it does work. Unfortunately, it works at twice the speed anyone would expect. Stories about auction bargains are often like fish tales. The bargain seems to grow larger with each telling, but that is half the fun.

Over the years I have had some good fortune, but I have yet to bid on a cookie jar containing enough money to pay the mortgage. That is only one of many stories I have heard — and it always makes me look twice when an auctioneer holds up an innocent-looking cookie jar.

Then, of course, there was the day the 1952 orange Dodge dump truck ended up in my yard, courtesy of a bidder cursed with auction fever.

I took a male companion to a farm auction and made the mistake of letting him wander off alone.

While I waited patiently for the auctioneer to hold up an old pickle crock, my fellow fell into the company of some farmer neighbours who were camped out on the other side of the barn where the machinery was being auctioned. I guess they spotted the city slicker and decided to have some fun because the next thing he knew they were offering him a little sip of something from the swish barrel out behind the chicken shed.

I bid about as far as I was prepared to go on the crock, and added a few extra bids for good measure in the ritual process of "bidding up." This is a form of "if I can't have it you are going to pay dearly" kind of auction revenge. Then I wandered off to find my friend.

There was a lot of machinery for auction. Rows of hay bines, wagons, manure spreaders and such. Smack dab in the middle of the row was a huge old dump truck painted cadmium orange. I heard a shout go up as it was auctioned and then the crowd moved on.

As I scanned the human mass, I saw my urban buddy and managed a wave. He fairly bounded across the field, grinning from ear to ear and positively glowing from his venture behind the chicken coop.

Sure enough, he had become the joyful owner of an uncertified, engine-seized, ancient orange dump truck.

The story was rather jumbled, but it seemed his newfound friends had told him it actually worked, but no one else knew that it did. They had also told him that it would not sell for more than 60 dollars because everyone just thought it was scrap. So the boys dared him to buy it, and he did — for just 55 bucks.

The boys were rolling with laughter by this time and as they ambled out the laneway they were snickering heartily at my dilemma. After all, what do you do with a dump truck that hasn't worked for a quarter of a century?

It all worked out in the end. My neighbour Elmer, who collects old dump trucks for usable parts, traded me a new hitch on my pickup for the orange nightmare. Then he turned around and sold the antique ram-head hood ornament for 125 dollars.

My foolish friend recovered from the swish with fond memories of owning a dump truck for a day, and I vowed never to allow city slickers to wander off at auctions.

MY GRANDMOTHER'S HOUSE

When I was a kid I used to go to my Grandmother's house, just outside of Stratford, Ontario, in a village called Staffa that consisted of the joining of two roads where there was a General Store and a Post Office.

My Grandmother lived down the road, and most of her children, my aunts and uncles, lived or farmed nearby. The cousins who taught me how to swing on a rope over the haymow still live there.

Many of my fondest childhood memories are set in my Grandmother's house. It was a big, old, two-storey, wood frame house with a cement porch overlooking the front lawn right next to the well pump where Grandmother would crank out her daily water. This was almost forty years ago and the idea that water came out of the ground instead of a tap was fascinating to a kid like me who grew up in the suburbs.

The outhouse was another mystery. It always seemed to take forever to get to the little shed that had two adult-sized apertures and one little hole for kid-sized bottoms.

There was a well-worn path through the raspberry bushes, and once you got there, you stayed until you were done your business even if it meant reading the linen ads in the Eaton's catalogue. The outhouse excursion was my first lesson in planning a daily schedule.

Grandmother's house was basically her kitchen. The other rooms were barely used, or bed chambers. After church, the aunts and uncles and cousins might spill over into the parlour and sit on the good velvet sofa and big stuffed chairs, but the heart of the house was the kitchen.

Everyone would crowd around the kitchen table and talk, while Grandmother quietly went about the business of making pies and cookies and bread. You would rarely see Grandmother without a rolling pin in her hand, or a vegetable peeler, or a boning knife. And she always wore an apron with big pockets that seemed to hold endless supplies of jujubes for us kids.

The meals we had at Grandmother's house were major affairs — meat-and-potato eating at its most gargantuan. The aunts would arrive with salads. Big leafy green salads, tart spicy bean salads, and impossibly colourful Jello salads that trapped everything from shredded carrots to pineapple and marshmallows in huge molds.

Everything was organic in those days. None of us even knew what a chemical additive was.

While Grandmother supervised the slicing, dicing, boiling and mashing, the uncles would teach the cousins how to play baseball, or show us where to look for turtles and frogs in the pond across the road. By the time it came to actually eating the supper, I remember being almost too tired to chew. No one ever left Grandmother's table hungry, and there was rarely even a wedge of pie left over.

There was always something to do at Grandmother's. Everything from crokinole to cribbage and croquet. Long after we kids had been banished to our quilt-covered beds we would hear whoops of laughter from the kitchen where the adults were playing games of Euchre, Crazy Eights and Hearts. The sound wafted to the second storey through strategically placed holes in the floor that were covered with perforated metal grates that allowed the heat from the wood stove below to rise into the bedrooms. "Listening holes," we called them, and more than once Grandmother's broom handle would poke against the metal advising us nosey children to mind our own business.

You could not sneak around Grandmother's house, because everywhere you went there was some creaking floorboard that would give you away. And once you were in bed, there was no foraging through the raspberry patch to the outhouse. There were "thunder mugs" under the beds to take care of eventualities that could not wait until morning. Even when Grandmother finally got an indoor toilet, we kids would always check under the bed for the thunder mugs, just in case.

You did not loiter in Grandmother's house. You could read a book. You could try to figure out how to make a cat's cradle with your yo-yo. But if you decided to hang out on the sofa in the kitchen doing nothing, Grandmother would scoot you outside "to get the stink blown off."

The same thing would happen to older cousins when they were caught listening in on the telephone party line. I think Grandmother's ring was two long and two short, but it didn't much matter what the ring was if the older cousins were there. They would just quietly pick up and listen to whatever real life neighbourhood soap opera was burning up the lines. Heck, they would even listen to someone else's grocery list — until their cantankerous Grandmother got a hold of their ear, that is.

Grandmother believed in privacy and good manners and order. It was a rare day when even a wisp of her long hair escaped from her hairnet, and no child ever left her table without asking to be excused.

Today, all that remains of my Grandmother and her house are old photographs, artifacts and genetics. But memories of her strike me constantly.

If I could relive just one moment in that creaking wooden house that filled with light and love every time some family member slammed the old screen door behind them, it would be one specific wet summer afternoon. Rain pelted down on the old shingled roof and Grandmother sent my father and the grown boys to the dark, dank attic to catch any leaks with pails and thunder mugs.

My mother, and her mother and little me stood at the kitchen door watching rain bounce off the fresh-cut grass.

"Go on and do it then, Margaret, I know you want to," said my Grandmother to my mother. "And take her with you," she added, meaning me.

Next thing I knew, my mother, MY MOTHER, was stripping off her clothes and Grandmother was telling me to do the same thing.

The screen door opened and out we ran. Leaping over the croquet hoops while the warm rain drenched us, we ran around the yard like naked dervishes.

I will always remember looking back at the doorway of the old house and seeing my Grandmotherin her familiar apron. I could hear her laughing, and my mother laughing in the same voice. My own laughing became a part of theirs. I might have been five or six, but I knew that in that one wet and wild moment, we were having the time of our life.

Nothing again will ever be like the times in Grandmother's house. But every time I smell vanilla, I think of Grandmother Fitzgerald because she used to daub it behind her ears as perfume. When I see an old well pump, I can hear the creak hers would make in the morning when the washing-up water was set out. Hollyhocks, delphiniums and climbing roses were the first perennials I planted at my own farm, because I wanted to look out of my kitchen window and see the same riot of colours that sparkled in my Grandmother's eyes.

I think I was about eight years old when I realized, for the first time, that my Grandmother's face had wrinkles. Until then she never seemed to change.

There are many lines from Shakespeare that strike a common chord in all of us. I think of the comic Nurse in *Romeo and Juliet* who notes, "With mirth and laughter let old wrinkles come."

In Grandmother's house, there was always laughter.

OF MINT AND MAYHEM

I have never begrudged the odd week in the garden. A little mayhem adds some humanity to those straight neat rows that start out looking like something from a trigonometry book. If there was nothing to do in the garden except admire the neatness and pick the bounty, I might as well go to the supermarket. And who can ever tell where the wild pumpkin is going to crop up.

My first few gardens were so huge I could spend half a day rototilling between the rows and still have hoeing to do. Then I tried all sorts of weed-free methods, including laying down thick beds of straw between the rows to smother the weeds and mulch naturally. This worked brilliantly until the stray seeds in the straw came to life and I had a sprout festival at hand.

I learned to use a combination of whatever I think will work, including chickens and disincluding chickens at my whim. You see, chickens love weed sproutlets and they love to root out the assorted bugs in the ground. They also create their own nitrogen-rich fertilizer. So if I want to clear a plot of ground for future gardening, I confine the chickens to it as their range. Every week I rototill the chicken range, turning up bugs and worms for the chickens. The weed seeds sprout faithfully, only to be recycled by the chickens. By fall the chickens are fine, fat and well pleased with themselves, and after a final tilling the plot will be virtually weed-free and fertilized for spring planting.

That is the theory. It usually works well until the day before I harvest the tomatoes. Then the chickens break through the mesh that separates them from the real garden and they peck holes in every other ripe tomato. So I plant extra tomato plants on the other side of the house, where the chickens cannot see them.

I am now so accustomed to growing "secret" gardens that I do not even think of them as secret anymore. Ask me why a plot of corn grows behind the flower bed where poppies, yarrow, lilies and red hot pokers form the backdrop, and all I can say is, "The horses won't think to look there." This is because just as sure as biennials bloom every other year, the horses are bound to find their way into the garden for half an hour when the corn is ripe. If I am not fast enough, the whole crop will be trampled or digested. Then there will be some salvation in having the secret plot. If the horses fail, I will have all the more for the freezer.

I no longer even think about the fact that there is a small plot of red-leaf lettuce in the flower bed next to the pansies, just in case some groundhog finds the real stuff in the garden. Basil and parsley grow just beside the front steps where even the most bold goose will not nibble it.

And flowering cabbages smile out everywhere, their huge heads bowing like something out of *Little Shop of Horrors.*

Years ago a friend gave me a pot of mint. She warned me to plant it far away from anything I treasured and to confine it strictly to the pot. But it looked so lame, so harmless and so small. I whacked its tiny roots into a flower bed, expecting nothing but a small whiff of fragrant green to emerge in one quiet spot.

But mint is the wildest and most wiry of all herbs. It has survival instincts that are so profound one suspects that it could survive a nuclear holocaust. You can pull it out of the ground by its roots and sift through the soil until you truly believe every fibrous strand is gone for good — two days later there will be a brand new sprout of mint.

I have tried releasing the chickens in the mint. But they do not care much for the peppermint-scented sprouts. The horses will not touch the stuff. Even the sheep deliberately graze around it. So today, I have a mint garden.

It is bounded by rocks and anything else I can think of to confine the pervasive stuff. It just spreads. After years of cursing it, of trying to control it, stop it and kill it, I have decided to simply contemplate the mayhem that is mint.

There is some satisfaction in freely scattering mint leaves around a dessert of baked pears with ice cream. Tarting lamb up with mint sauce has always seemed an abomination to me. If it must be done, all the better to be able to add the authenticity of chopped green leaves to the sweetness. Mint adds zest to tea, and a julep is nothing at all without a large infusion of leafy juices. When the mint garden overtakes all reasonable boundaries of companion living, I mow it down.

Like the wild pumpkin vine that spreads across the middle of a garden row, the mint is a reminder that nature has its own mysterious survival mechanisms. Once triggered, the greater one struggles against it, the larger it looms. Far better to sit back and accept that some roots grow deeper than others.

BARNYARDS
AND BASKETBALL HEADS

One of the things I disliked about working in an office was the politics — the politics of appearance, the politics of promotion and the politics of windows, coat racks and corner offices as definitions of worth. Every day some backstabbing plot seemed to be hatching in some cubicle.

Allegiances, allegations and arbitrations can make the workplace almost as treacherous as an abattoir. Skirt too short, off with her head. Voice too squeaky, banished to the mail room. Getting long in the tooth, bite the early retirement bullet. And the boss is seldom a hero. I once worked in an office where the titular supervisor was disrespectfully known as "Old Basketball Head." The primary function of the staff seemed to be constructing scenarios that would spell his demise. The cruelty of office life was something I thought I could avoid on the farm.

But even the barnyard has its politics. Witness the phenomenon of chickens in a pen. If one decides to lie in a corner, ten others want to be there as well. So they pile on top of each other, suffocating the bottom layer. The only way to survive is to claw your way to the top of the heap. Sound familiar?

And chickens do not tolerate weakness any more than office "team players" tolerate slackers. If one bird develops a bad leg, for example, word spreads through the coop with the same speed as derogatory e-mail. The injured bird is on the outs. The others stand apart in groups, clucking privately. Then they take turns as tormenters. At first, they just sneak up from behind and peck the weak one. Then they progress to bullying it in packs. Without supervision, such behaviour leads to murder. In an office, it becomes a pink slip or a transfer.

Pigs raised in confinement are the biggest bullies of all. Once they are weaned, the future wieners are corralled in fattening pens where the only thing they are supposed to do is eat. Like workers assigned to an assembly line, boredom sets in. Soon they are quite literally at each other's throats. You do not find this behaviour in pigs that are left to roam in a pasture where they can root around and explore their own creativity. Diversification of routine creates happy production units — Principles of Management 101.

Horses are the same. My friend Cheryl's extremely sociable equi turned to vandalism when she left them alone during the day to go to work. Even though they had a whole pasture to roam, Sunshine and Morningstar would stand in the barn and apply themselves to the task of pulling boards away from the stall walls. They were afflicted with the same loveless boredom that turns office workers into pencil pilferers and washroom graffiti artists.

Cheryl solved the problem by hanging two Frisbees from the barn ceiling. The horses had hours of fun whacking them around with their upraised noses. Show them something new, show them that you care — put a ping-pong table in the lunchroom.

Cattle and geese may look as though they move in cohesive groups, but spend some time watching and you will observe a hierarchy of authority. It happens quickly and often without warning. Two geese will fly at each other, honking and screaming. Then they will walk off in different directions, with the gaggle following the one who made the best display. An old cow will look up from the salt block and make a beeline for the heifer grazing ahead of her. After broadsiding the innocent youngster into a windless state, old Bossy goes back to licking salt as though nothing had happened. It is called learning your place.

Sheep may be the most corporate of all animals. Innovation intimidates them and they would follow a leader over a cliff to avoid making a false step. Rams only bang heads when there is a threat of a merger or takeover. However, ewes butt each other over serious things such as, "whose blade of grass is this anyway." To the victor go the spoils, and so on.

Yet sometimes I walk through the barnyard and all I see is a well-integrated community of gentle creatures involved in pastoral pursuits that I have established for them. Heads turn, ears perk and they greet me in their languages of contentment. At least I hope that is what is going on. I would hate to think that every "cock-a-doodle-doo" actually means, "Here comes Basketball Head."

THE LITTLEST SHEARER

In the world of sheep, shearers are a universe unto themselves. Usually they are shepherds, who strip the wool off other people's flocks to generate a second income. Good shearers are like good plumbers. You book well in advance and give them anything they want when they arrive.

Over the years I have had a number of shearers. Irascible might be the best description. But holding down 250-pound rams and bucking ewes carrying twins while flies hum around and novice shepherds ask dopey questions could make anyone irritable.

Women shearers are at a premium in the rarefied environment of sheep shearers. When I found my shearer, Judy, I felt simpatico, and so did my sheep. She has been shearing the flock ever since. We have sheared with helpers and sheared alone; sheared when we were both having life crises; and sheared when life was perfect. Sometimes there are more sheep, sometimes there are fewer. The one consistent factor is that I collect the dung tags.

Judy was single when we first met. Now she is married and starting to raise a flock of her own. Nicole was born three years ago. Judy was shearing almost up to her due date. Nicki did not change her mother's schedule much. The sound of clippers and the baa of sheep became the baby's lullabies.

At a year old, Nicole watched the shearing from her car seat set on a bale of straw. At two, she stood on the bale, sucking back bottles of juice and pointing her father Steve in the direction of the next sheep she wanted to see sheared. "Get that ewe, Dad," and he did.

At three, she is truly following in her mother's hoofsteps.

"Your sheep should be dry," she said when she disembarked from the shearing truck in the summer. "Can't shear wet sheep." Her phrasing was exactly as her mother's had been in April.

Cowed by a kid, I assured her that after a wet spring and several missed shearing dates, my sheep were finally dry.

Small and big-eyed, Nicki sat next to her mother on the shearing box where clippers and blades and extension cords are stored. On one sheet of paper, she drew pictures of what she saw. Baby barn swallows in an overhead nest revealed themselves in her hand as a series of open beaks. A wavy line was a rooster's comb, and a collection of round dots signified a sheep sneezing. It all makes perfect sense when Nicki explains it.

On another piece of paper, Nicki draws straight lines. Four in a row and then a diagonal line across. Each line represents a ewe that has been sheared. Each diagonal is a five, two fives are as many fingers as Nicki can count. So each set of two boxes of lines is a bundle. At three, the child has mastered the principles of "the new math."

When the fleeces have been "skirted" (the polite term for removing dung tags), they are folded and stuffed into caterpillar-like burlap sacks. Compacting the wool is an art. One shepherd I know built a twenty-foot tower specifically for stuffing wool bags. Each fleece was drawn to the top of the tower through a series of ropes, pulleys and hooks. Then a designated wool stuffer at the top of the tower loaded the wool into the hanging bag, poking it to the bottom with an extendable window-washing handle fixed with a weight instead of a wiper. Inevitably, the handle ended up lodged in the bag with the wool when the wool bag fell to the ground.

Instead, Judy uses Nicki. Dad Steve rolls back the burlap sack to a manageable size and he and I start stuffing. Then Nicki dances and prances on the wool, gyrating it to the bottom of the bag. Judy calls it the "wool war dance."

Each sack can hold twenty fleeces comfortably, but Nicki sees this as a challenge. When it is time to tie off the giant bag and hoist it into the truck, she crawls in sideways and pushes the core of the wool down. At twenty-three fleeces she is usually satisfied.

Nicki has lambs of her own at home, and bunnies and a cat named Rags. Doing chores is as natural to her as breathing. Every day she watches her parents work together. She is never bored.

Judy tells a story about taking her daughter into a coffee shop in the middle of a day of shearing.

"Your child smells like a sheep," the cashier said snootily when they picked up their take-out lunch.

"Thank you," said Nicole, without missing a beat. "I'm a little farm kid, you know."

THE BAT WHISPERER

You don't hear them twittering like birds and you don't see them fluttering like silent butterflies. Instead, bats tend to surprise you.

One evening you might leave a neighbour's house and look up at the moon, and see them zipping across its luminous face like little clouds of teacup-sized asteroids.

You might be out standing on a cottage dock watching the stars, when all of a sudden some small, dark, winged thing whips past you.

Or you might be in the parlour of an old farmhouse when one sneaks its way in and starts zooming around looking for a way out.

Bats generally keep their distance, but they do show up at the oddest of times in the oddest of places. And, even though I like bats, they always leave me with an eerie feeling and goosebumps as though I have been the subject of a visitation.

My first bat in the parlour was a comedy of errors that I am sure has been repeated in countless households.

We had not yet "settled" on the farm and the furnishings were as scant as a university student's first apartment. In fact, we joked about the ancient, round, wooden hydro spool that we used as a coffee table for the first year.

The kitchen, the family room and the bedrooms were equipped, but the parlour was so vacant that we installed a ping-pong table for rainy weekend recreation.

The bat appeared during a particularly rousing, four-handed game. I had successfully pinged the ball over the net and Moose raised his racket to pong it back when his partner, Mike, took a heck of a whack at something in midair. My partner, Janet, let her paddle drop to the floor and commenced jogging in place with her lips pursed, all the while emitting a back-of-the-throat hysterical hum.

Moose was under the table looking for the ping-pong ball, while Mike held his racket over his eyes and squinted into the distant corners of the room.

I was preparing to utter a statement akin to "Pray, what was that?" when the thing made another pass over the table. Between Janet's humming and Moose's sub-tabular fumbling for the ping-pong ball, it was hard to detect any sound associated with the assault. It was like a zipper opening in midair. Then it was gone.

Mike, an advertising executive who had been to summer camp as a child, immediately identified the creature as a bat. Those of us familiar with *Dracula* (the movie) immediately dove for cover. Three of us were still cowering under the table when Mike walked into the room with a kitchen broom which he planned to use to flush the bat out.

No sooner had Mike waved his corn-husk wand than the bat exited the parlour, looped through the kitchen and headed for the family room.

In the space of a short eternity, we learned everything Mike knew about bats. They are not the evil, bloodsucking things we imagine, unless you happen to be out in some disappearing South American jungle, where the spread of rabies and other blood-borne diseases was once, allegedly, a cause of concern with so-called "vampire bats."

They eat millions and millions and millions of mosquitoes, so in my book bats are a very good thing.

Hundreds of them can live in a small space, where they sleep during the day, hanging upside down, enclosed in the leathery membrane that creates wings between their long spidery fingers.

They are the only mammal that flies.

Most important, they don't bump into things because they bounce a high-pitched sound frequency off objects and they can judge by the echo how close it is, in a bizarre sort of rodent radar. But this very unique built-in radar makes confined airborne bat behaviour a little bizarre and erratic.

As a teenager, Mike explained in a quiet almost reverent tone, he had done a whole summer camp project on bats, but he had never actually seen one in the flesh.

Equipped with flashlights, binoculars and a trout fishing net, we repaired to the family room to capture the bat.

Janet tentatively, reluctantly, looked behind the sofa. Nothing.

I swatted cushions with the broom.

The men illuminated the dark corners of the fourteen-foot ceiling with a flashlight, discovering a variety of bat-like cobwebs.

Janet was bravely lifting the hydro spool, when Mike shouted, "Got 'em."

We followed his finger to the gaping mouth of the stuffed, twenty-pound salmon which was the first *objet d'art* to hang in the farmhouse. There was a brownish blob about the size of two walnuts clinging like a leech on the inside jaw.

This was no time for brooms.

Janet was again jogging in place, trying not to hum and give away her location. Both men wrestled for the fishnet, until it was mutually agreed that Moose, being the taller and the more experienced fisherman, would try to "capture" the now motionless bat.

He did manage to loop the fishnet over the salmon's mouth, but then the bat moved. Moose jumped back and the fish fell head first into the net which could only contain one-third of its hand-painted corpse.

In the meantime, the bat zipped out through a hole in the net and flew directly at Janet, who instinctively raised the ping-pong paddle to which she still furtively clung, like some anti-bat talisman. It was a futile gesture. The bat simply zipped around it.

The light in the room was not the brightest, but we all caught shadowy glimpses of the bat as it flew erratically around our heads.

Sharp-eyed Mike spotted it leaving the room through an open window, and we all gathered to look for it but, alas, it was gone and our game of ping-pong had some-how lost its lustre.

Years later, bats became a trendy eco-species. En-vironmentally friendly nature stores and catalogues became purveyors of bat houses.

Laws were passed in certain states against the arbi-trary poisoning of bats.

Even though the parishioners might have had other thoughts, bat rights were entrenched in many a New England church belfry.

But the blood-sucking, rabies-invested bat mystique lingers on.

I was quietly fingering through the ladies' athletic socks at my local Stedman's store when a curdled cry rang out from the back storage room. A shaken teenaged clerk emerged wringing her hands, close to tears.

A "thing" had flown at her from behind a box on the top shelf where the Christmas tree lights had been stashed six months earlier.

It was no bird, she knew that much.

It had a face; beady eyes, flat-sort of nose, pointy lit-tle ears and a mouth, maybe even teeth. She was describ-ing a teacup-sized flying animal that looked like a cross between a monkey and a Chihuahua, so I knew it had to be a bat.

The assistant store manager, a mature woman with years of retail experience, called the store owner for advice. No answer. Then she called the Town office to get them to send over the animal control officer. Alas, the animal control officer in the town of Mt. Forest does not "do" bats.

The next step was closing up the store and calling in the cops. Two young mothers had already given up on buying diapers and fled to the safety of the street. The only shopper left in the store was a light-fingered youth, who sucked in his breath so hard when the clerk described the beast, that the CD he had tucked in his pants fell right to the base of his pant leg.

If it had been a skunk, I might have thought twice, but, having had previous bat invasion experience, I figured I could give it a go.

Deborah, the shaken teenaged clerk, pointed me toward a pile of fallen cardboard boxes where she had seen the thing headed.

Sure enough, under a wad of tissue paper at the bottom of the third smallish box that I examined, there was a small brown blob lying with its back to me.

I went back into the store and found one of those splatter-screen kitchen utensils you use to keep frying oil at bay with, and fixed it over the top of the bat box.

By this time the assistant store manager had managed to get her brother-in-law on the phone. He was a Town Councillor and vowed to send over a road maintenance crew who were on their lunch break to straighten things out. No doubt his next call had been to the local newspaper, with the potential headline "Councillor Rids Town Store of Bat" looming large in next Wednesday's town weekly, *The Confederate*.

Stedman's back door opens out onto the local tavern parking lot. I eased the box outside and turned it on its side. The blob slid to the bottom. No sooner was the splatter pan removed than the bat whizzed out of the box, across the parking lot, over the dumpster, around the laundromat air vents and into the surrounding tree branches.

The road crew greeted me on their way out of the tavern. I told them the bat had escaped, so they could go back to their lunch. There were no headlines about flying mammals that week, but I did get a free pair of athletic socks and a toque for my troubles.

THE HUMPS OF THE HOLSTEIN

I like to go to the feed mill in Holstein, about eight kilometres from my farm.

It is an old-style feed mill, with huge timber rafters, the smell of grain in the dusty air and a regular sort of tricolour cat lounging around waiting for the sign of a single mouse.

At the mill they will mix up any sort of feed you want and give some advice to anyone willing to listen. Big blue salt blocks are lined against one wall, and notes are posted on a huge beam listing the various mixtures for dairy cows, pigs and poultry. There are other feed mills closer to me than Holstein, but none that has the same charm.

I guess a lot of it has to do with the village of Holstein itself. It is a really nice place to visit even on a rainy day. There aren't any subdivisions in Holstein, just houses that have big front lawns and more rocking chairs per porch than I've ever seen.

Main Street is just a stretch of road with a gas station and a couple of garages with signs that proclaim the owner's name. The general store is appropriately called "The General Store" and you can buy everything from pork chops to paper clips there. Holstein even has its own clothing line of sweatshirts and T-shirts, featuring its namesake black and white cow.

A stream bisects the town, and there is a big park which is home to many a family reunion and baseball tournament. People still tell fish tales about the monster pike that once got trapped near the dam.

And Holstein has a camel, a regulation two-humper named Baxter, who is featured in every local parade. He is owned by a local farmer who established a sort of wildlife preserve along with his sheep and cattle and poultry farm. At one time he had a herd of bison, but that ended when one of the beasts decided to attack him on his tractor.

There are quite tame white-tailed deer in a wooded setting at the edge of the road, and many a local child has marvelled at their velvety noses while feeding them a handful of grain. Zebras and elk have graced the fields, and peacocks seem to free-range in the ditches.

Tuesdays and Fridays are big days for traffic in Holstein because those are the only days that the local credit union is open. It is a two-woman operation with a lot of personality. The tellers know me by name and there is always time for a chat about the weather.

On Sunday the church bells peal and the parish pioneers gather like something out of an old movie.

A kind of infectious whimsy is always in the air when you drive into this village, and a palpable sense of indeterminate history seems to overtake the sensibilities. I guess that is why I never buy too much feed at one time.

There is something secretly wonderful about knowing that when I make up my official morning chore list of "Things to Do Today," I can write "pick up grain" and "do banking" and know that it also means I get to give a camel a carrot.

POOR LITTLE LAMBS WHO HAVE GONE ASTRAY

You can get lost in the country. One dusty sideroad is easy to confuse with another dusty sideroad. If you are finding your way for the first time, some fool is sure to give you directions that say "turn right at the red barn" and, sure enough, every corner you come to has a red barn on it.

Sheep, on the other hand, do not get lost no matter where they wander. They are not born with a compass rose etched in their brains, and there is no one genius sheep in the flock that knows all, sees all and finds all. Sheep navigation is more sensory than scientific. They smell their way home.

Between the toes of every sheep's cloven hooves, there is a nubbly little nodule that excretes a waxy substance. In technical shepherdese, it is called the foot gland.

You would never see it unless you knew what to look for, and sheep do not tend to stand quietly and allow you to pick up their feet as a well-trained horse should.

But that little nodule prevents the sheep from forgetting where it lives.

As the sheep stroll through the meadows, the reflex action of walking or gambolling or trotting along renders the scent. Little lost sheep can follow it home like lucky Hansel and Gretel. Once enough sheep follow the same path they stick to it. So it is that all summer long I watch the sheep wander off to their pasture along the same route and return each night the same way.

What I had not known one particular summer was that they had been wandering a longer path than the one in their enclosed pasture for several weeks. They had become rural explorers.

Every morning I innocently opened the gate and watched them amble off for a day of dining from the land. Like clockwork, when the sun was set low in the afternoon sky, they would trundle happily back to the barnyard, skipping along in single file like happy kids getting off the school bus. All seemed right with the world.

Then the policeman came to the door.

He was a bright, shiny young man, but I immediately began feeling guilty of something.

"Do you know anyone around here who has sheep?" he asked.

It seemed an easy enough thing to confess to, but I wanted to test the waters of justice.

"You mean white ones with black heads?" I asked.

"That's them," he said.

My fevered brain began to broil with visions of sheep rustlers, or escaped circus animals feeding on helpless woolly creatures or known bank robbers escaping in sheep clothing.

"Saw them in a field up the road and it doesn't have any fences, so I thought they might be lost or something" the young officer offered.

I felt better and worse simultaneously. Thanking him for his concern, I prepared to round-up my wayward flock before he called in the paddy wagon.

There is nothing my old horse Lady likes better than asserting her authority over sheep. We cantered into the neighbour's field where the sheep were casually grazing on the leftovers of a harvested barley crop. When the horse stopped, she snorted at them.

All their little black heads turned to look at us. Not an innocent face in the lot. I might as well have caught them smoking cigarettes behind the barn.

Lady started to dance in excitement. She got about three high-stepping prances in before the sheep turned and fled.

They all ran through the same little trampled area in a thicket between two old apple trees. Lady and I kept our distance as the flock settled into a slow jog back along the same route they had come.

If they had been cattle, they might have strayed from the beaten path. That is why we have expressions like, "You could wait till the cows come home." Sheep on the other hand "follow like sheep," and they followed their own footsteps with the same unwavering confidence that robins show when they fly off to Costa Rica for the winter.

At the fenceline, old ewes and young lined up smartly to take turns jumping over a section of cedar rail fence that had collapsed under the weight of a fallen tree branch. It was not their fault that a window opened on a whole new universe.

When they were all safely in the barnyard, I gave them a serious talking to. Haranguing sheep is about as effective as lecturing a Teflon frying pan. Nothing sticks and nothing is absorbed.

Once the fence was repaired, the walk-about sheep contented themselves with strolls through a new gate into fresh pasture. Every evening they dutifully returned, following their scented trail and taking a routine right turn at the red barn.

It is a small comfort to know that while you and I can get lost in the country, ewes can always find their way home.

MANURE SPREADING DAY

Between haying and harvesting, summer can move fairly quickly on a farm. The garden always needs weeding, grass grows like weeds and it becomes nearly impossible to keep up with the zucchinis. Cucumbers may grow from gherkin-sized to salad slicers overnight, but if you don't catch a zucchini in time it can grow into a small canoe.

Today I was in the midst of contemplating taming the zucchinis when Jim's Manure arrived. Complete with two manure spreaders and a front-end loader.

I never know exactly when to expect Jim's Manure. The machines are busy from April through November, travelling all over, cleaning out barns and spreading you-know-what over the fields. Jim just puts your name down on his list and when he gets to you — well, he gets to you. Jim himself drove one of the spreaders this year.

First he surveyed the job, in the process lamenting not having taken the day off to go fishing. It seems I'm a small fish in a big pond in terms of manure spreading jobs. But just consider the fact that one of my sheep management books suggests that half a ton of sheep produce eight and a half tons of manure annually. Roughly translated that means that my flock of 50 or so ewes had produced more that 42 tons of excrement since Jim's last visit, and approximately 35 percent of that was solid waste with nowhere to go until jim arrived.

Jim and crew got right to work. I don't know who invented the manure spreader, but the light bulb that flashed above that person's head must have been quite something.

A spreader is a sort of a big iron box on wheels with paddles that toss the manure out the back. I don't know how the thing works, but pretty soon all three spreaders were spitting last year's sheep left-overs all over the pasture. It is a very organic business.

It took about five hours to finish the job, and Jim figured he'd have just enough time left in the day to make it to his secret fishing hole, where a big bass had been playing hard to get for weeks.

I was not so lucky. Although machines can do wonders, they can't get into the corners of a barn. So I spent the rest of the day up to my boot-tops in sheep poop — shoveling as fast as I could. It is kind of mindless work. I try not to think about what I'm doing while I'm doing it.

Good things can happen in the detritus of a job like that. For instance, I found a long-lost screwdriver, a great chunk of rubber hose and my trusty Buck knife — all of which had somehow wound up buried in the sheep pen.

Now the barn is clean and I am about as filthy as my Buck knife. The sheep are confused by a landscape without a manure pile, and the pasture field has been fertilized within an inch of its life.

My muscles tell me that they have done an honest day's work. There will still be weeds in the garden tomorrow, and grass to cut, and zucchini to be plucked and relished. But maybe I'll take a cue from Jim of Jim's Manure, find myself a cool bank on the river, forget about sheep and just go fishing. There are options on the farm.

RUB-A-DUB-DUB, TWO SHEEP AND NO TUB

You never know how dirty and smelly a sheep really is until you wash one. I discovered this one fine summer day when I was getting two ram lambs ready to go to a sheep show.

The rams looked clean. Sheared in the spring, they came out looking as white as lilies. Then they cavorted in the pasture in all kinds of weather. I thought of them as naturally rain-washed and sun-dried creatures. But going to a sheep show requires more primping than Mother Nature had in mind. In fact, it practically requires a beautician's licence.

When I told a few of my senior shepherd friends that I planned to show my fine rams, they all had tidbits of advice.

"Walk them on a halter every day, or they'll run you around the ring," said one sage. So I made a rope halter and started taking the boys for a daily turn around the paddock. I learned to wear old clothes while doing this, since the young rams seemed to get a kick out of dragging me around. They were outlaws. So I named them after my favourite country and western renegades, Willie Nelson and Waylon Jennings.

"Get them to stand good and square" was another piece of wisdom. How this guy thought I was going to get the darn rams to hold still when I couldn't even get them to heel, I do not know.

Then came the concept of "fitting" the sheep for the show ring, an exercise that comes close to preparing a model for a Paris runway. In the course of events, I learned that before a perfectly good sheep could enter a show ring its feet had to be manicured, its wool cleaned and fluffed and its head suitably shined. I swear that if sheep had eyebrows, someone would have told me to pluck them.

I was about ready to abandon the whole idea when I thought of Judy, my shearer. She has been showing sheep all her life, and in her spare time she teaches 4-H'ers the tricks of the trade. Hearing my dilemma, Judy agreed to "fit" the rams, but I would have to do the washing. I felt sort of like the shampoo person for Vidal Sassoon.

I bought a big jug of gooey, greasy livestock shampoo and lined up the garden hose. The day was hot and ripe for lathering. Willie knew the game was afoot when I flopped him to the ground in the corral and trimmed his tiny perfect hooves with garden pruners. Sheep do not like having this done. Waylon responded by trying to kick the bejeebbers out of me.

Wool soaks up a lot of water. By the time I got them drenched to the skin, Willie and Waylon were literally wet blankets and they smelled like dirty sweaters. I lathered them up, down and sideways. Dirt and grime flowed out of their wool. Mother Nature was obviously not fastidious when it came to rainwashing sheep.

Before they started sun-drying, I called Judy to find out whether cream rinse was in order.

"What? You've just washed them once?" she asked. I winced as dribbles of shampoo and grunge caked on my face. "Wash 'em again and be sure you scrub their equipment. That's what the judges will be looking at for sure."

I might not have been raised on a farm, but by now I knew enough animal anatomy lingo to catch her drift. Off I went with hose in hand to re-wash my rams and consider the most mannerly method of scrubbing their equipment.

The boys seemed to relish a second chance at the massage that goes with a full-fleece shampoo. Willie mellowed right out when I lathered his privates, but the cold-water rinse put some bounce back into his attitude.

By the time I was ready to tackle Waylon's scrotum, I felt that I was getting the hang of the whole sheep-washing thing. I was down on my knees scrubbing away like an old washerwoman when I heard a car barreling up the laneway.

It was the dreaded insurance agent.

There was nowhere to run, nowhere to hide. He was at the fence in a flash and I was fully exposed.

"Picked a nice day to wash the flock," said the cheeky little monkey. I focused all my energy on the job at hand.

"Just need you to initial something on the truck insurance policy," he snickered, waving his ball-point as though a soaking wet woman shampooing the nether parts of a male sheep had three hands.

Waylon let out a guttural baa. I clenched my teeth in anticipation of some blinding display of sophomoric wit.

"Guy's got a good set of windpipes, heh, heh."

Fully lathered, I rose from the muck and reached for his dangling pen. Waylon gave me a playful butt from behind.

"Looks like you might need something a bit more in the collision insurance department. Heh, heh," he chortled.

"Wrong," I offered impassively, as I swirled my initials on the designated page.

I expected him to leave, laughing all the way. Wrong again. As I commenced the rinse cycle on Waylon, the insurance agent clung to the fence as though he had front row seats at a Tijuana side-show.

"Might need some extra coverage, though," I shouted back at him. Without even looking, I knew those were sweet words to his perky, insurance agent ears.

"Whaddya have in mind? Sheep blanket coverage, heh, heh," he crowed.

"How about All-Perils," I said turning quickly, hose in hand and nozzle adjusted to full-stream ahead. Got him dead on around the mid-section before he could run.

Judy was pleased with my ram laundry job. She did not say much, but I got the feeling that she would have graded me well in her 4-H class. As casually as though they were born with halters on, the boys walked obediently to her trimming stand and posed stock still, legs squarely planted, backs straight and chins up. Using her clippers, hand trimmers and various combs, Judy method-ically tailored their wool to the specifications of the show ring. A little off here and a bit plumped up there made a world of difference. She used a pump-spray bottle of water and other secret ingredients to work the wool into place. I caught a glimpse of a jar of Dippity Doo.

When the rams were finally "blocked," we stood back to admire her handiwork.

"Bit rough but we're getting there," said Judy. To me they already had the stamp of Grand Champion on their shiny black heads.

FEAR AND LOATHING FROM THE GARDEN OF EDEN

The snakes seem to be in full form this year.

Since early spring I have been catching them napping in the full sun and finding shed skins around the base of trees where they like to rub.

They surprise me now and then when I am walking through long grass, but I cannot get too excited about a garter snake. Call it Freudian, but I have been a snake fan since I was a little kid and lived near a ravine which all manner of snake, salamander and newt called home.

My parents, who seemed to have nothing for or against snakes, were wise enough to foster my early childhood interest in species other than my own. We would go on family outings to creek beds, and while the others were having a picnic, I would be turning over rocks in search of squirmy things to bring home for further examination.

Mother put her foot down when she found the bathtub filled with tadpoles, but as long as I cleaned my terrarium she was amenable to gathering a few earthworms from the garden to help feed my "collection." Dad introduced me to an elderly man who was a naturalist, and we would spend hours talking about everything from what happened to the dinosaurs to the changing colours of chameleons. Those were the days before *Sesame Street* and Nintendo.

By the time I entered grade three, I had accumulated about 35 domestic snakes through zoos and "snake trades" and scavenging. I seemed to have a knack for acquiring snakes named Samson who had to be renamed Delilah the moment they gave birth.

My snakes-in-the-basement thing tended to divide my little friends into two distinct groups — those who wanted to come for visits at my house after school and those who would not even attend a birthday party in a house that harboured snakes. This was my first encounter with irrational fear and intolerance. It could have been a lot worse. The snakes were not offended.

When I grew out of the herpetological hobby, my pets were released into suitable habitats, where I hope they lived happily ever after.

Moving to the farm provided an opportunity to reacquaint myself with creatures of all kinds, including my legless buddies. A farm can be a hazardous place for snakes. I discovered this after routinely ploughing a field and churning up a few garters in the process. And then, of course, there is the fear and loathing syndrome.

Early on, while rebuilding an old cedar rail fence in a back pasture with some helpers, I chanced across a very large brown snake with an interesting black geometric pattern. Even coiled, I could tell it was about three feet long. When it seemed to rattle its tail, the others jumped back and hid behind the pick-up. Then one macho man got a rail about 10 feet long and tried poking the snake. Its head snapped back as though striking.

A general consensus formed among the fearful that they were confronting a deadly rattlesnake, but I just did not buy it. I didn't see any rattles on the big snake's tail, or any fangs. Furthermore, no one had ever heard of rattlesnakes in the neighbourhood.

I made a rough sketch and ran back to my library to identify the snake. There are similarities of colouration between the massasauga rattler and the common milk snake — even overlaps in territory — but the milk snake is as harmless to humans as a garter snake. It is a well-adapted snake, however, and it copies the behaviour of a rattlesnake right down to vibrating its tail to make an intimidating warning sound when it is startled. Leave it alone and it goes about its business, the upside of which is keeping the rat population in balance. Altogether, the milk snake is about as dangerous as a pointed finger pretending it is an Uzi.

By the time I returned, the anti-snakers had killed it. No doubt the poor creature was as frightened of them as they were of it. It had tried to nonchalantly slither away and they perceived that as some form of sneak attack. When I chastised them for killing a simple milk snake, I was countered with a cockamamie story about "milk" snakes preying on the udders of dairy cows at night. Having tried my hand at milking, I can tell you that not even the most lackadaisical old cow would stand for such nonsense.

After that I heard a number of snake stories, most of them second- or third-hand and all virtually clouded in the kind of superstition that has hounded snakes ever since that alleged incident in the Garden of Eden.

For instance, I heard the one about snakes that bite hold of their tails and move across fields like self-propelled hula-hoops. The unspeakable viciousness of snakes was attested to by the belief that mother garter snakes will eat their babies at the approach of danger. However, my experience indicates that snakes are just like the rest of us, and when danger approaches they adopt the sensible position of "run away, run away." The fact is that if a full-term pregnant garter is killed and cut open, the unborn young may survive. Such is the stuff that creates old wives' tales.

You can generally challenge misinformation with correct information, but when it comes to snakes I have found that being "right" does not necessarily change attitudes. It's a lot like talking politics or religion.

Even though I can hold a snake and offer disbelievers the opportunity to touch it to prove that it is not slimy, they will still feel what they want to feel.

So now I keep my snakes to myself. My wild pregnant garters like to snooze on a rock pile overlooking the Pond. Their young will be born — alive and slithering. They will abandon their mothers immediately and begin fending for themselves. Like everything else in nature they will become a part of a food chain — some will live but most will die. I think about snakes when the ploughs hit the fields, and I will never turn a harmless snake out of my garden.

THE EMILY FISH

Shortly after the longest day of the year, the bass fishing season opens and I can catch Emily again.

Emily is a small-mouthed bass, or a "smallie" as we accomplished bass fisherpeople would say. She lives in a nearby river, in the shadow of a towering concrete bridge connected to a gravel road that hardly anyone uses. It must have cost a million dollars to build that bridge and I cannot help but feel that it was tax dollars well spent if it protects Emily. The sheer magnitude of the bridge and the steep drop below it is enough to dissuade all but the most intrepid intruder.

When I was a kid, fishing meant taking a spool of cotton thread and a bent safety pin to a sliver of a creek that passed through a pasture across from my Grandmother's house. Cousin Elgin would come with me, but only if I dug the worms. We would sit on a makeshift wooden bridge a few feet above the little ripple in the stream and I would wrestle the worms out of the coffee can. Sometimes we dropped a few over the edge to wake the fish up.

Although I was the kind of kid who cried if anyone so much as tried to disfigure my Mr. Potato Head doll, putting a worm on a hook did not faze me. Elgin and I would lower our tortured charges into the water slowly. Then we would watch as little minnows swarmed around, grabbing at bits until there was nothing left. We never did catch a fish in that stream, but we fed a whole lot of them.

After that, I forgot about fishing for several decades, until the Moose decided that he would fish. This resulted in the determination that we would fish. It has become a passion. We fish together, or we fish alone. We have fished all over the world, from jungle rivers in Central America to the great expanses of Georgian Bay. Salted or fresh, if it is wet it is one big fishing hole to me. But country folk hold their fishing holes as close to them as they do their poker hands, so when I found the spot under the bridge, I did not tell so much as one ewe.

This makes catching Emily a secret ritual. When bass season opens, an ultra-light spinning rod is rigged with two-pound test line. I have gone beyond the worms of my childhood, having graduated to plastic cases filled with rubbery jigs in colours that would define a rainbow. Emily prefers yellow. Before I make my cast I squeeze the barb on the hook into oblivion with pliers so it will be easy to let Emily go once she is caught.

The she-bass lies in the deepest part of a pool at the river's edge. While I stand amid the wild iris and shoulder-high grasses, a muskrat sometimes swims across nonchalantly. The sound is of the river and the plopping frogs.

It might take half a dozen casts before Emily rises in a burst. Small-mouthed bass are fighters and she is like a Ninja acrobat. I have seen her leap straight out of the water and soar before flipping backwards and diving deep. Light line sings off the reel. She leaps again, shaking her fishy head. We battle this way through at least three mosquito bites. Then she either escapes or I bring her to the river's edge, cradle her in the flow of the stream and watch her disappear with a tail flash.

I would never eat her. I would never stuff her and put her on a wall. If the river ever flooded, I would look for her. But I would never tell anyone if I found her, or where. That is a sacred vow I made when I named her.

The first time the fish thrilled me with her power and feist, I heard a voice behind me calling, "Emily, Emily." A rather large man appeared through the underbrush just as she was returning to her pool.

"Name's Brain," he said, brandishing a friendly hand for the shaking. "You know, like in your head. I'm looking for my cat, brown cat, name of Emily."

"Haven't seen any cats," I told him, wondering what kind of man looks for cats beside a difficult stretch of river.

"She's probably home by now anyway. Comes down to the river to watch frogs, I think. Me, I fish," he said.

Then he asked, "You any good at fishing?"

"I couldn't catch a minnow with a worm if I tried," I told him.

"Yeah, I didn't think there'd be many fish in this part of the river," Mr. Brain said as we walked back toward the bridge.

Emily Fish is safe with me.

GOD GAVE US A HORSE

It was one of those glorious summer mornings. The sun was shining, a light breeze rippled through the maple trees and you could almost hear the corn growing in the field. So I slept in.

However, my companion "the Moose" had decided it was such a fine day that he would venture to take his annual horseback ride.

Moose is not what you would call diminutive and he is also not exactly an equestrian. These are two features that Lady the Horse spotted right off the bat. She is one of the smoothest riding horses I have ever sat on, but with Moose on board she turns into a stilt-legged trotting maniac. Thus the annual ride is generally brief and to the point.

So I was quite surprised when I rose from my bed to hear the thunder of galloping hooves beating a path to the front door. Breathless would appropriately describe the condition of both horse and rider. While Lady snorted her discontent, the Moose managed to wheeze: "Come quick! God has given us a horse."

Sure enough, tethered to a wild apple tree on the back 40 lane, he had discovered a shiny brown horse.

While it's always been my fantasy that more horses would casually wander into my life, the only thing that people seem to freely deposit at a farmer's doorstep are unwanted dogs and cats.

We looked for signs of human tracks near the unknown horse and found a path worn into the cornfield. There we found, half-hidden, a polished black Mennonite buggy with the bridle and driving lines hanging from a tree branch.

The birds twittered from the trees; otherwise there were no signs of life around the buggy. Since we're both from the city, immediately our thoughts flew to foul play. There is a large Mennonite population in my area and so little is known about their religious ways and personal habits that prejudice occasionally surfaces and takes odd forms.

Mumbling about pranksters and rednecks, we prepared to take the horse back to our barn while we sought out its gentle, peace-loving owner who was probably attending a prayer meeting or helping with a community barn-raising.

Just as we were leaving, a rustling came from the bushes and a tousled, teenage Mennonite lad appeared. He was barefoot and buttoning his shirt. Sheepishly, he explained that he was new to the area and had not been aware that anyone lived here, so he had parked in the shade to cool off his horse for a few minutes.

Knowing something about horses and the deposits that they make over a period of time, it occurred to me that the bone-dry horse had been cooling his heels for several hours.

Then we heard another rustle in the bushes, and out she came: an apple-cheeked lass of about sixteen, who busied herself with brushing grass from her long dark skirt while she thanked us for our concern about the horse.

Moose and I managed to walk halfway back to the barn before we dissolved into laughter. The next time God decides to give us a horse, I think we will call it Romance.

WALLY'S WORLD

I was told in no uncertain terms by the breeder, when first I dared inquire after a Bull Terrier puppy, that one does not "just *have* a Bull Terrier, you have a Bull Terrier *experience.*"

Then, of course, there is the issue of who has who.

The story of Bill Brodsky, a long-time Bull Terrier owner, was conveyed by way of illustration.

Bill Brodsky said, "Bull Terriers? Had 'em all my life. I was twelve before I had realized he wasn't my brother."

In the beginning, I did not quite understand what Bill was getting at.

For the first three months of their lives, Bull Ter-riers are more piranha than puppy. Underneath that loopy nose lies a mouthful of miniature harpoon tips in search of a juncture to puncture.

It took Wally less than an hour to rip the voice box out of the fuzzy-wuzzy squeaking teddy bear that was to have been his first toy. And he would have eaten that had I not risked my digits to pry it away.

That's another thing. Bull Terriers will eat almost anything.

In Wally's first week at the farm, a number of things went missing. For instance, the rubber lamb nipple on the bottle I keep in the barn to feed milk to orphaned lambs.

Where oh where could it be, I wondered, until the mangled nipple turned up in Wally's stool.

I am still looking for a blue sock. And there is missing lingerie that I do not wish to discuss.

Nails, rocks, tree branches and car keys are just a few of the things that have been recovered from intrepid Bull Terrier guts. If they don't eat your wallet, as a consequence of these extreme gastronomic tastes, they can readily negate its reason for being.

When Wally was a puppy, he woke up one Sunday morning feeling a little bit peckish. That is to say that instead of leaving the house like a Stealth Bomber launched off the front porch, scattering all the guinea fowl into the branches of the maple tree, he just walked.

Because of its shape, the face of a Bull Terrier looks like a bicycle seat with eyes. I looked deeply into his. Normally, there is a certain look, a devil-may-care glint that now just wasn't there. All was not well in Wally's world.

He did not have a temperature. No agonized howls. Just not right. When he would not eat, I feared for his life.

I called Dr. Ron, my small-animal vet at home. Dr. Ron loves Bull Terriers. If it were not for his allergies, he would probably have as many bullies as he has children — which is quite a few. Having Wally as a client gives Dr. Ron great pleasure, but he did not like the sound of what I was telling him over the phone.

The upshot was that Moose and me and Wally ended up spending Sunday afternoon in the Emergency Ward of the University of Guelph's Veterinary Clinic.

If Wally had a blockage or an obstruction or something else too hideous to contemplate, the university, and one of the finest animal clinics in the world, would have whatever tools might be necessary to deal with it.

That day we considered ourselves very fortunate to be living only 40 minutes away from Guelph. How ironic, I thought, that I should be revisiting my alma mater, where I first learned about sheep, with a dog who some people think looks like Babe, the sheep-pig, of Hollywood fame.

When the doctor came into the examining room, Wally perked right up. Pretty women have that effect on him.

His vital signs were good. His tail started wagging again. Sprawled on his back, a trance-like ecstasy spread over his face when she palpitated his stomach. Then we faced her for the diagnosis.

"There's no question he's got into something but it's just given him an upset tummy," the good doctor said. She had perched on the examining table, cross-legged. Wally was beside her, sitting as he does, like an old Italian gentleman with legs akimbo, contemplating a bocchi ball game.

The prescription: soft food, plenty of fluids. Wally lifted his head and looked back at her adoringly. Then Moose and I noticed that he was experiencing his first erection and the glint was back in his eyes.

All the way home, Wally rolled happily in the back seat, yelping joyfully until he finally decided to rest his head on Moose's shoulder with his paws dangling behind the head rest. It looked as though Moose had grown a second head. Wally stared intently at the road ahead, as though *he* were driving the car. He remained in that position for the remainder of the trip back to the farm.

I was starting to understand what Bill Brodsky meant.

We never did find out what made Wally peckish. He ate a whole bowl of chicken soup that night and proceeded to hucklebutt the house.

Hucklebutting is a bully thing. It involves running at top speeds, making impossible U-turns around table legs and rearranging cushions. Sometimes whole furniture patterns are rearranged. The dog resembles a snub-nosed torpedo with legs and a twisted sense of direction. It is all part of the "experience."

In keeping with the nature of his breed, Wally likes to dominate everything in his environment. That includes us.

We were told: Rules must be made and stuck to or the bully takes over as pack leader. "No" must mean "no"; be firm but friendly, and so forth.

That worked with Wally for a while, until he caught on. Once he figured out how malleable companion humans can be, how putty-like in the paws of a puppy, he seemed to instinctively understand how flexible those things called rules really are.

Yes, he sleeps on the bed.

Okay, so he also sleeps under the covers.

And when Wally gets too warm, he tunnels to the bottom of the bed, pushes the sheet open and spills onto the floor in the middle of the night with an unceremonious "thud."

Shortly thereafter, he recklessly jumps across the pillows and tunnels back in place.

Wally also snores. Loudly. And he burps and does other things that are all too human.

Then there is this thing about balls and Bull Terriers.

Anything round that has the potential to roll captivates them. The problem is that most balls cannot withstand bully play. Tennis balls split, baseballs shred, all of which can lead to a dreaded "blockage" if the remnants are swallowed.

Enthusiastic loving chomps altered the form and function of dozens of basket, volley and soccer balls. After far too many trips to the sporting-goods store, I decided to dominate.

The rule I set sounds demanding, but the power of the orb was such that Wally quickly learned and obeyed. He can play with a ball *only* if he has something else in his mouth to act as a tooth guard. And the only tooth guard strong enough to withstand the jaws of an 80-pound Bull Terrier is a brutally tough rubber thing called a "Kong."

Wally has Kongs in various sizes and shapes. Large black Kongs are for outdoor play, red Kongs stay inside. Kongs are not allowed in the barn. And without a Kong, a ball cannot be in play. Simple.

There is nothing simple, however, about the way Wally plays with his balls. Having decided to abide by my rules, he has created a whole playbook of his own.

Wally's game of soccer involves controlling the ball with his front paws and propelling it toward its goal with his nose. Throw it and he does headers as good as anything you will ever see in World Cup play. He leaps into the air, rising twice his height and smashing the ball with his head. He is without question the Pele of the dog world.

His field of play is the front lawn of the farmhouse. His boundaries are a walkway, the lane way and the shadow of a large cedar tree. Within these self-imposed confines lies "the goal," a raised wooden flower box that runs the length of the front porch.

Human companion players should not set foot on Wally's field. They must stay in the lane way. Wally shoots the ball at them. If the human misses, he scores an automatic goal and wags heartily. Then the human must shoot the ball back, trying to propel it into the side of the flower bed goal while Wally fields and guards. As games go, I must say I quite enjoy it.

When he is not playing soccer, Wally also bounces tennis balls off his nose. And basketballs, volleyballs and even this fall, a football.

Another game is ball-in-the-pail. Wally started out rolling my hard plastic barn pails with his chest around the yard at a furious rate. This was most disconcerting, since it is the mark of a farmer that we never willingly part with any five-gallon pail. For the first time in my life on the farm, I began hanging my pails on hooks drilled into overhead barn beams.

Then Wally discovered my grain pans and such. A hard black plastic pan with low sides proved the perfect tool for Wally to scoop up his soccer balls. With the ball balanced in the pan, he proceeds to run around the property in ever-expanding figure-eights. Sometimes for hours on end.

Moose actually believes that Wally communicates with him through the ball, any ball. Bull Terriers raise anthropomorphism to a mystical level.

It is not a dog I would recommend to just anyone. Keeping up with "the experience" takes a certain energy and you have to have room on your face for a lot of laugh lines, but I have come to know exactly what Bill Brodsky was talking about.

As far as I'm concerned, one can never have too many brothers.

THE SOAKING
BABY-DOLL DEFENCE

The sheep hit the front lawn at 6 a.m.

I awoke from the leaden sleep of someone who slogged 400 bales of hay into a dusty barn the day before to find all 50 woolly beggars eagerly foraging through the petunias.

By the time I hit the front door, a handful of lambs had taken over the porch of the farmhouse and secured rights to the leftover Kibble in the dog's dish. Stella the dog, a 100-pound hairball Akita who lives to eat, nearly had a heart attack but managed to refrain from chomping wool.

The sheep scattered like pool balls when they saw me. Something about being on the other side of the fence must charge them with adrenaline because even the old reliable ewes began bouncing around and kicking up their heels. The lambs divided into two squadrons: one dedicated to devouring geraniums and the other focused on discovering the garden.

The garden! All my neatly tended rows of green beans, peas, lettuce and sweet corn rising. There is a Chinese proverb that says to be happy for a week you take a new concubine. To be happy for a month you kill a pig. And to be happy for the rest of your life you build a garden. I have not tried the first two proverbial suggestions, but I heartily subscribe to the last.

In an instant I saw the ewes lift their heads from the petunias in unison. If they had been cartoon characters they would all have sported a light bulb turning on in the balloon above their small brains.

"Please," I begged them. "Not the garden!"

Sheep are not revolutionaries. They are not like chickens who will spend weeks plotting their way out of a coop, or pigs who will bide their time waiting for the instant a gate opens to make a squealing exit. Sheep do not make plans. But when they find themselves outside the fence, sheep are born anarchists.The overthrow of my garden appeared inevitable.

Running about and screaming has never served me well with sheep. It seems to amuse them and provides them with an incentive to carry on exactly as they please.

I leapt barefoot into my trusty Wellingtons and pursued the only option that seemed quick at hand — the sprinkler system. I had laid perforated hoses throughout the vegetable rows in the early spring when I thought we might have a dry summer. Within seconds of turning on the tap, the garden sprouted with fine streams of H_2O.

Sheep hate surprises and it was only a minute before they bounded back to the gravel lane in confusion.

Five minutes and a pail of grain later, the whole crew was quietly returned to the field. Sheep will follow you anywhere for a handful of oats. And they do follow like sheep. As soon as one ewe heard the rustle of grain in the pail, the rest trailed along behind with petunias still clinging to their lips as they fertilized the lawn at will.

With no time to spare I settled into repairing a two-foot gap in a cedar rail fence that had allowed just enough space for the entire flock to belly-walk their way to freedom. Sheep are creatures of habit who do not take defeat well, and petunias hold an odd allure for them.

The sun was at about seven o'clock when I finished. Dusting off my knees, I walked back to my soaking garden and cooled off in the misty spray from the sprinkler system. The sheep had been outwitted again, and I felt like the Schwartzkopf of garden defence strategy.

Stella sat grimly on the front porch beside her empty dish casting me baleful and inquisitive looks. I guess she has never seen a soaking wet woman wearing pink baby-doll pyjamas and Wellington boots eat a freshly washed carrot so early in the morning.

SHE SWIMS WITH THE TURTLES

While farmers around me are busy harvesting and the combines churn in the fields, the vacationers are busy getting on with the task of having a holiday at a furious pace.

Just down the road there are a couple of little lakes and an eighteen-hole golf course surrounded by several thousand summer campers who lodge themselves in all manner of tent or trailer in a sort of stacked-together-out-door-experience whose common bond is *eau de mosquito* repellant. They stake their place on a few feet of sand and try to commune with nature.

Occasionally, I will slip the bridle on the horse and ride bareback over the hayfield next to the golf course to see how the nature lovers are doing. I get a fairly good view of the seventeenth hole from a hilly mound where groundhogs lie around in the sun. The little carts tootle from hole to hole with foursomes and twosomes in pastel shirts, shorts and visor caps. Old Lady has no idea what to make of it.

I cannot get too close to the campground itself. The sight of a palomino horse causes a sensation. The campers swarm out of their canvas and tin abodes at the sight of anything that could potentially become part of their vacation experience.

Kids always want a ride and everyone has a million questions about what horses eat and how long they live and why do they sleep standing up. Then there is a general scramble to find a carrot to feed the sleeping horse, but in my experience I find that summer campers rarely travel with carrots. Lady often ends up nibbling on a hot dog bun.

I once caused a real kaffufle by taking the horse swimming.

My neighbour, Elwood, shares a wide pond with the campers. It is a shallow, mud-bottomed affair that supports a small school of fast-swimming, multi-coloured little fish that we call pumpkin seeds because they are oval-shaped and flat as flounders. Mostly, the pond is home to actively breeding colonies of mosquitoes and deer flies, which is what drove Lady and I plunging into the water.

Nobody goes swimming in the pond because of the snapping turtles. Legend has it that the entire bottom of the pond is covered with toothsome turtles just looking for a juicy ankle to chomp. There is nothing Elwood likes better than telling a bunch of greenhorns about the time a posse of snapping turtle hunters came all the way from Tennessee to harvest the hard-shelled horrors.

"They were snapper hunters. That's all they did. Took the live turtles back to Tennessee and sold them for gumbo stew — big bucks in turtles. 'Course it's illegal these days," was his usual opening.

"They had steel snares and sabres and long poles with knives stuck to the ends, but they couldn't get old Horace."

Anyone who has heard the story knows that Horace is the turtle equivalent of the Loch Ness monster. The first time I heard the tale, Elwood said Horace was the size of a snow-shovel scoop. In subsequent tellings, he has grown to have the circumference of a tandem-truck tire.

"They'd go out at night on a big old raft with lights to draw the turtles to them," Elwood would explain. "Turtles'd pop their heads up and then they'd lasso them, jump in the water and wrestle them into burlap sacks — turtles clawing them up and down their arms. One of the snappers chewed his way out of the bag and bit a hole right through a steel-toed boot. But it didn't bother those fellas, no sir. Not one of them had a full set of fingers."

As the story goes, the Tennessee turtle hunters had a raft full of bagged snappers on board when Horace reared his fearsome head.

"Those boys never saw the like of it. Old Horace headed for that raft so fast that he raised a wave behind him. They didn't have a snare big enough to fit over his head. Horace rammed into the raft and started ripping chunks out of it."

There ensues a good deal of thrashing, gnawing and tearing. In the end, Horace sinks the raft and liberates his fellow turtles, leaving the turtle hunters to hightail it back to Tennessee with a variety of appendages missing or damaged.

To prove that Horace is still out there, Elwood points out that loons will not land on the pond, and loons are smart birds.

So folks got fairly excited when they saw Lady and me swimming across the pond on a hot and buggy day.

A hoard of mosquitoes and deer flies had descended on us when we rode through the woods to the pond. Lady's tail was swatting double time and I was trying to hang on to the reins with one hand and clear a path through the bugs with the other. By the time we got to the water's edge we were both quite loony.

Horses do not generally take it upon themselves to go for a swim, but I had no trouble coaxing Lady into taking the plunge.

Once we got past the mud bottom, it was clear sailing. I kind of floated over her back, clinging to her mane and plucking the deer flies from her tender ears. The water was cool and clear. Lady had no trouble galloping weightlessly through the water as we headed for the far shore.

The whole swim might have lasted ten minutes, but it was enough time for a crowd to gather. People were waving their arms and shouting. Two golf carts left the fairway in mid-hole to follow the commotion.

Dripping, Lady and I emerged from the pond. I slid off her back and she shook her whole body like a wet dog, sending droplets flying all over the pristine pastels of the golfers. My soaking blue jeans suddenly felt like a dead weight. But at least we were surrounded by campers coated in bug repellant. Not a deer fly in sight.

"You sure are lucky Horace didn't get you," said a freckle-faced kid as he stroked Lady's neck. Someone pulled out a bag of marshmallows and the horse glommed them down like Pablum.

I had not even thought about the snapping turtles. I remembered looking into the water and seeing nothing on the bottom, just an underwater moonscape without so much as a rock or a weed in evidence.

Then Elwood roared up in his pickup truck.

"You are one lucky woman," he announced. "But that horse is even luckier."

I knew something was coming, but with Elwood you just never know where the ball is going to land. He circled Lady slowly, making sucking sounds through his pursed lips and rubbing his cheeks in wonder.

"He almost gotcha, didn't he darlin'," he said clapping his hand on Lady's damp rump and holding her dripping white tail. "Don't worry, a horse's tail grows back in no time and it looks like he just got a grip on a few inches — good thing you kept movin'."

Now I know for a fact that Lady's tail was the same length it has always been, although Elwood's nose seemed to grow with every word. But there is no point in desecrating a legend, especially when you have become a part of it.

Lady and I dried in the sun while we rode home.

My last vision of Elwood was of him perched on a picnic table with a hot dog in one hand and the other pointing to a spot at the far side of the pond.

"Notice there's no beaver dams in the whole pond," I heard him say. "That's cause old Horace is always biting their tails off. Yessir, people think we got a lot of groundhogs around here but all we've got is a bunch of beavers without their tails."

OWLS IN THE CHICKEN COOP

There is a pair of Great Horned Howls that live in the bush at the back of the farm. I hear them "who-who-ing" at night. It is a low, haunting sound that reminds me of sitting around the Girl Guide fire and telling ghost stories.

I have only seen the owls a few times on moonlit nights, swooping across the pasture fields looking for their prey. They are big birds and they hunt in silence. When they spot something tasty moving in the grass they descend on it with surprising speed, talons first. It is quite a dramatic sight, powerful and terrifying, but somehow defined by an overwhelming grace. I like having the owls around, but I wish they would stick to the pastures for their evening meals and stay away from my chickens.

I must admit that I am not a big fan of the white Leghorn chickens that I raise for meat. They are noisy and stinky and I have no doubt that their IQ is a heck of a lot lower than their body temperature.

But, whatever endearing qualities these creatures may lack in life, there is really nothing quite like a plump, farm-grown, corn-finished roaster chicken to make Sunday dinner something special. So it should come as no surprise that I am willing to put up with their cannibalism, stupid chicken tricks and constant squawky crowing. I see them as much more than a life-support system for the elusive owl population.

The problem is that I started out with 100 chicks but I am now down to 89 full-feathered juvenile birds thanks to Mr. and Mrs. Horned Owl.

Chicken brains must be some sort of owl caviar, because they only take the head. As you can imagine, it is most disconcerting to discover the decapitated victims of these flying guillotines.

Local farmers have advised me that the only solution is to lock the chickens up at night. This would be well and good but my chickens are the organic type, and they free-range in their fenced area. They do not come when they are called and they are not partial to curfews.

A large maple bough shades the open-sided coop where they roost at night, and I suspect it provides the owls with an ideal lookout and launching post, but I am not prepared to cut it down.

I have talked with my local conservation officer, who advised me that since the birds are preying on my livestock I could legally shoot them. Unfortunately, everything I learned in my hunter education course would indicate that firing a shotgun at night is not a safe practice.

And I do like the owls. Somehow I cannot rationalize reducing them to puffs of feathers because they like chicken as much as I do.

The nature narc told me that it is fairly difficult to trick an owl into a humane trap, and they are not shy about dining out in well-lit areas. However, they do not care for noise and they are wary about attacking in the same spot when things physically change.

That's when I thought of the sleigh bells and the pink flamingos.

Covering the chicken range would be a costly affair, but if there is one thing I have accumulated yards of, it is baler twine. And the one thing I could not resist at a garage sale was a basketful of jumbo-sized sleigh bells.

I rigged strands of twine across the chicken range and tied bells to each strand. Then I took out the pair of plastic pink flamingos that have been living in my basement since my farm helpers parked them on top of the manure pile as a joke. I planted the flamingos in the chicken range at dusk and left the chickens to enjoy sweet dreams while the sleigh bells jingled in the breeze.

Nothing happened for a week. I kept moving the flamingos and ignoring what I am certain was the sound of chickens laughing. Finally, one night around midnight there arose such a clatter that I went to my window to see what was the matter.

Suffice it to say, the bells were ringing for me and my owls.

I still hear the owls at night, but they seem to have altered their diet and returned to foraging in the pastures and fresh-mown hayfields. And thanks to sleigh bells and pink flamingos, my chickens can keep their tiny heads — for the time being at least.

IN CLUMPS AND BOUNDS

The voice at the other end of the phone line sounded frazzled.

"I need clumps. You have lots of them, don't you?" asked Lela, an old friend from the days when I was acquainted with socialites and the whims of those who entertain in a grand style.

The "clumps" in question were large masses of flowers. It was the early 1990s and gardening had suddenly become ultra-fashionable among ladies-who-previously-lunched. Lela was hostessing a backyard fundraiser, and the pedestrian planting of pansies and geraniums she had at poolside just would not cut the mustard. Instead, Lela wanted to have massive displays of peonies and poppies, lupins and lilies.

"A sort of flagrant Olde English garden," was how she put it.

Well, my flower beds at the farm do tend to have a "clumpy" look, I suppose. But as I explained to Lela, it is simply not possible to dig up "clumps" in full bloom and expect them to survive a two-hour drive to new digs without having them suffer collateral wilting.

"Clumps," I told her, are the consequence of allowing a plant to put down roots, grow strong and spread. A decent clump can take a few years of nurture. Then you divide the clump and create some more.

A finely clumped garden can take years to develop. But to the gardener, there's a story behind each clump, and every gardener surely knows which clump is the mother clump and which ones are the siblings.

For instance, I can trace all of my clumps of bushy bleeding hearts to one bush planted at the side of the farmhouse. Her progeny are everywhere. Some live in my mother's garden, one lives in Toronto and the other lives beside a neighbour's mailbox. The mother of all clumps is often the pride of the garden.

Lela ended up going to her local upscale nursery and commissioning large clay pots, overstuffed with annual blooms that managed to approximate the image of flagrant something-or-others. She was happy.

As the millennium rushes to an end at the speed of data through fibre-optic cable, the concept of "instant gardening" seems to have taken a stranglehold on urbanites, a phenomenon which is both amusing and disturbing.

For the price of enough seeds to populate a garden for a century, consumers are invited to subscribe to glossy magazines that promises to tell them how to spend their way into an "instant" garden.

Books, television programs, whole satellite television networks are devoted to making the solitary and contemplative pursuit of a private haven into a burden-free hobby that takes about as much time and effort as flipping a burger on the barbecue. Where's the fun in that?

It gets worse.

My friend Claire, a woman who is as urban(e) as women get, who I suspect subscribes to several glossy gardening magazines, who I know maintains a library of books about things like "You and Your Patio-Stone-Friendly Garden," has somehow managed to create her own oasis of charm and maintain a devoted interest in each and every one of her plants.

What she discovered in the affluent back alleys of her neighbourhood was a shocking disregard for life forms that do not eat pâté.

"My gawd, they dumped a dozen rhododendrons in a bin behind the new condo," wailed Claire. In broad daylight, she executed a rhododendron rescue. Four of the mature plants fit comfortably in the trunk of her Audi.

It seems the rhododendrons had flowered suitably on the rooftop garden, but their residual leafy green was no longer required. Someone decreed: "Out with the old, in with the new," and showy annuals likely replaced the uprooted rhododendrons.

Eight out of twelve rescued rhododendrons are now thriving in Claire's garden.

In fact, she has made the pursuit of homeless plants something of a hobby.

Dried fuchsia hanging baskets in need of a drink find themselves drenching at the edge of her backyard lily pond.

One whole section of her garden is devoted to "found bulbs," leftover municipal daffodil and tulip residue that would otherwise be composted into flowerless obscurity in some landfill.

Claire's garden is full of surprises, a riot of colours bound by the theme that every plant is a wanted plant, even those that are unwanted by others.

She is as proud of her urban clumps as I am of my country clumps. Our gardens have deep roots and character. That's what makes us happy — gardens, rural or urban, that grow flagrantly, in clumps and bounds.

OF BULLS AND VARIABLES

One midsummer day, I had a call from Big Tom, a downtown friend who puts together deals. This is the kind of a guy who makes money by generating ideas on paper and letting other people buy into the idea of trying them out. It is what you might call "creative" work. Some of my farmer friends who are out there bouncing through the fields on their tractors baling hay might have another word for it.

Tom was generating an idea about farming. To do this, he needed to create a model, showing profit and loss and capital gain and depreciation, and all of those other things that I'd rather not think about when the strawberries need picking.

His model had cows and sheep and pigs and chickens, and he needed some advice about the sheep part.

"So how many pounds of lamb meat can I get from one, whaddya-call-them — youses — in a year and how much can I get per pound?" he asked.

Now I was once a city girl myself, and I always figured that if anyone would have an answer to a question that would be the soul of brevity — it would be a farmer, one close to the simplicity of nature. But 15 years on the farm has taught me that there is nothing simple about nature, and there is virtually no easy answer to any question about farming.

"Well, that depends," I answered, in the best tradition of my neighbour Hooter, the horse farmer, who answers every question with a "depends" caveat. "It depends on what type of ewe you are breeding, what size of lamb you are marketing, when you are selling and who you are selling it to. For starters."

"Okay, okay, so there are variables," my eager friend replied. "Just give me a top end scenario."

We shuffled a few numbers around. We talked about the Dorset breed versus the Suffolk, the difference between Easter prices and August prices, and the dressed weight of a lamb as opposed to its live weight.

I could hear Big Tom pounding the numbers into his computer as we talked. Variables, these guys love variables. When I told Tom that one ram could probably service as many as 40 ewes, all he could say was "Wow."

"So, what have you got for pigs?" I asked, when we'd finished figuring out that there was hardly a penny of profit in sheep.

"Looks good so far," he said. "I start with one female pig called a sow, and she has two babies . . . "

I had to stop him before he got into the second year projections.

"Thomas," I interjected, "a breeding sow in my uncle's barn is usually good for at least 16 piglets a year."

"More variables, " he muttered.

The problem here is one I've seen before. There are a lot of variables to farming, and unless you investigate them one at a time, there's always a variable out there that leaves you looking like a model of lunacy. I've been there, seen it, done it too many times to be embarrassed anymore. Chalk it up to the 4-H Club slogan "learn by doing," but I always hope someone can tell me before I do it badly.

For instance, a lawyer I know once bought a farm as a country retreat. He had only good intentions for the buildings and the land. Contrary to what many people might think, he wasn't buying a tax dodge. So called "dodges" are as mythical as the brown cow that gives chocolate milk. Truth be known, he was trying to buy some sanity with after-tax dollars.

The lawyer liked cows. He didn't want to start a cattle empire. He just liked the notion of having a few cows.

So he went to a neighbouring farm and bought a dozen of the colour that appealed to him. He put up fences, and he hired a lad to care for the cows. It gave him great pleasure to see the cows grazing in his fields.

Then came the question of breeding the cows. And all of a sudden, the lawyer became a farmer. "Of course, I'm having them bred," he told the neighbours. And he asked for the name of the best bull seller around.

Like a lot of city folk who come to the country, this was one urbanite who wasn't going to let country folk tell him what to do every inch of the way. They were his cows, goll-darn-it, and he was going to see that they were bred to the best dam bulls around.

Even though he was a lawyer, this guy had never seen a real bull in the flesh. Still, he spent a fine Saturday afternoon selecting bulls from a purebred breeder with a wall full of ribbons to show the excellence of his stock. He bought 12 bulls for his 12 cows and ordered them delivered the following weekend. Although the bull breeder attempted to explain the non-monogamous nature of cattle, the lawyer's insistence and the looming financial bonanza mitigated further protest.

When the truck pulled up, the lad who was tending the cows was a bit disconcerted.

"You can't put them out there, no way," he advised as the truck eased into the pasture field where the cows were grazing.

"My cows, my bulls, nature's way," said the lawyer, fully believing that the boisterous boys and the comely heifers would pair off equally and go quietly into the sunset to make little cows.

Well, all hell broke loose when the gates were opened. The bulls bolted like something out of a Merrill Lynch commercial — all wild and bucking, with fury in their crazed loins. The cows froze. Then the bulls decided to run at each other. After all, when a bull sees a dozen cows he wants to make each one his own, and he's not about to share with his brothers.

It took six good men and three good cutting horses to straighten out the donnybrook that ensued. Some of the bulls were taken to isolation stalls in other barns and the rest were tethered by nose rings in the lawyer's barn. The cows just shook their heads in disbelief. The neighbours wandered off with a story they knew they could supper on for the next decade. The lawyer acknowledged that maybe he had taken on more bull than he could handle.

The lad selected one of the bulls as the herd sire, and the rest were sold at auction. But the lawyer never saw the fine calves that resulted. After the Great Bull Fiasco, he couldn't even go into a supermarket without hearing whispers behind him as the story spread.

He sold the farm and bought a ski chalet.

At least with skiing, you know that you only need one ski per leg.

I hope that Big Tom's farm model works out. The country can always use an infusion of capital from city people who want to get closer to nature and understand a few variables. But if Thomas ever calls me with a truck-load of rams for sale, I'll be the first to tell him he's got the wrong number.

A CASE OF
DOMESTIC SHELL SHOCK

Proving that you can recycle almost anything, my neighbour Sarah has found a market for infertile goose eggs.

Every year Sarah hatches hundreds of goslings and other waterfowl. What most people would consider a living room is her incubator. Whole walls are lined with hydro-sucking egg warmers. If it contains life in a shell, Sarah can hatch it.

But some eggs do not contain life. All sorts of variables from a change in feed to a change in season can result in an infertile egg. Those that fail to show signs of embryonic life after a certain number of days are rejects. Having been subjected to slow heating, they are no good for eating, but Sarah turns their loss into a profit by selling the big eggs to a woman who hollows them out and paints them for Easter. Sarah makes more selling one barren goose egg than most farmers make selling a dozen fresh chicken eggs.

I wish she could figure out a way to turn my dormant wild turkey eggs into gold.

The problem is that my wild turkeys are an oxy-moron — domestic wild turkeys. Hatched in incubators themselves, they are strictly specimens of what used to grow abundantly in the wild. Gradually, the natural wild turkey population is increasing, but my domestically raised wild turkeys would not have a clue about what a balanced diet is if it does not come from a feed mill.

Still, the hen turkeys lay eggs. I have harvested some and hatched a few. As day-olds, the poults show some hint of the wild. Baby cock birds, for example, will lower their tiny wings and shake them along the top of the wood shavings as notice of their territorial rights when the great giant hand fills the feeder in the brooding cage. The wattles of full-grown males turn from purple to red when they feel threatened, and the display they make with their wings sounds like the rattling of tree branches. But if you put a pair of domestic wild turkeys two storeys up in a tree, I venture to say it would take a forklift to rescue them.

Turkey eggs taste almost the same as chicken eggs, a touch darker in the yolk, perhaps. When they are laying, my two hens produce an egg a day. Usually they stop in the late spring, but one year the eldest bird, Hortense, decided she would keep on laying and sit on her eggs.

The broody hen flattened herself over a shallow de-pression in the earth where she laid her eggs. For weeks I did not see Hortense move. The cock bird flew at me when I filled their feeder, which was highly uncharacter-istic for him. One male, Bourbon, has been noted for dis-plays of violence, but his son Hector actively enjoys human company. He once attempted to grab me by the back of the neck and mate with me when I was painting the base of the pen.

Hortense was truly dedicated to her eggs; the problem was that she did not rotate them. The heat eggs need to develop is one thing. Distributing it evenly involves turning the eggs every few hours, no matter how slightly. My incubator has a small motor attached to the egg trays that tilts the egg racks automatically. Hortense just sat there, hugging herself to her eggs with a maternal deliberateness that was not going to hatch a thing.

Six weeks went by. The eggs should have hatched after twenty-eight days or so. Armed with a garbage can lid and sporting a hard hat, I entered the pen. Hector made no protest. Apparently he had grown tired of playing protector. When I took off the hard hat, he tried to mate with it.

Hortense held firm to her eggs. I shoved my hand underneath her and felt roughly a dozen eggs. When I tried to gently remove one, she grabbed my wrist and nearly broke the skin. I got the message. Hortense sat and sat and sat on those eggs. No amount of cajoling or poking from outside of the pen could convince her to give up the ghost and get on with her life.

Then one day I heard a loud bang from the turkey pen. Then a squawk, another bang and a flutter of wings. Hector was terrified. Hortense was flapping around frantically, jumping up to her perch and then returning to her eggs. When she saw me she plopped on the eggs and tried to pretend nothing had happened. Bang! It happened again. This time I watched her go straight into the air. What we had here was a hot egg explosion.

I wore industrial-strength gloves and two layers of sweatshirts along with my hard hat and coveralls when I retrieved Hortense and put her into another pen with the shell-shocked Hector. The only thing I was missing was a gas mask, and I sorely missed having one. Rotten eggs are one thing, exploding rotten eggs are more like stink-bomb grenades.

Hortense did not lay another egg all summer. I would not blame her if she post-traumatically suppressed eggs for the rest of her life. If she ever decides to lay more than an omelette, I plan to diffuse the whole lot of them and paint them for Easter.

THE EARLY BIRD
CATCHES THE WORM-PICKER

One of the mythic stereotypes about life on a farm is that the cock crows at dawn, triggering the happy farmer into a joyful tumble out of bed to do chores. I have had crazed roosters that crow at four a.m., and at that time of morning I'm not ready to tumble anywhere. The fact is, roosters crow anytime they want. Light can trigger their crowing, but roosters do not differentiate between moonlight, sunlight or, as it happens, flashlight.

My friend Ron had an ongoing war with marauding worm-pickers. One of his back fields was flat and fertile, perfect ground for night-crawlers. On a moist summer night, he was driving home from a late meeting and saw an unfamiliar van parked on the concession road be-side his field. Half-a-dozen worm-pickers with tin cans strapped to their waists and flashlights mounted on their caps were feverishly harvesting a bounty of limbless fish-bait. When Ron stopped to confront them they leapt over his fence and drove off.

Installing a "no trespassing" sign did no good. The pickers were nimble and quick. The fenceline was sagging, and Ron was starting to boil at the illicit harvest of "his" worms. The more he thought about the problem, the madder he got. No one from the police to his neighbours could control their mirth when Ron went on a "worm rustling" rant.

"What're you going to do? Catch 'em slime-handed?" joked one of his erstwhile buddies.

In the coffee shop, the fellows who fish the local streams would trade stories about what lure or which fly was working. Then as Ron strolled by, they'd let it be known in loud voices that the only thing that was really catching fish was "Pride of Ron." When Ron found out that good worms were selling for more than a dime apiece, it pushed him over the edge.

Although he wasn't about to get into the business, he started thinking of worms as money in the ground. He installed a strand of barbed wire to protect his worms and his fences, but the night-crawler vigilantes clipped their way through it with wire cutters. That was tantamount to a declaration of war.

When Ron asked his neighbour, Derek, if he could borrow the meanest bull in his barn as a worm protector, it was apparent that he had reached the end of his tether. He was thinking dangerous thoughts. He had even been overheard talking to veterans at the Legion about minefields.

"You want to catch them, not kill them," Derek offered, hoping that he was right. "What you want is an alarm system that no one would suspect."

Derek's wife, Kathy, raises prize-winning chickens and she clued them into the rooster defence. In half-an-hour they'd constructed a two-rooster-capacity cage made of chicken wire. They placed it in an unobtrusive stand of tall grass at the edge of the field and installed a pair of Kathy's cockerels.

Two days later, there was a light afternoon rain. It was just enough to call all crawlers to the surface at midnight. Ron notified the authorities to be on call, because he was certain he would be worm rustled that night. He wanted backup.

Sure enough, in the dead of the night those roosters started crowing their beaks off. Ron called the cops at the first crow. Derek was roused from his bed to block the worm-pickers' escape route at one end of the concession road, and Ron rushed to close off the other end.

By the time the boys-in-blue arrived, the worm-pickers were cowering beside their van. There were kids and women and little old men in the crew. Many of them did not speak English, and all of them were scared to death. Ron decided to let them off the hook. If there was a profit being made in worm picking, it was obvious that this motley crew of fish-bait rustlers was not getting the lion's share.

Under the glare of the headlights of assorted friends and passersby who gathered to witness the worm-picker bust, Ron did a reasonable pantomime explanation of his concern about fence damage. The confiscated worms were returned to the flat, fertile field. Remorse and apologies were expressed. With a stern warning, the rag-tag worm-pickers were sent on their way.

"They never saw it coming," chuckled Ron, as he regaled the coffee shop with the tale. "They might as well have rung my doorbell. As soon as those roosters caught sight of those flashlights they wear on their heads, they started crowing as though there were six suns in the sky."

Ron's worms have thrived without intrusion ever since. His fences are straight and stalwart. He still has the rooster cage and Kathy sold him a couple of big-time strutters for the barnyard, just in case. As the saying goes — the early bird catches the worm. But if you want to catch worm-pickers — get a rooster.

ANTI-NOAH'S FARM

When the two reverends, Doris and Daniel, were granted a rural ministry, they thought their prayers had been answered.

They had ministered in inner cities, outlying suburbs and small towns. Wherever they were asked, they went. But in their dreams, they imagined serving a peaceful country church, the kind where every family has its own pew and the organist knows all the hymns by heart. Somewhere nearby the church, they dreamed of having their own little farm.

And so it came to pass.

The church was a fine yellow-brick building with an unimposing steeple and a gleaming oak door. Sunlight dappled through the stained-glass windows into the sanctuary, and well-worn hymnals and prayer books lined the pews.

In the lower level, the Sunday School rooms and kitchen/dining area looked out on a country road and a pasture field, where curious cows gathered on the Lord's

Day to watch the comings and goings and listen to the joyful sounds.

Along with the church, the two reverends were provided with their ultimate fantasy. It was a small house by most standards, but the front porch looked out over a pond draped with willow trees.

On warm summer afternoons, the reverends would sit in their rocking chairs, counting the turtles sunbathing on a log and listening for the *plop* of bullfrogs. At dusk, the deer would come to drink.

Behind the plain frame house, there was a small red barn with three horse-sized stalls and a couple of open pens. The mow could hold about a hundred bales of hay and still leave the pigeons with fluttering space.

There was a fenced paddock and a small pasture facing onto a maple bush that turned the colour of fireside flame in autumn. Between the house and the barn, a path was lined with knee-high sunflowers called "Teddy Bears," bordering a garden plot that was twice the size of the ground floor of the house.

In all the years of their marriage and their ministering, this was exactly what the reverends had hoped for.

Neither of them knew much about country life or farming, but they found themselves embraced by their neighbours. Everything from firewood to fresh eggs showed up on the stoop of the veranda, with a friendly face behind it all, asking only a blessing in return.

Often, after the Sunday service, a parishioner would offer an invitation to come for tea, to help celebrate an anniversary or just to take a tour of the farm and stay for a barbecue. It was at a barbecue, when Doris mused aloud about how she had always wanted to know what it felt like to care for animals.

The Velkon family farm was a devoted dairy operation, but the children had their own "special projects." In an old driving shed, Billy Velkon and his sister, Mary, raised rabbits and an assortment of exotic chickens. When the kids took Doris on a tour, she spotted one huge grey rabbit sitting forlornly in a pen all by itself.

"That's Mambo," explained nine-year-old Mary, solemnly. "She can't have babies anymore, so we have to get rid of her."

Doris furled her brow into a question mark. Billy, who was a few years older than Mary, whispered in the reverend's ear.

"Dad's gonna shoot her. It won't hurt or anything."

Doris reached into the pen and stroked the old rabbit's fur. Mambo raised her twitchy nose, revealing clear blue eyes circled with pink.

"You could have her if you want. We have lots of extra pens, too," said Mary. "She never bites."

Doris did not hesitate. She knew Daniel would agree that it would be a sin to leave a creature awaiting certain death for the sole crime of infertility, especially when they had a whole empty barn at their disposal.

The two reverends left the Velkon farm with Mambo in the back seat.

One barren bunny was just the beginning.

At church the next week, Reverend Daniel delivered a sermon titled "A Second Chance for All God's Creatures."

He trod a delicate furrow in farm country, where the dead-stock trucks routinely pick up any half-dead "downer" cows, and the last thing some crippled piglets see is the head of a shovel.

Later that Sunday, the widow Rachel Hunter stopped by, ostensibly to drop off a peach pie for Doris.

"I enjoyed the sermon," she told Daniel. "It reminded me of how my late husband Bill kept an old blind boar in the back of the piggery for years after he served any useful purpose. Huge old boar, he was, but a gentle soul. Used to come when Bill called to him."

Then she paused, lost in memory, and rocked her chair.

"Suii, Suii, Here come, Chop, here come," whistled Rachel, recalling the sing-song call Bill had used to summon the blind pig. Then she sighed. "Bill died a year to the day after he buried Chop. He always said he wouldn't go before that pig."

In the week following the sermon, the two reverends heard many such stories — about old faithful ploughing horses, dried-up milk cows, three-legged barn cats and even a flightless barn pigeon. They were all long-gone animals, remembered from a time before "the bottom line" was a serious threat to every farm, a time when love and loyalty were weighed along with Total Daily Nutrient Consumed and Estimated Value of Production.

Before long, the reverends ended up opening their barn to a few more strays. From the outset, Daniel and Doris made one simple rule: since they were not in the business of farming, they would not be in the business of breeding animals. They would take one of any creature, and do their best to find homes for the rest.

That was the beginning of the Anti-Noah's Farm.

The animals came in one by one. There was Pouch, a miniature donkey who had arthritis. Doris simply could not resist the mouse-grey, long-eared creature. The fact that he enjoyed having his back massaged made Pouch even more endearing. Of an afternoon, Doris would look out her kitchen window and see the donkey sitting contentedly on his rump, like a large dog. It always made her smile.

Then a really large dog came to join Pouch in his reveries.

Tiny's owners were almost frantic when Reverend Daniel answered their advertisement in the weekend edition of the city newspaper that the church organist passed along to him each Sunday. They were computer specialists who had been transferred to assignments in Asia. Tiny was their Great Dane, a six-year-old spayed female who could knock Mambo the rabbit off her feet with one giant lick.

The only creature that Tiny did not try to lick was Iggy, an old white goose, who hissed and snapped anytime the black dog's shadow crossed his own.

In a cage beside Mambo, a male guinea pig and long-haired female hamster snuffled around in a bed of shavings that was cleaned twice a week by eleven-year-old Kelly Lambert, whose younger brother had severe allergies.

Kelly was also happy to tend to the needs of Melissa, a Vietnamese pot-bellied pig who once lived in town, but outgrew her circumstances and enraged her owner's neighbours by rooting in their gardens.

At the reverends', Melissa rooted around Pouch and wallowed with the turtles in the pond, where a mateless Canada Goose endlessly cruised.

A one-eyed goat named Sam and a grandmother ewe named Flossy shared a stall in the barn and a bounty of windfall apples in their pasture. If a shepherd was too busy to keep a bottle-fed lamb, Doris would take it and raise it for a while until it could go back to the flock. When she nurtured a runt calf, the weaker of a set of twins, she impressed everyone. The buttery brown Jersey named Daisy became Jennifer Talbot's 4-H calf and they took first prize in the fall fair, with due credit given to "Reverend Godmother Doris."

Every once in a while, someone would drop off a kitten. Doris and Daniel found homes for them, except for Cal, a calico cat, who was the resident mouser and lap cat. Cal eyed each new addition to the farm with suspicion but, as long as they stayed off his cushion on the front porch, the kingdom remained peaceable.

Semi-regulars became regular attendees at the church and the Sunday School was packed. The reverends' kitchen was always open to anyone who just wanted to talk. People often stopped by to check on the animals and offer advice, as well as everything from feed to fencing.

News of Doris and Daniel's success in the rural community reached the church hierarchy. Doris and Daniel received a formal request for a delegation of observers to attend a service.

This made the two reverends nervous. They well knew success often spelled transfer. They broached the possibility with a few of the church elders, concerned only about what would happen to the animals if they were required to move on.

Doris delivered the sermon on the fateful Sunday. The leader of the church delegation, Reverend Ron Whipple, and half a dozen assorted observers were duly welcomed and presented with gifts, including a selection of homemade preserves.

As her theme, Doris chose "The Farm as Sanctuary," which seemed appropriate since afterward the congregation and the visitors were all invited to attend a tea at the reverends' homestead which, after all, was nothing if not a sanctuary.

Doris and Daniel did everything they could to minimize the visibility of the animals, but, on a farm, out of sight is seldom out of mind. There was nothing they could do to minimize the smells and sounds of their growing menagerie. Pouch brayed from his stall, while Sam and Flossy *baaed* anxiously and the old goose squawked.

In the kitchen and in the yard, people sipped their tea and chewed their cookies as though oblivious, while the observers twitched and arched their brows.

"I do so love to see the pig. Where's the pig?" inquired the widow Hunter. Then, realizing she had interrupted a potentially religious conversation between Reverend Daniel and Reverend Whipple, she whipped out her hand and introduced herself.

"Rachel Hunter," she said. "My late husband Bill had a blind pig named Chop." Then she wandered off, calling "Suii, Suii," under her breath.

The Sunday Schoolers broke the lid off things. They excitedly rushed the barn to see what was new and revisit what was old. Soon the paddock was full and kids were sitting on the porch, legs dangling into the petunias, petting

Mambo and crew, along with a squirmy ferret named Fuzzbuster. Hammy Hamster ran up Mary Velkon's right arm, under her blouse, and down the left, dangerously close to Cal's cat cushion. There was a momentary panic.

Then Pouch sat down and brayed, distracting everyone, except for the untended pig who discovered that rooting in Doris's garden was much more rewarding than rooting around Pouch.

The Reverend Whipple and his gentrified delegation were somewhat taken aback. They frowningly sipped their tea and watched as Doris and the choir mistress chased Melissa the pig out of the garden and then plucked a few carrots for a donkey that apparently did nothing except sit on his hind end and *hee haw*.

Sam the goat tried to nibble one of the delegate's patent-leather shoes, a material that interested him greatly since he had not seen such shiny potential food on the farm.

"It's eating my foot," screamed the patent-shoed woman, who jumped back, leaving the shoe in Sam's bearded mouth. Young Kelly Lambert grabbed it away.

"Sam just wanted to nibble it," he muttered, wiping the slightly scarred shiny red pump on the thigh of his good Sunday pants and handing it back to the hobbled delegate.

Then Kelly stroked old Sam's head and the goat rubbed against him.

"Sam's only got one eye," he said to no one in particular. "He's no good for anything and he should be dead."

Reverend Whipple took a step forward to hear the boy more closely.

"Fact is, everything on this place would be dead if it weren't for the reverends," Kelly continued, shoving his hands deep in his pockets and talking to the ground.

"My brother coughed real bad because he was allergic to Hammy and Ginny, and my dad told me to say goodbye to them. They would have had their skulls crushed with the mallet, sure as anything, if the reverends didn't take them in. Not to say my dad's bad, he didn't think he had a choice. Just like Mr. Velkon would have shot Mambo soon as look at her because she was just taking up space. And old Pouch, he can't do much of anything."

Kelly's father joined him and put his arm around the boy. Don Lambert, like his son, was spare with his words.

"Kelly's right," he said. "Until the reverends came, we all tried not to think much about animals — I mean, a pet is a pet, but if it interferes with your life it's got to go, that's how I thought. Farmers can't have animals taking up space and not producing, not when feed's as dear as it is."

"Don's right," said a voice from the crowd. "The reverends raised two of my orphan lambs and now those lambs have lambs of their own."

Jennifer Talbot told her prize-winning calf story.

"Now Daisy gives so much milk that I bring some extra over for the pig every week," she said, and there was a small, spontaneous round of applause.

"The reverends are godparents to all these animals," said Jennifer, "so if you make them leave, you make all of the animals into orphans. Then everything will go back just the way it was."

People left quietly after that. Falling away in tidy knots, they seemed to melt down the lane. Alone with

Reverend Whipple and two carloads of delegates, Doris and Daniel shivered under stoic skin. The yard was still.

"You've done a fine job here," began the Reverend Whipple, in a solemn tone that matched his grey eyes.

"I mean it's fantastic what you've done. Just to see those people and the connection you've made and the obvious Love the good Lord bestows, and the animals . . . "

He was clearly touched.

In the paddock, the pot-bellied pig started rooting. Her steady *unh, unh, unh* grunts forming a background rhythm section to the chorus of praise from the chattering visitors.

By the time they were done, Fuzzbuster the ferret was stuffed with pound cake and draped around the collar of one of the visiting dignitaries.

The patent-shoed observer fed the goat a carrot and quietly took Doris aside.

"I don't want to impose," she began, "but my sister is quite ill, in and out of the hospital all the time. The problem is, she still has this budgie, but she thinks the world of him."

"We've never had a budgie," says Doris. "Tell your sister we would be happy to take care of the little fellow for as long as she needs. That's what we're here for."

The two reverends were not going anywhere.

Instead, the Church sent them a brass sign to hang on their mailbox. All it says is "Sanctuary."

THE FARMER GETS A TAN

By July the first round of haying is complete and there is a sort of breathing period on the farm. In this window of time, I can actually block off time to ride the horse for fun, wander through the garden just to look at the way things are growing, and generally stop to smell the peonies.

Around this time of year, the level of water in the pond naturally drops. The frogs take over, plopping for cover when they hear footsteps. So this year I decided I would do something a little different — I would go to an actual beach.

At the beach you can always tell a farmer from the rest of the crowd. We are the ones with the unusual suntans. You will notice, for example, that a farmer will generally have an excellent tan on the back of the neck — just below the baseball cap line and just above the T-shirt line. Some pejorative folks would call it a "redneck," but a friend of mine calls it "farmer's neck syndrome." The tan stops where the T-shirt begins and proceeds again from some point just above the elbow.

The tan of the hand is another matter. When you handle bales of hay or straw, it is a good idea to wear a pair of durable gloves with the fingers removed so that the twine doesn't cut into your palm. Under a beating sun this leads to tanned digits and white hands. Likewise, since I don't tend to wear socks, my tan ends where the running shoes begin.

So when it came time to don my beachwear and sandals, I realized that I might just as well have tattooed "farmer" on my forehead.

Beach scenes are pretty much the same everywhere. Seagulls cruising overhead. The smell of hotdogs and burgers. Miles of faces in sunglasses and floppy hats. The lapping of water and the crunch of sand in your shoes — not a cow, chicken or sheep in sight or sound.

There were a lot of very good tans on the beach. In fact, there were some tans that looked darned-well professional. In contrast, my thighs and upper body were very pale, my toes white and my knees and lower arms bronze. I realized that I stood out like a thistle in a wheat field.

To disguise myself just a bit, I decided to at least keep my baseball cap on while I set off for the shoreline. No one even noticed me. Small children did not ask their mothers why that lady had two skin colours. There was no giggling behind my back. No one asked me if I shouldn't be at home milking the cows.

Floating in the big water of Georgian Bay is different from drifting on a farm pond. There are waves that roll, and that faint feeling of undertow that comes with a horizon where water meets sky. I was casually practising my crawl stroke when an ambient wave caught hold of my baseball cap and washed it out of sight.

Half an hour later, I felt cooled enough to return to the beach. The water had rinsed away a lot of daily strife. Not once had I considered the plague of potato beetles in the garden, or contemplated the logistics of moving turkeys into a new pen, or dwelled on the cost-effectiveness of buying a post-hole digger versus renting one.

I had barely reached my towel when a young man with a perfect tan came bounding over.

"Think I found your hat, ma'am," he said. Producing a damp mess with a red brim. At least the colour was right.

I took the hat and examined it. Mine had come from a farm-equipment dealer and featured a tractor on it. But the sodden cap I held in my hands just had the words "Farmers Do it in the Hay." I'd been found out.

By then the bronzed boy had disappeared into the herd of tans. Some farmer left the beach hatless that day, but it wasn't me.

THE SOUP LADLE RESCUE

The barn was empty. The Sheep and the horses had all taken it upon themselves to spend the late days of summer in the shade of the back pasture, where they forage for fallen apples from the wild apple trees. So I was surprised to hear a small racket of peeping coming from the far corner of the barn. The baby barn swallows had long ago swooped from their nest in the rafters. I wondered what could be left.

That particular area of the barn is rather dark. In the spring, it is the favoured spot for ewes to lie down and deliver their lambs. But in the summer, it becomes what a neighbour's little girl calls, "the place where spiders live." In the few rays of sunlight that filtered through to the corner, I could see the big, filigree webs the spiders had been spinning. With some regret and some timidity, I chopped my way through their handiwork with my broom, looking for the source of the peeping.

The peeping was loudest in the corner, where a covering of plywood separates the exterior metal barn wall from damage when the tractor clears out the manure. At the bottom of the four-foot high plywood — in a gap about the diameter of a garden rake — I could see the soft beige feathers of a tiny Old English Game hen, puffing her wings over a fresh hatch of thumb-sized chicks.

As I walked back to the house to get a flashlight for a better look, I pondered the dilemma. The secretive hen had selected a truly secretive place to brood her eggs. Unfortunately, she had also selected a space that offered no exit until her chicks could fly. No exit also meant no food and no water.

Moose joined me to analyze the problem. The whole idea of a new batch of chicks so late in the season had him all excited.

In the glare of the flashlight, the hen moved. We counted eight tiny heads. But the narrowness of the gap and the height of the dividing wood was such that even the long arm of the Moose could not reach them. We contemplated ways and means of lowering food and water. We thought about cutting a hole in the wood so the birds could make their escape.

Nothing seemed practical, until I thought of the soup ladle.

Moose could not ease more than his arm down the wooden wall. However, I figured if I stood on a tall metal pail I might be able to lean further down the gap with my short arms and use the ladle to scoop the chicks out.

So, while he trained the flashlight, I balanced myself on the pail and hoisted my right shoulder up into the breach where I slashed through a cloud of cobwebs with my soup ladle.

I was standing on my tiptoes and the ladle was just inches away from scooping up a chick when my right breast shifted down into the gap, giving me just the depth I needed. A brownish ball of fluff fairly rolled right into the ladle and I tried to draw it slowly up.

Quickly I discovered that any movement I might make would have to be sideways, since the shift of my bosom had lodged me firmly in the gap. So while I teetered on the old bucket, I ladled the chicks sideways into the Moose's waiting hand.

The hen found all of this most distressing, and made several assaults on the ladle with her beak and her tiny wings. When the nest was empty, I finally managed to clutch her back and pass her up to be reunited with her babies.

Extricating me from the gap was another matter. I wiggled and teetered on the bucket to no avail. Finally, Moose suggested greasing me with salad oil, which started us both laughing. Then something shifted, freeing my boob, soup ladle and all.

We put the chicks and the hen into the pail and took them to a pen. Game birds are smaller and even more delicate than the Banties that strut around farmyards like miniature chickens. The babies were so tiny that even the smallest of chick waterers that I had on hand would have been so deep that one false step could lead to a drowning.

Moose solved the problem with shallow pop bottle caps, weighted with pennies glued to the bottom so they could not tip over.

In no time, the hen was wandering around scratching in the dirt and pecking in the feed dish — teaching and eating at the same time. When the chicks rest, they flock under her wings.

Sometimes all you can see of the eight of them is one little head with blazing dark eyes or one little chick foot straggling beyond its mother's fine feathers.

People occasionally ask me where I go for a summer vacation. Well, I do not go much of anywhere. Maybe, like the sheep and the horses I will wander to the back pasture to find apples, but otherwise, it is best to stick close to the farm.

After all, a hen with a new brood in a no-exit zone cannot call 911. And a farmer never knows when it might be time to get out the soup ladle and perform a rescue mission.

THE SQUIRT

Mabel was the youngest of a family of five. Her nearest sibling was six years older, and she was the only female. The boys called her "Squirt." She had always been tiny. Mabel enjoyed the privilege of being pampered and cooed over when she was a toddler, but by the age of five she began to feel left out of the pack.

Her brothers all had barn chores to do before they cleaned themselves up and headed off together for the school bus. When they came home, there were more chores. Then they all sat down for the evening meal, and it seemed to Mabel that her brothers had their own secrets and their own language.

They talked about teachers and compared notes. They told their father about a calf with a sore leg or a plan they had for a new gate. When they went to their rooms to do homework, Mabel would listen through the door and hear them talking about everything from hockey players to girls.

That summer, Mabel decided to become one of them. She pulled her hair back into a tight pony-tail and announced that she was ready to help with the chores. Tagging after them toward the barn, Mabel suddenly found herself scooped up in the firm arms of her father and deposited squarely back in the farmhouse kitchen.

"Barn's no place for a squirt like you," he said.

There were things that Mabel was allowed to do. Under the watchful eye of her mother, she trailed around the garden pulling weeds and picking peas. Perched on a soda pop crate, she reached into chicken nests and gathered fresh eggs. When the dog's water bowl was half full, she filled it.

Still, the brothers seemed to stream through the house and fill it with life and excitement that Mabel was missing. They would come bursting through the screen door, dusty, tanned and poking each other to be the first to get into the refrigerator. They placed bets with each other about who could load and unload a wagon fastest. Everything about them seemed larger than her own life.

As the summer drew to a close, Mabel felt more and more left out. No one seemed to care what she did, as long as she didn't do it near them.

The last job the boys had to do on the farm that summer was setting a row of fence poles along a stretch of hard gravelly ground.

The poles had to be set into the ground a good three feet and they were to be placed no more than twelve feet apart.

Once the boys had dug the holes, using a combination of the tractor and auger along with pick axes and shovels, their father said he would measure each one and, if the job was done to his satisfaction, the whole family would spend the last Saturday of the summer in the big city watching a professional baseball game.

Mabel's mother gave her a wink and told her that she would have to work with the boys to qualify. The four brothers groaned, mumbling about the "Squirt" getting in their way.

The boys had three days to dig the holes while their father was away at a cattle sale. It was dry, miserable work. Mabel helped the boys pile rocks at the edge of each hole. The rest of the time she had to stand three holes away from them when the tractor was running and the post-hole digger gyrated its way through the tough clay ground.

"Not deep enough," said Mabel sitting on the edge of one of the first holes.

"What would you know, Squirt?" the boys said, almost in unison.

Then Mabel slid into the hole.

"See, half-my-head short," she said, peering up at them with her nose on a level with the lip of the post hole. "I'm just exactly three feet tall."

When Mabel's father came to inspect the fence line, he found the holes neatly dug with a post lined up next to each one.

"Looks good, but the tape will tell a truer story," the farmer said, taking out his faithful tape measure.

Mabel's oldest brother pushed her forward. She looked up at her father shyly.

"I'm the fence measurer," she said, "and the hole measurer, too."

Mabel's father gave her a quizzical look, and then the boys took over.

One grabbed the tape measure and, while Mabel stood on the tab at the end, he ran it to the top of her head.

"Squirt's exactly three feet," he said.

The two other brothers picked Mabel up and lowered her into the hole. The earth around it was perfectly level with the top of Mabel's head.

Outside the hole, Mabel crouched down and rolled four somersaults, landing her exactly at the opening of the second hole.

Again two brothers lowered her, patting the top of her head to show their father that the hole had met the measure of his daughter.

"A full Squirt" the boys called it, and Mabel gritted her teeth.

The job was pronounced well done and Mabel rode back to the farm house on her father's shoulders. Her mother was waiting on the porch with a small package wrapped in shiny paper, a present for Mabel.

It was a tape measure tucked inside a baseball cap.

"Being a Squirt only lasts so long," said Mabel's mother.

Sure enough, when Mabel was measured in her fine new cap she was a full tick taller than three feet.

No one ever called Mabel "Squirt" again.

THE SUMMER OF LOVE

It is hard to leave the farm for long periods of time. I have been lucky enough to have neighbours who are willing to pinch-hit on overnight trips, even weekends, when business, family obligations or windfall World Series tickets demand a sojourn. Still, it takes days of preparation. You try to think of anything that could go wrong and cut it off at the pass — replacing that barn light bulb that must be on the edge of virtual burnout, for example. If an animal is sick or due to deliver, you just do not go.

Even in the summer when the sheep and horses are in the pasture feeding themselves and drinking from an automatic waterer, there is always the chance that a lamb will stray or a gosling will fall into a groundhog hole. Such worries have caused me to have guilt attacks in the middle of a Rolling Stones concert and have prompted the urge to phone home as soon as a bride and groom have said "I do."

I can take a writerly meeting in the city, but the follow-through is something I can do from the farm. So when the career opportunity of a lifetime presented itself, I was in a quandary because it meant I would have to spend five days a week for half of a summer working in the city.

Farm economics being what they are, I did not have much of an option. So, I started looking for a full-time relief shepherd. I might as well have been looking for ears on a snake.

Coincidentally, one of my closest high-school friends called. Angie has always been a manic whirlwind. She is the kind of woman who will do backflips down a bar on a bet. I have seen this, personally. She writes poetry and music, which she recites, sings and plays with the passion of her Russian ancestry. A quick study, she once married a chess player and in no time she herself was representing Canada at chess Olympiads. The marriage ended in checkmate, but her board game skills led to a job in Europe managing the World Chess Federation. She has sold everything from pianos in Brussels to BMWs in Hong Kong.

I have learned that her phone calls can be anything from a 2 a.m. "Psst Marsha, I'm calling from Rick's Cafe. I'm with Bobby Fisher and he's wearing a fake beard" to "They want me to go to Beijing. I can't go to Beijing. There's no night life, just one darn Planet Hollywood." But this time her phone call was about coming home and being in love.

From my standpoint it was perfect. She and her first high-school flame, Derek, had reacquainted. While they were sorting out where and how they would plan a life together, they would be delighted to spend the summer taking care of the farm. On weekends, I could come home to all things bright and beautiful, and they could roam the countryside in search of their own heaven on earth. I breathed a sigh of relief. One hitch: they had no experience whatsoever.

Angie, Derek and a monstrously huge cat named Charlie arrived a week early to acclimate themselves. They brought Wellington boots, an electric piano and a wok that came all the way from Macao. Angie wanted to start farming immediately. She rushed to the paddock where the horses were grazing and leaned over the fence calling, "Here horsie, here horsie." I did not have a nanosecond to warn her about the strand of electric fencing at the top of the fence. That was her first shock of farm life.

Angie and Derek spent the next few days following me around and making lists. They listed the number of scoops of grain I gave the horses and the bin that it came from. They listed the number of brown eggs that we collected. They noted the identifying marks and location of animate and inanimate objects. The red-golden pheasant was "male: red and gold with some blue and green feathers; female: brown, no long tail. 2nd bird run. Name: Mao and Mrs. Mao, from Manchuria!" A chicken feeder was, "metal, hanging in back coop. Fill from blue container, wash weekly, use side hose."

And they asked questions. Does the ram bite? Do bees sting chickens? When I told them to toss some grain to the duck every day they asked how many handfuls. Angie started reading sheep health books and querying me about things like the difference between foot rot and foot and mouth disease.

At night, Derek drew maps and Angie made schedules. They charted every inch of the farm, noting each and every strand of electric fencing. A blueprint of the garden recorded the rows by number and tabled the dates when the peas and carrots should be ready. Chores were equally divided. Derek to brush the horses on Mondays, Angie on Tuesdays. Mow the lawn — Derek; weed the garden — Angie, and so on.

All of this attention to detail made me start to realize how complex the whole operation actually was. I made up my own list of contacts and phone numbers in case of any emergency from dishwasher meltdown to rabies.

My first week of city work passed uneventfully. I called home morning, noon and night. All was well. Diva Dog chased Charlie Cat up a tree, but everything else was tickety-boo. When I arrived home that first weekend, vegetables from the garden were steaming in the wok and Derek was grilling lamb chops to perfection. The sheep grazed happily in their field and the horses shone golden in the sunset. Diva sat obediently when Angie told her to, even though Charlie and the barn cats careened right in front of her after a chipmunk.

The lovebirds loved farming. It suited the bloom of their mood. The next day they showed me their routine. Hand in hand they strode to the barn, calling each passing chicken by name. Groucho the duck quacked happily in their direction. He never did that to me. One little lamb — a darling thing with a button of a nose — came over to the fence to give Angie a nuzzle.

"There now Chelsea," said Angie, bending to give the lamb a hug. "I hope you don't mind, I just call her Chelsea because she's sweet, like the buns, you know." I knew.

Assured that they had done a terrific job, off they flew to spend the day antique hunting. I plopped myself on a lawn chair and wondered which big heavy book I should start reading now that I worked in the city and had time on my hands.

And so it went for weeks on end. I reduced my telephone calls home to one a day. On weekends, I puttered around in the garden and watched the lawn grow. There was plenty of time left over to go horseback riding. Angie made enough strawberry jam to last for two winters and Derek rebuilt the barn door that had been sticking for years. When it rained, they went outside together and danced through the flower beds, singing and laughing like Dead Heads at a sixties love-in. They had terrific suntans.

By the time that my job assignment ended, Angie and Derek had found their dream homestead. When they drove down the laneway with Charlie sitting in the back window, the egg-fed barn cats came close to tears. I turned around to find perfection in whatever I beheld and wondered how I could possibly manage to keep it that way.

The next day, potato beetles invaded the garden. Two nights later, raccoons levelled half a row of corn. A heat wave followed and the chickens were of no mind to lay. One ewe started limping. Diagnosis: foot rot. I treated the whole flock by walking them through a formalin foot bath. Those who did not want to walk through, I pushed through. Consequently I was also foot-rot free, and knee-rot free and elbow-rot free. Then it rained for three solid days and the lawn grew a foot.

The summer of love had ended. Chelsea had doubled in size. Groucho duck went back to being grouchy. it was back to life as usual and I was not about to leave it soon.

Fall

THREE STRIKES
AND THE SUMMER IS OUT

Summer officially ends for me with the final game of the Slo-Pitch League. It is a game that is sure to happen long before the World Series gets underway, while the sumach bushes are still tinged with scarlet and the geese are gearing up for the flight south. It is also a "sure thing" because there will never be a baseball strike in the slo-pitch league. Millionaire baseball players and owners may think it is okay to huff and chew when they should be playing ball, but at diamonds in every rural town the boys and girls of summer have never stopped trying to whack the ball over the cow palace building.

When I was a kid I used to watch my six uncles play baseball on a dusty old diamond that didn't have any fancy lights for night games. The village bleachers would be packed with families. If a game went on past sunset, cars and trucks would scatter around the diamond and we would watch the finish of the game through a blaze of headlights. The crack of the bats, the whistle of the pitch, the endless moment of a fly ball dropping slowly from the sky, and my strapping big uncles charging from base to base in a swirl of dust — that's the real field of dreams.

Now I am not a baseball player. My one season of play ended when I ploughed into a first baseperson who had the specific gravity of a brick outhouse and injured my knee. Then a cow kicked the same knee, and I have been on the injury reserve list ever since.

I am a fan, and my team of choice is the UIC Flyers. The team was formed about a decade ago when most of the guys relied on the Unemployment Insurance Commission for their daily bread. Things change. Now they all have jobs and families, but they don't have full baseball uniforms.

There is nothing fancy about small-town baseball. The Flyers wear T-shirts sponsored by their watering hole of choice, a construction company and a guy who kills lawn weeds. Instead of the usual player numbers, they decided every shirt should just have a Number One on it. Of course, they all have baseball caps, which are worn backwards unless there is a brutal sun.

Baseball doesn't need to mean fastball. That's really a young person's game. Slo-pitch is a kind of genteel baseball, a sort of a signpost on the geriatric coast toward lawn bowling. Instead of blinding pitches, the ball is thrown underhand. There are no dramatic belly-skinning slides into home plate — that would be too dirty and dangerous. Instead, runners just trot past the plate. At that rate, you can keep players going well into their 60s.

I knew of a team that called itself La Bats, and they thought they were hot stuff. They tried to stack the roster with youngsters and hard hitters, which earned them the nickname La Dorks. Slo-pitch is meant to be fun. When a team by the name of the Master Batters went to the finals one year and heard their name incorrectly pronounced as one word over the loud speakers, everyone was laughing except for their wives.

Each season there is one perfect game. One game in which everyone on the team plays like Robert Redford in *The Natural*. It's the kind of game where double-plays happen every other inning and home runs abound.

The fans go wild, and a sort of baseball-speak takes over the English language. A ball hit low to the ground, for instance, is a "worm burner." And a pitcher doesn't throw the ball, he "tosses the dark one." There is always one guy in the league who yammers non-stop through every game in an idiom that goes something like: "Have an eye, this is the one. The sticks are ready. The sticks are hot. Just give it a nice light poke. Touch a bit of green."

One year the UIC Flyers lost 14 games in a row, but they still managed to win the championship. They took this as an omen and promptly declared themselves World Champions.

A celebration was in order, and the team asked for permission to party for a weekend at my farm. Younger people might call this a "field party," but the Flyers took it one step further. For instance, I was somewhat surprised when a full-blown work crew appeared on the scene and spent a non-stop weekend erecting a 20-by-30-foot covered stage, complete with an electrical system capable of handling an eight-piece orchestra. They even installed an outhouse with a dandy crescent moon on the door.

On a Saturday afternoon, a steady stream of campers poured up the laneway with all manner of tents and trailers, kids and barbecues in tow. Someone rounded up a wagonload of picnic tables that were strewn in a clearing in front of the stage, and the decorating committee installed Christmas lights through the evergreens. It was a nippy evening, and everyone assembled down in front around a bonfire, while the second baseman acted as deejay, playing everything from Bob Dylan to Bob Wills.

It didn't take long for real musicians to appear. Country and western guitarists and Irish minstrels play slo-pitch. At one point, everything from a mandolin to a penny whistle were blended in harmony. Before supper was served, "Amazing Grace" was rendered in a bagpipe and saxophone duet. Then there was a talent show and the first baseman won with a mean display of break dancing. By the time I went to bed, the embers were cooling to the last strains of "Kumbaya."

The next morning, while the smell of bacon and eggs filled the air, the Flyer kids were playing baseball in the pasture. Shortstop Craig announced his engagement to Miss Ellie and the World Champion UIC Flyers toasted them. I kept expecting Shoeless Joe Jackson to wander out of the cornfield.

By Sunday night, my fields were once again my own. Soon the empty stage was packed with hay for winter feeding. Summer had ended appropriately with a celebration of baseball.

A LABOUR OF LOVE

On Labour Day, I like to turn the tables a bit and make the laziest guy on the farm do some work. On that Monday, the ram gets down to business.

It isn't much of a strain. After all, the guy only works two or three times a year for a maximum of about 30 days, and none of those are exactly what you would call manual labour.

In fact, the working conditions are a kind of macho ram's dream.

All the big fella has to do is make love to his flock of adoring ewes. He's a stud, plain and simple. Two hundred and fifty pounds of paternal genetics waiting to happen. Once he's completed his task, he can lie down in green pastures until the next season.

The terms of employment are, however, very strict — get the job done or face extinction. The odds are heavily stacked against the male of any species living a long life on any farm. Heck, you don't even need a rooster to get eggs from your hens.

On a dairy farm, only the most exceptional males will ever qualify as breeding bulls. And even those fortunate enough to qualify often end up never actually enjoying a romantic moment. Their seed is collected into sterile tubes that are divided into smaller units called "straws," which are used to artificially inseminate the great mothers of milk.

Beef bulls are tending to go the same route. Making the grade is rigorous. The best of the crop of purebred bull boys often end up on test station farms where they are evaluated for everything from how much weight they gain on an average day to the size of their breeding apparatus.

Size does count on the farm. For instance, I would never consider keeping even the most charming of runt ram lambs as flock sire. As they say in boxing, truth is in the "tale of the tape."

Years ago I was attending a sheep show and sale where the competition was fast and furious. One fellow in particular was promoting his ram as the best thing that ever walked on grass. And it was a pretty animal — washed white as snow, with shiny black hooves, a gleaming black face and a pedigree as long as a rack of lamb.

The sad truth came when the veterinarian who was inspecting all of the animals called for "the tape" and discovered that the fancy ram was a few critical centimetres shy of the scrotal circumference that makes or breaks a breeding ram.

The poor owner threw a woolly fit when he was told of the disqualifying characteristic. Manhood and ramhood melded as one.

A recount was demanded. But the tale of the tape was just as damning the second time around.

"Nothing personal," the vet kept saying, as he backed away from the enraged owner who had worked himself into a stomping, red-faced, testosterone-fuelled rage.

The undersized ram was led quietly from the building, while his charged-up owner required a three-person escort who were subject to a freewheeling range of expletives. It is one of the few times I have seen a shepherd truly lose it. And I never saw that shepherd or any of his sheep in the show ring again.

With some pride, I can report that my ram, Magnus, survived the tape. He is fit and handsome, and there's a gleam in his eye. On Labour Day Monday I will dress him in his breeding harness, a leather affair that holds a bright crayon marker at the front of his chest. Then he will be taken to the breeding field where the chosen ewes have been gathered.

From then on, it is up to him to do his job without supervision. The crayon is my only intrusion. Each time Magnus works his charms, it will leave its mark on the ewe. In a few weeks, the whole group of ladies will be sporting a red streak on their backsides.

I like to think there will be romance — and tender moments of baaing and cooing— but that is something only the sheep will know.

I will know if Magnus is the worker I think he is sometimes late in January, probably during the half-time ceremony of the Super Bowl. From start to finish, it takes anywhere from 148 to 152 days to make a lamb. So I figure that one or two of the ewes who catch his eye on

Labour Day will inevitably be giving birth as the last game of the football season plays out.

At least, that is what Magnus had better hope happens. Otherwise, he's out of a job and off with his head.

FOLLY COMES TO FRUITION

I have eaten an apple. To most it would have seemed a rather ordinary fruit; red, round. No big deal. But I have been waiting a long time for this particular apple.

It is not as though there are no apples on the farm. I can view the aged survivors of a pioneer orchard from the kitchen-sink window — gnarled boughs glazed with ice in winter, pink-white blossoms in spring, green fruit trinkets, through the leaves of summer and rosy, swelling apples in the fall.

And there are wild apple trees all over the place, on fencelines and in the middle of pasture fields. They have a certain mystery. I wonder what seed they came from and how long they have lived here? Nothing about wild apples is predictable. They come in all sorts of flavours from sugary smooth to mouth-puckering tart.

I have always liked apples, but seldom craved them because they seem to be so predominant in my life. From a couple of trees, I can gather hundreds of apples of all sizes. Over the years I have had larders filled with apple derivatives — apple jelly, apple chutney, apple butter and, of course, applesauce.

Still, gathering apples is a lot of work. And wild apples tend to be a bit rough. They can be pockmarked, nibbled by bugs or worm-eaten. The biggest, brightest fruits always seem to be at the top of the tree, one ladder step out of reach.

Every year the apples seem higher and the ladder seems shorter. And something is getting rickety — it could be the ladder, but maybe it is me.

So I decided to create an orchard of dwarf apple trees that would flourish right next to the garden at the front of the house. I have watched all sorts of people as they age and there seems to be a certain amount of shrinkage that goes on over the years. At least with dwarf trees, I figured I might still be tall enough to pick apples when the pension cheques start.

The orchard was planted eight years ago. Five trees is all that it is. The whole deal cost me about $150, and I do not expect my apple harvest will ever pay me a dime. The trees have taught me about pruning and fertilizing. I have stripped and burned the dreaded tent caterpillars from their slender boughs. I have wrapped their trunks to protect them from the ravages of winter bunnies and frost. In times of fungal peril, I have mixed organic pesticides with water and washed the leaves of each threatened tree.

Eight years of this, and finally, one tree on the north side of the orchard produced an apple.

It was a McIntosh.

I looked at it for a long time, hanging there from a delicate stem, defying gravity. When I finally reached up to pluck it, I had visions of Eve in the Garden but I knew that my apple was imbued only with good intentions. I nudged it gently and the apple plopped into my hand.

After holding it for an appropriate time and marvelling at the perfect imperfection of its beauty — one side larger than the other and the red skin somewhat streaked with gold — I cored it and cut it into bite-sized strips.

The Moose has always considered my little orchard something of a folly — a non-event — a bit like growing sunflowers only to have all the seeds devoured by blue jays before we even get a few to add to the granola mix. But when folly comes to fruition, the reward is sweet. I shared the bounty of my harvest with him, and we both pronounced it the best apple ever eaten. Next year I may have enough to make an apple pie.

Almost certainly, by the time my pension cheques start arriving, the dwarf orchard should be producing bushels of apples. It is hard to envision it happening right now, but there is some comfort in knowing that as I shrink into my Golden Years, I will always have apples within easy reach.

GETTING THE LINGO
AND THE LAY OF THE LAND

It was my first autumn in the country and I was preparing for winter. Everyone said we were headed for a doozie. One farmer could tell by the texture of his cattle's coats and another cited the early departure of the geese. An organic farmer spent hours explaining the physical changes in the appearance and depth of earthworms. Obviously, I was not the only one with winterization in mind. The plumber was so busy that he could only make time to set up a heated water bowl in the barn after dinner. The sun went down and I waited, watching for headlights to wind up the lane. No one came.

When I called the next day, he told me he had been at the farm after dinner, but no one was there. He looked in the barn and figured he knew where to put the water bowl. There was no question he had visited. He described the dogs, the sheep and the scarecrow in the garden. I felt as though I was living in the Twilight Zone. How could I have missed him?

"Well, I was there about 1:30," he said. I thought for a moment.

"Sorry," I offered, "I was out because I thought you were coming after dinner."

"I did," he said.

That was my first lesson in rural-speak. In my part of the country, dinner means lunch and supper means dinner. Lunch is a big midday spread that you have on a weekend with family or friends attending. Lunch is also the sandwiches, salads and desserts that "ladies" bring to evening parties. It is usually served around 11:00 at night when things begin to wind down.

Country language can become a complicated affair. Nothing is quite as simple as just a "chicken." For example, there are pullets, which are female chickens that are old enough to lay eggs. Then there are layers, which are chickens that are in the process of laying eggs. There are roasters (which are usually roosters) that you grow into Sunday-supper-sized birds, and there are broilers that commercial growers feed to supply fast-food restaurants and such. Then there are capons, which are roosters minus hormones, which means they grow big breasts like hens. The whole lot of them are called fowl.

The local newspaper carries all of the social news. If I want to know who took tea with whom or who is planning a reunion or having a baby shower in my area, I must look under the column labeled "Little Ireland." It seems the Irish first pioneered the neighbourhood. Although it is now populated by everyone from Mennonites to Portuguese and Scots, the social identity is still related to the century-old cemetery down the road. Similarly, ancient school districts that have long since gone the way of amalgamation are used to describe certain neighbourhoods — Greenbush, Beehive and Poplar Grove. None of these identities exist on any map.

Directions can drive one to distraction.

"You go past the old Ross place, where Eldon Weber lived before the barn burned," my chicken plucker once told me. "Then turn right at the new silo that the Crispin boy is building and drive past where the old Greenbush school was before they put up the white house where Mrs. Reid lived until she went into the nursing home. I'm the next lane to the south." It took almost as much time for me to find his farm as it did for him to pluck the darn chickens.

Unless your deed goes back to the time that the Crown granted it to your family, you do not live on your farm. If the person who owned your property had it for a few generations, then your farm will bear their name for your lifetime. If the person who owned your property only owned it briefly or (heaven forbid) it was owned by a numbered company, then your farm will be named after the person who owned it the longest before you did. You can put up signs galore. You can paint the barn turquoise and write "Brady Bunch Farms" in eight-foot-high purple letters. The locals will still tell You that you live on "the old Tilden place."

This is exacerbated by the fact that many people go by different names than those that appear on the mailbox, especially the men. I had a few of these nicknames explained to me in the pub.

Take a guy known as Spider. His real name is Thomas Noonan, but even when his mother gets formal she calls him Tim. He is also called Tim-Bob, because during the peak of the TV series *The Waltons* someone decided that he resembled the lanky character called John-Boy, but Tim-Bob sounded better. It was his gangly height that earned him Spider.

Rooney, who is actually Richard Young (even though everyone from his boss to his girlfriend call him Rick), earned his title because he has a tendency to whine in the tradition of *60 Minutes* television commentator Andy Rooney. The local disc jockey, Doug Kerr, has always been known as the Suds or, affectionately, Sudser. To the roads superintendent falls the title Pothole King, but if you want to point out a pothole to him, you have to ask for Demo. It seems after one particularly long night in a pub, he required a designated driver. However, before anyone could be designated, he managed to demolish a quantity of other vehicle bumpers in the parking lot. Hence, Demo.

My neighbour Ken Houston pronounces his name "house-ton." But I named him Hooter because come haying time he starts hooting and hollering. It stuck. In return, he named my companion Moose, which automatically designates me Mrs. Moose. All and any names can be followed by the word "cat." I doubt that this has anything to do with the beat generation or "hep cats," but you end up having a beer at the tavern with the likes of Bob-cat, Tom-cat and Moose-cat.

There is no such thing as an unwed couple in the country. If a fellow parks his car in your driveway for three nights running and you attend at least one social gathering in his company, you might as well get hitched because explaining anything different just will not wash. If two men live together in any sort of relationship for a long period, they will end up being called "the bachelors." Young men who live together are likely to be called "the fellows." Two unrelated women who set up house are called "the girls," no matter how old they are. Sexual preference is rarely discussed outside of the privacy of the coffee shop, where everything and anything is reported, discussed, condemned or supported.

If you are new to the country, you can expect to be stared at, but not spoken to unless you say something first. This can be too much for some people. I had a painfully shy acquaintance who bought a big old house in town as a renovation project, but she left halfway through the job because she just could not take being stared at constantly. If she had told people who she was and what she was doing to the house, they might have stopped staring.

You can expect to be granted privacy in the country, but that won't stop people from finding out who you are. They just won't bug you.

Years ago, actors Michael Sarrazin and Jacqueline Bisset spent a month living with their friends Robert and Marlene Marklein in Egremont Township. Sarrazin had recently starred in the Academy Award-nominated film *They Shoot Horses Don't They*, and Bisset's film *The Deep* was playing at the Roxy Cinema in town. They were movie stars. When they strolled into the drugstore, they positively twinkled. No one in town so much as asked for an autograph. When Robert introduced Jackie to Bill the supermarket manager while they were waiting for some chicken breasts to be boned, all he said was "Nice to meet you, ma'am." To this day, ask Bill and he can show you the exact spot in the store where he met Jacqueline Bisset and feigned indifference out of respect for her privacy.

Once you get used to the lingo and the lay of the land, the country is just another living landscape. The problem becomes one of translation. It is up to you to remember that if city friends are invited to dinner it means that they are coming for supper. Directions are best provided in map form, along with a full description of property and the number of mailboxes to pass before you get to the correct lane. You may get used to telling people that your place is the first on the left after the railway tracks but is impossible to find a farm that exists along the railway tracks now that the railway tracks don't exist any more.

In the end, you just have to go with the flow and all things will be revealed. One day you'll wake up with a nickname that you can't get rid of. And no matter how hard you try, you will never get an egg from a capon, but once a layer quits laying, she's headed for the stew pot no matter what time of day you decide to eat.

And every winter is bound to be a doozie.

GLASNOST CAN BE DUCKY

It was a fine and sunny autumn day when we plucked Gorbachev.

Gorbachev Duck, that is.

I was just starting to batten down the barnyard hatches in preparation for winter, when I had a semi-frantic call from my friend Mia, a poet and shepherd who moved to the country about six years ago. Since I have been on the farm twice as long as she, Mia assumes I know a lot more about farm-type things than she does. So when she decided that Gorbachev was ready to become dinner, she called to request a hands-on demonstration of the delicate art of plucking a duck.

I have plucked my share of waterfowl, and the one thing that I have learned is that I would far rather buy a fully naked bird at my local supermarket. But Gorbachev, Mia's singular duck, had been grain-fed and deliberately raised for a feast. So we gathered in the woodshed and assembled the tools of the trade: an axe, a few sharpened knives, pails of various sizes and, of course, a hair dryer.

Mia's husband, Tom the Philosopher, fetched Gorbie from the barn. He was a fine big Muscovy duck with a kind of huge red wattle on his bill, which spread in a red patch over his white head and earned him his name.

I expect Tom and Mia had discussed the actual killing of Gorbachev from a variety of philosophical, poetic and moral aspects. Although I volunteered to do the deed and thus absolve them of guilt, Tom had obviously contemplated the awesomeness of the task at great length and determined that he should take responsibility for his duck in death as he had in life.

Once Gorbie was released from this veil of tears, the business of plucking began.

Mia provided a large bucket of warm water. The theory is that the water helps loosen the feathers. Getting a duck soaking wet is another matter. Ducks are virtually waterproof if you soak them head first. So we stuffed the duck in the pail tail first and swished him around until the water penetrated layers of feathers. A couple of tablespoons of laundry detergent helped to disperse the natural duck oils.

Then we put the wet duck on a table and six hands started to pluck. Feathers were flying and for the first five minutes we were going great guns. Half an hour later, no one was in that much of a hurry. A 12-pound duck packs a lot of feather. And under the feathers there is down — tiny fluff with an uncanny ability to fly directly up your nostrils as soon as it is plucked.

I tried to save the down from a half a dozen plucked geese. Many years ago I had *Harrowsmith* visions of creating my own duvet, but in the end there was not even enough for a whoopee cushion. Plucking gives you a lot of respect for feather pillows.

We were picking out pinfeathers with tweezers when Tom decided he had to go to his study and memorize *The Critique of Pure Reason*.

I cleaned the inside of the duck, while Mia marvelled at the various entrails — brilliant coral lungs, a sleek and slippery liver and the hardened block of gizzard. She examined each organ like some kind of Greek oracle as I explained what it was. It turned into a sort of Duck Anatomy 101 session. Although I take the business of evisceration quite seriously, I did find myself having to laugh when Mia gingerly touched the two almond-coloured, walnut-sized globes that I removed from the mid-section of the duck.

"These are remarkable — almost opalescent, so very delicate. I wonder what they are?" she exclaimed, cradling them gently in the palm of her hand.

As it happens, those were Gorbie's testicles, which caused Mia to drop them very quickly.

Tom hung the duck from a beam in the root cellar while Mia and I proceeded to blow-dry Gorbachev and pluck the remaining downy feathers. It worked quite well. One year I tried covering the down with melted wax. Theoretically, it is supposed to harden and then it can be peeled off with all the down cleanly affixed. However, I ended up with a sort of duck candle.

The final step was singeing the bird. Underneath all of those feathers, ducks have a smattering of hair that has to be burned off. It just takes a flick of the Bic to come up with a totally bald duck.

It took about two hours to get Gorbie ready for the roast pan. I'm sure that he will make a fine feast. As I left, the look of the poet crossed Mia's face and she set off to compose a poem of grace for her Gorbachev dinner party. I wonder if there is a word that rhymes with glasnost?

THE WORLD'S LARGEST ALL-FEMALE MARCHING KAZOO BAND

It started in the Mount Royal Tavern, where many things are started and few are realized. Tim "Spider" Noonan and the boys were halfway in the trough on a warmish sort of evening, when an attractive young woman known as Spike dropped by with a few girlfriends. Boys being boys, they got a bit giddy thinking of ways to engage Spike and her entourage in conversation. Spider drummed his fingers so hard that every glass of beer on the table became effervescent. Then he came up with the idea.

"Can you ladies hum?" he inquired, raising his eyebrows expectantly.

"Anyone can hum," said Spike.

"Good. You can try out for the marching band," came his rejoinder.

The women laughed, as he knew they would. Thus engaged, someone asked, "Who ever heard of a marching band that hums?"

"The band doesn't hum, exactly," said Spider. "They hum into kazoos and march. Haven't you ever heard of the World's Largest All-Female Marching Kazoo Band?"

There is nothing quite like the thrill of a marching band. But once you reach a certain age, the dream of ever being part of one dissipates, especially if you play the piano. The kazoo was a back door to a dream and the Homecoming Parade for the Old Boys and Girls Reunion was fast approaching.

The first gathering of aspiring marching women kazooists took place at Minto Meadows, the activities headquarters of the U I C Flyers Social Club, of which Spider Noonan is convenor. About fifty women showed up. Some came with their mothers, some had children in tow and some just brought a cooler. Local retailers noted a run on kazoos the likes of which they had never seen. By the end of that first day, everyone knew their instrument. As Bacall said to Bogart: "You just put your lips together and blow."

The kazoo marching band evolved into a model of democratic procedure mingled with chaos. Two drummers, a cowbell player and a triangle tinkler volunteered to set the pace. Spider got to play the cymbals because it was his idea. Women who had been passing each other in supermarkets for years without speaking marched side by side, touching fingertips to maintain proper distances and debating the arch-support merit of various types of running shoes. At least a dozen women could do a passing impression of Phil Slivers as Sergeant Bilko. "To the leeheft, right, leeheft. Leeheft . . . Leeheft."

Selecting marching music was another matter. Someone suggested the Disney theme "It's a Small World" and kazoos were heard to gag. The Irish contingent lobbied for "MacNamara's Band," and won. Polka enthusiasts fought for "Roll Out the Barrel." Everyone agreed it gave them happy feet. "Three Blind Mice" as a rondo worked at a standstill but floundered when married to marching, as did The Beatles' "Oo Blah Dee." Everyone agreed that "When the Saints Go Marching In" was a natural. Three songs would do it. The whole parade was only about six blocks long.

Word spread and soon the ranks of the kazoo band swelled to one hundred strong. Friends brought friends into the band and co-workers brought co-workers. Spider's two daughters joined the band, as did his ex-wife and his ex-girlfriend. The ex-wife brought her three sisters, and one of them ended up leading the band. If there was nepotism, it took a circuitous route.

Leading the band was a bit like organizing a daycare centre for a bus trip.

"Everyone hold your kazoo in your left hand," Band Leader Vi would begin, waving her baton. "No not that left hand, your other left hand."

Vi's baton looked suspiciously like a broom handle with a gold papier maché knob on the end, which was exactly what it was. Sometimes Spider had to crash cymbals to bring order.

"Watch the butt in front of you and keep your distance," Vi commanded as one hundred kazoo-blowing women marched on, five abreast, down the curved laneway of Minto Meadows. When they reached the turn at O'Dwyer's Sideroad, one hundred heads, some permed and some in ponytails, turned to check for traffic — to the left, right, left. And the kazoo band went marching along.

The neighbours came out to watch, and the thrill of having a crowd enthused the marchers. Kids and dogs were a distraction. One entire line of marchers fell out of step and the band had to mark time until they regrouped. The smokers in the bunch heaved and wheezed. Even six blocks was going to be a challenge, but if men in skirts blowing sheep bladders could make it . . .

"Remember to breathe before you blow," advised one nursing kazooist. "Don't just assume it's a hot flash if you feel red in the face and woozy."

The subject of uniforms arose. To put it delicately, the general consensus was that the supplier would have to understand the meaning of "Extra Large." There was not going to be any spandex marching in this band. The name of the band was printed in hot pink on white T-shirts featuring a kazoo with musical notes over top of it. Co-ordinate this with white pants, white running shoes and a hot pink visor and you had one sharp-dressed marching kazoo band.

At the hot dog roast following the final rehearsal, children ran around playing their mothers' kazoos under shady maple trees. There was discussion about where the band would be positioned in the parade. No one wanted to march behind the riding horses, and especially not behind the draught horses.

Some distance had to be drawn between the kazoo band and the calliope or both musical art forms would be compromised. It would be a health concern to march in the wake of the exhaust fumes trailing behind the huge transport truck that always gets into the parade just because it is too big for anybody to say "no" to.

"And remember," advised Vi, "the most important thing is to go to the bathroom before the parade starts."

Homecoming celebrations kicked off three days before the parade with a Gigantic Bingo. The next day out-of-town campers began setting up their tents on the front field of the Stinson Farm. Friday was Old Boys and Girls Registration Day, sidewalk sale day and dedication of the Town Bell day. Swimming at the public pool was free and there were almost as many pies at the Presbyterian church salad supper as there were salads. Before the Welcome Home Dance started, the Beard Growing Contest was judged followed by the offer of free shaves for all competitors courtesy of Floyd's Barber Shop.

Only a few kazooists showed up for the pre-parade breakfast at the Legion. Most were too busy pulling out hair curlers and putting in a few final minutes of practice. A sea of pink visors collected in the roadway where the parade was forming. There were a few nervous Nellies in the pack, but they soon got down to focusing on "Lee-heft, right, leeheft." The Porta-Potties across from the ambulance garage did a brisk business.

Band Leader Vi sported a plume that looked a lot like a feather duster in the back of her visor. Before the parade took off Spider crashed his cymbals.

"Remember it's your right hand that you raise when you say 'hey' at the end of each song," shouted Vi. "If we don't all do it together people will think we're drunk."

Someone reminded her that it was eleven o'clock in the morning and the Bavarian Beer Garden at the curling rink did not even open until two in the afternoon. Some-one else suggested marching straight to the curling club. Then the convertible carrying the Dairy Princess started moving and the Largest All-Female Marching Kazoo Band in the land went into parade mode.

To say that it was glorious would be an understate-ment. They marched with pride, strutting all of their stuff and breathing deeply through their smiles. When the par-ade came to a brief halt while a Shriner replaced the wheel on his go-kart, the marching band marked time and sang a few choruses of "When the Saints Go Marching In" to the delight of the crowd. Adolescent sons cringed at the sight of their mothers making such a display of themselves. Grandchildren cheered their grannies on. The Old Boys and Girls saw so many familiar faces that their hands grew limp from waving.

At the fairgrounds where the parade ended, the band played "Oo Blah Dee" and a jived-up version of "Three Blind Mice." Husbands congratulated wives, boyfriends were kissed and kids carried on shoulders.

"I love a parade," shouted Spider, and the kazoo band looked up in unison.

"If you can hum a few bars, we can play it," said Spike.

NO RAM OF MINE

I've been thinking a lot about sex and sheep recently. This is not as unhealthy as it sounds, since the breeding season for sheep is coming up soon. As soon as there is a nip of chill in the night air, some trigger in their brains activates sheep hormones and translates into lust. The ram is the best barometer of this.

And all of that nasty business with President Clinton caused me to have even greater admiration for the ram who serves as the sire for my flock than I already did.

My ram never lies.

He never makes excuses.

And he is unabashedly polygamous. The worst thing that he could admit to a Grand Jury would be his incessant, libido-inspired penchant to jump fences.

I've known sheep sent to the wool factory for much less.

Obviously sheep and other animals have simpler lives than the President. So I have resented certain American news reporters who have compared the behaviour of

Mr. Clinton variously to that of a dog, a goat and, yes, even a ram.

Sheep don't have sex for fun. At least, I don't think they do.

And there is not much romance involved. Certainly no exchanging of gifts.

There is nothing furtive about what they do in virtually any aspect of their sheepish lives.

Quite simply, sheep have no shame and a ram would not know how to look embarrassed if he tried.

You would never find a ram looking apologetic about having had sex with a young ewe.

And since the whole flock is his harem, there is no First Ewe to answer to.

It is perfectly natural for a ram to have sex in his workplace, since sex is his one and only job in life.

Mind you, I don't think a ram could pull off serving as the leader of the most powerful nation in the free world — but I do resent the American media comparing the behaviour of their wayward President to that of an innocent male sheep.

I've kept a dozen or so rams on the farm over the years. My first was a feisty fellow called Cronkite, because I wanted him to be as trustworthy and steady on the plough as his newsman namesake. Then I had my *Star Wars* sire, Jedi, followed by the outlaw brothers, Waylon and Willie.

Be it from Rambo to Lord Randall, none of my rams would consider to give the time of day to the likes of Monica Lewinsky, even if she was to be wearing a blue wool dress.

All of the tawdry, mawkish, demeaning news that has emerged about what goes on behind closed Oval Office doors has nothing to do with the morality of sheep. Sheep have no morality, which seems to be the only thing that Bill Clinton and my present ram, Cisco the Kid Maker, have in common.

I was watching the flock one evening last week. Some people might think that watching sheep is about as interesting as staring at wallpaper, but it is a very important aspect of shepherding.

There is almost as much reading between-the-lines to do with watching sheep as there was in having to translate an American President's version of certain events.

It was chilly that evening. I sat on the edge of a cedar rail fence listening to crickets. A few ewes came over to watch me watching them. Then in the distance, the sound of things to come — honking Canada geese circling a lake nearby where migrating flocks would soon congregate.

That's when the ram's lip curled upward, crinkling his nose and revealing his toothless upper gum. Thus self-disfigured, he arched his opened lips skyward and weaved his head back and forth slowly, like a dog wagging its tail on a hot day.

The first time I saw this behaviour I thought something was terribly wrong. Sheep yawn, but this was ridiculous. And it was only the ram doing it. I checked his nostrils for foreign objects, and soon learned that rams, like certain children, do not like to have their noses blown.

Then I called the shepherd who sold me the ram to find out if there was some treatment for the chronic curling of the lip.

Had I done something wrong?

Was the ram in pain? I tried curling my own lip up and found it distinctly uncomfortable, serving no purpose I could possibly think of.

Well, it turns out that the curling lip is all about sex.

Unlike the American President, rams don't try to fool anyone when they are thinking about fooling around. They don't wear silly neckties to send messages. They just curl their lip and stand there, waggling their heads like goofs.

The lip thing actually has a purpose. Believe it or not, rams have an olfactory sensor in the roof of their mouth. They use this during the breeding season, to check the environment for significant scents regarding the ewes' potential disposition toward mating.

Nothing scandalous about that. Rams don't act on impulse any more than ewes kiss and tell.

I managed to lock the ram in the barn by himself after I saw the lip curl.

I didn't want to interrogate him. That wouldn't do either of us any good. Rather, because I am a good shepherd, I want to make sure that when breeding takes place, it is all aboveboard and all of the animals are in the best condition they can possibly be.

So for the next month or so, the ewes and the ram will receive a special ration of grain. Cisco will not be happy in the barn, no matter what I feed him. In the crisp night air, I will hear his growling *baa* of longing as the sexual tension heightens.

When I decide the time is right, I will strap a leather harness around his chest. It has a large crayon marker fastened to it.

When Cisco is freed to meet his waiting harem, I will walk away from the field of the curling lip and let him do his job.

Unlike the independent prosecutor, Kenneth Starr, I won't need a DNA sample to know what goes on in the privacy of the pasture. The crayon leaves its own evidentiary stain.

Maybe there are things that President Clinton could learn from spending more time with real animals.

Or maybe the American people should be looking for different signs the next time he or any other politician decides to say something such as "Read my lips."

What sheep know to be implicitly true — and what Bill Clinton should have learned long before Ms. Monica curled his lip — is that a good shepherd never betrays the flock.

APPLE ANNIE IN EDEN

Sheep are curious creatures. If one member of the flock develops a particular interest in something, all of the others are sure to follow.

One fall a ewe, whom I now call Apple Annie, developed a passion for finding fallen fruit. After most of the apples had been picked from the rambling ancient trees in the small pasture outside my kitchen window, I let the flock roam through to find sweet windfalls in the afternoon.

Apple Annie decided the orchard was Eden. Every day at 2:30 p.m. she would stand at the orchard gate with an expression of anticipation as fervent as that of a 10-year-old waiting in line for a hockey star's autograph.

Naturally the rest of the flock saw her standing there, and they were curious. Soon the entire flock started joining her at the gate — baaing and shuffling — with visions of apples dancing in their small brains. Annie led the charge of the wool brigade into the orchard. Keeping her nose close to the ground, she sniffed her way through the grasses to find the last apples of fall.

These were the runtiest of apples, smaller than a cue-ball but easy to crunch. Gluttonous cattle have been known to try gulping apples whole. As the story I heard goes, one poor cow managed to get a large fruit lodged in her throat just behind her windpipe. Her owner tried all sorts of methods and potions before calling a friend for advice. They ended up holding a plank against her backside and giving it a heck of a whack with a sledgehammer. Out popped the apple. A vision of that fiasco was lodged firmly in my mind as I watched the flock mindfully chewing their "finds."

A few good winds blew most of the straggling apples down with the last of the autumn leaves. While most of the sheep had the sense to retreat to the barn, Annie and a few of her faithful followers convinced themselves that foul weather simply meant an apple bonanza.

Snowflakes had fallen, but Apple Annie continued begging to enter the orchard. I humoured her, although her nose snuffle through the frosty grass was usually fruitless. One day I spotted her standing perfectly still under the oldest apple tree, looking at its great curled and gnarled boughs.

After an hour of watching her standing like a statue, I decided to find out what her problem was. Sure enough, swinging in the breeze from one of the top-most branches was an apple that would not fall.

Now I am no great marksman, and there are many healthy groundhogs on the farm who can attest to the poor shots that I have made. But for Annie I figured I could probably wing an apple. I took steady aim with my faithful .22, and the crack of the rifle sang out high above Annie's head.

The apple twirled on its stem and seemed to waft to the ground. Annie was on it in a flash, apple juice dripping from her jaws. If sheep can smile, she was grinning from ear to floppy ear.

A BARN IS A BARN
IS A SHED FOR TRUTH

One of the first realities that I had to confront when I moved to the farm was the fact that I did not have a barn. A falling-down chicken coop, yes. A barnlike structure sinking into a swamp, yes. But there was no sign of the bulky round-roofed buildings that seem to define the term "farm." This was surely an oversight on my part and one that I realized I would have to rectify before the sheep needed a winter home.

I had one quote from a construction outfit and realized that the cost of building a two-storey barn was significant. The term "pole building" began to have an appealing ring. My neighbour Elmer was of the opinion that building costs could be kept to a minimum by using previously owned materials. He offered to help co-ordinate the scavenging and found that much of the stuff I needed was lying in various yards at various farms that he owned. Soon wagonloads of wood were stacked up in my yard. I learned how to remove previously installed nails with hammer claws, crowbars and combinations thereof. Moose and Elmer dragged huge spruce and cedar poles out of a local pond where they had been curing for some time.

One of the good things about sheep is that their housing requirements are fairly basic. Give them some space in a dry place out of the wind that has plenty of fresh air and they are happy. We settled on a simple rectangular structure with a large sliding door on one side. It was the kind of shape that would be easy to add on to and straightforward to construct. Elmer installed the strategic posts and suggested Mennonite builders to do the framing and finishing. They were private people, he explained. He would tell them what I wanted done. Otherwise, I should not interfere.

When the harvest had ended and I was packing up the scarecrow, two buggies pulled up filled with men named Martin — there were Edwins and Harveys and Sidneys and friends of Ananias Martin. They brought their own hammers and mallets and started right at it. At lunchtime, I asked them if they wanted to eat their dinner in the house but the weather was so fine that they opted for the picnic table, divvying out loaves of bread made into hearty sandwiches.

Halfway through the second day, there was a knock at the front door. It was a young Edwin who was acting as assistant to his taller relative, Sidney.

"We were wondering," he began in halting English flavoured with a German accent, "did you want the barn to last for forty years or one hundred?"

This is a question whose strength of character I would ruminate on for many years to come, but at the time I did not hesitate.

"One hundred would be best," I told him. Edwin smiled and nodded his head. I was given a list of building materials to acquire.

Sidney, Edwin and I went shopping for steel siding to put on the building. This meant taking the truck. We loaded into the front seat and Sidney gave me directions. We seemed to traverse every sideroad in the county to get to the place. As we bumped along dirt trails marked "No Winter Maintenance," Edwin and Sidney pointed out various of their relatives' farms. Occasionally, they would say, "That's new," and then they would break into German. Later, I learned there was a direct route to the steel supplier that took about ten minutes, but from the truck Edwin and Sidney could conduct a neighbourhood tour that would take days by buggy. I discovered roads I never knew existed.

Construction dictated the gauge and quantity of steel we would need. The only variable was colour. Edwin, Sidney and I walked past a rainbow of shades until they planted themselves in front of panels of plain galvanized metal. When the salesman calculated the price for coloured steel versus plain steel, the builders Martin gasped audibly.

I paused. Did I need a red and green barn? Would the sheep care if their walls were plain old steel? Would the Mennonites respect me if I proved so spendthrift as to fall prey to installing vanity steel? The salesman seemed to sense my dilemma.

"You can always paint the galvanized after it's weathered a few seasons," he whispered. I ordered the plain steel. Once again, Edwin nodded.

Cold weather was closing in fast. The men agreed to eat at the kitchen table. An offer of hot coffee was welcomed but when I served my potent brew the Martins' eyes bulged. After that, Edwin was designated as the coffee foreperson and I showed him how to make weak coffee. My rudimentary knowledge of German caught me understanding a jocular comment about Edwin being a better woman than the woman. When I nodded at Edwin, the comments stopped abruptly.

Finishing the roof involved the help of Martin children who scaled the steel and pounded nails like pros. My job was passing the nails. No one even asked my name. Finally, one of the bolder boys called down to me, "Do you like this shed for sheep?" and I responded over the rat-tat-tat of hammering with a thumbs-up gesture. When the kids left that day, I waved to them and they all raised their mittens in a thumbs-up. I had unwittingly corrupted the gesticulation of a generation.

The final touch was installing the sliding barn door. Edwin and Sidney did it by themselves. When they came to the kitchen door to tell me they were finished, a heavy snow had started to fall.

"You tell us if it is not good. Goodbye," said Sidney, handing me the bill solemnly.

"For truth, it is a winter wonderland," I heard Edwin say as they clip-clopped away.

"For truth, it is," said Sidney.

And, for truth, I hope that when the sheep shed celebrates its centennial, someone gives the old building a thumbs-up salute — even though the red and green paint is cracked and peeled.

A HUNTING SHE WILL GO

It is getting to be that time of year when a country girl's thoughts turn to guns.

The goose and duck hunting season has opened in my neck of the woods. You can always tell its starts because people who normally tend their businesses closely sometimes disappear for days at a time. They always seem to be a few guys short at the lumberyard, and sick leaves rise dramatically at the factories in town. The Canadian Tire store usually runs out of shotgun shells.

Unlike my rural friends, I wasn't raised with guns. The only gun I had seen first-hand before coming to the farm was the revolver the police officer wore to my public school when he came to talk about Elmer the Safety Elephant. I subscribed to the Freudian notion that men who used guns were trying to extend their penises, and considered hunters to be a Neanderthal form of life, probably poorly endowed.

One thing country life has taught me is that an outsider shouldn't criticize blindly or try to impose alternative values before understanding the ones that exist already. Conventional wisdom boils down to two facts of life: having a gun in your possession is a serious business and being around guns without knowing how to handle one is just plain stupid.

I hated the notion of having a gun in the house, but you cannot use sweet persuasion to move groundhogs, and the holes they dig in the pastures where my sheep and horses cavort are leg-breaking deep. The country boys hunt groundhogs with .22.250-calibre rifles that blare like cannons. They use mushroom-head bullets that explode internally. As the saying goes, "They blow 'em up real good."

My decision to learn about guns was the culmination of a lot of things, including groundhogs. A pack of wild dogs ripped apart one of my sheep, leaving a tumble of entrails for me to find before breakfast. A rabid skunk bit one of my cows and led to her demise. Cantering along the edge of a hayfield next to groundhog mounds made me wary.

And being alone made me feel vulnerable. During a full moon, I could hear neighbours who I'd been warned were "a bit slow" literally howling at the moon. One of them took to walking the road at night and leaving mash notes in my mailbox. One midnight, a man I barely knew arrived drunk on my doorstep demanding beer. Another drunken local showed up wanting to waltz in mid-afternoon. I felt a sense of the film *Deliverance* in the air, and with it, my own defencelessness. Not that you can use a gun to defend yourself in this country. The issue for me was more letting it be known that this woman living alone in the country wasn't about to let varmints of any sort overrun her property.

I called the cop shop and discovered there was no handy-dandy, one-day, all-you-ever-wanted-to-know about-guns course, so I enrolled in a provincial hunter education program. This five-week, 15-hour course was conducted in the basement of a United Church. My fellow students consisted of 30 guys wearing Penzoil and STP T-shirts, as well as a handful of women who were the wives of hunters hoping to save their marriages.

We studied everything from the five different types of gun actions to the habitat of upland game birds. Some sessions were spent looking down the muzzle of guns and crossing imaginary fences safely, others included films with titles like *Shoot, Don't Shoot* and *Ducks at a Distance*.

The final test wasn't easy. There were 60 questions that covered topics ranging from the essential parts of a cartridge to the environmental ramifications of hunting. About 20 percent of my class flunked before they even got to the practical part of the exam.

The "practical" consists of handling guns and moving with guns under the watchful eye of a conservation officer named Sir, who asks a barrage of questions. He can ask you to do anything from loading a gun to unloading a gun, to demonstrating all manner of gun carries. Then, out of the blue, he might ask the bag limit for black ducks on any given day. If your gun barrel wavers in the direction of anything human, you are simply asked to leave.

I came away a licensed hunter, with a code of ethics and a knowledge of guns that made me feel a whole lot safer. Word of my achievement spread like wildfire. While my city girlfriends teased me with nicknames like Bambo and Duckbo, the bag boy at the supermarket showed me a new respect and the town newspaper publisher clapped me on the back. I found out that one of the top trap-shooters in the local sportsmen's association is a woman who works at the drugstore, and there is considerable respect for her ability. When men find out that another woman is learning to shoot they just wrinkle their brows and mumble something like "hope she leaves a deer for me."

That year, I hunted for the first time, going after the Canada geese that make annual predatory swoops on the local cornfields.

Don't get me wrong. I like geese. They are magnificent birds. But my cousin, who crops his land for a living, figures the annual migration of geese through his fields can cost him up to one-quarter of his cash crops every year. This means his wife takes a nightshift job at a factory and he takes handyman jobs just to keep the kids in decent winter boots. So it is that I came to understand that shooting a few geese and scaring off the rest is something of a survival tactic. No wonder I have no trouble getting permission to hunt on my neighbour's land.

I fired three shots but nothing fell from the sky, so my hoard of wild goose recipes remain untested.

I probably will try again this year. My shotgun is cleaned and gleaming. I've done some target practice and reviewed all my safety lessons. One of these crisp autumn mornings a small group of us will don our camouflage gear and traipse off to the edge of the cornfield in our bright orange hats. By sunrise we will be laying low, sitting on tree stumps, some on one side of the field and some on the other.

We will hold perfectly still and watch the frost on the boughs of ancient apple trees dissolve as the sun comes through the clouds. In that enormous quiet of dawning we will hear the cornstalks creak and the sparrows start their morning twitter wars with the starlings and crows. Far in the distance we will hear the honking of geese, and as the sun crests, the leader of the flock will fly over on a reconnaissance mission.

Then we will blow our goose calls making odd squawks that will recall childhood memories of New Year's Eve blowers. The sound will drift over the brown-flowered heads of fenceline burdocks and purple thistles until the V-shaped flock of 200 Canada geese passes overhead so close that we'll hear the feathers beat against the din of their honking.

I might take aim and shoot, and I might not. The mere sight of me at that hour of the day in such ridiculous clothing should be enough to scare my neighbour's marauding geese away from his fields forever. Ultimately, just being there at the edge of a cornfield at dawn is enough of a trophy for me.

HAUTE HEADGEAR

When I lived in the city, I hardly ever wore hats of any kind. Something furry in winter and something breezy in summer were about it. But on the farm, to every season there is a hat.

Variations on the old baseball cap are universally accepted, whether or not baseball is in season. Long into October, the baseball cap is worn. In winter, a version of the baseball cap comes with earflaps. In spring and summer, baseball caps are aerated. A baseball cap can be worn with the brim frontwards, backwards or sideways. In terms of cap etiquette, the sideways wearing of the brim indicates that the bearer is on "half-lock," while a complete reversal of the brim is a "full-lock" situation. These variations generally display themselves in social circumstances involving libations.

Some hats are "for good" and others are working hats. Straw hats with broad brims are for gardening, while straw fedoras are often suited to haying. If you take the advice of old-timers, a burdock leaf placed in the dome of a straw hat will help to wick away the steam that rises to the top. However, straw hats generally have a limited lifespan, particularly when they are worn in the company of goats. Cowboy hats are ideal for attending cattle auctions, but unless they are tied down like the Lone Ranger's they often hang up in trees during trail rides.

Winter hats are purely practical. It is written somewhere that 90 percent of your body heat escapes through the top of your head. Toques are essential and the nice thing about them is that you can layer them under or over other hats. Hats with Velcro fixtures for holding up brims and letting down earflaps offer a whole world of adjustable warmth. Gore-Tex hats and Thinsulate hats start getting pretty fancy for wearing in the barn, but in the howling dead of winter such extravagance can be forgiven. The only winter headgear that can be disconcerting is the full face mask. I wore one in the barn once and the sheep thought I was a stranger.

Still, of all my millinery treasures, it is the shower cap that has proved to be the most universally indispensable. You can be all done up to head for a dance or a visit with friends and decide to take one last trip to the barn to check on things without fear of getting barn-scented hair if you wear a shower cap. Any plain old plastic shower cap will do, as long as the elastic stays firmly in place. And because a shower cap is looser than a bathing cap, your hair stays approximately the way you have styled it. You can even wear curlers under a shower cap.

Unlike fabric hats and caps, a shower cap can be rinsed in soapy water after each use and towel dried, completely odour-free. This makes it particularly attractive during lambing season when rounds of the barn are made every few hours. There is no point in sullying fresh pillowcases with barn hair when a shower cap offers a cheap and easy prophylactic solution.

On a farm, headgear is a way of life rather than a fashion statement. At least that is what I tell myself when I find myself reaching for the faithful shower cap beside the alarm clock at 2 a.m. Something furry or something breezy may have a time and place, but something plastic can come in awfully handy.

PUPPY SCHOOL DAYS

Farm dogs have to be sociable and well behaved to co-exist with livestock and humans ranging from the unannounced hydrometer-reading person to the uninvited Jehovah's Witnesses, who frequently parade unabashedly up the lane way.

Likewise, farm dog owners can often use some socialization to modify behaviours that result from dealing exclusively with livestock and strangers.

Wally was four months old when we went to puppy school.

"Is that a puppy?" his classmates' owners asked curiously.

Wally was the certainly the largest puppy in the class, which consisted largely of younger puppies, limber little puppies and one Jack Russell Terrier the size of a running shoe.

In the meantime, Wally was at that awkward age for a Bull Terrier. His head and his paws seemed huge. His tail wagged his whole body.

"That dog looks like a pig with big feet," one juvenile handler whispered to her mother. Children can be so cruel.

Classes were held in the high-school gymnasium. There were seven pages of introductory notes, starting with an admonition: "This course is a COMMITMENT."

As per instructions, I brought a "puppy mat" with me — a salmon pink carpet remnant that was all I could find at the last minute.

Puppies being puppies, the whole room was in chaos. A Miniature Poodle tried to tear a strip off the Cockapoo. Two Golden Labs ran laps around their owners until their leashes were impossibly tangled. A mixed breed named Griffon kept leaping on a squeaky toy shaped like a fire hydrant that belonged to a very possessive Beagle. At least two puppies peed themselves.

Wally sat there looking miserable. The pink mat was definitely a mistake.

The Instructor strode confidently into the middle of this cacophony of youthful canine enthusiasms accompanied by a black and white Border Collie who walked perfectly at his side and sat immediately when he stopped.

Every owner in the room had the same fantasy — simultaneously — My dog: perfectly behaved.

I looked at Wally. He was rolling on his back, chewing on his choke chain.

We worked the puppies for a good half an hour that night, learning to use food treats as "drivers." By the end of the session, some puppies had learned to "sit" on command. We left with homework.

I learned a lot over the next few weeks. For instance, I learned that expensive dog treats, such as "Snausages," drove Wally to better behaviour than dry doggy biscuits.

Snausages are moist brown jobbies, shaped like cocktail wieners. They come in little tins with snap-off lids. When I first got them, I left them on the kitchen table. The next time I went into the room, there was a jar of mustard sitting beside them, next to an empty beer bottle.

Moose had made a natural mistake.

There were times when Wally seemed to really enjoy himself at puppy school. He liked the "Down" command. When the Instructor came to inspect Wally's progress on that particular exercise, I was determined to do well.

"Down," I announced forcefully, giving Wally a flat-handed hand signal. And down he went. And further down, until he was lying flat on his stomach, back feet splayed, like some kind of large squashed bug.

Then I stood six feet away and gave the "Come" command. Sure enough, Wally began paddling toward me like an army commando — elbows grounded, butt raised.

"At least he understands," the Instructor said, gritting his teeth.

That evening we were given our long leashes. Wally's was lavender.

"I think this instructor has it in for you, Wally," Moose wryly observed.

Teaching Wally to heel took hours of practice.

I walked him beside me as we did the chores, making him sit and stay while I filled buckets of water for the sheep.

I walked him up and down the lane way.

I took him to foreign places, like the supermarket parking lot, and worked him on turning corners with me expertly.

Regardless, Wally always seemed to want to be two steps ahead of me or two steps behind. Snausages weren't working. Wally had so many Snausages he was starting to look like one.

The solution was "pop correction."

I was supposed to give Wally a sudden sharp jerk on his leash every time he was out of step. Thus, the puppy would then learn exactly where he should be in relation to my body to avoid the "pop" he would otherwise receive. I was to look straight ahead, maintain my direction and "pop the pup" whenever I felt he was out of step.

At the beginning of the next class, the Instructor asked me to demonstrate the "pop" heeling process.

"Heel," I commanded, leading off with my left leg as though I were a Polish riding instructor.

Wally was perfectly aligned with me for about ten steps. Then I felt a drag on the leash, so I "popped" him. No response. I "popped" him again and kept moving, even though there seemed to be a dead weight at the end of the leash.

"Oopsie," said the Cockapoo owner, zipping by me with her mop-sized puppy dancing daintily at her side.

"Poopsie," said Griffon's owner, giving me a frazzled look.

I turned to find Wally at the end of his tether, hunched over in the midst of a substantial bowel movement directly beneath the west basketball hoop. His face was etched with distress.

"Clean up," the Instructor shouted.

I didn't "pop" Wally again that night.

The note on the lesson sheet at Week Four said, "Puppies learn at different rates, so please do not get discouraged if your pup is not doing as well as a classmate's pup."

Hah. Make no mistake, life in Puppy School, despite polite appearances to the contrary, is a cutthroat competition.

Sure, I behaved as though I liked the curly-haired black puppy, Griffon, and as though I liked his owner, but, let's face it, Griffon couldn't hold a candle to Wally when it came to doing the "down/stay" exercise.

The Jack Russell did everything perfectly, until he got bored and started attacking his owner's shoe laces.

The Poodle was jumpy.

The Beagle was a barker.

The Golden Labs wriggled.

With a lapse here and there, Wally was perfect. And the test at the end of the course would prove it.

"Your puppy may fail," the Instructor solemnly told the Class at Week Five, "but that is just a sign that you need to do more homework because every puppy can pass."

All owners left the building with a mantra: "I will not fail my puppy, therefore, my puppy will not fail."

Week Six was intense. We entered the gymnasium to find a minefield of puppy temptations.

Bounded by fluorescent highway markers, the basketball court was laden with all manner of puppy toys.

The exercise worked this way: Puppies were expected to sit at one end of the gymnasium while the owner stood at the other end and gave the "Come" command.

Puppies were supposed to stay within the highway markers, ignore the toys and, on the "Come" command, go directly to their owners' side.

Of course, the jumpy black Poodle did it perfectly, treading carefully through the toys and arriving brightly exactly where he was supposed to be. His owner beamed with pride.

I looked at Wally. His eyes were glazed.

Surveying the gymnasium full of doggy toys — stuffed Garfield the Cat toys that meowed when they were chomped by little puppies and colourful plastic squeeze toys in the melt-in-your-mouth shape of hot dogs — he had become unhinged.

There were hard plastic bone-shaped toys, toys that rattled when they moved, and, from Wally's perspective, there was the finest toy of all — a tennis ball.

I kept Wally to the very end, hoping that he would "get it" through a combination of repeated example and osmosis.

Finally it was Wally's turn. A crowd of spectators had gathered at the end of the gym — family members, loved ones and a whole troop of Air Cadets who stopped by after training to watch the puppies.

Then Moose walked in. Wally briefly wagged his tail and went back to hypnotically staring at the tennis ball.

Wally knew that all eyes were on him. He sat reluctantly, without letting his bottom touch the floor. When I called him, loudly and firmly, he started off in my general direction.

Other class members had given the "Come" command with varying degrees of success but, by-and-large, all the puppies made it to their owners' sides with little fanfare.

It took three full minutes for Wally to finally get to me.

But that was not the worst part.

One of Garfield's legs trailed from his muzzle, where it was lodged between a rattling dog bone and a plastic hot dog. Mashed somewhere in the garbled mess was the bright yellow tennis ball.

In the doorway, Moose lowered his eyes. The Instructor sighed a Saint Bernard-sized sigh. The Jack Russell started pulling on Garfield's leg and Wally finally let go of his treasure trove.

It was then revealed that Wally had also managed to stuff a sock in his mouth.

From that night forward, the Puppy School Test loomed large in front of us, like Mt. Everest. I knew it was going to be a daunting challenge. By the time test day arrived with its majesty and oppressive threat of failure, Wally could stay for a full minute without breaking position.

After the puppy toy-course fiasco, I literally spent days and nights providing Wally with all manner of distraction.

Sheep walked around him. Cats walked in front of him. Moose yelled things in the background such as "Hamburgers, bacon, bologna, Get your, hamburgers, bacon, bologna."

Through it all, Wally just sat there.

When I called, he came, tail whipping like a helicopter. We were as ready as we were ever going to be.

As anticipated, the Test was torture.

When the Jack Russell broke his "down/stay," Griffon's affable owner let out a low growl. The Instructor wove his way through the puppies, a judicious and disgruntled General Patton.

Sometimes he clapped his hand unexpectedly and a puppy would jump toward him unthinkingly. He tossed bags filled with puppy treats past little puppy noses to see if they would budge.

Many did.

When he got to Wally, he suddenly emitted a high-pitched whistle. Nary a twitch.

He waved his arms and shouted, "YOU HOO!"

Wally was bemused but unmoving.

Then came the *coup de grâce.*

The Instructor flipped out a brand new, day-glo yellow, perfectly manufactured tennis ball and gently tossed it toward the centre of the gymnasium.

Wally hit it in mid-bounce, projecting it under the Poodle. Result: airborne Poodle.

Still at full tilt, Wally tried to pounce upon the ball, which had been propelled by the sheer velocity of his attack into the vicinity of the Golden Labs.

Soon both Lab owners were wrapped in an unintended embrace.

Choosing Wally as a role model, Griffon dashed after the ball too.

The Beagle barked, the Cockapoo peed.

Sensing something run amok, the Jack Russell chomped on its owner's shoelaces and missed, drawing blood at the ankle.

Wally's lavender long leash trailed after him as the tennis ball careened around the gymnasium as though driven by a McEnroe serve.

I froze in place, until the incident finally ended with the ball trapped behind a bench which had been, blessfully, bolted to the floor.

While the Instructor stood off in a corner grading his scorecards, anxious owners subdued their puppies.

The excitement had been too much for Wally. He promptly fell asleep on his pink mat.

The Instructor called the puppies names, one at a time, a final roll call. He shook their paws and spoke quietly to their masters and mistresses.

Wally stumbled forward, half asleep. Then when he wouldn't do the paw thing, the Instructor grabbed his foreleg and Wally collapsed in a heap. He looked like I felt.

"Interesting animal," he whispered, and slipped something into my hand.

It was a whole chicken wiener. Wally quickly came to life and inhaled the whole thing.

In the truck, I sat exhausted, while Wally tried to lick Moose's ears.

"How did it go?" he asked.

"He got this," I said, handing him a crumpled ball of paper, which I expected contained a screed about Wally's unsociable Puppy Class *interruptus* behaviour, or lack of behaviour and commitment papers to the nearest Puppy Reform School.

Instead, it was a Graduate Certificate, complete with Wally's name, "Rather's Wallace Stevens," just above my own. It had gilt edges and a little drawing of a Border Collie sitting alertly, as a good dog should.

A note was enclosed. It said: "For best results, limit access to tennis balls."

PUMPKIN MOUNTAIN

It must have been a good year for pumpkins. At my local Co-Op store, they gave them away with every tank of gas. Roadside stands were chock-a-block with pumpkins of all shapes and sizes. And then, of course, there was my neighbour Joy's manure pile, a veritable Pumpkin Mountain.

It is hard to imagine a manure pile as a thing of beauty. But last autumn it seems Joy and her girls made a batch of pumpkin pies for a church supper and deposited the pumpkin entrails outside the barn on Dad's front end loader, from whence they ended up atop the manure pile.

Then in the spring, the manure pile started to sprout. Hundreds of pumpkin seeds came to life in the warm compost of the two-storey-high pile. Soon there were vines cascading down the slopes. Great leafy jungle-type vines that seemed to grow overnight. It was a magical thing.

Somehow Joy convinced her husband to let the manure pile stand for the summer, while we all watched and waited. Sure enough, the pumpkin flowers appeared throughout the summer, big horns of yellow blossoms amid the dark green foliage.

The triumph of it all came in the autumn. A true mountain of pumpkins graced the barnyard — big ones, little ones, grumpy-looking ones and pudgy little round ones. It was the kind of sight that makes you just stand back and grin.

I don't know why, but there always seems to be something laughable about pumpkins — maybe it has to do with the concept of growing a vegetable that is bigger than one's head, but about the same shape.

Still, there is only so much you can do with a mountain of pumpkins. Joy and the girls harvested a huge batch. They hosed them down and had a pie-making bee. Then they stacked a jumble of them up at the end of the laneway along with cornstocks and a straw man dressed in Dad's old coveralls as a kind of display. But even that left dozens of homeless pumpkins to be dispersed around the neighbourhood.

I am not a big pumpkin pie fan, but my sheep just love the flesh of the big squash. So I loaded up a pickup truck full of pumpkins and took them home for the flock. For a month, I hauled four or five pumpkins into the pasture every few days. After scattering them around, I'd get out my axe.

The guinea fowl thought this was a great amusement. Five of them perched on the rail fence to watch me wander around whacking pumpkins to pieces. As each pumpkin split, they would squawk with delight and run like fiends to poke through the pumpkin pulp and gulp down the slippery seeds.

The sheep think pumpkins are just grand. They ran through the orchard gnawing and nibbling at the sweet orange flesh. The vitamin boost was good for them, and they surely enjoyed the change of menu.

My horses, on the other hand, have no pumpkin appreciation. They found the sheep's treat a rather stupid joke on my part. The only orange thing they find worthy is the carrot.

By late October, I had just about exhausted my pumpkin supply, and Joy's once joyful pumpkin mountain was relegated again to a plain old manure pile waiting to be spread on the fields. In the meantime I carved two big, old, grumpy-looking pumpkins into smiling, square-toothed wonders with lopsided eyes and triangle noses. They sit on cinder blocks on the front porch waiting to glow on Halloween night.

Chances are that I will be the only one to see them. Kids don't tend to trick or treat in the country, where pickings are few and far between. The best I can expect to see are a four- and six-year-old ghost and goblin team from down the road, who will make a quick stop before heading to town, where they can fill their bags in an hour by leaping from door to door.

Come the witching hour, I expect to be in bed. When I blow out the candles in the old jack-o-lanterns, I'll make a special wish. You see, I buried their bountiful seeds at the top of my old manure pile this year. And I hope the guinea fowl don't find them, because I'd really love to see a mountain of grumpy-looking pumpkins in my barnyard next year.

A TALE OF TWO TICKETS

Country roads have a natural slowness to them that comes with bumps and ruts and loose gravel. There are no lines drawn neatly down the middle. Unless a passing horse and buggy has left some equine marker, country roads tend to be bare of anything except the cloud of dust that flies in the wake of everyone who passes.

You get to know the shape of roads that you travel most frequently. Two deep tracks in the ditch near the end of my lane mark the spot where the carpenter's truck ended up one icy day. That was more than five years ago, but I can still recall how blue the February air turned when the carpenter found out that he had skidded into a swamp.

Along the edge of a hayfield further down the road there is a stump of a maple tree that is a constant reminder of the night there was a stag party at the pig farm. One of the celebrants backed his truck clear across the road and into the tree before leaving. That collapsed old maple kept the wood stove burning for half a winter.

I drive slowly on country roads because that is part of the joy of them.

The plain fact is that I did not even learn how to drive a car until I moved to the country. In the city, I took taxis or found obliging men with cars to take me places. It worked quite nicely. Besides, why would anyone want to drive in the city when all the people who do drive do nothing but complain about traffic and the absence of parking spots?

But the country is different. There is no such thing as a convenience store on the corner. After one week without wheels I was close to having a tizzy. Mennonite children on bicycles had more mobility than I did. So the Moose and I decided to forgo putting a Jacuzzi in the master bathroom. Instead, we bought a turquoise pickup truck for me to use.

It was what you would call an aged pickup truck. At least it was a Ford, which the neighbours thought showed a modicum of taste. I waxed her the first day we got her and the turquoise paint fairly shone.

The truck was a standard, which did not mean much to me at the time. Soon I was shifting gears as though I was born to hand-foot co-ordination. I passed my driving test in the old truck and we were bonded. Slow and steady was our credo. I do not think we went further than twenty kilometres in any direction, but that was all we needed.

So about three years later, I was ashamed when I was stopped for speeding on a sideroad that did have a nice neat line painted on it. I was also surprised.

It happened on one of those late autumn days when nothing seems right and every radio station you switch to has a weather announcer who forecasts snow in the cheeriest of voices. Worse, I had decided to do the laundry. Two full hampers of barn clothes, long johns and stiff woollen socks joined me on the front seat of the ancient turquoise pickup. She was still running like a top, but her body was fading fast. I was dressed about the same way the old truck looked, wearing the only clean clothes I had left in the house and hoping the patches would hold.

I could not put the hampers on the floor because certain areas had rusted clear through and the plywood that covered the holes was always shifting. I tried it once and lost two perfectly good socks through the floor.

When the police cruiser passed me coming the other way, I thought the officer who waved at me was just some guy I foxtrotted with at the Kinsmen's beef barbecue in the summer. In fact, he was. I gave him my usual two-fingered salute from the steering wheel. The disconcerting part was that a minute or so later, he was following me with his lights flashing and his hand still waving.

I geared the old truck down and pulled over, checking to see if the laundry was still intact, imagining that I might be trailing some sheet out the window, or worse under the floor board.

Once we got over the formalities of remembrance of barbecues past, the young officer — whom I remembered as exceptionally light on his feet — advised me that I had been going a full twelve kilometres over the speed limit.

Well, I was astounded.

"I didn't think she could go that fast," I told him, in all honesty.

"Well, you seem to be in an awful hurry and you know this truck can't take that kind of driving," he said, scanning the plywood flooring.

I knew I was supposed to say something about the urgency of my mission and my laundry-distracted feminine state, but I was so darn proud that the old truck had managed such velocity that I forgot my lines. Besides, the smell of stale socks was filling the truck cab sufficiently to impress the officer with the notion of urgency.

"Okay, we'll let you go this time, but slow down and let this be a warning," he said.

The idea of getting a speeding ticket had not caught up to me yet and all of a sudden I realized I was being I let off the hook. I was so excited that I knocked over the laundry detergent when I put my ownership papers back into the glove compartment.

I left the scene of my crime in a cloud of dust mixed with laundry detergent that was sifting through the floor boards.

The turquoise truck held on for a couple more years, until she finally fell prey to the rust that never sleeps. I do not know what the final mortal wound was but I do know that she "popped a rad," needed a "valve job" and was "misfiring on three pistons." I suspect any one of those could bury even the most stalwart pickup half her age.

My next truck was the spiffiest thing you have ever seen. I thought that no truck could ever replace the turquoise Ford in my heart, but this new little filly was a heartbreaker. She was navy and cream, the same colours as the flags at the ploughing match that year. In fact, she was an official ploughing-match truck before I got her —

complete with ploughing match emblems beside her tail lights. No holes in her floor, in fact, her half-ton bed was lined with rubber and she had a tarpaulin top to keep out the rain.

I did not even need to wax the new truck before I took her for that first spin into town. It was a fine fall day. I wore sunglasses and lip gloss and a perfectly matched ensemble.

The unmarked cruiser passed me at the bottom of the hill and there was no waving. By the time I got to the top of the hill, there were flashing lights behind me. An officer who I knew I had never danced with came up to my open window and his portly belly nudged the shiny door of the truck cab.

"Clocked you going ninety-two in an eighty zone, Miss," he said, and I felt ashamed. Surely this new heap could go faster than that on a downhill grade even with me at the clutch.

I retrieved my documents from the pristine dash compartment and watched the officer dutifully note that the ownership had been transferred within the past forty-eight hours.

"Nice truck," he offered and I imagined him on the car lot kicking new truck tires. I was glad my truck would never have to surrender to that sort of abuse ever again.

Briefly, I considered saying something in my defence. But he was watching me, waiting for my learned feminine lines. I could not do it, to myself or to the new truck.

"Just going into town, sir," I said.

From behind his badge, he was sizing me up. Even though my driver's licence showed I was living in the country, it was obvious from my get-up and my gloss that I had come from outside and thought I was pretty hot stuff, new truck and all. He reached into his pocket and I knew that the law had me in its sights. While he wrote the ticket, I swear I watched a dozen old pickup trucks zoom past us at speeds far exceeding my downhill effort.

The fine was roughly equivalent to the profit I might expect from the sale of one lamb. I accepted it as a sacrifice of some sort to the memory of the old turquoise truck who never got me a ticket.

After that, the new truck and I were bonded in our infamy. At the top of every hill, I would rein her back and check the speedometer, recalling the time that we both seemed fast and far too glorious to be "country." Over the years, we collected a lot of dust together on the sideroads, but we never got another ticket. Country roads bring you down to speed — at the best of times . . . and the worst.

WINNERS, LOSERS
AND HERMAPHRODITES

Farmers are a bit like gamblers. We tend to remember the wins rather than the losses. For example, I thought the hermaphrodite sheep was sure to end up as mutton. Instead, I ended up selling "it" for twice the price of a purebred breeding ewe! It was a glorious reversal of fortune, since economic success stories are all too rare on the farm.

The animal in question was one of a fall-born set of triplets. A little dumpling of a lamb, it always looked stout and square. I recorded the sex of the lamb as female. Obviously, I acted in haste, but there were not any telltale testicles to cause me to think the lamb was anything else. "She" grew at a tremendous rate and she came from a good family, so when it came time to decide which lambs would be keepers and which would end up fetching a fine Christmas price at the butcher's, I decided to keep her.

It was spring shearing time when the duplicitous nature of the lamb's sexuality reared its ugly head, so to speak. Underneath the winter wool it seems the lamb had been developing male apparatus, albeit quite small. "Saw one like this entered in a fall fair once," said Judy the Shearer, who has seen just about every form of sheep and shepherdly quirk that exists. "This guy had entered a huge yearling ewe and everyone thought she was sure to be the top of the class. Then the judge ran his hand under her belly, and sure enough he found a surprise. I don't know who was more taken aback, the judge or the sheep."

I did some checking and found out that hermaphroditism occurs in sheep with about the same regularity as snow in June, but it does happen. The hermaphrodite sheep may have two sets of organs, but neither of them usually develops sufficiently to fulfill any particular function of reproduction. So it is really neither here nor there. I was stuck with an infertile sheep of questionable sexuality — too old to qualify as lamb to my trained palate, and too big an eater to keep as a curiosity.

Before I could decide what to do with the sexuality-challenged animal, a sheep breeder of some distinction scheduled an appointment to see the purebred stock I had for sale. I wanted the whole flock to make a good impression, so I hid "Hermie" (as I called "it") in a back pen behind a stack of straw. I did not want one mutant animal to put a potential purchaser off his cheque book.

The visit went well. My secret was never discovered. By the end of the day, I was helping the breeder load half-a-dozen lovely ewes and a top-of-the-line ram lamb into his trailer.

"Now all I have to do is find another 'it,'" he said, as he wrote me a solid cheque. "Mine finally died after 14 years and I sure could use another."

Two weeks earlier I wouldn't have had a clue what he was talking about, but now my interest was piqued. Sheepishly, I told him that I just happened to have an "it," but I had never considered selling "it."

"Sure you won't reconsider?" he asked. "I'll pay a good price for a new 'it.'"

It seems the dual sexuality of a hermaphrodite sheep enables an "it" to detect sheep that are cycling and ready to breed. The male component of the "it" apparently comes into play during the breeding season. When the testosterone kicks in, the "it" responds as though it were a bona fide ram. Fitted with a breeding harness, the hermaphrodite will dutifully mark ewes that are ready to breed. Thus forewarned, the good shepherd can then deliver the ready and willing females to the service of the "real" ram.

In a one-ram operation this would not seem to have much advantage. However, in a large purebred flock, knowing when a ewe cycles and directing her to the sire with the most complementary genetics is a big advantage. In a way, the process is the same for thoroughbred racehorses. A "teaser" stallion of indiscriminate breeding generally susses out the mare. Then he works himself into a frenzy determining precisely when conception is most likely to occur, only to have the job completed by pricier horse flesh. This must be particularly frustrating for the teaser stallion, but it would not faze a sheep like Hermie. The other advantage of an "it" is that when breeding season is over, the feminine aspect of the hermaphrodite returns. This incarnation is a more docile, manageable animal to work with than a strong-willed, potentially dangerous ram.

I had not intended to be cagey about selling Hermie so that I could drive a better bargain, but that is what I had unwittingly done. The breeder examined "it" from top to bottom and announced that "it" was exactly what he was looking for. My embarrassed reluctance only fuelled his passion for full possession. With the cheque handsomely revised, Hermie left my barn to enjoy a long and leisurely life that would include total freedom of sexual preference. The breeder gave "it" a name: B.C.

"I name all my sheep after movie characters," he explained. "I just couldn't decide whether to call this one 'Bonnie' or 'Clyde.'"

I have not bred a hermaphrodite sheep since. Years have passed, and I still double check the sex of the lambs from that particular genetic line. I guess that's the farmer in me — always looking for a loser who could turn out to be a winner.

TALKING TURKEY

When I say grace over the Thanksgiving turkey, I always add my own private thanks that I did not have to grow the confounded bird.

I tried raising my own turkeys a few years ago, but once was enough. I was placing my spring order for day-old chicks and I noticed that the hatchery was also selling baby turkeys, so I ordered a dozen. With a hundred or so chickens ranging around the farm, I figured that a few turkeys could not do much harm.

My pal, Henry the Chicken Farmer, happened by the day I was installing the fluffy yellow chicks and the gawky, bald-headed baby turkeys in their pen. He laughed, called me Pilgrim, and told me he gets a real good chuckle out of young idiots from the city who haven't got the sense to just buy a Butterball when they crave a feed of turkey.

Henry then proceeded to offer me a quick course in turkey maladies and idiosyncrasies, along with some plain language talk about what he calls "the stupidest bird ever created."

First off, I quarantined my turkey poults. It seems turkeys and chickens just do not mix, and turkeys can give chickens a deadly disease called Blackhead. That meant building a new turkey pen, at a cost of about six store-bought, table-ready birds.

Chickens never impressed me as mental giants, but at least they have enough sense to eat and drink. I had to physically impel each baby turkey to the feed trough and provide the occasional refresher course in water drinking.

During the summer, the turkeys gobbled around in a pen next to the garden. They would flap their wings, but they weren't much for flying. About the best they could manage was a wild hopping gallop when they saw me coming with fresh carrot tops or corn cobs. All seemed right with the world, until we had a drenching rain.

The chickens were smart enough to run for the cover of their coop and perch on their roosts like sensible birds. The turkeys, however, stood in the middle of the field with their beaks upraised, swallowing the pouring rain. Two of them literally drowned themselves before I could herd them to safety. Another one had to take a spoonful of vodka before jump-starting to a sputtering revival.

While I was towel-drying the survivors, I began to wonder which of us had the smaller brain. Henry the Chicken Farmer told me he has seen flocks of 200 turkeys drown themselves in the rain. Great.

And turkeys are vicious. Chickens will occasionally rumble and rooster feathers will fly, but given enough space to range they tend to be fairly peaceable. The turkeys, however, literally pecked one of their own to death and tried to eat him!

"Cannibalism is just a phase they go through," advised Henry.

You would think that turkeys who could shred a fellow egg-mate into bits would be tough guys, but give them a few claps of thunder and watch them turn into total wimps. They would cower in a corner, piling on top of each other, and I had to wade through and separate them before they suffocated each other. A woman gets to feel a bit addled when she rides out a lightning storm making soothing gobbling sounds to a bunch of terrified adolescent turkeys.

If you live with turkeys long enough, you finally reach a point where you start asking basic questions such as, "Why do they exist?"

Consider the fact that the basic construction of a turkey is totally silly. The big white gobblers we devour at Thanksgiving are genetic hybrids of the original lean, dark-meated wild turkeys.

The fact is that not everyone wants a drumstick, so breeders have developed turkeys with a lot of breast meat. As a result, commercial turkeys cannot even reproduce without a helping hand. There is simply too much breast meat on a good breeding tom turkey for him to accomplish what nature intended, and the poor hen turkeys' legs were not designed to support heavy loads. So breeding hens must be artificially inseminated.

I found this out from my friend Susan, who spent one less than idyllic summer working as a "turkey jerker" at a big fowl breeding farm. Talk about a career opportunity. Ultimately, Susan became a blacksmith. She has strong arms.

The best time I ever had with my turkeys was stacking their plucked and vacuum-sealed torsos in the freezer. For once, they did not smell rude or gobble back at me.

From that day forward, I have stuck to raising chickens. When a turkey is called for, I do the simple thing. I make a pilgrimage to the supermarket and pluck a prime one out of the cooler.

PATRICK, HE DEAD

Patrick was a beagle. He was full grown with floppy spotted ears and paws that seemed disproportionately large in contrast to his snakelike tail. Just a kind of regular beagle, he came to live with my neighbours, the Houstons, some time after the family observed a mourning period for their first family dog, Buford.

It is unlikely, however, that Ken Houston — the patriarch of the clan — will ever stop grieving for Buford. The long-haired, sandy-coloured dog of unknowable breed was a puppy when Ken brought him into the marriage. When "the Buf" finally sighed his last sigh, he was three years older than the eldest adolescent Houston daughter, Amy. Ken buried him in a special spot that only he knows.

Patrick was no Buford, but he managed to develop his own special character and carve his own special place in the affections of the Houston females. Ken's wife, Joy, found the dog pleasant and goofy enough. Amy and her younger sister Angie found it refreshing to have a dog that could keep up with them on a walk. Buford's pace had been rather slow in his latter years.

The fact that Patrick could walk quickly was not missed on Ken or the rest of the folks on the concession. Up at dawn to do his chores in the horse barn, Ken would see the beagle trotting down the road, or crossing it and bounding into a vacant field to check out the groundhog holes.

Dogs that run off their own property are frowned on in the country. Ken knew this very well. Buford had been a stay-at-the-barn, inspect-the-fenceline and go-no-further kind of mutt. Patrick was more like an aborigine called to stroll the neighbourhood by some primordial muse that only he heard. At least, Patrick never seemed to hear Ken when he tried to call him back home. He just wagged his tall when Joy wagged her finger at him for breaching the property line.

Not that Patrick ever caused any harm in the neighbourhood. He was a gentlemanly beagle, not a vagrant. Sometimes he would come up my lane. Dopey and drooling, he would visit my dog's water bowl and take a great slurp on a hot day. Then he would tour whatever tires and trees that held some peculiar fascination for his right leg. He would walk among the chickens without so much as a nip, and he had no inclination to chase sheep. He seemed to like horses but he stayed away from them.

Car tires, truck tires and tree trunks seemed to be the motivating factor behind Patrick's wandering. He liked meeting new people, too.

That weakness for new people proved to be Patrick's downfall. One day, Ken watched as the beagle sauntered along the road beside a young girl from the trailer park campground down the road. She was probably a summer camper, up with the family to enjoy a few weeks' holiday in a tin can bungalow overlooking a fetid lake, polluted by camper sewage and chemical run-off from the fertilizer ladled on the adjoining golf course. Patrick could have been the highlight of her vacation.

Visiting the trailer park was something everyone in the Houston clan did regularly. As a nurse's aide, Joy went down twice a week in the evenings to replace the Band-Aids on young boys who attended hockey camp. Amy and Angie both worked at "the lodge" changing bedsheets in the few units that operated as a motel for people without tents or trailers. Ken was known to stop by the golf course restaurant for a beer and a burger at lunch time, but he never went back in the evening because of the karaoke machine in the lounge. Ken was never the sort who could stand to watch people humiliate themselves in public.

Joy tried tethering Patrick to a rope on the front lawn, but he would always slip his collar. Not that his collar identified him in any particular way. Ken hid the dog when the township dog-licensing servant came up the driveway. When Buford died he still had nine months left to go on his dog licence. No way Ken was going to spend eight dollars on the beagle, even though Buford's nine months were more than a year old.

That summer was a busy one. Rain plagued the haying, so when a good patch of weather came along Ken and the girls worked like fiends to fill the horse barn for winter. Ken is into standardbred racing as a full-time occupation. In some ways, that takes a lot more courage than other types of farming, which at least enjoy the prospect of having a product to sell.

Every decade or so, Ken breeds himself a champion. He still focuses on the bloodlines of Black Mist, a mare who died at twenty-six in 1990. He had sold one of her offspring for $100,000 — hence the new drive shed and Joy's expanded kitchen. Two of Black Mist's grandnieces were showing some speed, so twice a week he was truck-ing them around to various racetracks, hoping against hope that someone would make him an offer he could not refuse before a pebble in the hoof or a splinter in a shin bone ended the dream.

Nobody paid too much attention when Patrick dis-appeared for a few days at a time. Someone would spot him — or at least the tail end of him — sticking out of a groundhog hole. One night he woke Joy up when she heard him off howling in the bush, no doubt stalking the jackrabbits who were claiming the Houston lettuce patch. His food and water were on the front porch. Sometimes there was less there in the morning.

When round, open-faced Angie heard the dog catcher had been called to take Patrick away from the trailer park, the Houstons realized that no one had seen the beagle for about a week. The odd thing was that everyone who worked at the "recreational complex" knew that Patrick was the Houston dog who lived just up the road, barely a nine-iron shot from the fourteenth hole.

A camper probably called in Wilf Hall without telling anybody. All it would take was a call to the township office and the clerk would have dispatched the legendary dog catcher. Mr. Hall was not a legend because of his skill, but rather because of the lack of it. He was best known for having murdered two dogs in cold blood.

Minto Township had not had much luck with dog catchers. One of the ones before Wilf Hall had been raided by the Humane Society. She lived in an abusive relationship with a town cop, but that was no excuse for the way she managed the puppy mill and menagerie she kept in her barn, which also served as the township dog pound. Cock-a-poos and collies, poodles and spaniels had to lie down in small, dark pens filled with feces. Sometimes dead puppies stayed with their living siblings for days until they were chucked onto the dead pile at the back of the barn. When the Humane Society descended on the place they found that an injured dog who had been taken into the pound had been shot. The bullet was said to have come from the cop's service revolver, which was a no-no.

Wilf Hall heard the job was open and he just applied for it and got it. Nobody asked him a lot of questions about his experience; dog catching being about as simple as it sounds. He was given a copy of the township bylaws, which list regulations pertaining to dogs running at large and licensing requirements. There was even something in there about a township prohibition on keeping meat-eating cats over a certain poundage, marsupials, pachyderms and undesignated odd-toed ungulates.

One of Mr. Hall's early assignments was a report of dogs running at large. The neighbours had called it in; one of the dogs had even taken a nip at them. They were likely from the city. A farmer would not have done such a thing — the rule of thumb being that dogs running at large should be shot and then buried with their collars. Nothing more need be said.

Mr. Hall attended the slightly dilapidated home of the dogs' owner, Wayne Cook, and advised Mr. Cook to restrain the animals and get them proper licences within a week. Mr. Cook dutifully fixed his German Shepherd, Max, and the smaller, excitable English Bull Terrier, Dylan, on long chains next to the house. He was working during the day and he did not make it into the township office to buy the licences that week.

After seven days, Wilf Hall checked and found out the licences had not been purchased. He saw it as a sign of failure to co-operate. Anyone could have seen there was going to be trouble. Mr. Hall was on a mission. He was not quite up to going it alone, however, so he enlisted the aid of the township road superintendent, Neil Murray. Together, the two men road out to the Cook place in Hall's pickup truck, in the middle of a September afternoon. Neil Murray knew every pothole on every concession. He had worked for the township for more than twenty years, and he knew just about everything about everybody going back a few generations.

No one was home at Wayne Cook's. Max and Dylan were tied up. They strained at their chains, barking at the two strangers. As their master would admit, he had trained them to "put up a show," but they were friendly to people they knew.

Since the dogs had no licences, Mr. Hall got it into his head that he would impound them. Later he told a court that he thought such action would encourage their owner to understand the seriousness of the situation with the dogs.

While the road superintendent stood by, Mr. Hall tried to get control of the dogs using a long pole with a rope-snare on the end, but he had never been trained in the use of a rope-snare so it did not work. Instead, he went back to his pickup truck and took out his .22 calibre rifle and shot both Max and Dylan in the head. As he explained it to the court, "I destroyed the dogs for the safety of the people in the neighbourhood."

When Judge H.A. Rice convicted Wilf Hall of unlawfully killing the two chained dogs, he left the matter of restitution up to the civil court. So far as anybody knows Wayne Cook never took the matter any further. Instead, he moved away.

Mr. Hall's lawyer, Ernie McMillan, argued that his client really thought that he had the authority to kill the dogs. He put the blame for that on Minto Township for not bothering to explain the duties, rights and privileges of dog catching under the bylaw, and then not bothering to provide instruction in the craft of actual dog catching. It must have been quite a presentation for Mr. McMillan to make, since his general practice mostly involves real estate transfers, traffic violations and wills.

Wilf Hall was given an absolute discharge, leaving him free to tell the world he has no criminal record so he can enter foreign countries with impunity. But instead of leaving so much as the county, he stayed on as the township dog catcher. At an "in camera" session, the local council voted to keep Mr. Hall on the payroll. They sent him on a two-day dog catcher training course — at the taxpayers' expense. Most of the taxpayers never knew what hit their mill rate, since the case of the canine homicides was scantily reported in the local newspaper.

Ken Houston only knew about Mr. Hall's misadventure because his pal, Mark MacKenzie, sits on the Minto Township council. He also boards a few standardbreds at Ken's. Mark told Ken that he had been the only dissenting vote at the in camera council session. Being a MacKenzie, Mark takes the task of being an elected officer very seriously, even though as a junior member simple mathematics would tell him that he can dissent all he wants and it will not change the way the old guard votes. And, since most of the important political decisions in the township are made in camera where taxpayers are among the great uninvited, there is no podium from which the dissenter might grandstand. Except, of course, for the fact that information about who says what about whom and what to whom at the in camera sessions quickly becomes the talk of the coffee shop as soon as the road superintendent leaves the meeting.

Mark regularly unburdened his angst on Ken over a case of cold ones in the empty box stall where the racing harnesses are stored. Information being a commodity, these sessions served to bond the two men, and Ken rather liked having a friend in "high places." Mark even managed to have Ken appointed to the arena board, which added $300 a year to the Houston coffers and allowed Ken to have some say in the management of the ice hockey food booth. It also meant that Mark had someone to talk to at the annual township employees' Christmas party.

High places could not help Patrick. Ken asked Mark to make inquiries, and Mark determined that the unlicensed beagle had been duly dispatched by Wilf Hall exactly three days after he was impounded. Everything was done in accordance with the bylaws.

Of the two girls, the youngest, Angie, was the most upset. Ken figured she was misty-eyed for about a day. Amy, the more analytical of the two, just could not figure out why somebody had not said something before calling in the dog catcher. Joy shrugged and threw out the stale dog food that was collecting flies on the porch. She grew up in the country. When a dog runs, something like this is bound to happen.

Mark bought the Miller High Life the next time he saw Ken. They disposed of it in one afternoon, while Mark expounded on his theory of events. At least one citizen had written a letter opposing the retention of Mr. Hall's services and suggesting that the township dock a day's pay from Neil Murray, who had been neglecting his duties as road superintendent by attending the execution of Wayne Cook's companion animals. But Patrick was still dead.

Privately, Ken has confessed that the beagle was never much of a dog. He caused more trouble than his feed was worth and he was always chasing after the tractor tires, trying to bite them, or pee on them, or just bark at them because they were in motion. Sure, he spent a lot of time around groundhog holes, but there was never any evidence that he ever caught one. Even worse, when a friend of Joy's employed Patrick as a beagle stud, he failed. In Ken's world, where a consignor pays big fees based on the delivery of a "live foal," Patrick was nothing less than totally useless — an embarrassment to boot.

The other Houstons tried to get Ken to reclaim the body so Patrick could at least have a proper burial, but Ken already had closure.

"I'm not going to pluck him out of that pile they've probably got stacked and ready for the bulldozer," he said. "He'll go with the rest into that Rwanda-style mass grave, and no more talk about it."

Only Ken knows where Buford is buried and only Ken can visit with him. A dog can be a sacred trust, a friend that stays in the heart long after its heart stops beating. But as for Patrick, he dead.

APPLE ALVIN

You cannot spend half a day with Alvin Filsinger without coming away a more healthy individual. Just keeping up with Alvin is an aerobics exercise, especially if he decides to show you his farm — all 4,000 fruit trees worth, plus the trout pond and the vegetable plots. And, of course, there's that unforgettable compost heap teaming with red-wriggler worms.

The farm is set back from a quiet road just outside of Ayton, Ontario, on gently rolling land. In the barns and assorted outbuildings there are cold-rooms for storage next to the apple-packing room and the juice press.

Somewhere on the place Alvin keeps seventy-five wooden barrels full of apple cider and somewhere else there are twenty beehives for pollination. If you make the trek all the way to the far side of the property, where a hedge of multiflora roses, thick enough to keep the neighbours' cattle out, rises like heaven on earth for hummingbirds — you start to get a sense of the Filsinger farm, and Alvin himself.

"I had apples in my blood from a kid," Alvin shouted to a couple of dozen organic farming enthusiasts, who had travelled from as far away as Windsor and Hamilton to take a tour of the farm.

At approximately three score and ten years, Alvin has some personal auditory challenges, but it is no problem at all for anyone to hear him.

With a spring in his step that would daunt a Bay Street bond trader half his age, Alvin fairly bounds through his orchards.

Picking his way through a windfall of apples, pointing out sweet red orbs in the grass, he urges those who aspire to organic practices to do the organic thing by eating one.

When he was a boy, Alvin started working on apple trees. There is a McIntosh behind the barn, a few tree rows in, that he started himself.

"It was the first week of May, 1937, and I asked my dad and my uncle to teach me how to graft a tree," he says, sidling up to a gnarl-limbed tree laden with fruit.

The tree in question was a transplanted wild sapling with a trunk about an inch thick at the time. Alvin describes his elders using frying pans coated with beeswax to prepare the McIntosh graft. He knows exactly where he put it, and he remembers the cow that chewed a bit off the crown of the growing grafted tree. Then he's off again.

Not just McIntosh grows in his orchard — there are early apples, mid-season and late apples. Some of his root stock is of Russian origin — winter-hardy, Siberian crab apple trees.

He has Yellow Harvest apples, Empires, Spys, scab-resistant Liberty apple trees and dwarf Joni-golds that boast apples the size of George Chuvalo's fist.

If you get tired of apple trees, he has plum trees and pear trees and rows of grapevines in another spot.

Some of his apples end up in tidy cardboard palettes for shipping to commercial supermarkets. These are what Alvin calls "the pretty stuff." Pesticide free, chemical free, unadulterated apples picked at the height of their sweetness according to Alvin's scientific tool called a refra-cameter, and his own unerring sense of all that is apple.

But most of Alvin's apples end up as sauce, or juice, butter, vinegar or cider because according to Alvin "the public is getting harder to satisfy. If there is a bump on an apple, people don't think it is good. Today, everybody wants picture-perfect fruit."

If you ask Alvin why that is, he might just tell you that it's because "the human beings did not take care of things."

The way he sees it, the mass of big red apples on produce counters that weren't allowed to hang on the tree long enough to earn the sweetness of their appearance are, likely as not, never eaten to the core.

"Kids only take about six bites of a big store-bought apple," he declares. "By then they've started to fill up and they know it doesn't taste too good."

But Alvin does not dwell on the dark side of non-organic food. That he leaves to the individual, although if you press him about the processing of modern food, he is just as likely to pull back on his suspenders and say something like, "The whiter the bread, the sooner you're dead." And then he marches on.

Alvin is big on compost. Bits of pruned tree branches and twigs litter the floor of the orchard, along with cut grass that mulches naturally.

"Here," he says, bending over suddenly and coming up with a handful of black guck. "Smell this — that's biodynamics for you. Biodynamic people love that smell." Then he points to the place the guck came from, and shouts with glee, "And look at all those worms."

Politely, the organic enthusiasts lean toward the dark clump and, sure enough, a few earth worms struggle to find a hole away from their hole.

Alvin calls his farm a research centre. He has been farming organically since 1953. He has battled gnawing mice, coddling moths and the dreaded oblique leaf roller with everything from blackstrap molasses to soya oil emulsions and tricgrama wasps.

"I'm learning all the time," he told the weary marchers in organic soil, as we trudged across a knee-high alfalfa field beside rows of lush carrot-tops flagging in the breeze over their foot-long orange roots.

Back at the store, where Alvin sells everything from juicers to books about juice and puff balls and spaghetti squash and garlic, the organic wannabe entourage paused to catch their breath.

Then anxious shoppers buzzed around the store, filling up their plain paper bags with packages of buckwheat and brown rice. Juicers were crammed into trunks and vans for the gas-guzzling journey home.

The fall air was heavy with the smell of apples. Alvin was standing off in a corner, looking across the lane at a field full of fruit-laden trees waiting to be picked. All the while, his gnarled fingers beat a gentle rhythm on the shiny skins of a bushel of apples at his side. He looked like a man with apples in his blood.

THE CEMENT TRUCK COMETH

Could someone please explain to me the relationship that men seem to have with cement? The combination of grit, stone and water in the giant tumbler on wheels that we know as a cement truck seems able to capture some primeval masculine heartstring and pluck it directly.

I discovered this phenomenon when we were attempting to construct a pad of cement about the size of a bathtub on which to set a brand new, weatherproof, never-freezing, Jim-dandy, yellow automatic waterer for the sheep. Expert help was called upon to construct the frame which would contain the cement. It took Mr. McCutcheon and his helper half a day to build a frame worthy of containing the volume of cement required.

You can always rent cement mixers and do it yourself, but that route has its own follies. Inexperience can lead to cracks and other horrors too awful to contemplate.

The key word became "pour," and the source of "the pour" was a cement truck. So I called the sand and cement company that operates within half a mile of my farm and described my needs.

Well, it seems you do not just buy as much cement as you need, instead you must buy a "yard" of the stuff. No one ever adequately explained to me the dimensions of a yard of cement, but they were able to tell me that I would have about half a yard too much.

When a woman starts fooling around ordering cement pours, word gets around. My neighbour Ken "the Hooter" Houston soon caught wind of the plan since he pals with Paul O'Dwyer who drives truck for the cement plant that borders his beef farm.

"Hear you're planning a pour," Hooter said emerging from his truck with his shovel in his hand, even though the cement was not scheduled to arrive for two days.

After inspecting the frame that would enclose the pour and dutifully adding a few shovelfuls of dirt to shore the whole thing up, Hooter turned his attention to the question of what to do with the leftover cement.

Where I would put cement if I had it is not a question that I had ever considered. Perhaps a nice walkway in front of the pheasant pens, maybe a really big bird bath.

Ultimately, Hooter decided we should build a ramp into the barn, smoothing the way for the tractor which had been bumping and jumping every time it went in and out during the barn cleaning days. Hooter brought over some gravel, since apparently cement does not cling well to plain old dirt. Then we took a few pieces of lumber and framed the ramp.

The day of the pour dawned brightly. Hooter came early to announce that Paul O'Dwyer himself would be driving the cement truck, so I had nothing to worry about. Mr. McCutcheon just happened to drop over to check on the frame and my neighbourly town road maintenance supervisor came by to make sure the pour went as planned. As more and more neighbours arrived, I began to wonder if I should be selling tickets.

A cement truck is an impressive sight at close range. The fact that the huge drum rolls slowly at all times gives the whole vehicle an odd appearance of life. Red-haired O'Dwyer waved to the assembled crew from his perch in the truck cab as he rolled toward the waiting frame.

The first pour took about ten minutes. The cement wriggled and rattled down a sluice that came out of the cement truck like some kind of grey elephant's trunk. Once the frame was filled the men gathered to tap it lightly and smooth the top with trowels. They looked a little bit like pre-schoolers playing with Play-Dough.

The creative work came when all hands gathered at the barn door ramp. Discussion ensued about whether or not the frame Hooter and I had constructed was up to the test, but we decided to pour anyway. The cement truck drum hummed away and the cement oozed out in irregular clumps which were quickly raked and shovelled into an even shape.

"She's a darn fine pour," Hooter proclaimed loudly, turning the rake over to the road maintenance supervisor who was anxiously awaiting his turn. Mr. McCutcheon muttered something about amateurs and ran back to his truck to get a huge nail to shore up the frame. There was no way I was going to get to touch the actual cement. Wavy lines were pressed into the grey matter so that the ramp would not become an icy peril in the winter. It was finger-painting on a grand scale.

Paul O'Dwyer drove off in a cloud of dust and the sheep gathered at the gate to watch the cement dry. This prompted a fine story from one of the gang about a cow that had wandered into a fresh cement pad and fallen asleep while the concrete dried around its hooves. I moved the sheep to a far pasture.

Everything was perfect until the work of art was sullied by Groucho the duck that walks like a man and thinks he is a rooster. Groucho was faster than the four men chasing him when he caught sight of his favourite hen standing inside the barn at the edge of the ramp. Duck prints in the concrete added just the right amount of character to what was heralded as "the Boulton pour."

That night I went to the barn to see how things were settling. Concrete looks like concrete even in the moonlight. I thought I would close the barn door and let everything get back to normal.

Then I realized why there had been no ramp to the barn in the first place. The barn door closes sideways on a large sliding hinge, and its bottom was now six inches lower than the cement ramp.

Maybe I would have been better off with a giant bird bath.

ANOTHER
ROADSIDE ATTRACTION

How the cow got the pail stuck on her head will always be a mystery. What is known is that it was a rather large metal pail. Somehow the handle became lodged in the cow's mouth like a horse's bit, while the bucket itself was firmly lodged over her horns. This combination effectively blinded and enraged the brown cow, who was known as "Betty."

Cattle can behave in irrational ways without any complicating factors. As a heifer, Betty had stolen into an orchard and consumed an idiotic quantity of apples which nearly killed her.

After the birth of her first calf, she seemed to develop a modicum of cow sensibility, behaving as part of the herd and seldom drawing attention to herself.

Unlike dairy cows, who are milked twice a day and regularly enjoy human contact, Betty was a beef cow. Her sole purpose was to create new cows for human consumption. She did not know this or she might have become enraged much earlier. Instead, Betty plodded through life and seemed happiest of all when she was out standing in a summer field swatting her tail around and licking the calf standing at her side.

The first person to discover Betty wearing the pail was a passing motorist. He was driving by the Hadley farm when he noticed a gaping hole in the straight, white wooden fence. Betty was swinging her head in the ditch. The rest of the herd kept its distance, as if severing themselves from this unusual event.

Mr. Caldwell knew nothing about cows. He sold business forms and rarely came close to anything resembling a farm. Still, he stopped his car and rolled down the window. Betty heard a rumbling in the gravel at the edge of the road and charged toward it, bumping her knee on the bumper of Mr. Caldwell's blue Ford Escort.

A pickup truck was coming in the opposite direction. Mr. Caldwell waved his arm out the window and started honking his horn to warn the driver. Freaked, blind Betty swerved into the roadway.

Earl Rapp saw the whole thing coming and slowly pulled his pickup truck across from Mr. Caldwell.

"Best to stay in your car, Mister," Earl told Mr. Caldwell, who had no intention of getting anywhere except out of there.

"I know, it already attacked me," shouted Mr. Caldwell.

Earl didn't believe that, but he did know that a cow with a pail stuck on its head in the middle of the road was an unpredictable predicament. Betty had worked herself into quite a sweat. Her mouth was agape. She kept trying to spit out the metal — to no avail. At the sound of the men's voices she flicked her head, took four steps sideways and stumbled into the opposite ditch, where she slipped on some wet grass and landed on her rump.

"What's it doing now?" Mr. Caldwell asked, leaning out the window.

"Just having a sit down," said Earl. "You stay here and I'll get some help. And don't honk your horn, just flick your lights. Okay?"

Earl found John Hadley working on his tractor.

"Hate to tell you this, John, but you've got a cow with a pail on its head sitting in the ditch by the side of the road back there," Earl announced.

John absorbed the information. His lower lip rose to the base of his nose and his teeth chattered.

"I'm coming," he said, tossing his tool box into the back of his pickup truck. As he drove out of the laneway he told his wife to call the neighbours.

"Tell them we may need a hand with a runaway," he said. "And maybe someone brings a gun, just in case."

A gun was just what Mr. Caldwell had in mind when he saw the cow lurching toward his car after laboriously lifting herself from the ditch.

"There's a mad cow with a pail on its head out on Sideroad Two. It just attacked my car and now it's coming back," he shouted into his cellular phone.

"You might want to get out there, sir," said the police dispatch officer on the other end of the line.

"But it's right in front of me," cried Mr. Caldwell.

Betty followed the sound of his voice and the pail clanged against the hood of the car.

"Arrgh," was the last sound the dispatcher heard. The cow rammed the vehicle with such force that it knocked the phone out of Mr. Caldwell's sweaty grip and sent it flying into the roadway.

Earl and John approached the scene slowly, driving on opposite sides of the soft-shouldered road, hazard lights flashing. Mr. Caldwell had rolled up his window and climbed into the backseat of his car, where he pressed his face into the back window shouting something that could not be heard, which was probably best.

Betty walked uncomfortably on the roadway and nearly slipped when her front hoof skidded on the shattered cell phone. Mr. Caldwell pressed his hands to his ears and slumped into the backseat.

John Hadley recognized the cow and immediately understood how stressful and potentially dangerous this situation was to Betty. He rolled down his window and tried talking to her.

"Soo boss, soo boss," he crooned in a low gentle voice. John had no idea where the phrase "soo boss" came from, but he had been using it all his life whenever he wanted his cattle to feel some measure of comfort.

He would certainly have used it on Betty when she was straining to give birth or when he was moving cattle from one pen to another in the barn. The brown cow lowered her head, sides heaving, and she listened.

"Thing would be to try to get her back in the field," Earl Rapp called from out on the roadway in an even voice.

John nodded and both men gently nudged the doors of their trucks open. They were just beginning their approach when three of the Daillard boys pulled up in their truck and the youngest idiot started shouting.

"Heard you had a cow loose, what can we do for you?" shouted Ned Daillard, the youngest of the well-known, semi-demented clan of pig farmers.

Betty whirled toward the unfamiliar voice, sending a spray of cow slobber across the driver's side window of Mr. Caldwell's shiny new blue car. He glared out at her through the green-foam spittle as though she were an alien.

John and Earl motioned the Daillard crew to stay quiet. More trucks arrived, lining the road-edge as they do at auctions.

Earl then moved over to John's truck, which was roughly established as headquarters, and farmers crept silently along the edge of the ditch to confer on the tailgate. In the distance, there was the sound of a siren.

Passing traffic was neighbourly about stopping for the cow. But Mrs. Betelmayer was bound and determined to get her school bus through come hell or high water. She nudged the bus along in first gear, while the kids pressed their noses to the windows and giggled.

As expected, Betty moved away from the sound and the fumes of the school bus. The brown cow banged her knee on Mr. Caldwell's front bumper. She appeared to be heading awkwardly back into the ditch leading to her pasture when the bus back-fired, sending a ton of un-ground hamburger straight up in the air like a rodeo bull.

"Whoa," someone on the tailgate cried, and blind Betty ran toward the voice.

Men scattered, leaping into the backs of their trucks. Mrs. Betelmayer shifted into second and pulled away.

Betty shook her pail covered head and zig-zagged along the centre of the road.

The police cruiser pulled up a safe enough distance away, with its lights flashing to alert any other traffic. Constable McIntee had grown up on a farm and he had enough sense to adopt a "wait and see attitude."

The men were trying to figure out how to get close enough to the cow to tie a hobbling rope to her back legs, so they could immobilize her while they snipped the pail handle with long-handled, metal shears. In theory, once the cow could see, she could be herded back to where she belonged without incident.

Unbeknownst to anyone, 14-year-old Amanda Hadley had exited the school bus and headed directly for the scene. Constable McIntee was the first one to spot the slight, blond teenager running through the long grass. Grown men taking their chances with a crazed cow was one thing, but the Constable wasn't one to allow a child to be at risk.

Although he had never had occasion to draw his weapon in more than 20 years of serving and protecting his community, Constable McIntee showed no fear when he opened his cruiser window and fired a shot into the air. Once deafened, the air grew still.

"There's a kid behind you," he shouted in the general direction of John Hadley and the rest.

Betty was fear-frozen by the blast. And it was all quite too much for Mr. Caldwell, who crawled back into the front seat of his car and purposefully fastened his seat belt.

At the roadside, John Hadley whisked Amanda into the back of his pickup truck with one sweep of his strong right arm. She was crying.

"Did he shoot her, dad, did he?" she asked in a panicky whisper.

"Naw, just be quiet, stay down and don't move," John told Amanda. But she persisted.

"That's Betty, my Wilford's mother, I know her," said Amanda. "She'll come to me and Wilford, no matter what. Don't let them shoot her."

Wilford was Betty's most recent calf, and when he had been weaned he became Amanda's 4-H calf. On any given day after school, Amanda and Wilford practised walking together as they would in a show ring, him responding to her gentle tug on his white and green calf halter. At 600 pounds, Wilford was hardly a "baby," but when Amanda brushed his coat she always tied him next to the pasture, where he could nuzzle his mother. Betty would lean her head through the wood slats on the fence to lick him.

"She knows me, dad," Amanda said in an echo of the same forceful tone her mother used when she was making a point.

In his car, Mr. Caldwell watched the cow zig-zagging in his direction. He turned on his windshield wipers and tried to clear the slowly drying cow slobber.

The *whish, whoosh* of the wipers attracted Betty and she stumbled toward the blue Ford. Four steps later, Mr. Caldwell fired up the ignition and grabbed the steering wheel. Betty turned away when she heard the roll of the tires. She snorted and trotted in what she thought was the opposite direction. Ramming into Constable McIntee's cruiser was not intentional.

The cruiser door swung open, blocking Mr. Caldwell's escape route.

With his gun drawn, Constable McIntee positioned himself behind the door. In his first ever, Clint Eastwood moment, the police officer was facing down a cow with a pail stuck over her head.

"I've got her in my sights," shouted Ned Daillard, who was crammed into the front seat of his father's pickup truck with two of his brothers, all of them bearing arms ranging from a .22–250 varmint rifle to a 16 gauge shotgun and a 50 lb. crossbow. Alec Daillard made a heap of noise when he dropped the crossbow out of the back window into the truck cab, and then got himself stuck trying to squeeze through the window.

Betty broadsided the Daillard truck, denting the door and scraping off a swath of red paint.

Alec waved like a sock on a clothesline in the back window, while his brothers tried to haul him back in.

"Y'all wait right there," shouted John Hadley, cupping his hands into a megaphone. He swung his truck into the roadway and headed back to the farm.

"Don't shoot, don't shoot!" shouted Ned Daillard, when he saw that Constable McIntee turned his weapon on the cow that was now leaning unsteadily against the truck door.

Without a "clear shot" Constable McIntee stepped back into his cruiser, motioning Mr. Caldwell to stay calm and shut off his windshield wipers.

Betty backed away from the Daillard truck, nudging her hind end against Constable McIntee's trunk, where she deposited a moist cow-pie, and sighed audibly. The Daillards rolled up their windows, so did Constable McIntee.

From the Hadley farm laneway it was a good quarter mile. John Hadley was slowly backing his truck and livestock van down the middle of the road, while everyone watched and wondered what was coming next.

He got as close as he could and pulled to a stop, motioning for Earl Rapp to join him. At the back of the trailer, the two men opened the door and adjusted the ramp as quietly as they could. Inside the two-stall van, Amanda was holding Wilford by his halter.

The calf was coloured a redder shade of brown than his mother and his long tail had a flaxen tip.

Wilford backed out of the van noisily, and John Hadley took the rope lead from his daughter and told her to get in the truck. Standing in the centre of such focused attention, Wilford bawled as if on cue.

Betty knew that voice.

"Soo boss, soo boss," called John and he walked the calf toward its mother, singing the words softly, hoping the cow would pick up the sound of her son's advancing hoof-steps.

But Wilford stopped when he saw the cow with the pail on its head. Mother or not, this was one strange sight, not to mention the flashing lights on the police cruiser.

"Gee haw!" Amanda's voice rang out. "Gee haw, Wilf, gee haw!" Betty knew that voice, too.

When mother and son finally inched close enough together to hear each other's breathing, Earl moved in with the metal clipper.

Later, John Hadley said it was like watching an owl pluck a rabbit out of a field. So fast and so smooth, it was over before old Betty realized what happened.

With a lick of her thick pink tongue Betty had the handle out her mouth and the pail tilted to one side, allowing her to see Wilford out of one eye. He touched his nose on hers, and she moved forward to lick his neck as she had ever since he was born. John came around to remove the pail, and she paid him no mind.

For a minute or two, people just looked on. Amanda joined her father and took Wilford's rope. She led him down the ditch and into the pasture, with his mother following like the contented cow she had been before the pail got stuck on her head. Engines were started, and the Daillards unlocked and unloaded.

At the edge of the road, Mr. Caldwell finally gave up on trying to recover pieces of his cell phone.

John Hadley asked him if he wanted to come back to the farm to use the phone there, maybe stay for supper considering what he'd been through. But Mr. Caldwell was determined to put as much distance as possible between himself and anything to do with cows. He kicked the pail into the ditch and took off.

Constable McIntee pulled himself to his full height and accepted John's offer of the use of his garden hose on the cruiser. He was glad things had worked out. Still, he would have to file a report since he had fired his weapon. John assured him that all the witnesses present could be called on to verify that he acted in the line of duty.

At school the next day, Amanda was hailed as a heroine. When she took Wilford to the fall fair, there was applause for them even before they won first prize.

Betty grew round and prepared to deliver another calf. She never went near a metal pail again.

THE BAREST HOLE OF ALL

Groundhog holes, rabbit holes and snake holes — there are all sorts of holes in the country and all sorts of critters who live in them. Then there was the day we found the hole of all holes.

My neighbour Elmer found it out in the corner of a hillside where he was digging out sandy soil to even the landscape. Elmer is a fairly laid-back fellow. He handles big machinery with easy grace, but when you see him sitting under his apple tree, leaning back with legs crossed, you would swear he was more akin to a leprechaun than a heavy machinery operator.

Elmer came booting up to the house to announce the discovery of the hole. It was a bigger hole than he had ever seen in these parts and he has been in these parts all of his life. He had never seen the like of it. It was a hole so big it was almost a cave.

Essentially, he wanted a flashlight and some back-up. One never knows what could be in a hole that size. Moose unlocked the shotgun. Although there was no direct talk about it, we were all thinking the same thing. This could be the home of the legendary bear of Minto Township.

I heard about the bear during my first lonely winter on the farm. I was not used to the depth of the silence in the country. Some days the only sounds I heard were the creaking of tree branches and the cries of the blue jays. At night, the great stillness was rarely broken by anything more than the distant hum of a snowmobile, but sometimes I would hear sounds coming from the forest; rumblings that would set the dog barking.

Everyone seemed to have a different version of the bear story but no one had seen it first-hand. The colour of the bear ranged from black to reddish brown. Its size was anything from adult grizzly to cuddly cub. Some folks said it had escaped from a zoo, but there were no zoos for miles around. By my reckoning of the stories I had been told, the bear was now approaching middle age.

We got to the hillside and found the fine deep hole tunnelled into the hill. At first we did not venture close. No sound came from the hole and even the dog was not terribly interested. Every once in a while some loose dirt skittered down the hill and we all leapt back, fearful of an avalanche or some sort of curse that would befall any who entered, just like in the Egyptian tombs.

"Well, we best see if that tunnel from the hole goes anywhere," said Elmer, and we bowed to his authority.

I ran back to the house to get some newspapers. The idea was that we could shove them in the hole and burn them to see if smoke came up anywhere else. We all knew such things could happen, because a hole that deep in the ground had to have an air feed from somewhere. I was selected to install the newspaper because I was the smallest and possibly the quickest — if something should happen. Armed only with a childproof lighter, I entered the hole and did the deed.

We all ran over to the other side of the hill to look for puffs of smoke, but there were none. Elmer examined a few groundhog holes and tried to calculate which one could be the exit point of the main hole, based on the trajectory of the arc from the hole to the hillside and such things.

We became more bold and brought a few shovels down to the hole and started digging. The hole was about an oil barrel in diameter, nothing but gravel at the bottom and sandy soil above. Finally, Elmer decided to dig the thing out with his bulldozer to find out where it went.

The machine roared to life and leftover starlings blew out of the trees. He ploughed the bulldozer into the hill and lifted the hole out. It crumbled and the whole hill shook and groaned. I held the dog back, just in case the old bear came out with the hole.

No bear. No bones. Not so much as a sleeping raccoon lived in the hole. We walked away slightly disappointed. Now we had a story to tell at the pub, but no bear to go with it.

A few weeks later, I heard that the bear had been spotted in a neighbouring township. Someone else thought they saw the bear at the dump. Children walking home from school claimed the bear walked right past them and went into a ravine. Goose hunting season was about to open and there was concern about the safety of the hunters in a bear-infested landscape. Some folks talked about some animal rights activists coming to town for a rally to urge the humane capture of the bear. No one seemed to recall that bears begin their hibernation in the autumn.

Halloween came and went. Still no sign of the bear. After the destruction of the hole, Elmer left the site alone. In the spring, we will have another look. Holes like that one do not happen for no reason at all. And in the country, there can be bears that live forever, in the barest of holes.

REFLECTIONS ON A THIRD EYE

It took me quite a while to realize that I had a mark on my forehead. Invisible to the naked eye, it flashed like a beacon when I showed up at any community function remotely affiliated with a walk-a-thon or a pancake breakfast or a bingo for a good cause. It revealed itself to organizers desperately in search of another body to help with hot dog day in the kindergarten class and hospital administrators in need of impartial judges for logo-design contests. The third eye of the volunteer was visited upon me.

From the very first question I asked at my local lamb producers' association meeting, I believe I was looked upon as future fodder. Less than a year later, I was invited to stand for election as the group's secretary. Resumé in hand, I showed up at the meeting wearing a dress rather than my usual blue jeans. After the retiring secretary nominated me, I addressed the group briefly, confessing my shepherdly inexperience but drawing attention to my note-taking abilities. This was greeted with quiet smiles.

There were no other nominees. I served as secretary for six years before I could find another novitiate who bore the mark.

Newcomers to the country are of particular interest to the volunteer sector specifically because they have no history in the community. They have not spent an Arbour Day planting trees beside the river, so they do not recall the year that the Arbour Day planting took place in ankle-high poison ivy. A newcomer can canvas door-to-door raising charitable funds and she will be hearing all of the stories about all of the ailments of the housebound for the first time. New volunteers can suggest things that seasoned volunteers would never dream of making. They can be pardoned for coming up with a craft sale alternative to the fuzzy, imitation poodle, Kleenex box cover that the association's president designed personally a decade ago.

I suspect it was my newness that attracted the attention of the local historical society. A neighbouring township had compiled a local history and it had been a great success. Now it was time for our township to go them one better. Committees had been formed, grants allocated and quotes solicited from printers. Senior citizen historians had been combing the community for old photographs and reminiscences. What they wanted was someone who could help organize the material into a book. I was appointed as editor.

It seemed like something I could handle. Dotting a few i's and crossing a few t's was about all they said they needed. The group calculated that finishing the book would take about eight months. It would be called *Minto*

Memories and launched at the fall fair. The parade float was already in the planning stages. The book's cover would be royal blue with silver lettering. Did I think that was a good idea?

I was given a filing cabinet and boxes filled with family histories and photographs. No one told me that there were almost five hundred historic families in the township. And no one could have known that more than nine hundred photographs would be submitted.

There were family histories that had been generated on computers. Family histories that had been beautifully scripted in calligraphic hand. Family histories stained with gravy and family histories with addenda written on the back of telephone bill envelopes. Special committees formed to gather information on schools, churches, veterans, railways, sports, Women's Institutes and industries. There were poems and maps and stories about sleigh rides in buffalo robes. School children were invited to submit drawings. Little Larry Dean drew a picture of a log cabin, two men on horseback and what appeared to be an outhouse. "The pioneers had no TV so they just played games and sang," he wrote.

Twelve full pages of the book featured pictures of twins and triplets.

Whole meetings were devoted to figuring out who was who in photographs. Tempers flared in debates over who begat whom or who had the first automobile on any given concession. When sensitive subjects arose, committee members would sometimes visit me privately to explain the whole tangled story of the skeleton in the closet and the reason it was going to stay in that closet no matter what so-and-so had to say. That was where being a newcomer helped. The committee could have inbred the entire township and I would not have known the difference. In the end, it was determined that stories about things such as moonshine stills would be bylined "Totally Anonymous."

It took us two and half years to complete the book.

"Bet you never thought it would take this long," said Mary Seifried, the wife of the committee chairman, as we watched a line-up of book buyers form in the arena after the parade. Mary always brought home-baked cookies to the meetings. I realized how much I was going to miss everyone. What would I have to do now on Monday evenings? Was it possible to have a kitchen table that was not covered with file folders and photocopies of Crown Deeds?

Then I felt a light tap on my shoulder. "We are having a fundraiser banquet this fall, and we just wondered if you would mind . . . "

HEDGEHOG FUTURES

I called my neighbour Rick the other day to find out how the great Minto Township hedgehog-raising experiment was going. Every fall, it seems Rick tries out some new critters as ongoing investment strategies. One year it was bronze-back turkeys, and another time it was African cats with super-long tails.

As you may have noticed, the raising of exotic species has become somewhat of a trend in the country. A farmer on a main highway close to where I live regularly stops traffic with his long-necked, puff-bodied llamas. And every summer, miniature horses are a big hit at the senior citizens' picnic. While "real" farmers have concentrated on building cows the size of a townhouse, those who dabble often end up channelling their efforts into Dexter cattle, a rare Irish breed that stands about waist-high.

Behind tall fences there are beefalo, buffalo and bambis chewing hay where dairy cows once roamed. These days, you can find everything from Vietnamese pot-bellied piglets to full-grown wild boars ranging in fields and barnyards. There is a whole contingency of bird-raisers who are convinced that ostrich could be the Thanksgiving dinner of the future. I'm not sure what sort of stuffing you would use on an emu, but I know a woman who paid $9,000 for the privilege of trying to hatch some. Of course, when I consider some of the "exotics" I have kept, I have to be the last one to say that there isn't a market somewhere for everything.

So when Rick announced he was getting into hedgehogs, I tried to nod politely.

"Gonna sell them to pet shops," he said.

It seemed almost logical. After all, if people are willing to keep ferrets on a leash, the market in hedgehog futures could be a goldmine. But something about hedgehogs bothered me.

So I went home and looked them up in the encyclopedia. Sure enough, they were exactly what I thought they were. Funny-looking, rodent-type gaffers, covered with sharp spines that protrude nastily when the pointy-snouted beast is scared and curls into a pincushion. You could fit one into a lunch pail.

I'd only seen a hedgehog once in person, on a moonlit night in Denmark some 20 years ago. They are nocturnal creatures that spend their day hiding out, quite literally, under hedgerows.

The next time I saw Rick, I asked how the hedgehogs were going.

"Great, just great. Got them set up in a terrarium in the living room," he said. "But don't they sleep all day?" I asked cautiously.

Rick's a private sort of person, and in the country we just don't pry directly into private affairs all that much.

"Yeah, but they wake up around midnight and then they're really fun to watch," Rick told me. "That's why they'll make good pets for shift workers." Logical, once again.

Rick himself had a nightshift job, so he was just waking up when most us were starting to dream. At that giddy hour, apparently the hedgehogs were merrily rooting around their terrarium, digging for earthworms and playfully nudging each other the way buddy hedgehogs do.

By November, I figured Mrs. Hedgehog might be about ready to have a litter, and I hoped to have a peek at what could be the pet-trend of the 90s. Nope.

Rick had already taken his profit in the rising hedgehog market. He'd shipped the four-legged urchins to Alberta — where hedgehog fanciers are apparently clamouring for pets that go bump in the night.

MIRACLE ON MAIN STREET

Drive through almost any small town these days and you will see vacant storefronts. You will also see storefronts that have clearly been occupied by the same business for years. Then there are the storefronts with spanking new signs — those are stores occupied by either the bravest, most naive or the dimmest entrepreneurs in the world.

Starting a new business, particularly a retail business, is a risky enterprise anywhere. In a small town, anyone who opens shop is well-advised to have a long line of ancestors buried in the local cemetery and a heap of prosperous cousins who are active in the local service clubs.

When I first moved to the country, I fearlessly explored every new shop in every nearby town. A new shop opened and I would march right in. After a while, I began to wonder why I never saw anyone else in these testaments to mankind's capacity for hope in the face of insurmountable odds.

When talking with neighbours I began to notice that they would often ask me if I had been into such-and-such a shop yet. When I answered in the affirmative I would be prodded for a detailed description of inventory and a list of the prices.

Six months later, I would discover it was all for naught because the new store had closed.

It took me years to understand what was going on.

Like the first Mennonite who ever wore a zipper, I had been breaking an ancient rule of conduct.

My transgression did not stop the curious locals from wanting to know what the experience was like. After all, I could be excused. I didn't know any better. I was from "away."

The rule in question is the one that prohibits anyone from going into any new shop or patronizing any new business for at least six months, with a few exceptions. For example, if you are collecting rent or carrying the child of the proprietor, you would be exempt.

If a new business somehow miraculously survives the six-month rule, a trickle of customers gradually begin to tentatively tiptoe onto the premises.

This provokes talk in the coffee shop, and plenty of reminiscence about whatever business was there before and how much it is missed, but the locals will gradually start patronizing the joint.

Prices are pressure points. A new restaurant opened in a town I frequent. A month or so later, the woman who manages the convenience store where I buy the newspaper asked me if I had eaten there yet. I allowed I hadn't.

"Well," she said in a conspiratorial whisper, "They're selling potato skins with cheese — for $3.95! How long can you stay in business doing that?"

Good question. How long, indeed?

I started hearing about those pricey potato skins everywhere I went.

Since then, the restaurant has changed ownership three times in three years.

The first thing everyone does when they see a new name on the sign is ask someone they suspect may have eaten there since it changed hands whether there are potato skins on the menu.

"There aren't? The cook is married to a local girl, you say? Who would that be? The owner coaches pee-wee hockey?"

With certain conditions finally met, this incarnation of the restaurant has an odds-on chance to survive.

If a new business owner/operator "comes from away," it is crucial that they establish some timely or long-lost link to the community. Any straw is worth a grab.

One relative who served in an army battalion that even one ancient Legionnaire still remembers creates an instant, *bona fide* connection.

If your mother's brother married the 1962 Dairy Princess and they still visit the family farm at Easter, someone will think they know who you are talking about. If all else fails, it will be necessary to marry someone who is related to the Mayor or change your name to Tim Horton.

Even with the endurance and nepotic conditions satisfied, new businesses often have to be diverse operations. Hence, you will often find interesting retail combinations under the same roof.

Photo-finishing and framing is a natural enough link to something like book selling, but pets and video rentals is something else: "Specials Today: New Schwarzenegger blockbuster/Ragdoll Kittens Ready to Go."

Overnight successes are as rare on Main Street as in Hollywood. I have only witnessed one, and it put the lie to another enduring myth of country life in the process.

In my 20 or so years on the farm I have seen things and been told many stories. The old adage that one sees the damnest things when unarmed has stood the test of time.

However, the most persistent falsehood, the most overweaning myth surrounds the idea that there is actually something called "good ol' down-home country cookin'."

The proprietors of the new business that illuminated this impenetrable secret for me were not only from out of town, they had immigrated from the big city with no blood ties, or anything.

Then they had the unmitigated gall to buy a building on Main Street that once housed one of the most popular beauty parlours in town.

The beauty parlour's demise caused such an enduring wave of discombobulation that certain ladies still inadvertently walk into the store expecting to see Adele and get a perm. They often become thoroughly disoriented when they see loaves of bread rather than hair rinse products on the shelves.

Worse, these urban interlopers planned to open a bakery in a community where baking cakes and cookies was not only a ritual, it was a sacred right.

The rural countryside, according to the myth, is the home of "country cooking," an enduring symbol of family values, goodness and light.

In such a landscape, people know how to peel a potato within an inch of its life, and they can incorporate a marshmallow into anything from a fruit salad to a cream pie.

The actual fact is that anything involving the joining of the words "country" and "cooking" should be avoided at all costs.

The worst examples are found at events billed as "suppers." These are invariably hosted by a church group, civic organizations or local clubs.

They may be touted as "fowl suppers" or "roast beef suppers," but whenever a food classification is followed by the word "supper" and the address is rural, my best advice is to opt out by booking a medical procedure that entitles you to an official paper stating that you must *fast* for at least 12 hours.

It is not that country people do not like to eat. They do. These suppers are prime examples of that. They will eat anything that is put upon their plate and declare it delicious, even when it is unknown grey meat topped with a gelatinous substance of questionable origin. Chicken, pork or beef might be mixed on a plate, but one gravy serves all.

With gusto, those who attend these suppers welcome what are hailed as mashed potatoes, usually identifiable by their lumps.

The whole mess is surrounded with khaki and rust-coloured vegetables, topped with some limp, sweetened cabbage and a dill pickle the texture of liver.

Then there is the matter of dessert.

At most suppers, there is an early "buzz" about pies.

It is almost guaranteed that any cherry pie served in March involved someone opening a can of cherry-pie filling.

The "homemade" designation is derived from the fact that someone purchased a frozen pie shell into which they poured a tin's contents and took responsibility for the hydro bill necessary to bake it.

Anything covered in meringue has something related to Jello underneath.

Nevertheless, there is seldom a flake of pastry left in the building when any supper is over.

Why? Any pies that remain at the formal end of the supper are invariably set on the long, wrapping, paper-covered industrial tables. Then they are set upon and devoured as though they were the last pies on earth.

"Country cooking" seems to be more about quantity than quality. Why else would people stand in line to heap their plates with huge slabs of perfectly good meat that has been cooked into something the taste and texture of corrugated cardboard. But, by golly, it's a tradition that belongs to country people and is inextricably linked to the collective sense of identity.

When city folk want a good meal, they go out to eat. Country folk go home.

When city people dine out, they eat food that is most often prepared by well-schooled men wearing starched white hats who care deeply about things like ingredients and presentation.

Country people eat what's on their plate.

Upstart urbanites, who come from a world where words like "gastronomic delight" and "culinary experience" are dished out along with double-digit priced appetizers, are not welcomed. Crème brûlée doesn't cut it at the coffee shop stolid rice pudding with a few whacked out raisins does. That is why I was certain that a bakery founded on urban principles would never succeed.

Other bakeries had tried and closed. Two supermarkets sell baked goods and there's a Tim Horton's at the crossroads. And then there's the perennial bugaboo of price point.

Jeannette and Doug, the couple who started the Village Bakery, knew nothing of these things about which I speak. If they had, they certainly would not have done what they did.

Hail and handsome mid-life folk embarking on a second career in what they thought was a quaint, quiet, beautiful small town (one, surprisingly, without a bakery), they earnestly began renovating their shop on Main Street.

When I say they lived their business as it took shape, I mean it literally — in the two storeys above the shop.

Two years after the Village Bakery had opened, I picked up my Thanksgiving order.

It was a good thing I had called a day ahead because the bread racks were bare by the time I got there in the mid-afternoon.

Every pumpkin torte had been spoken for. Every last crumb of the best cranberry and blueberry pound cake ever to come out of a loaf pan was boxed and labelled for pickup. Doug told me he could have sold everything twice.

It has miraculously been like that ever since the bakery opened.

But their success was not the result of something as ebullient as a complicated strategic marketing plan. It was, in its way, pure genius and a business lesson for anyone who might care to pay attention. It was impulsive, sincere and deceptively simple.

Being from the city, and children of their age, Jeannette and Doug took cooking seriously and knew something about it from books. But they had no hands-on experience.

While figuring out the craft of baking, testing recipes and searching out the best combinations for the finest ingredients, they often ended up with a surplus of experimental product.

"We gave the stuff away where we thought it would be most welcomed and useful," laughs Doug, a jovial former commercial photographer, whose specialty today is making round loaves of spinach, garlic and cheese bread that have to be eaten to be believed.

Loaves of flax bread fresh from the oven found their way to the hospital cafeteria — for the staff.

Pans full of double-chocolate killer brownies were dropped off at the police station which just happened to be a regional centre. That meant about three hundred uniformed and well-armed men with spouses and families in the immediate vicinity had an exclusive preview of Jeannette and Doug's wizardry.

Not knowing any better, Jeannette even went so far as to accost Town Councillors in their cars at the stoplight outside the shop, thrusting butter tarts through their window.

"Let me know what you think," she'd say.

What did they think?!?

First, they thought, what cheek! I don't know that person.

Then they thought, Wholly smokes, free stuff.

Then, Hmmm, hmmm good.

Then they realized that their spouses, their mothers and sisters really had never really known how to bake anything, and from that day forward insisted that the family start buying all their pies, cakes and bread at that new bakery by the library,

"What's it called, Town Bakery or Village Bakery? Nevermind. It's right there just north of the Town Hall. You can't miss it."

Even badly baked cookies can be addictive. Great baking can blow the mind.

And boy, did Jeannette and Doug's ever do just that.

When the "OPEN" sign finally appeared, without any fanfare or hoopla, customers came in droves.

In fact, opening day was one of the biggest Jeannette and Doug have ever had.

"Townies" and farm folk found themselves stacked side-by-side in front of the bakery, waiting their turn and admiring a fanciful collection of cookie jars that perch on a shelf above the bread racks. Price became no object.

People were paying more for one of Jeannette's pies than they would ever consider coughing up for a whole "supper." I've never heard a word about price in relation to the Village Bakery.

A little cartoon on the cash register about sums it up:

One image shows a pie on a table with the sign, "Mom's apple pie: $2." Next to it is the same table with a better looking pie. The sign reads, "The pie Mom thought she baked: $5."

It does the heart good to see a new business in a small town achieve its goals and add a new dimension to the community.

"I need a good pie," I overheard an elderly lady lean into the counter and whisper to Doug the other day. With a twinkle in her eye and the demeanour of an experienced bargainer, she added, "It's for the church supper,"

"Oh, we've sold lots of pies for that supper, dear," chirped Jeannette, as she emerged from the back room with a tray of three lattice-work encrusted beauties fresh from the oven.

The old lady handed Doug the money without further comment and hurried out of the store. I suspect that pie never made it to any church supper. I doubt it even made it to dinner time.

KISS A PIG FOR A CAUSE

If you want to raise money for anything in the country, you need to get the local bankers on your side. Not because they are pillars of the community or persons of great charity, but rather because they are generally and roundly despised.

Charitable groups, recreation committees, hospital boards and youth committees all suffer when farm commodity prices are low. The tightening of farmers' belts ripples through the community. Banks are generally the first to respond by reducing lines-of-credit, insisting on added security, or simply foreclosing.

So when a "dunking" game is featured at a fall fair, you can bet that the star attraction is going to be a banker. Dunking contraptions are fly-away chairs or bars set over large tanks of water. You pay a buck for a ball and try to hit the pie plate that releases the seating contraption and plops the subject into the water. Large crowds gather to observe this humiliation, and long lines form to risk a loonie on the chance of satisfaction. When a banker is scheduled, some joker is almost certain to dump a few bags of ice into the tank to add to the "vig."

During periods of killing interest rates, whole baseball teams stand in line to dump the banker. If you get a hot-shot, never-miss pitcher at the front of the line, it can be splish-splash-banker-takes-a-bath time for two solid hours. Teenage boys may get a kick out of dumping the Dairy Princess, but anyone old enough to have applied for a loan waits for a banker.

I gather that this was not always the case. There was a time a few generations ago when some rural bank managers inspired certain veneration. The bank earned the trust of farmers, and cash that once lived under the mattress went into the bank. In those days a banker might live out a lifetime serving the same clients, but in these times knowing the client too intimately is considered a disadvantage. The unseen evil known as "head office" makes sure that bank managers change every few seasons. This allows the banks to remove any notion of consistency. It also supplies a steady flow of fresh fodder for the dunking tank.

Communities are always trying to figure out new ways to raise money. A few years back, the idea of the duck race took hold. This involves selling bright yellow rubber duckies and letting them loose on the stretch of river that runs through most towns. Then someone decided that teddy bear picnics could be a grabber, and soon Bear Days were popping up everywhere. Such themes are worked to death, until another genteel idea springs forth. They work but, without revenge on a banker as the finale, they're about as exciting as watching bubbles rise in pancake batter.

Bingo is a main staple of fundraising. The most innovative variation on that theme is Cow Bingo. This involves a heifer and a controlled area that is divided into squares, which are sold by number. The heifer is fed and watered substantially, and let loose on the gridded plot. The game involves selecting the square where the first cow pie lands. Sometimes the judges have to wait for hours before they shout "bingo!" On the rare occasion when a banker is the winner, the local newspaper tries to run a picture of the winner beside the "deposit." Then, there is general praise for the acumen and aim of the heifer.

One contest that bankers always win is Kiss a Pig. In fact, if there is more than one financial institution in town, you can bet that those managers will place first, second and third, relative to their general foreclosure rate. For the price of a loonie, the populace is invited to nominate and vote for the local person they would most like to see kiss a pig. Tax collectors, police chiefs, school principals and dentists usually capture a fair share of the votes. But since there can be only one winner, it is the abused clients of the banks who dig the deepest.

"The nice thing about Rollo is that he doesn't care who he kisses," said the swineherd, who offered his prize boar to buss the people's choice. Bank managers have been known to apply for transfers when confronting Rollo. Let's hope that automated tellers never take control of the world.

A HANDS-ON LEGEND

Legend has it that country folk are by nature a more decent and honest lot than their urban cousins. It is a pleasant enough legend, and I have found it can be worked to one's advantage. I used it once when I was researching the wool industry at a reference library in the city. All I wanted to do was photocopy an arcane article about felt-making in Great Britain, which I found in an obscure sheep journal.

"Sorry the photocopier is broken and we do not allow materials to be removed from this department," the library technician told me. "People steal things like this all the time. You will just have to come back tomorrow, or take notes."

I explained that this would be impossible, since I was from out of town. Notes were just not feasible since the text in question was impenetrably mathematical. The wool-washing instructions alone dealt with tempera-tures and tonnage and soap to litre ratios that would take me an entire winter to analyze. Then I waved the article in front of her as evidence and asked if I could please use the working photocopier in the adjoining department.

"You in the clothing business?" she asked with some suspicion, her tweedy eyes narrowing as she examined the object of my desire.

"Oh, no, no, nothing like that," I said. "I'm a farmer. I raise sheep. That's why I'm reading up on wool."

She eyed me with even more suspicion. I guess I had "warshed up real good," as they say in the country. At least, I did not smell like a sheep. My polished leather boots bore no trace of the barnyard and the neat folds of my skirt showed no signs of recent tumbling in the hay. I had no alternative but to produce my hands as proof positive of my profession.

Mine have always been active rather than elegant hands. No square French manicures for these fingernails. What kind of psychotic lambing midwife would subject her trusting ewes to long nails of any shape? And since you cannot pour hot water on frozen taps while wearing unwieldy mittens, the texture of the surrounding flesh becomes somewhat roughened in rough weather. My hands are only truly soft when the lanolin in the sheared sheep's wool has drenched them in smoothing oil. Unfortunately, that only happens one day of the year and there is plenty of sheep by-product that comes with the lanolin.

A scar marks the right palm where a horse inadvertently kicked me. Another ragged mark distinguishes a different horse who mistook my left thumb for a carrot. Various bumps and gnarls come from long-forgotten incidents that involve everything from scrappy chickens who refused to surrender their eggs to hammers that eluded nails. All ten digits are in working order, however, and working is what they reveal.

"Goodness, you must be a farmer " said the clerk widening her eyes and lowering her chin.

To brighten the light bulb that was dawning over her head, I produced a photograph of a newborn lamb that I carry in my wallet like a doting parent.

"I promise to return the magazine right away," I assured her in a whisper appropriate to the location.

"You know, I believe you," she said in the same tone that teachers use on errant students to whom they are giving one last chance before calling for parental intervention.

I scurried over to the next department and inserted my quarter. Two minutes later, I was back at her desk replacing the well-travelled document. The library technician smiled at me as though I had sprinkled her with fairy dust.

It might not work with automated bank machines, but there are times when belonging to a profession that has decency and honesty as its legend can sure come in handy.

THAT CHAMPIONSHIP
SEASON

While the farmers were taking off the second cut of hay and worrying about rain, I was putting makeup on my dog and worrying about rain. Go figure. I was going to a dog show.

At sheep shows, I have seen that it takes a fair amount of primping to make a sheep a champion. Fluff the wool a little here, trim it back a little there — use a black felt-tip marker to disguise a few white hairs where there should be only black. In dire straits, go for the Miss Clairol.

Cattle breeders use vacuums and hair blowers on their prize beef. They have trunks full of clippers and hair shiners, hair spray and hoof gloss. And, I hate to tell you this, but there was a scandal in the dairy industry when certain competitors were accused of enhancing the udders of prize-winning cows with silicon injections.

People will go to ungodly lengths to try and win a silly ribbon. That notion really struck home for me when

I found myself wiping a cosmetic sponge covered with clown makeup over Wally the Wonder Dog's gigantic nose.

It started innocently enough. A few Bull Terrier owners complimented Wally's good looks and said he had "show potential."

That was some solace to me, since he had shown no sheep-herding potential. Lambs stamp their hooves at him and he runs away — at top speed, usually aiming for my knees. He tries to engage the horses by squatting in front of them and wagging his tail like a helicopter ready for take-off. They just snort in his general direction. He's good at chasing chickens across rows of round bales of hay, disrupting the stacking of anything, and jumping into puddles.

"Show potential" sounded soothing.

It took a year for me to figure out how to enter Wally in a dog show. When I told his dog-obedience instructor what I was planning, I was dispatched to a store that specializes in dog show equipment, where I could find fancy, thin, show leashes and a chain so fine it could be a silver necklace.

There were aisles chock-a-block with doggy things, everything from life-sized plastic fire hydrants to bags full of those impossibly tiny little bows people use to hold the hair out of the eyes of furry little lap dogs. There was even a special counter for pet perfume and hygiene aids, including "whitening, brightening" toothpaste to go with curved canine toothbrushes.

Dog foods ran the gamut from puppy to geriatric, with all manners of gummy bone, raw hide bone and fake salami in between. Then there was what must be the ultimate in the waste-not-want-not category — dried pigs' ears.

Real late-pigs' hearing devices dried to a crisp for Fido's pleasure.

Perhaps that explains the toothpaste.

Before I could grab a shopping cart, Moose bagged the fine chain and leash and whisked me out of the store, muttering something about turning Wally into some kind of "girly dog."

On the day of the dog show I got out the garden hose and gave Wally a bath. I brushed him until he shone and clipped his toenails. That was it, I thought. Ready for the show. I had a fresh package of something called Beggin' Bacon to make Wally stand prettily and my secret weapon — a lacrosse ball.

I was totally unprepared for what greeted me at the arena that day. A thousand dogs of every variety imaginable stared out of metal cages, plastic dog houses and little pens. There were trailers and vans filled with dogs in the parking lot. In one corner of the arena, huge Old English Sheepdogs stood on sturdy stands while their personal groomers worked the hair dryers. Scissors and shears trimmed Poodles in some sort of art form, while every silky strand of Lhasa Apso was carefully combed in place. Impossibly tiny bows were everywhere.

Moose thought taking Wally to a dog show was the biggest waste of time I had come up with since trying to get chickadees to take seed from my hand in the winter. We waded through a sea of dogs and dog owners before reaching the ring just as the Bull Terrier class was called. I examined Wally. His paws were still white.

Having watched a few dog shows on satellite television, I had some idea of the routine. My numbered armband was adjusted and I swung into the ring with Wally. He was perfect. Trotted around looking joyful. Stopped dead still like an alert statue when I pulled out the lacrosse ball. The judge patted his body and, at the appropriate moment, Wally looked deeply into the judge's eyes and wagged his tail. What showmanship!

Wally won a ribbon. It was unreal. We kept going back in the ring and winning some more. In the end, Wally got a trophy and a handful of Beggin' Bacon. Moose was jumping up and down like a bee-stung goat. I shook the limp hands of the losers and realized that these were professional dog handlers. Wally the Wonder Dog had emerged from nowhere and ruined their day.

Alas, we never regained our early glory.

The professionals would always top us in the final round. It was going to be a long limp toward winning the title of champion.

Moose started developing conspiracy theories, drawing charts showing which judges favoured what handler and griping about American dogs stealing the thunder of Canadian dogs.

Once, when Wally seemed sure to take the top prize, we were called into the judging ring at the precise moment that a neighbouring dog had what would be called a rather large "accident."

"Clean up," shouted the professional handler without a hint of embarrassment.

I looked at Wally. His almost-champion face was a twisted grimace that said, "Somebody's in a lot of trouble."

It was the same look he gave the Basset-faced judge. Then he tried to hide from sight by burying his head under her skirt.

"Control your dog," she commanded.

Wally looked up.

Moose added that judge to his list of conspirators.

Our final show was an outdoor extravaganza that promised to bring out the *crème de la crème* of dogdom. Wally was ready in spirit, but not in form.

By mid-summer, he had developed a fair-sized callus on his nose from heading off soccer balls. Then he chased a chipmunk into a woodpile, adding splinter wounds to go with whatever damage a cornered groundhog can do.

Bluntly put, Wally's nose was a bloody mess of bumps, bruises and scabs.

I thought of forfeiting the entry fee. Then I remembered how things work in sheep shows and cattle shows. I checked with a friend who is an old hand in the world of doggy showing and discovered that the remedy for Wally's nose was clown-white and a dusting of corn starch.

Where in a small town in southwestern Ontario was I going to find clown makeup? Stedman's, of course.

Sure enough, there on the toy rack facing the vegetable peelers and potato mashers, I found a tube of clown-white Halloween makeup, non-toxic to children. Stedman's never lets you down.

Applying makeup to a teenaged Bull Terrier is not an easy matter. By the time I finished, my arms were streaked with clown white, and a whole section of the kitchen floor was covered in a fine dusting of corn starch.

Moose surveyed my handiwork.

"He looks like a girl," was the verdict.

On the drive to the dog show, Wally rolled in the back seat. When we arrived, the upholstery was clown white.

I registered, leaving Moose to exercise Wally. When I found them, they were in the middle of a crowd of children putting on a show of their own.

"Batter up!" Moose cried. Then he lobbed a tennis ball at Wally, who promptly hit it back with his nose. More clown white was applied. Dusted in corn starch, I looked more like Bela Lugosi than any show-ring belle.

Spectators in lawn chairs lined the show rings.

Chihuahua owners carried their dogs in vest pockets to keep them from disappearing in patches of long grass.

A Yorkshire Terrier passed by, carried aloft as though it was a stuffed toy.

Elegant Afghans paused to have their paws groomed before stepping daintily into the ring.

Apparently sensing the odds of an "accident" occurring in such a large number of dogs, Wally commenced howling and barking.

Reluctantly, he followed me into the show ring, squirming to check out the dogs behind him.

Then a child on the sidelines shouted, pointing at Wally: "Mom, it's the dog that hits balls with his nose!"

Wally heard the word "ball" and promptly went into a crouch waiting for the games to begin. I tried straightening him out and instead he flopped down on all fours.

I looked down the row of dogs. Professional handlers in tweed suits held skinny leashes over still-as-stone, perk-eared Bull Terriers.

"Round the ring," said the judge.

Wally lurched to his feet. The idea is for the dog to show off his gaits. But Wally was having none of it. He wanted to sniff the grass for underground moles before he took another step. Behind us, a line of dogs jogged in place like finely tuned dressage horses.

Wally jitterbugged all over the ring somewhere between a trot and a gallop. He jumped in the air and kicked out his hind legs. The crowd loved it, especially when the leash became tangled around my leg, and Wally barked while I twirled around, trying to free myself.

With an arch of his finger, the judge called us for inspection. Beads of sweat formed on my brow, sunglasses hung askew.

"Teeth, please," said the judge. I wrested Wally's jaws open, revealing a Beggin' Bacon strip glued to his incisors.

The judge patted Wally's head and a cloud of corn starch poofed in his face.

At the tail end of the examination, the judge tried to check Wally's breeding equipment. Wally suddenly reared back and gave the judge such a look as though to say, "What the hell do you think you're doing, you pervert?"

"To the corner," said the judge curtly. I felt as though I was tugging an anchor. I went the wrong way.

"Miss, diagonal, please," called the judge. I turned too suddenly and tripped. Wally stopped my fall by jamming his head in my face, followed by a full body licking.

"You two are a pair, aren't you?" noted the judge.

We waited in line while the other dogs performed beautifully. My nose was bleeding. Nothing a makeup sponge covered in clown's white makeup couldn't absorb.

Bored, Wally decided to dig a hole, apparently to China.

To distract him and spare the spectators from flying clods of dirt, I pulled out his favourite thing in the entire word — the lacrosse ball.

Bingo, he butted it out of my hand where it rolled under the belly of an American bred Bull Terrier whose owner had travelled half a continent to see his dog win a ribbon. The Yankee dog lunged backward in an unseemly fashion. So did the judge, whose heel slipped on the ball, propelling him into the lap of a large lady who may have had a Chihuahua in her vest pocket.

We did not win that day. By some miracle, Wally placed third. The crowd applauded. I wiped my brow, smearing clown white across my forehead.

"Looking more and more like your dog, Miss," said the judge when he handed me the ribbon. "Pervert," I thought.

That was the end of Wally's career as a show dog.

Outside of the ring, Moose took Wally on a tour of the grounds. Man and dog trotted in a straight line.

A crowd of children gathered and Wally shot tennis balls off his nose until it started to rain.

Our makeup melted and that was fine with Moose. I went back to worrying about that second cut of hay, and Wally went back to soccer and searching the barnyard for moles.

THE GREAT MINTO COW HUNT

There is nothing like a cow on the loose to turn grown men into frustrated children.

The other day, driving along the gravel roads on the outskirts of a small town, I observed such a phenomenon in action. Five men were chasing a dairy cow around the front lawn of a farmhouse in an attempt to move her back into the barnyard.

I pulled my truck up, knowing that a loose cow is the equivalent of a loose cannon and she could decide to bolt across the road at any given moment. True to form, old "Bossie" was soon joyfully kicking her heels sideways, throwing up stones like some bucking rodeo steer.

The men knew what they were doing. They fanned out and moved slowly, trying to surround the cow without alarming her. But something seems to snap in the mind of a cow when it realizes a taste of freedom. Even though she had probably been trained to head to the milk parlour morning and night along with the rest of the docile milking herd, in the outside world the cow became a maniac.

However, the calm containment method of herding was working — until the cow saw some laundry flapping on the line behind the house. She bolted through the blue jeans, running full-bore around the house via the clothesline and ending up beside the front porch draped in a flannelette sheet.

At this point an angry woman appeared on the porch, brandishing a broom. One firm shout from her scared the cow enough to send her ambling off to the barnyard, shedding the sheet in the autumn leaves.

Five men ran shouting and waving as they dashed to close the gate behind her. Then they perched on the fence looking at their captured quarry, no doubt having words about her parentage.

It reminded me of one of the reasons I don't keep cows anymore.

Years ago, I bought Hazel the Hereford and Lindy the Limousin from Henry the Chicken Farmer. Along with Hazel and Lindy came their calves, Herman and Heathcliffe, two funny-looking gaffers whose father had been a Highland bull, a pedigree that gave them long shaggy coats and the nubby beginnings of horns.

Henry drove his livestock truck into the pasture and I prepared to photograph the arrival of my first cows. I have pictures of the truck doors opening with the cows and calves wandering out. The rest of the pictures are of their backsides as they ran to the top of the field, jumped the fence and headed off over the neighbour's fields.

I didn't find my cows for three days.

A full-scale cow hunt ensued. All of the neighbours were on the lookout for the travelling foursome. Posses in pick-up trucks toured the gravel sideroads. The police were notified. The local country and western radio station carried a public affairs announcement about "four stray cattle beasts in Minto Township," and I got out the horse.

You can cover a lot of distance on horseback, and I rode from dawn till dusk. We jumped fences, forged creeks and interrupted many sunbathing groundhogs. After two days of tracking and finding tufts of shaggy hair on fenceposts, I figured they were still somewhere in the area, which was small comfort to my saddle sores.

Phone calls were coming in from as far as 30 miles away, reporting possible sightings.

Finally, a young couple from Toronto called to say they had enjoyed watching my cow family graze peacefully in the back field of their hobby farm near the highway for several days.

With the help of Henry the Chicken Farmer and the horse, we herded the renegades back on the truck and took them home, depositing them in a pasture with fences that were reinforced and had a single strand of electrified wire around the top.

Hazel, as belligerent a cow as I have ever met, immediately headed for the fence, but one touch of her nose on the electric wire was enough to send her dancing back into the pasture. All of them had a go at sniffing the strange wire, and after a couple of high-stepping bovine tangos, they determined the boundaries of their new home and settled into eating and mooing and doing regular cow stuff.

I never trusted the cows after that. I could feel them watching me every time I opened a gate. I could tell by their sneaky cow faces that they were just biding their time for one lax moment when they could once again bolt their way to freedom and make a fool out of me.

The Great Minto Cow Hunt made good conversation in the neighbourhood for months. I could not go to an auction without someone chuckling and making inquiries about the present address of my cows. The only comfort came when I discovered that virtually anyone who has ever had a cow has at least one tale of a merry chase of hamburger on the hoof.

So when I drove away from the scene of the escaped Holstein, I felt a certain camaraderie with the five men perched on the barnyard gate. I knew that once they retired to the kitchen for coffee, their stories would start about cows that had escaped, and quite possibly they would recall the three-day cow hunt in Minto Township by "that lady with the sheep."

ELWOOD'S UFOs

These days, one of the cheapest forms of entertainment in the country seems to be the attending of public meetings where land severance applications or zoning changes from agricultural to residential are hot topics of discussion. Public meetings are most often held in a township municipal office, where elected officials meet once a month to discuss burning issues such as where a drain should go and whether or not a dog catcher who has been convicted of unlawfully killing dogs should be re-hired. Anyone can attend such regular meetings, but the real fun is when a "public" meeting is called because there is bound to be controversy between the pro- and the anti-development forces.

And then, of course, there is the question of what's going to happen to the UFOs if all this development takes place.

Almost every month there is a notice in my mailbox informing me that someone nearby is applying to sever a lot or two off their farm. This raises all kinds of environmental questions about land use planning, sewage percolation rates, the right to farm and the right of farmers to make a buck by selling off a bit of real estate.

All things considered, my neighbour, Elwood, is more concerned about the effect all this development is going to have on the UFOs that rely on his private lake as a water refueling centre.

Elwood is the kind of aggressive old-timer who will sit in a wooden chair and rub the arms and claim that he can tell you how old the tree was. When a man claims to know the age of trees by touch, you are best just to nod in agreement. That's also the best response to give regarding discussions of the UFO water refuelling issue.

A few years ago, a group of neighbours got together and formed an association with the unwieldy title of Concerned Citizens for the Pike Lake Area and the Environs. We get involved in local issues like preserving agricultural land, maintaining wetlands and generally keeping a watchful eye on anything that threatens to pollute our water or our way of life.

We added a concern for the UFO situation after a discussion about the wisdom of placing an 18-unit subdivision on a provincially significant wetland, which just happens to be next door to Elwood's private lake.

The Indians used to call Elwood's 15-acre lake Spirit Lake and later the pioneers called it Ghost Lake. It has always had an aura of mystery. The lake is set back from the roadway and you could drive by the fieldstone house Elwood built by hand and never know that paradise was only a few hundred yards away.

I first visited the lake when I was about five years old, on an excursion with friends of my parents who were friends of Elwood's. From Scarborough, it seemed to me that we drove for hours to get to the "wilderness."

There is a trail cut through the bush where pheasants and grouse hide. At the lake, a rustic cottage sits perched at the water's edge, and I remember holding my fishing pole out the window and reeling in fish that Elwood cooked as fast as we could catch them.

When I discovered that Elwood was my neighbour after moving to this neck of the woods almost a generation ago, it brought back all kinds of good memories.

Elwood's lake is unchanged; the trees just keep getting bigger. Nearby, progress has taken a certain toll. On a lake a few hundred acres away there is a huge trailer park. Nature just doesn't look right with 400 mobile homes racked up side by side. No self-respecting pheasant would want to nest amid that accumulation of barbecues, and all those septic tanks can make the air smell distinctly unnatural.

Elwood, however, has guarded the pristine nature of his lake. He has pet names for the catfish that live under the dock, and he claims they come when he calls. One year he announced that there were five bullfrogs missing at the lake. It seems he also counts his bullfrogs every spring.

Eccentricities aside, this was the first any of us had heard about Elwood giving the UFOs permission to stock up on water from his pond.

"All I can say is that if they build houses, the extra-terrestrials won't be coming back," declared Elwood, during a discussion of the effect of development on waterfowl nesting sites. "They don't like a lot of people around watching their spaceships," said Elwood, leaning back into an 102-year-old maple chair.

According to Elwood, ET and his buddies have been bringing their frisbee-shaped spacecraft to his property for over 40 years. They suck water out of his lake and carry on with their journey. Makes me wonder if they didn't make a mistake once and suck out five bullfrogs while they were at it.

"If they can't get water here in privacy, I guess they'll just die," advised Elwood. "They won't go near a lake with a subdivision on it, no sir. They won't even come near while the trailer campers are around in the summer."

We all quizzed Elwood about the logic of what he was saying, but he refused to budge.

If Elwood is right, this could be as important as discovering the Lost City of Atlantis next to the Dome Stadium. It could certainly create quite a stir at a public meeting.

If it went to a judicial hearing, it could be even more interesting. Imagine trying to explain to a judge that, sewage percolation rates aside, a development should not proceed because it will disturb the aliens' watering hole in Minto Township.

I'm convinced.

THE LAST GARAGE SALE

When I was growing up in the suburbs outside of the major urban centre we rural folks call "the Big Smoke," everyone had a garage. Some were tidy affairs lined with hooks for mounting ladders and garden tools. Some were messy affairs filled with work benches and kids' bicycles and the usual detritus of outgrown toys. Old end tables and couches that might one day find their way to the dream of a cottage could be stacked in the garage, just like yesterday's news. More often than not, there was even room for a station wagon.

No one in the suburbs of my youth would have ever considered dragging the garage dreck onto the front lawn and trying to fob it off on the innocent for a few bucks. In the polite society that played the unspoken game of "my barbecue is bigger than your barbecue," garage contents were as furtively secret as the family treasures that were hidden in the parents' underwear drawers.

Times change. Today the first sighting of a "garage sale" sign is almost as revered as the first robin of spring.

City people are so accustomed to surveying their neighbourhood garage sales and finding the same assortment of rusted TV-tables and bad lamps that they have been compelled to move further afield. Now entire rural towns designate garage sale days and vans filled with urbanites descend in search of quaint, faintly amusing, trinkets from a lifestyle less familiar than the guy next door's.

One person's junk becomes another's obsession. My friend Bette collects waffle irons at garage sales, second-hand stores and auctions. She has a shed full of them. Some with frayed cords, some with rusted bits and some that just need a bit of cleaning up. I have never seen Bette eat a waffle, but that is not her point. She thinks of the old waffle irons as potential gifts for acquaintances and relatives. Reconditioned waffle irons have come to represent her stab at frugality in retirement. And, it makes her happy.

Grandpa Bill and Rick Rooney are another matter. Both grown men, more often than not gainfully employed, they view garage sales as a sort of independent business opportunity. In the world according to Bill and Rooney everything costs a quarter, or it is not worth ten cents. Up at 5 a.m. on garage sale Saturday, they generally have a route all planned out. If they can, they try to sneak a peak when people are setting up tables the night before. Nothing excites them more than the creak of a virgin garage door opening to reveal its world of wonders.

Most of the stuff they collect in their rounds ends up at Grandpa Bill's, stuffed in the basement or covered with tarpaulins outside. The organization of material is loose. Old books are favoured, along with old signs and lawnmowers that just need a part here or there. "Perfectly good" is their watchphrase.

What Bill and Rooney discovered after years of garage sale haggling is that most people who hold garage sales are so fed up with nickel and diming at the end of the day that they just want whatever is left over to disappear. So, after spending the morning collecting a total of about four dollars worth of "good stuff," Bill and Rooney spend the late afternoon revisiting garage sales and offering to remove the remainder for free, or a quarter.

By fall, the pair have accumulated a mass of garage sale excess that rivals what most rural towns can offer in a weekend. They wait, biding their time through September and October when the garage sale phenomenon starts to wane. By November, most people have packed up their garages for the winter and farm auctions have about come to a standstill. There exists a void in Saturday mornings. It is time for "the last garage sale."

Alex, a local fellow who has a lawn maintenance business, keeps Bill and Rick posted on weather patterns through the Internet. When that one sunny November weekend is headed our way, the tables begin to appear on Bill's lawn and the signs go up on the highway with arrows directing the traffic. Cars line Bill's long lane and families trudge across the frosted lawn for one last fling at a bargain.

At the last garage sale, books are a nickel. A whole carton might go for a quarter, especially if Bill and Rick have already read them. Kids' bikes, playpens, toys and mismatched China pieces end up in car trunks and tucked into back seats. The packrat pals gleefully note that they have sold the same end table three or four years in a row, for a profit of about a dollar in total. One ancient hockey net has made the rounds five times. A bad watercolour that was a bad watercolour in 1992 still sells for a quarter every year. And as long as there are garages, there will always be one more "perfectly good" waffle iron for Bette to add to her collection.

CASKET LIDS AND OTHER FOUND TREASURES

Pack-ratism is rampant in rural areas. One of my neighbours collects old doors. Another keeps a trailer full of abandoned windows of all sizes. If I ever need an anvil, there's a retired Irishman two townships away who keeps a shed full of them, for reasons known only to him.

Every farm I have ever visited has a designated area for "stuff." In a shed or a corner of the hay mow or stacked behind the barn, there's always a pile of wood left over from some project, various roll ends of different sizes of wire and snow-fencing, windows, odd-sized doors and baskets of nuts and bolts picked up at an auction that might come in handy some day.

I inherited just such a pile of debris when I moved to my farm. At first it just looked like a mess, but when I needed an instant panel to divide a pen, there were always a few pieces of lumber that could be sawed and whacked into shape. Old windowpanes made perfect coldframes for spring vegetables and the odd pieces of barnboard were made into handy shelves, saddle racks and chicken perches.

The farm has provided me with the impetus to develop skills I never thought I would have. One year I put a new floor in the chicken coop. It still surprises me that I know what to do with a mitre board. When I conquered the use of a drill, I put screws into everything. None of this is art, mind you, but it does have a lot to do with form and function.

My neighbour Alex tells about his great-grandfather building a stable entirely out of wood. The only things that weren't wood were the door hinges. Those were made of leather. Alex's grandfather swore that all he needed to make a log cabin was an axe. The handle was used as a measure and the width of the axe head was used as the depth of the dovetail on the end of the logs to be fitted at the corners. In those days, they didn't have a pile of "stuff" to rely on.

Left to my own devices, I have been known to build some pretty funny-looking things out of scraps of wood. My first A-frame chicken house was rather lopsided, but it served its purpose.

When you are forced to improvise for economy's sake, a lot of things can be recycled. An old shower curtain stapled to the windward side of my pump house wall has stopped the wind and rain for ten years now. One of these days it will be replaced by proper insulation and an interior wall — but that could be five years hence. In the meantime, every time I see the shower curtain holding firm, I take a peculiar pride.

The township dump has proved somewhat of a treasure trove. I have come up with discarded twin bedframes that make ideal lightweight lambing pens. Buckets, barrels, leftover steel siding and fence-roll ends that have all been another person's junk have found a useful purpose in my enterprise.

When I needed a few small pieces of quality wood for some kitchen cupboards, I let it be known throughout the neighbourhood. Sure enough, an offer presented itself. You can imagine my surprise when I found myself in an empty hay loft that was stacked with beautiful pieces of oak and cherry wood. The only thing was that they were discarded casket lids.

"Too good to waste," said the owner, Elmer, who is a practical man.

Somehow I could not countenance the notion of having coffins as kitchen cabinets.

My friend Clare ended up with a real boondoggle on his hands when his dad died and left him a farm that had hundreds of ancient vehicles simply left hither and yon. Just when he thought he had found everything, Clare would look over the crest of hill and find another cache of rotting metal on wheels. There was everything from Model-Ts to early motorized milk trucks. Some of the rusting heaps from the 30s still had the original gangster bullet-holes in the bodywork. What seemed at first like a disastrous removal and disposal proposition turned into a gigantic antique car and car parts auction that brought buyers from all over North America.

The best I've found on my farm is an ancient plough hidden under wild grapevines, and a pile of old car licence plates amid some smashed whisky bottles that somehow ended up in the middle of a swampy patch of forest.

Apparently, our forbears were not always the most ecologically minded citizens. Under aged mounds of moss, I have unearthed everything from rotting tin cans to green-glass mason jars that someone felt comfortable ditching in a cedar bush clearing. Of course, some of this historic debris now qualifies as "antique." I can perch etched-glass medicine bottles, defunct milk bottles and oddly shaped pop bottles in front of a window and the sun streams through their coloured glass and hand-hewn shapes, beautifully belying their garbage-pile origins.

Every fall I am tempted to cart the "stuff" I have been hoarding to the dump. But somehow I know that I would miss it in the spring when I need the odd piece of two-by-four to shore something up, or a sliver of plywood to cover the wear in a certain step. So far I have eschewed casket lids, but there's always next year.

THE UNPREDICTABILITY
OF A FARM WEEKEND

On a cool country weekend at the farm, what could be better than a cosy fire crackling, while a simmering stew bubbles and the smell of fresh-baked bread floats in the air?

Sounds good to me. I sure wish someone would come over and set things up just like that for me.

When you actually live on a farm, weekends just can't all be the "over-stuffed plaid sofa, window-box herb garden, long, quiet communes with a book" lifestyle that you see in magazines. Weekends are not necessarily reserved for finishing that tranquil needlepoint or creating some marvellous hand-hewn bird feeder. Nothing is that predictable.

Take the dogs on a rambling hike through the woods and you are just as likely to find yourself mired knee-deep in bog or burdocks as you are to interrupt a small herd of deer peacefully wading in a stream.

Plan to attend an auction that is fully stocked with antique crockery, hand-tatted lace and oodles of those quirky old rug beaters that can positively define a room, and — just as you intend to leave — the phone will ring with a neighbour in crisis requiring an extra hand to steady a horse that's having trouble giving birth.

These are things that happen. But when you try to warn city friends that a "weekend at the farm" means anything that goes on at a farm will keep going on — well, they just think you're kidding. The funny thing is that once a city person arrives in a country state of mind, they think that just about anything that happens is quite marvelous. For instance, I remember the day that Herf got out.

"Herf" was only a few days old. I bought him at an auction, a mistake I tried not to make — but there he was, a little Hereford bull calf hiding off in a corner away from the larger, black and white Holsteins.

He was such a little guy, no doubt a classic runt or the weaker half of a set of twins. He seemed to cower in the corner as though he wanted to hide from the auctioneer's gavel. When I caught his eye he looked so forlorn, so motherless.

My maternal instincts found me stopping for a bag of calf milk replacer powder while I drove home with the hapless Herf in the back of the truck bawling his brains out.

We arrived at about the same time as the guests. Herf descended from the truck like a good little orphan and we took the baby boy to the barn and gave him his first bottle.

The city folk loved that. The red and white calf, so soft and trusting, nuzzling and thrusting away at the big bottle with warm milk supplement in it. He lay down in his straw and gave a great burp.

"Terrific," said the city folk. "We've done some farming already. Now where's lunch?"

We were well fed and ready for the mandatory walk in the woods when one of the urbanites decided to check on young Herf. In doing so, the city person made a crucial mistake and left the door open. Out of the barn in a flash, what had once been a sad-eyed, motherless bull became a frisky, mooing little butthead. Herf wanted to play. So off he ran, with the five folks in their Eddie Bauer footwear — and me in my Wellington boots — giving chase.

Now you can't chase a cow, no matter how small. They just don't respond well. We would all have done much better to stop in our tracks and leave the poor, confused Herf to stand stock still and consider where his next bottle was coming from. But I could only convince my urban friends of this when they had finally reached a state of exhaustion after criss-crossing a 50-acre field like errant Pac-Men, while Herf bobbed and bucked ahead of them.

Finally, they retired when I promised to make them raisin-and-cheese scones and herbal tea flavoured from the window box garden.

Herf showed up on the front lawn by the time we had finished. Two urbanites proceeded to charge at him with love in their hearts and a big hug in mind. But cows — no matter how little — have a privacy zone. Just like people on a subway, they like to think that some of the space they occupy is their own.

Herf's privacy zone involved not being hugged around the neck. He bolted. And again, five sets of Eddie Bauer boots and one set of Wellies set off in pursuit.

This time we stalked the little dickens. He was mooing for more milk and feeling forlorn. So we fanned out around him, crunched into commando poses, and moving ever so slowly, each one of us mimicked his mournful, Munchkin moo.

One of the ironies of life in the technology age is that every time you should have a video camera, you are part of the action.

As we funnelled the little Hereford back toward the safety and warmth of the barn, I watched a heavy-duty mutual fund manager hide behind a gatepost making soprano mooing sounds. His buddy, an expert in Egyptology, balanced the scene with an alto moo from behind a lilac bush. Shadowing them were assorted wives, lovers and children, all mooing intensely in an effort to make Herf feel as though he was part of a herd.

Heavy, wet snow and freezing rain began falling just as the diminutive Hereford entered the barn. Someone thought he was a bit wet, so I discovered the whole lot of urban cowboys massaging the baby bovine with my best bath towels when I got back with the warm bottle.

By the time Herf had sucked the whole thing dry, we were ready to repair to a crackling fire that I had managed to light, and a bubbling stew that I had managed to thaw in the microwave and transfer to suitable antique crockery. One of the guests had brought a basketful of fresh-baked breads.

As it turned out, we had a wonderful evening of needlepoint instruction and birdwatching discussion — but who could have predicted that?

Winter

FLANNELETTE DREAMS

The first day of winter on the farm is the day that I put flannelette sheets on the bed. Usually, it is also the first night that snow blankets the ground and stays there. It is the night when the one garden hose that escaped the autumn garden clean-up freezes into place until spring.

That first lasting snow brings with it the mixed emotions that challenge everyone who lives with the stuff. Something about it recalls the rapture of childhood excitement over being able to make snowballs any time you want, building snowmen and designing snow forts. It also recalls the wind-whipped days, windshields blinded by a cataclysm of falling flakes and sludge falling from encrusted boots onto so-called draining trays by the front door.

And then there are the flannelette sheets. To me, they are second only to homemade stew with dumplings as a cure for any winter day. There is an air of comfort about flannelette sheets that makes you feel that the misery of the weather cannot get you. And, of course, if you sleep in the nude, flannelette sheets are mandatory in any house that takes on a chill at night.

The question then becomes: what has happened to flannelette sheets in modern times? The flannelette of my childhood seemed so much thicker, so much more cuddly. Every winter for years, they were the same flannelette sheets as always — plain white, trimmed only with a line of pink and blue at the top. They were washed a zillion times in the same washing machine, by the same mother, year after year, and they always felt the same. Smooth.

However, the flannelette sheets I have acquired as an adult are not like those of my youth. Granted they do come in a riot of colours to mix and match and co-ordi-nate with nude, or whatever colour you sleep in. These new-fangled flannelette sheets start out just grand but after a few washings they start to fizzle into a fuzzy-nubbed surface. I think the formal word is "pilling." The principle is the same one that applies to certain sweaters, which develop pesky "pills" of wool at the worn bits around the neck and at the wrists. In between the fuzzy bits on the sheets, the layer of flannelette is skimp and limp, so you have to try to wrap yourself in the fuzzy bits to get that feeling of flannelette security.

Complaining about the declining quality of flannel-ette gets you absolutely nowhere. I know, I tried.

"You can see that the flannelette is all fuzzy right here," I said to the clerk in the "major retail shopping store," where I had purchased a set of cornflower-blue flan-nelette sheets. "In fact, you can see it quite clearly because the fuzzy bits are still cornflower blue, while the unfuzzy bits are more of an azure blue."

"Well, they *are* a year old," sniffed the clerk, without even bothering to touch the freshly laundered sheet I had trucked all the way to the big city, lugged from a parking lot across four intersections and hauled up four escalators. Instead of sympathizing with me or even apologizing for the poor quality of the product, this whippet-thin clerk with skin the texture of 200-thread percale and attitude worthy of a bank manager was trying to make *me* feel like some sort of slob because my sheets went fuzzy halfway through the winter.

So I asked to see the linen supervisor, thinking that perhaps I would find satisfaction with a more mature individual who understood the true nature of flannelette.

"How did you wash this?" was the first question that emerged from the lips of a thirty-something supervisor. I noticed that he had pills on the wrists of his cardigan.

This was obviously a trick question; but before I could pick the lint out of my thoughts, the truth was on the table.

"Warm water, tumble dry," I sputtered.

"Bleach?" he asked, twisting the word as though anyone so stupid as to add bleach to a load of laundry had the personality potential to poison the entire city water supply.

"No, never," I responded, perhaps too quickly to make even the truth believable. I stuck my chin out to emphasize my point.

Stymied but unmoved, the supervisor deigned to actually touch the fuzzy sheet, which I thought would be a defining moment.

"Well, it *goes* like this when you use it," he said, stroking the sheet as though it were a sick puppy. Then he started to leave.

"But you're supposed to use it, that's why you buy it and now it's all fuzzy and my mother's flannelette was never fuzzy and it's just not the same . . . " or words to that effect burbled out of me as he walked away.

"Sorry," was all he said as he headed for the duvet aisle and the perfect oblivion of goose down.

All the way home, I kept thinking of snappy retorts and clever rebuttals to arguments that had never been made. I even contemplated writing a letter to the store's president suggesting that he inspect his linen department employees for wrist pills, because if they are satisfied wearing pilly clothes, they surely do not give a yahoo about selling flannelette that goes fuzzy after a few washings.

A few days later, I went to the big pre-Christmas sale at my local Stedmans store. Stedmans is like a small-scale Wal-Mart, except that you are likely to find the owner working the floor. You can find almost anything in Stedmans from bikini underwear to clothes pegs and shower curtains. The pre-Christmas sale is usually a jumble of stuff that has been stacked up in the storeroom, for longer than anyone can remember.

That is where I found my "real" flannelette sheets. On the bottom shelf of the linen aisle, there was a clear plastic bag with a set of white sheets trimmed with pink and blue. Nothing fancy marked them, no designer label, no nothing. Ruth, the owner, told me she found them in a box in the back room and that they must have been left by the previous owner. Heck, she even found a carton of Pet Rocks back there. I opted to buy the flannelette sheets.

After going through the washing machine ten times, those sheets are still smooth. They tumble dry into fluffy perfection. One touch of them makes you a nighttime nudist for the whole winter.

When I close my eyes at night and briefly ponder ways of extricating the garden hose from its frozen resting place, the flannelette sheets take hold and lull me into dreams that are as cuddly as a childhood memory.

THE HAIR DRYER — MY INDISPENSABLE FARM TOOL

When I first left the family home, twentysomething years ago, my father gave me a hug, a hammer and a multi-head screwdriver. My mother offered the same gesture of affection along with an electric kettle and a hair dryer.

I was on my own, and my family had prepared me with tools and appliances to cope with the world at large.

Today, after a decade of urban life and more than a dozen years on the farm, those implements (albeit slightly updated) remain indispensable. I keep them all together in my barn where they enjoy constant use.

The hammer and screwdriver have been joined by all manner of other small tools and corresponding sizes of screws, bolts and nails. I am still not what you would call "handy" with them, but I have come a long way from my first attempts to hang a picture. The kettle is good for a comforting cup of tea during winter lambing, and for heating up cold buckets of water during difficult animal births or making a warm mash for the horses.

It's the hair dryer that confounds almost everyone who visits my sheep barn. But of all my family tools it is the one I find most indispensable.

I first discovered the many applications of a hair dryer in the barn in the middle of a particularly active party, which included a house full of guests. Naturally, there was a blizzard featuring a minus 20 windchill factor, but being a good shepherd I thought it prudent to take a quick barn tour before partying hardy. I had checked to see that the mangers were full and the hatches were battened down, when I heard a small high-pitched bleat from the back of the barn. There I found a ewe milling about a frost-encrusted newborn lamb.

Lambs were not scheduled to arrive so soon, but I vaguely remembered one early August day when the old ram had built up enough steam to leap the fence and join the ladies. Obviously, I did not catch him before at least one unscheduled romantic interlude occurred.

I tried rubbing Frosty the Snow Lamb with straw, but I could feel that he had already taken a powerful chilling. My trusty kettle was frozen solid, so a hot water bath was half an hour away. As quick as I could, I set him and his mother up in a portable pen with a heat lamp and I dashed back to the house through the swirling snow.

My guests were swinging by this time. As I slipped inside via the mud room, it occurred to me that they had not even paused to miss me. I sashayed into the bathroom and stuffed the hair dryer casually into one pocket and a hand towel into the other. My guests were having such a good time that they didn't even pause to question a hostess departing their midst with a small appliance protruding from one hip and bathroom linen from the other.

Back at the barn, the heat lamp was casting a warming glow and the ewe was licking the lamb to stimulate it. All the right things were happening, except now the frosted lamb was glazed with ice.

That's when I started blasting away with my trusty hair dryer, moving it in slow circles and rubbing the towel over the lamb. In about 10 minutes Frosty was dry, warm and eager to stand up and find the faucet of life. I gave the ewe some molasses water, warmed from the finally thawed kettle, daubed Frosty's umbilical cord with iodine and left them to get acquainted as ewe and lamb have done so well for thousands of years.

When I rejoined the party, no one even noticed the mild scent of *eau de sheep* on their smiling hostess.

Since then, the hair dryer has enjoyed its own peg on the barn wall. It has warmed countless lambs, thawed water pipes and pumps, and even blown-dry a few baby turkeys who were too stupid to come in out of the rain.

So frankly, when I visit a barn that doesn't have a hair dryer, I wonder what tools and appliances that farmer left home with.

HERE COMES THE JUDGE

I do not know who suggested that I judge the snowmobilers' chili contest, but if I ever find out my revenge will
be the reverse of the ancient Sicilian adage "Revenge is a
dish best served cold." Balderdash. My revenge will be
swift, and served hot, very hot, at least as hot as chili pot
Number I7.

There were twenty-eight Crock-Pots laden with chili
when I arrived at the tasting — nary a snowmobiler's helmet in sight. The jolly trailblazers were all out zooming
over their carefully groomed trails in packs that sounded
like a jet airplane accelerating down a twisted runway.

I was watching the chili co-ordinators connect a
dazzling array of extension cords and multi-plugs to the
Crock-Pots when my co-adjudicator arrived.

"Call me Ted," said the politician, who is the local
sitting Member of Provincial Parliament. Then he
promptly sat down.

I could understand why Ted had been anointed as a
chili judge. Community service is part of political life

and most of what politicians do involves bilious bursts of hot air and laying the blame on others.

I guess I was selected because everyone knows sheep hibernate for the winter and writers are always game for a free lunch. My only experience with snowmobiles ended decades earlier when the one I was a passenger on, an ancient Bombardier infernality, stopped dead in the middle of a frozen corn field — far, far away. Then and there, I took an oath that I would rather be stuck on a horse in a snowdrift any time. Unrelated, unprejudiced and able to swallow seemed to be the criteria for selecting me as a judge.

Fortunately, politicians are masters at these things. "Call-me-Ted" had obviously been to a few goat ropings. On top of first, second and third categories, he added three more potential vote getters — hottest, best looking, and most politically correct. We had two hours, four jugs of water and a box of unsalted crackers to get us through the job.

Each pot was numbered and the ingredients were carefully listed on the back. The organizers had specifically checked each entry to make sure that none of the ingredient lists contained subliminal messages, threats or specific pleas for consideration.

I did note that phrases such as "liberal sprinkling of" managed to compromise some of their best efforts. Ted agreed to ignore such self-defeating chicanery.

We started off on a lovely pot of chili — an ambrosia of beans and meat chunks in a sauce that clung to the wooden spoon with an easy grace. We swallowed. The finish of the chili had an appropriate rise in temperature that burst on the taste buds without damaging the will to continue. Ted gave me one of those "need we go on" looks. Nevertheless, we marked our scorecards rating the chili on a scale of one to five in categories ranging from texture to heat units.

And so it proceeded down the line. There were thick chilies and runny chilies. Chilies with chunks of tomatoes and chilies with catsup-flavoured sauce. Some had lots of meat, some had very little and a couple had no carne at all.

There were kidney beans, lima beans, pinto beans, chickpeas and baked beans from a tin. One chili even had noodles.

The spicing ranged from mild brown-sugar sweet to scorching. Ted and I learned to identify deadly hot jalapeno pepper pods. We wrapped them in our napkins when no one was looking, but there was no avoiding the soft-tissue damage inflicted by combinations of cayenne, Tabasco and some concoction called Dan T's Inferno. One chili had sweet pickle in it, another was adrift with baby corn cobs. Some had nuts. But the strangest chili of all was one that had sauerkraut as its secret ingredient. Cruel lot those snowmobiling enthusiasts.

We ended up awarding the grand prize to a chili that smelled darkly of beer. In fact, I think we only settled on it in the end because we were tired of swilling down chili with water.

Coincidentally — or not, perhaps — the winning chili was the masterwork of the town newspaper photographer, so Ted and I were guaranteed front page coverage.

The hottest chili was the two-alarm, arsonist's delight in Crock-Pot 17. It had a unique ability to cause the eyes to water and the toes to curl. The most beautiful was the first pot we gazed upon in all naiveté, and the most politically correct was vegetarian.

The snowmobilers arrived in time for the ceremony. I was slumped over a table covered with cracker crumbs, but Ted was still perky enough to pass comment on the great Canadian tradition of chili-making which unites our nation in both and several languages.

The aftermath of the judging was predictable enough. I am sure the house needed a new roof anyway. I will not be judging such contests in the near future, but I do have a better understanding of what fuels politicians to filibuster. And I will never again describe a cold day as — that word.

MAILBOX JUSTICE

When the township announced plans to widen the road in front of my farm so that it could accommodate two lanes of traffic comfortably, I just had one question.

"What happens to my mailbox?"

The box itself did not concern me, just the placement of its new post.

For many years, I have been lugging my mailbox up and down the lane way every day, setting it on its post an hour before Len the Mailman delivers and picking it up early in the afternoon.

This exercise was predicated by sporadic outbursts of mailbox murder. This is a ritual form of rural slaughter that often results in the residents of an entire concession awakening to find that their mailboxes have been bruised, battered or lopped off by young hooligans armed with baseball bats or tire irons.

As customs go, it is a primitive form of self-expression, which, I am led to understand, generally passes when the perpetrators master the art of shaving.

As crimes go, at least the immediate victim feels no pain. And the irritant to the owner is the same whether the fallen mailbox is the consequence of vandals or, as has happened far too often in my township, a snowplough operator runs amok in a new, unfamiliar machine.

However, there is something about mailbox murders that people take very personally. Firstly, the crime often tends to be a serial one. A dozen people along a single concession road may awake to the horror of felled mailboxes.

Secondly, mailboxes are alone and defenceless and, although we love them less when they hold bills, we cherish the notion far more than any urban-dweller of cheques in them and private missives from the loved or the long-lost. E-mail and voice mail will never replace the intimacy of real mail.

I have heard many a tale about mailboxes missing in action. In fact, you can usually count on a story about a mauled mailbox anytime you stand in line behind some beleaguered-looking person who is buying a new one. Usually, the story ends with some vigorous head-shaking and mumbled sentiments such as "and you know, they'll never catch the bastards."

(I know it is a sexist comment and politically incorrect but the country remains a stubborn bastion of reality-based sentiments. Recent studies have shown that most, if not all, mailbox murderers are adolescent males. There is something about the activity that seems to hold no appeal whatsoever for young women.)

When an evildoer gets caught, there is some satisfaction roundly felt by all who have shared the pain. Any person branded by such a crime would surely have to abandon their neighbourhood or pay a penance so public, the shame would melt his mother's heart.

So it was that a certain courtroom in a certain small town found itself more than half full of onlookers for the first time in anyone's memory.

The accused and a partner had apparently intended to steal a pickup truck from a farmer who they knew always left his keys in the ignition — not at all uncommon behaviour among farmers.

It was a dandy six-month-old, white king-cab, four-wheel-drive baby with four-on-the-floor and raised suspension.

The perpetrators had, in their fashion, thoroughly staked out the area and knew that every Thursday evening, the farmer and his wife attended church choir practice for several hours.

The farm was set back from the road, surrounded by trees, without a clear view of any neighbours.

The plan was for one of the scoundrels to drive the other to the foot of the lane, drop him off and park at the road's edge to watch for any ambient traffic.

Once the stolen truck was at the end of the laneway, the two of them would drive off and do whatever it is one does with a stolen truck.

Ultimately, the issue at trial had little to do with car theft, since the accused pleaded guilty. Stumbling along in the dark, the truck thief had managed to start the truck, but failed to calculate the treachery of the ice that lay under a few inches of fresh snow.

Perhaps nervous, or perhaps just stupid, he had gunned the spunky new truck down the lane with the lights off and ended up doing a doughnut that landed the vehicle squarely in the ditch.

His buddy dutifully drove over and turned on his truck lights to assess the situation. The fellow in the truck turned its lights on, too. Then he tried to gun the truck out of the ditch, and did it with such fervour that the forward thrust sent the truck skidding across the road, where he ran into the mailbox.

The hapless pair were attempting to dislodge the mailbox post from the truck's bumper when a neighbour happened onto the scene. Unfortunately for them, the neighbour also happened to be a cop.

Within the community, knowing the culprits as it did, guilt was presumed. So it came as no surprise that the truck theft charges went unchallenged.

However, to the amazement of all and sundry, when it came to the charge of property damage, the accused firmly responded, "Not guilty, Your Honour."

The prosecution's case seemed open and shut. Not only did they have an eyewitness, they also had Exhibit A, a green metal mailbox, bearing a mortal wound in its left side.

The defendant was representing himself, and the judge invited him to present his case.

"I've done some bad things, some real dumb things," admitted the accused, "but I swear, anything that happened to that mailbox was an accident, pure and simple. I am not the sort of person who whacks mailboxes. I stopped doing that when I turned 20."

In the after-court discussion at the coffee shop, it was generally agreed that the fellow was definitely an inept thief, but arguably not the kind of "so and so" who whacks mailboxes for fun.

The judge levied a fine instead of giving the guy hard time for the mailbox. Everyone agreed that a car thief would probably have an easier time in "The Big House" than somebody up for whacking mailboxes.

In the future, as in the past, victims of "battered mailbox syndrome," or BMS, as the resident experts have designated it, will be forced to live with a faceless enemy intent on destroying a container the size of a breadbox that is empty most of the time.

But even when the road in front of my farm is widened, even when it is paved and painted with a white line, even when the speed limit is raised by rote from 15 kilometres to 125, as appears to be inevitable if drivers' behaviour on the paved crossroads is any indication — making it impossible for anyone in the vehicle to even see a mailbox let alone whack it — I will not subject my old, battered, duct-taped mailbox to even the potential for irreparable harm.

Tucked safely under my arm, the box that has now served me faithfully for a record two and a half years, the fickle box that bears good news as stoically and indifferently as it does bills and flyers will serve its daily purpose and daily be returned to the safe harbour of my front porch.

Even though, from now on, I most certainly will have to look both ways before I cross the road to retrieve it.

JUST A PASSING WINDSTORM

On the farm lots of things happen that you tend not to discuss at the dining room table. I do not mean blood and guts stuff or digestion-inhibiting economic stuff — I just mean normal, biological, animal, vegetable and mineral stuff.

For instance, every so often I will cut the string off a bale of hay and find a dead snake that got stuck in the alfalfa as it passed through the baler.

Occasionally, rain water will somehow manage to seep into a barley bin and cause a fermenting process that turns it into the kind of mush that breweries distill. It sure stinks before it becomes beer.

While pigeons may create problems in urban areas when they unwittingly fertilize window ledges, farm animals also "go" where they live and the droppings of a half-ton horse are far more evident. Animals do not ask for permission and they are not shy about nature's call.

What brings me to this is a weekend visit by my Toronto lawyer, his wife and their children. It seems that the children, aged three and six years, had never been closer to farm animals than a television screen. As the visit progressed, I began to suspect that the same was true of the adults.

Although I always tell guests to dress casually for the farm and bring some old clothes if they want to feel comfortable in the barn, the allure of a "country" weekend seems to prompt urban folk to dress like British gentry rather than Canadian farmers. Fortunately, I have a stock of Wellington boots in various sizes for visitors, and the extremely active three-year-old male child was delighted to put on extra layers of socks so he could wear a bigger-sized boot.

There is this great thing that I do for city folk that drives them out of their minds. Long ago I developed a whistle call, based on the call of the killdeer. It is almost as haunting as a loon's cry.

From the empty barnyard I make my mournful whistle, and in the distance you can see the sheep and horses pull their heads up from the feeders in the snowy pastures and the next instant they are running joyfully toward the barn. City folks would not know it, but the animals come running because they are gluttons and they know their arrival at the barn means they will get a treat.

For my lawyer friend and his family, it seemed like some magical scene to watch the snow fly as the two palominos galloped in with their tails flying, while the sheep trailed after like so many white blips on a computer screen. Horses neigh and the kids scream. Sheep baa and the kids scream again. Geese honk and ducks quack, chickens cluck and fly off to their roosts. This I am used to. These are sounds I love.

But as fate would have it, at that exact moment of country frenzy, good old Ken "the Hooter" decided to roll up the lane on his tractor to deposit a big round bale of hay for the assorted livestock.

Hay deliveries drive my animals wild. Apparently tractors have the same effect on three-year-old male children from Toronto. The six-year-old female child clasped her hands to her ear muffs, finding the tractor noise quite impossible to deal with along with the rest of the racket.

"Hooter" made a suitable display of jockeying the tractor around the yard and slam-dunking the huge bale into a feeder. In reality he is a normal-sized man, but something about captaining a tractor allows him to masquerade in a larger persona. Shouting above the din, he proceeded to regale my guests with the challenges a man who has "been on the farm for 35 years" experiences trying to help a novice like me feed animals. "Hooter" left in a veil of snowflakes. The three-year-old thought he was a superhero.

By this time the animals were really revved up and they commenced doing what animals do when they are mildly excited. The sheep urinated, squatting neatly in no particular order. The horses entered into a magnificent display of spirited trotting, snorting and bucking which was accompanied by sporadic flatulence.

The little girl, who had obviously been conditioned to appreciate certain social graces, was appalled by the scene confronting her. Her brother, on the other hand, was thrilled to observe natural processes that television had failed to convey.

"Tooter, tooter," cried the young lad as the horses ran off to the back pasture farting in stereo.

I saw mother and daughter feeding a ewe some grain from a pail. The sheep stood back and chewed thoughtfully while they stroked her head. I cringed when I saw her stumpy tail raise for an emission. "Mom, I think the sheep just fluffied," said the girl, turning her head delicately.

I am sure that the parents were relieved when I suggested we retire to the kitchen for hot chocolate.

Dinner presented a few challenging moments. The three-year-old insisted on practising all of the farm animal sounds he had learned. His sister rolled her eyes and the parents shook their heads.

When I tell Ken that animals "tooter" and "fluffy" at the sight of him on the tractor, I can guarantee there will be a whole lot of hooting going on.

TREE THIEVES BEWARE— PALAMINO ON PATROL

Sometime soon the dogs and the horses and I will make the annual trek through the evergreens in search of the perfect Christmas tree. We will try to wait for a sunny day, with a few snowflakes falling and the kind of crisp snow that crunches underfoot.

I have a 20-acre field filled with thousands of evergreens that range from me-high to over two storeys tall. So it can take half a day to find the perfect conifer — the one that fills the living room and scrapes the ceiling so that the star on top bends sideways.

With red ribbons I mark eligible trees, but as we get to two or three, the horse and I make a few passes around each one, looking for bare spots and making judgements.

I cut my tree with a hand saw. Using a chain saw just would not seem fair to the tree or the tradition, and it might spook the rabbits. With a rope tied to the tree and anchored to the western saddle, old Lady and I will drag the tree home, with the dogs chasing behind.

If it sounds like something out of Currier and Ives, frankly it is.

My tree will not be the only one to leave the field. Although I am not in the Christmas-tree business, my neighbours, their friends, the local hockey team and a few church elders will all be driving up the lane with their saws and their toboggans and their kids to take a walk in the woods and find their "perfect tree."

When I am not around, I leave instructions on the front door. These are simple things like "cut your tree close to the ground, close the gate when you leave and have a Merry Christmas." Just below that I tack an envelope for donations so that I can keep replanting.

It warms the heart to come home from a day of shopping and find an envelope filled with money, along with little notes of thanks and the occasional crayon drawing of last year's Christmas tree from a child. Then there is the problem of the tree thieves.

Tree thieves do not respect signs. They do not pause to think about the damage they do to fences or the damage they do to trees. With thousands to choose from, it does not make much sense to scale a 20-foot tree only to lop off the top 6 feet — but I have seen it done.

It is not as though the tree thieves can't afford a tree from me — I am easy to negotiate with around Christmas. The local Food Bank knows that they have free access, no questions asked. I get so pink and squishy with the emotion of the season that I have even been known to cut and deliver for shut-ins.

But for the tree thieves in my neck of the woods, stealing a tree is also tradition.

I had this "tradition" explained to me in the local pub where all things are revealed, eventually.

"Don't ya know a tree is no good unless you steal it," a local golf course manager explained to me. He apparently had been stealing my trees for years and thought the trespass was a great game.

So I started the "tree patrol." I think the horse likes it more than I do. At random times of a weekend I slip on the bridle and we bareback to the fenceline, scattering pheasants as we canter.

The tree thieves are definitely surprised to be accosted in mid-hatchet-job by a mad woman on a charging palomino. I get all kinds of lame excuses like "I didn't know anyone owned this place" and "My friend said it was okay, his brother did this last year" and "We just thought we would take a look, but we found this one and liked it a lot. Who do I pay?"

It is Christmas after all, so I don't have the heart to call the authorities. Also, I have found that the first thing tree thieves do when confronted is reach for their wallet.

I enjoy knowing that Christmas trees from my farm are part of family festivities all over the township. The memories help in the spring when reforestation begins.

Still, the best part comes just before Christmas when the Food Bank gets a donation accumulated from the tree thieves.

It is enough to make a palomino smile.

THE MOMENT OF REALIZATION

In the country, community is a loosely defined term that starts with family and tends to spread itself around through a network of marriages, friendships and other relationships. When a stranger enters that environment, there is an uneasiness on both sides that only time and curiosity and the same sort of ritual sniffing that dogs partake of can overcome.

I do not know exactly when the community I live in accepted me as part of its fabric, but there was one epiphanic moment when I knew that I was home.

It happened a few years after I moved to the farm. I was still struggling to figure out who was who and what was where in my immediate neighbourhood. Making friends was not easy without the social life of a job, and so many things always seemed such a long drive away. In my first year I signed up for a water aerobics class a full township away. Everyone in my class was a good quarter-century older than I was and the sessions were more like Beginners Whirlpool than exercise. No one would talk to me because I was young enough to be their daughter, but I was nobody's daughter and I was from "away."

I mentioned this to my neighbour Gerry one day. Geraldine is a private sort of woman. Her husband, Jack, had been blowing the snow out of the lane for two full years before we met and discovered we were related. They had stopped in for Christmas tea and Gerry kept saying there was something awfully familiar about me. But they were pig farmers and they hardly ever went to the city, so we could not figure out what sort of sherry Gerry was sipping. But when she got home, Gerry found me in the family photo album.

I was about ten years old and I was standing in a cemetery. It turned out that my paternal grandfather, Harry, had married Jack's widowed mother, Edith, in their Golden Years. They had lived briefly in the town of Mount Forest until Edith's death. I remembered Grand-dad's wedding to a woman who smelled of lavender, and I sort of recalled driving for endless hours to visit them in a little town with one grocery store where people dressed in black and tied up their horses and buggies in the parking lot. All I recalled about the funeral was thinking it quite strange that anyone would want to take pictures, but I did not mention that.

Somehow, that vague connection made me close to being family. Gerry asked me if I would like to join the women's bowling league.

"Long as you don't mind losing, that is," she said.

Well, I never thought that I would find myself wearing shoes previously worn by others, but Wednesday at the bowling alley turned out to be a hoot. Our team was the Try Hards — and we did — but no one took it seriously. We played the five-pin game, not because we thought the big balls were for men, but rather because it was easier. There were young mothers playing with their mothers, middle-agers playing with their high-school chums and enough carbonated oldsters to keep things lively.

I stayed quiet the first half of the year, conversation being difficult at best in a bowling alley. But I picked up shreds of conversation and I learned about things that were going on — difficult births, mumps in the Grade Five class, anniversary socials for people celebrating fifty years of wedlock even though they had not spoken to each other for a decade — that sort of thing.

Then my doctor called me one Wednesday morning and confirmed my worst fears. I would need to have surgery for the removal of an early form of cancer.

"No big deal," my doctor said, "two or three days in hospital. You'll be back for Christmas."

So I had to tell my team that I would not be attending the bowling league Christmas party. They already knew something was wrong because I did not do a little dance when I bowled a strike. And they agreed with me that the C word was a very big deal, no matter how nascent. I had hugs and promises that they would freeze me a piece of cake.

The dawn of the day I was to go into the hospital was as grim as my mood. Worse, when I turned on the water tap, there was nothing but a sputter of air. My step-uncle Jack was blowing the snow from the lane when he spotted me leaving the shed where the well pump lives.

"Trouble?" he asked. I told him there was and he had a look.

Diagnosis: "Pipe's broke underground somewhere between the pump and the house. She's going to have to be dug up and replaced. Pipe'll be five or six feet down."

I had six hours to get it done, if I could find a plumber who was available four days before Christmas. And a backhoe operator and an electrician and anyone else who might be needed.

I started with the plumber. Busy signals, nothing but busy signals. When I finally got through and stammered out my explanation of things as I understood them, he asked me again, "And your name is?"

He repeated it slowly as I spelled it out. Then I heard a familiar voice in the background. It was his wife, the shyest Try Hard on the team, but I could hear her bellowing.

"You get out there right now, Marsha needs to have water, today, man." Then she came on the line and in her shy voice said, "Don't worry, he's coming right now."

Uncle Jack called to say that he was on his way over to Elmer's to help boost the backhoe. My next call was to Clarence the electrician, but he was already en route, courtesy of his wife Helen, the strikes-and-spares queen of the Try Hards. Word was spreading through the bowling league faster than a greased gutter ball.

Trucks and machinery started rolling up the laneway. There were people I knew and people I had never seen before. There were Mennonites with their lunches neatly packed in six-quart baskets and ladies carrying industrial-sized coffee percolators. Once the backhoe broke the frozen ground, a trench half as long as a hockey rink snaked from the house to the little metal shed housing the pump. Men jumped in and the shovel work began. It looked like a scene out of World War I.

By the time I left for the bus, a party atmosphere had taken hold. Kids were ferrying coffee to the workers and women were making sandwiches in an assembly line. I stood at the edge of the trench and shouted my thanks. Ken "the Hooter" Houston looked up at me, grinning, with mud glued to the stubble of his beard.

"And I thought I was just coming over to throw a few bales of hay at the sheep while you were off galavantin' in "the Big Smoke," he shouted.

"Git, girl," said Clarence. "If you don't make that bus, Helen will have my hide."

I returned to the farm two days later. The doctor was right, no big deal. On the kitchen table I found bowls of nuts and candies. Elmer's wife, Betty, sent a decorated fruit basket with a bottle of ginger ale wrapped in foil. Under the sheep fridge magnet, there were instructions about casseroles and pies in the freezer. Someone had tied a big red bow around the kitchen tap.

The note said, *"We always try harder. Welcome home."*

WHAT MY TRUE LOVE
HATCHED FOR ME

According to the song, on the third day of Christmas my true love should have given to me "three French hens," but instead he came up with three West African guinea hens that celebrated the season by chirping away under a heat lamp in the basement.

The week-old balls of brownish fluff and squawk look like a cross between a chicken and a pheasant. They run around their pen like mad, cocking their heads to catch a side view of the world and singing together at the oddest hours of the day or night.

The guineas in the basement came to be because "True Love" found a nest of guinea eggs hidden in the brush near a cluster of cedar bushes during a mild-weather patch in November. No one knows why my few guinea hens decided to go broody and lay a clutch of eggs when frost was threatening, but they did.

The hens were not sitting on the eggs, just sort of laying them and hanging around them and wandering off. There were six brown speckled eggs in the nest when we found them. Having no idea how long they had been exposed to the elements, my inclination was to leave them be or throw them away. But my true love would have nothing to do with that. He fetched the incubator and placed the little eggs tenderly in its care.

Guinea eggs are smaller than regular chicken eggs, but they take a few days longer to hatch. By the time the prescribed 28 days had elapsed, the man in my life seemed to be spending half of his day peering through the glass-topped incubator for signs of life.

"Number three is rocking," he announced with glee. But I put it down to too much time wishfully thinking that an egg would hatch.

"Number five is peeping," he advised me a few minutes later. But I put that down to the chronic squeak in the floorboards.

Not to say that eggs don't rock and chicks don't peep before they actually hatch. They do. Sometimes, before a chick hatches out of the egg or even makes the first nick in the side of the shell to let you know that it's going to hatch, you can actually hear the little birds peeping away inside their shells. And while the chick is actively pushing and poking to find the way out of the egg, it does often set the egg into a kind of rock-and-roll motion with its efforts.

Just in case he was not a victim of a cruel imagination, we moved the eggs to a hatching tray.

Not half an hour later, the first baby guinea popped out of its egg, splitting the shell into two neat little pieces. Within an hour, two more had joined it and they were drying off nicely in the incubator, peeping like mad to find out what life is like beyond the egg.

I always feel some moment of tragedy when I take a chick out from the incubator. Here is a newborn thing with all the natural expectations of being mothered. But instead of downy feathers to hide under and the cooing of a mother hen to comfort it, a big human hand scoops it up and plops it in some wood shavings with some water and some food and a bright light over its tiny head. Other similarly confused chicks soon join the first hatchling, and they start to figure out basic things like eating and drinking together. But they have no role model to follow, just a big hand that intrudes on their space now and then to replenish their bowls, and a big featherless face that looks at them through Plexi-glass and makes cooing sounds that don't sound at all like a maternal fowl.

The miracle of the Christmas guineas is that they hatched at all. Somehow, despite their fickle mothers and the vagaries of nature that should have stopped them dead in the yolk, they found a mentor who believed in them — a father hen, if you will.

The little dickens doubled in size in just a week, and developed tufts of feathers on their wings and tails. While their parents have dark grey feathers flecked with pearl-coloured spots and funny sort of purple helmets instead of feathers on their head, the baby guineas, who are called "keets," take at least a month before they begin to look like the birds they will become.

My true love, of course, is spectacularly thrilled with his little ones.

When he pokes his burly hand into their warm little brooding box, they crowd around it and poke him with their inquisitive beaks. He has hung a straw doll ornament intended for the Christmas tree in their nest area so they have something to play with. He shreds lettuce leaves into fine strips to make sure they get all of the vitamins they need. And instead of cooing at them, he makes appropriate guinea fowl sounds, which amount to a sort of sporadic, high-pitched repetition of the word "buckwheat."

Now I am on the look-out. After the three West African guinea fowl, it wouldn't surprise me to see a partridge take roost in the old pear tree.

DON'T WAIT UNTIL DARK

Living in the county during the winter also means living in a state of constant preparedness. One toque, one scarf, one set of mitts is never enough. There always has to be backup that is accessible — and dry. On a really ugly, soggy-snow day this can mean as many as three full changes of clothing, right down to the long johns. After a while, you start to feel like a giant baby.

Trucks and machinery need to have jumper cables and battery chargers at the ready. Logging chains become a standard piece of equipment to carry around in case someone needs a tow. And a big margarine bucket full of wood ashes comes in awfully handy when the old tires start spinning on ice. As long as there is room in the back of the truck for the dog and the groceries you know that you have not overdone it. I even find that the dog enjoys resting her head on the ancient Sesame Street sleeping bag I keep rolled up behind the truck seat — just in case.

Better to err on the side of preparedness is also true in the farm house, particularly when it comes to provisions and batteries. I have never been through a winter without at least one sustained power failure that threatens to wreak havoc on everything except the contents of the freezer.

The power usually fails after dark without warning. It never happens at a convenient time. For instance, one minute you are standing in the shower, beginning to rinse the shampoo out of your hair and, bingo, all of a sudden the water stops flowing and you are in the dark dripping bubbles. So you stumble carefully out and begin reaching for the towels that should be handy and you end up wrapping your head in the clean sweatshirt you brought to change into. A hand towel is usually the only thing that seems available for dabbing the remaining wet bits.

First errors aside, even the most lowly apprentice in the business of managing a power outage learns that at least one flashlight must always be stored in a hallowed place where it can be found without mishap. It should not be buried underneath the screwdrivers in the third drawer down in the kitchen. It should not be mounted on a wall with kitchen pots and pans, whose handles could be confused leaving you trying to find a switch on a wok in the dark. It should not be left anywhere near the television gizmo which is chronically missing in action. Instead, at least one flashlight with working batteries should be mounted permanently somewhere convenient to available candlesticks and communications devices — say above, below or beside the telephone in the kitchen, provided said telephone is not a travelling model.

This is all well and good, but unless one retains the control learned in military or reform school, it is difficult to enforce. So I always try to make sure that I know where last summer's barbecue lighter is situated, since it is not prone to temporary borrowing and provides just enough light to find a candle and light it.

I always keep three candles on the kitchen table. It looks kind of romantic, as though every dinner could be a candlelit rendezvous. Once I have them lit, visual sanity can prevail and permit a search for additional sources of light.

Living with power failures also makes you into a flashlight fanatic. Not for the little, two D-cell models, either. I like those flashlights that have snaky cords that you can wrap around things. I have flashlights with long incandescent bulbs that you can hang from coffee-cup hooks. If I need to light up the barnyard, there is a halogen light that plugs into the truck cigarette lighter and floods the yard like a movie set.

There are portable flashlights you can strap to your head, and mini-flashlights that you can attach to reading material. And it never hurts to keep a strand of battery-operated Christmas lights handy for general ambiance. One of my summer-use flashlights even has a built-in bug zapper. If you sit close enough to it, no creepy-crawly, winged things can get you.

Once you have light, ascertaining the magnitude of the hydro failure becomes a priority. Neighbours call neighbours, always with some trepidation since there is always the possibility that the Hydro Grinch has decided that the "cheque-that-is-in-the-mail" is long overdue, so they have arbitrarily pulled the plug. Anytime such an outrage occurs, there is plenty of shed talk about solar power and harnessing the energy of the underground springs to generate our own power and watch the hydro meters run backward for a while.

When a local outage is confirmed, I do what all my neighbours do. We head outside to see if we can spot the local "town" lights glowing in the distant sky. If there are no lights in town, it could be a long outage. The prospect of a long outage seems to have a direct effect on the bladder, which causes a panic in lavatories all over the county.

You see, in the country your water generally comes from a well, and the pump that brings that water to the house (and the loo) is powered by electricity. Hence, a long outage means that if you are caught in mid-shampoo that shampoo is going to harden dry before you can get it rinsed and that one flush that is left in the toilet has got to count.

Everyone tries calling the hydro company, but there is absolutely no point since the lines are always jammed. If you ever do manage to get a live voice on the other end of the line, all you will learn is that "trucks have been dispatched." You will never be told why trucks are needed or where they have been dispatched to or from. Apparently, the idea that there are "trucks" out there is somehow supposed to be a comfort while you slowly freeze and starve in the dark.

Large farming operations often have gas-powered generators to keep things going. Newborn piglets do not have much except the hair on their chinny-chin-chins to keep them warm, so heat lamps are essential.

Cooped-up chickens need warmth and light to keep their egg production to the maximum. And anyone incubating thousand-dollar ostrich eggs wants to keep those giant babies nice and warm.

But sheep do not fret much about hydro, and simple shepherds like me can usually manage in the dark for a few hours until the trucks work their magic.

This is where a wood-burning stove comes in handy. Candles, oil lamps and the crackle and glow from a wood stove create a homespun atmosphere. Until you find the batteries to fire up the transistor radio, it is about as close as you can get to life in pioneer times.

A good iron pot or frying pan is all you need to create a storm-stayed evening meal — canned corned beef with home fries, and scrambled eggs with a tin of baked beans. Something about it feels like chuckwagon swill.

Once you get into the spirit of a power failure, it does not seem like a failure at all. Without the use of a television and a VCR, conversation picks up. Half-read books find their way to the best lit spot in the house and the lovely tradition of reading makes a comeback. Neighbours phone neighbours with outage updates and rumours. If a hydro truck is spotted on the road, it is news that is passed from lip to ear without virtue of a Web site.

The hydro usually comes on halfway through some intensely pleasurable, after-dinner outage diversion. Suddenly candles seem redundant. Overhead lights glare and digital clocks flash impatiently while five CDs try playing at once. Immediately, there is a scramble to turn things off that were left on and to turn things on that were turned off. With each outage, a new instruction in "preparedness" presents itself. One year it may be a reminder to stock a few gallon jugs of water in the basement so that toilet flushing can be managed without trauma. Another year it may be a reminder to keep a manual can opener in stock because fancy electric ones will not open a tin of beans during an outage. Maintaining a stockpile of batteries starts to become as automatic as drying your toque.

SANTA CLAUS
IS COMING TO TOWN

Somewhere in a huge warehouse in Toronto busy gnomes spend months getting ready for the Santa Claus parade. Precision marching bands drill for hours practising those old familiar tunes, and the search goes out to find persons unknown to dress up as clowns that can walk on their hands for the entire parade route.

But the world doesn't stop or start in Toronto, and neither do Santa Claus parades.

In storage sheds and machinery shops all over the rural countryside, Santa Claus parade stuff happens at a furious pace. I know because I've been called upon to donate some old chicken wire and a bag of wool for a top-secret project that I suspect involves some sort of snow-man.

Every year "Grandpa" Bill, who lives alone on Side-road One, spends months working with a dedicated crew on the float to end all floats. Early in December, it will roll down Main Street with a variety of other homemade concoctions pulled by tractors and pick-up trucks and teams of horses in jingle bell harnesses.

Anybody can enter small-town parades — and whole families do just that. You can bet that in some hay loft in the vicinity, a few generations are collaborating on transforming a hay wagon into a thing of beauty that will feature everyone from great-grandmother to the latest grandchild in a warmth of evergreen boughs and toboggans decorated with big red ribbons.

And somebody is sure to come up with a big old St. Bernard or Newfoundland dog, sporting a red plastic nose and flannelette reindeer ears.

Last year three police cruisers and four fire trucks made it into the parade. And there are always a few antique tractors decorated with flashing lights, and an assembly of classic old cars carrying folks dressed up like something out of Charles Dickens's *A Christmas Carol*. School bands and pipe bands join in the chorus, and mini-majorettes twirl their stuff in the frosty night air. The Kinsmen, the Lions, the Oddfellows and the Women's Institute all join in to create some sort of tribute to Christmas.

The clowns may not walk on their hands, but they do shake hands — and if you look real close you might just find that the person behind the greasepaint is anyone from your plumber to your chiropractor. Candies are tossed from each passing float, and kids scramble and squeal with delight.

If it sounds unsophisticated, it isn't.

Just consider what Grandpa Bill and company have to go through to make it to the parade on time.

First comes the concept. One year the parade theme was "Christmas Is for Kids," and it worked so well that the parade committee decided to stick with it.

The hay wagon route is too mundane for Bill. The float he works on involves the developmentally challenged, so he likes to make the float itself a challenge — complete with lights, music and moving mechanical parts.

Last year this involved life-sized, dancing marionettes. Another year it was skaters rotating on a turntable; the year before that, a toy tower that spun around. Accomplishing this involves a lot of mechanical ingenuity, not to mention power generators and batteries.

This year Bill and crew are launching an aircraft float. The wings are welded out of scrap metal from an old grain bin and the hull is crafted from a discarded water-heater tank. The plane rocks and rolls courtesy of the hydraulics from a gadget that normally moves bales of hay into barns, and the nose propeller spins courtesy of a 12-volt battery. The "pilot" even gets to ride in comfort, on the padded seat of an ancient riding lawnmower.

After six men mount this assemblage on a trailer, the lights are carefully strung. Although it will stretch the budget, the plan this year is for "chasing lights" that zap around in sequence, giving a psychedelic effect while the speakers blare out Burl Ives singing "Have a Holly Jolly Christmas."

In the cockpit, some brave soul dressed as Charlie Brown's dog Snoopy will be dipping and diving and tossing out lollipops. Who knows, at the end of the parade they may win a prize. At the very least, they will get their picture in the local newspaper.

While a million people may see Toronto's Santa Claus parade, only a few hundred will line the Main Street in town to catch the spirit and wave to Santa as he winds up the parade in a flurry of "Ho-ho-hos."

Frankly, I don't think little kids see much difference. And for the bigger kids, there is always the fun of watching your local butcher dressed up like a jack-in-the-box, or your bank manager portraying the back end of a reindeer.

Those huge floats may fill the downtown streets with glitter and glam to draw the mongrel hordes directly into the prime shopping districts. But the sight of a full team of Percheron horses prancing in their jingle bells and pulling a wagonload of kids posing in the nativity scene does a lot more to fill me with Christmas spirit.

OF CHRISTMAS TREES
AND MEMORIES

When I first moved to the farm, there was a twenty-acre field that had been planted with white pine and spruce trees in neat rows. They were only about three feet tall, and it was hard to see them at times because leafy stands of Queen Anne's lace and Canada thistle could dwarf them. So that first Christmas, I scouted the fence row until I found a scraggly wild pine that was taller than me.

It took a few years, but the sheep managed to graze their way through the evergreen rows and nibble out the weeds, fertilizing as they went. There were great advantages to this, since I was teaching a young horse to neck-rein Western style and rows of trees were a natural training arena.

In the spring, the horse and I would wind our way through every other row of trees. Along the way, I would "candle" some of the trees, grabbing the shiny new growth at the end of the boughs and twisting off the soft evergreen ends so that the following year the new growth would be bushy — like a Christmas tree.

After a few years, the trees started growing grandly — tens of thousands of them. The Kinsmen and the Boy Scouts took hundreds off my hands, thinning them as they needed to be and raising money for their projects by selling them at supermarket lots. Neighbours, friends, church groups and passers-by drove up the lane and scouted the field for the perfect tree.

Still, there was always one man who came out every year with his little grandson and they would trudge off — hatchet in hand — to find a tree. But they could never seem to find one that suited them, so they packed up and left.

The problem is that Christmas trees that have not been picked for Christmas keep growing. So after almost twenty years on the farm, I find myself with a wondrous field of two- and three-storey-tall trees which looks more like Temagami than a neatly tended Christmas tree plantation.

People still slog through the bush looking for little ones. Sometimes they find one. And sometimes they let the Paul Bunyan in them come out and cut down a huge tree taking only the topmost part. Come spring, I always have a pile of Christmas tree bottoms to shred into wood chips for the garden.

I can always find a tree that suits me, even if it needs a bit of trimming. It might take days, but the horse and I will wander through the field dodging branches until one particular conifer catches our eye. Sometimes the sheep follow us, for no apparent reason other than curiosity. The final tree is always impossibly big, majestic, round on all sides — and heavy as all get-out to drag through the snow.

Years ago, the smaller trees could come through the front door of the house and be manoeuvred into position against the fifteen-foot-high brick walls of the living room. But as the trees grew, so did the dilemma of getting the tree through the door.

In recent years, the logistics have become impossible. So I have taken to bringing the tree into the house through the back way. This painstaking exercise involves removing an entire picture window and balancing the tree on a picnic table before it is gradually inserted and propped upright through a series of ropes and human willpower.

I was contemplating the calories this would burn up when a city friend called to ask how things were going. Nancy and her husband, Geoff, have three young children and a small house. The idea of such a huge tree seemed fantastical.

"How on earth do you decorate it?" she asked.

So I told her about using the extension ladder to install the star at the top. The lights, all 550 of them, sort of drape over the top and all the way down, followed by the ornaments. A collection of antiques, kitsch and baubles that all seem to have a memory behind them are hooked on at random, like the icicles that add the final shimmer. Then I offered the notion that I might not do it again. Maybe, I thought, it was time to give the Boy Scouts and the Kinsmen their chance to sell me a little tree.

Perhaps, I sounded weary. Perhaps, I was thinking about the way the hydro meter would start spinning around as soon as I plugged the tree lights in. Or perhaps, I had forgotten how wondrous a Christmas tree can be. Nancy with the laughing eyes would hear none of that. Her kids had never had a big tree to decorate. They could be the ornament elves. Together, we agreed we would lead the horse and the sheep into the forest and see what we could find.

I rearranged the furniture, so that a whole third of the room was ready to be covered in tree. Boxes of ornaments lined one wall, although I always know the exact location of the purple glass balls that my Aunt Jean gave me. They were wrapped in tissue right above the hanging musical Elvis. The 1993 World Series Blue Jays commemorative ornament was mixed in with ceramic Santa Clauses, shiny balls, plastic apples and the wooden sled ornament on which I painted the name "Rosebud." I love the stuffed penguins that have to be wired to each branch, and Snow White and her Seven Dwarfs — and even the Miss Piggy ornament that I bought on sale at the drug store.

There is nothing Martha-Stewart-correct about my Christmas tree, but it is the kind of tree that grows on you. The kids — Aurora, Olivia and Anna — swarmed the branches, hooking on ornaments and reaching deep into the tree to hide painted pine cones. All of the candy canes were placed within easy child reach. It was their tree, too, and that made it the best tree of all.

A few days after the tree decorating, a teenaged boy came to the door. Something about him looked awfully familiar. He told me that he used to come to the farm when he was a kid, with his grandfather. They were the pair who could never find a Christmas tree. He laughed with me over that one.

His grandfather was dead now, the young man explained. And the reason that they never cut down a tree was that his grandmother had terrible allergies. Now she was gone, too.

"Could I take a walk through the trees?" he asked. And that was all right with me.

I watched him walk off into the forest of Christmases past to commune with his memories, and I realized that the gift of a grandfather — of time spent in the woods, out of the pure spirit of caring — was a larger and brighter memory than any Christmas tree could ever be.

THE SHEPHERD IN WINTER

Some animals handle cold weather better than others, and that includes human animals. Given a choice, I find that my horses prefer to spend their days outside, unless the wind is particularly vicious. I can be freezing, but they will be happily rolling in the snow.

By mid-winter, the sheep are wearing five inches of wool. Unless there is a blizzard, the barn door is open and they are free to wander in the fields if they choose. Snow can blanket them and they do not even try to shake it off. If you dig your hand down to their soft pink skin, it is as warm as toast.

My fifteen-year-old barn cat, Webster, spends every winter night snoozing on the back of his favourite old ewe. Neither the cat nor the ewe ever so much as sneeze all winter long. And when there is a touch of a thaw on the pond, the geese are on it like a flash, swimming around like happy polar bears.

In the meantime, if my mitten gets so much as damp, my hand feels like it's stuck in an ice-cream sandwich. If

I do not wear two or three layers of socks my barn boots are perilously loose.

One blustery day, I was casually tossing flakes of hay into the feeders, when I noticed a ewe standing back from the manger while the rest chewed with a vengeance. Then I saw something small and black near her side, which I assumed to be Webster the Cat just waking up. But when it cried out in a high voice — a sound just like a baby wailing "Ma" — I knew it was a lamb.

Further inspection revealed it to be a female lamb, just hours old. She was dry, fed, warm and bright-eyed. The temperature transition from womb to barn must have been extreme; no one seemed worse for the wear.

I put the pair in a pen and the lamb curled up beside her mother in the straw to have a snooze without so much as a shiver. Transmogrification being what it is, I was tempted to run to the house to make her a hot water bottle to sleep with. But, unlike me, the lamb was thriving with just a simple layer of natural wool to keep out the cold; adding heat would just upset the balance of what nature had her prepared for.

The first time I had lambs born in the winter, I felt so sorry for them that I dashed off to the local thrift store and bought a stockpile of infant undershirts. I had outfitted about a dozen lambs in striped pullovers and pyjama tops imprinted with teddy bears when a local farmer stopped by and put an end to my foolishness.

"If they were meant to come with a suitcase full of clothes, they'd come that way," he announced. "What do you think they have wool for, anyway?"

Although the new ewe lamb adapted with ease, I considered her to be an accident. A good shepherd should have a management plan, and mine was to avoid sub-zero lambing — for the good of my own health. I went back to my warm kitchen to blow my nose and check my diary. Sure enough, on or about August the 20th for one brief but seminal moment, the ram had managed to escape from isolation. Obviously, his mission was romance.

I spent that afternoon on my hands and knees checking udders. In the event that the ram had managed to commit bigamy or polygamy, I wanted to be ready. Sheep cannot kick sideways the way a steer can and they do not pack nearly the wallop of a horse's hoof, but they will not line up quietly like dairy cows to have their udders fondled. Instead, they must be coerced into a narrow alleyway where they can be isolated briefly for purposes of medication or, in my case, palpitation.

Every once in a while, one would give a little jump and I would apologize while warming my frosty hands in my mitts for the next one. The only time I came in contact with anything unusual was when the ram slipped through. Oops. He did not like that much.

From the feel of things, it was apparent that only one accident had occurred.

Every time I see the ewe lamb running circles around her mother, I should be reminded of my failure to conduct myself as a proper shepherd and stick to my management plan to have lambs born in April.

Instead, I find myself spending a bit more time in the barn every day — watching her play, and checking to make sure she is settled and comfy when the wind howls at night. Webster sometimes curls up with her or sleeps on top of her mother. No duvets, no fossil fuels, no chicken soup required.

Even in the dead of winter, nature knows best how to take care of its own.

WAINSCOTING
OF MANY COLOURS

There must have been a big sale on green paint sometime during the past century. Not deep forest green or velvety emerald green, but rather a dull cross between minty and putrid green.

At least that is one of the many shades of paint I discovered when I spent one winter stripping the wainscoting and wood trim in the kitchen of my old farmhouse.

Two townships away, the same shade of green showed up when a friend did some renovating. Just about everyone I have ever talked to about the original colours they discovered after buying a Victorian country home has some recollection of stripping or painting over this exasperating shade of green.

My house was in pretty good shape when I found it. Nothing that a few gallons of white paint couldn't cure temporarily while the basic necessities of sheep farming were attended to. So while many of my urban friends were concentrating their efforts on installing jacuzzis and Italian kitchens, I was working on fencelines and sheep sheds.

I am glad that I did not make any sudden changes to the old house. Living in it for a while gave me a chance to appreciate its past. It was built sometime in the mid-1880s with the yellow bricks that were the pride of a long-departed brickyard a few kilometres away. After I had learned something about the families who had lived here, the children who were born here and the lively euchre games that had taken place in the parlour, the house came to remind me of a canvas on which other people had been designing, painting and wallpapering for a century before I arrived.

Any tinkering I do within these walls will end up being a message of some sort for future occupants. The marks I make on the house, just like the job of husbandry I make of the fields around it, become a part of a transformation that involves the history of all of us who have lived here.

This hefty, if somewhat sentimental, responsibility does not preoccupy me when I select new paint for a bedroom. However, there are elements of sincere craftsmanship that have gone into the old house and I want to maintain that integrity.

It was the integrity of the house that I had in mind one snowy day when I started to strip the kitchen wainscoting. In my experience these sorts of projects tend to start out small, and then take on a monstrous, never-ending quality. I found a tin of stripper and decided to find out what was underneath the dark brown paint around a door frame.

I uncovered faded yellow paint and some sort of cream-coloured paint before arriving at the dreaded green, but finally the wood was bare. It was a beautiful buttery oak, along with mixtures of other softer woods that had all grown in local woodlots over one hundred years ago.

The stripping chore took an entire winter, progressing inch by inch. It was a rubber-glove job that saw many pairs of gloves dissolve into gummy masses from the chemical stripper. All manner of tools were involved, including a kitchen sugar spoon that proved to be the perfect size to scrape between wainscoting boards.

You don't have to be a brain surgeon to strip wood. There is a certain skill in retaining the natural patina and texture of the wood without leaving it dry and raw, but other than that, simple patience and dogged determination seem to be all that is required. The greatest reward is living with the results.

So I was fairly taken aback when an interior designer acquaintance from the big city schmoozed into my kitchen one fine day and pronounced it to be a room "with a lot of potential."

Along with modern laminated cupboards and halogen light fixtures that look like aircraft, the designer envisioned "pickling the wood trim black to tie the whole room together."

At that point, I could easily have tied the designer up and installed him in a vat of brine.

As long as I am the custodian of this house, it will be proud of its age and happy to reflect its history without a lot of cosmetic surgery. The wainscoting will remain as naked as the trees from which it hailed. And for the sake of future generations, I will never buy green paint on sale.

THE TOLL GATE CHRISTMAS

Before he even asked them to Christmas supper in July, most people in Northcote already held that Old Jim was crazy.

"Just telling you, is all," Jim would say. "Christmas supper at my place. You're invited. All the trimmings. Gonna grow it all myself."

It was the longest speech that anyone had heard Old Jim give in years.

He lived in a squat stone house down at the edge of the village in a small-windowed structure known locally as "The Toll Gate" because about a hundred and fifty years earlier it had been the residence of the roads dues collector.

Jim kept to himself in the cool darkness of the Toll Gate, and he expected everyone else to mind his privacy. Only the bravest of children ever tried to take a short-cut across Jim's garden to the river.

"Hey, you there," he would shout from behind a cedar thicket. "There's a toll for crossing my land, and I'll have it out of your hide with my musket if you aren't gone by the time I count to ten."

By the time Jim got to "five" the intruders were breathless, past a raspberry patch that marked the property line. No one ever saw the actual musket. Someone heard that a newcomer woman from the subdivision, by the east side of the Northcote, had once knocked on Old Jim's door and told him that he should not be threatening children with firearms. She would report him to the authorities if he ever did it again. Jim swept her off the porch with a broom and told her she'd get hers if she ever set foot on his property again.

To most, he was just a harmless hermit. Picked up his pension cheque as regular as clockwork at the General Store post office. Always paid cash. Took the bus to the farmers' market every other Saturday and brought home whatever he bought in a heavy brown satchel that looked like it had been through the war.

Before Mother Purdie went into the nursing home, she told her son, John Purdie Jr., who everyone just called "Junior," that Jim had been a soldier once. That was why he sometimes dragged his left leg. Shrapnel shifting in his knee. Junior was also told that Jim had even won some medals.

Jim never took a wife. He worked at the feed mill, in the back-shed dust of the granary, until the day his pension kicked in. Then he limped down the hill to the Toll Gate house and slammed the door. A whole generation of villagers grew up after that and not one of them ever saw the inside of the tight, square building where the hermit lived.

Only eight of Northcote's "Old Guard" were invited for Christmas dinner at Old Jim's. Far from feeling snubbed, the rest were relieved.

Christmas in Northcote was always a family affair. People didn't leave Northcote for Christmas, they had relatives and friends come. Washed in snow, Northcote was a postcard from Currier & Ives — the snug gingerbread houses trimmed with holly and cedar boughs, snowmen in the front yards, toboggans stacked at the side door and skating parties with carollers in the Northcote pavilion.

In the evening, Northcoters retired quietly to home and hearth for their private meal and merriment. They did not abandon ship and crowd into a virtual stranger's house for no apparent reason except an invitation.

In August, a delivery van was spotted in the Toll Gate lane. Katie Purdie, Junior's 11-year-old, peeked through the raspberry bushes and saw Old Jim burning two huge cardboard boxes in his backyard fire pit. The next day, Will, the scrap dealer from Glengate, hauled an ancient Fridgidaire and a two-burner stove off old Jim's front porch.

Amelia Fudger waved at Jim as he lurched toward the General Store to pick up his pension cheque the next Tuesday. Her husband, Tom, had been so surprised when Jim actually talked to him in July that it wasn't until Jim was half a block away that he realized Jim had invited them for Christmas dinner. Amelia had been apoplectic.

Before she had a chance to burble something she had carefully scripted about having to go to the mother-in-law's that Christmas, family illness, could be the last time, grandkids coming from all over, so sorry, maybe next year . . . Jim was looking her square in the face.

"I'll be breaking in the new oven this week," said Jim. "Getting the kinks worked, figuring out the dials and such like. The turkey's at the Welch Farm. Say he's about six pounds now. I give them five dollars a week for feed. He'll be 25 pounds by Christmas the way I'm having him grown. Forward to seein' you, Mrs. Fudger."

He was past the picket fence and across the road before Amelia could speak.

"Well, I just wanted to let you know Tom's mother is sick," she called out.

"Sorry to hear that," said Jim, without turning his head her way.

That evening, Amelia and Tom invited the other six invitees to a Friday-night backyard barbecue to discuss the situation.

On Thursday, Lovett Allen saw Old Jim hauling something in big white pails up from the swamp bush near the river bend. Lovett had barely nodded at Old Jim before he and his wife, Wendy, were invited to the Christmas dinner. Now he was pulling his car over to the roadside to offer Jim a lift.

"Don't bother me none to carry some good black swamp dirt," Jim said, and he just kept walking. "It'll be lighter once I got it cooked anyway. See you in December."

When Lovett Allen shared that tidbit at the Fudger barbecue, the women's necks arched back into their shoulder blades and the men made puffing sounds.

"What in holy hanna's name is he doing cooking swamp dirt?" declared Farrah Carmichael, whose husband, Ned, claimed to have only heard the last half of Old Jim's invitation because he'd had his hearing aid turned way down. Junior was with him at the time, so Ned got the details second-hand. Farrah, his leonine second wife, had been chastising Ned ever since for not putting an end to the invitation right then and there.

"I get you fresh batteries so you can hear and then you don't use them," she sputtered. "Now some crazy old man is cooking us dirt for Christmas dinner."

After considerable delving into Long Island Tea and gin-laced fruit punch, the consensus among the women was that the men were responsible, so the men would have to deal with Old Jim.

Junior's wife, Posey, laid it on the line.

"You got us into this by listening to the old fool in the first place, so you can just get us out of it," Posey said, asserting the full huff of a middle-age-spread that started at her plump ankles and spread all the way to the chins under her chin.

The men stared into their drinks, plucking out imaginary bugs, and pulling on their ears. In the back of their minds each one was thinking the same thing. Christmas was four months away. Plenty of time. Strength in numbers. One of these days.

Labour Day came and went, along with Fall Fair Day and Halloween. Without the summer people passing through the village on their way to the lake, Northcote settled into a hibernation pattern. People trimmed their hedges for the last time, mulched their gardens with burnished maple leaves and checked their roofs for loose shingles.

Every Friday night, Farrah and Ned fought. It was a one-sided sort of affair. Farrah spat words at Ned, and he nodded in her general direction, careful to turn his "good ear" away from her volley. It was a trick he used all the time when salespeople tried to talk him into something at the hardware store he had managed for years.

Farrah wasn't just on about the Christmas dinner. She scattered her thoughts like a shotgun pattern. It was the usual second-wife stuff and nonsense. She first wanted to redecorate the bedroom. Then she wanted different towels. She wanted her own set of pots and pans. She needed to feel the house was her space, and on and on and on. If only *he* didn't have to make alimony payments, *they* could have a life, but what kind of a life was it when they could not even sit down together for a private Christmas dinner?

The other men suffered as well, to varying degrees. Tom Fudger was just into his second bite of Thanksgiving pumpkin pie when Amelia announced that he had already "spoiled Christmas."

The fact was that Tom's ailing mother had moved to California to live with his sister and her family. Too far to travel — Amelia worried that the separation might give the cats fur-ball attacks. The only Fudger child, Gordon, sent a letter in October saying that he planned to go skiing in Vermont with his university pals over Christmas. Since Amelia had come to what she termed "odds" with her side of the family, the Fudgers would be alone in Northcote for the holidays.

"I don't know about you, but I plan on having some virulent, contagious disease for Christmas," wailed Amelia. "And if you're just lucky, I'll give it to you, so we don't have to go to some stupid place where we don't belong, to sit with a bunch of spineless wimps and eat gawd knows what cooked by a psychopath."

Wendy and Lovett Allen were also considering disease options.

"We could say you've got the gout and I have to tend you," Wendy offered brightly.

But Lovett was organizing the Christmas Day skating party and Wendy was the only soprano caroller. They considered themselves indispensable to the community.

"Well, you'll just have to sprain your ankle or something when it's over," Wendy said. "I don't mean really, mind, just a pretend thing, so we can make our excuses and be done with the whole thing."

Posey and Junior had another problem. Early on, it was apparent to Posey that the men were a leaderless group, lacking in imagination and destined to fumble their way to Christmas dinner at the Toll Gate regardless of their instructions. Junior had even started saying aloud that it might be kind of interesting to have a look inside the Toll Gate house. They would be having Christmas lunch after church with his mother at the nursing home, so there was no need to do more than nibble whatever it was Old Jim planned to serve. Could be interesting, something different and for just a few hours.

"And what do you think we're supposed to do with Katie?" an exasperated Posey asked, after one of Junior's more elaborate rambles. "It's her Christmas, too. Am I supposed to throw a turkey TV dinner in the oven for her and leave her alone on Christmas night? Have you lost your senses?" Perhaps he had, Junior thought benignly. Christmas was already taking its toll.

A few days after the first snowfall in November, Posey picked Katie up from school and drove over to the Toll Gate. They walked up to the front door, Posey more purposefully than Katie, who clutched her backpack full of school books in front of her in case they were met by a musket.

Jim answered on the third knock. He didn't seem surprised to see them.

"Oh yes, Mrs. Purdie it is and you, you're that young one in the raspberry bushes I see now and then," he said, giving a wink at Katie that Posey judged wholly inappropriate.

"Well, that's just it, Jim," started Posey. "The Christmas dinner and all, well Junior and I just wouldn't feel right leaving Katie alone and I know how you feel about children, so I guess we just can't make it."

Jim didn't move to speak.

"Well, maybe you could come over to our place on Boxing Day for brunch or something and tell us all about it," Posey spouted. "Or another time, you know, New Year's or something."

She began backing away from the porch.

"Oh now, Mrs. Purdie, I didn't mean for you to take it wrong. Of course, Katie's invited, too. I mean the turkey's already 24 pounds and there's weeks of growing left to do," he said.

Posey's face scrunched involuntarily and Katie swished her lips from side to side, the way she always did when something wasn't quite going as planned.

"And I've an idea to go with that," Jim said, running his hand up over his smooth-shaven chin. "I could use a helper getting things ready. Of course, I'd pay you Katie and it wouldn't take much of your time. Help you get something a little extra for Christmas and you'd be helping out an old man. No muskets, I promise."

Katie Purdie was a willful girl. She had flecks of gold in her hazel eyes that her grandmother said meant she was destined for riches and glory.

"It'll be $6.35 an hour, that's minimum wage," said Katie. "And double if I have to do anything on Christmas Day."

"Done," said Jim. "Come over Saturday at noon and we'll figure some things out." He held out his hand to seal the deal.

Posey carried Katie's backpack to the car. She was so mad she could feel her feet swelling inside her fur-trimmed boots.

Katie knew better than to smile or even say a word. She didn't have to. Imagine being paid to get first-hand information about the Northcote Hermit and the Tortures of Toll Gate. Everyone would want to know. If there was a dungeon — and everyone knew that there must be a dungeon — she could draw pictures of it and sell them right from the back of the school bus.

Old Jim didn't scare Katie. He was right, she had watched him from the raspberry bushes and all she saw was an old man working in his garden, listening to old-time music and feeding the birds. Big deal, so he needed his windows cleaned or whatever, she had to do that at home for free.

Posey was poised when Junior got home that evening. It started with, "Now you won't believe what your daughter has gotten us into," and it went on from there. The last thing Katie heard before she fell asleep was Posey wailing: "Anthrax is too good for us. We are cursed."

Every passing day brought the Northcote Eight 24 hours closer to Christmas. Life went on. Christmas lights went up on the gingerbread. Flannelette sheets went down on the beds. The Santa Claus parade rolled through without a hitch, and pots of poinsettias could be viewed through most front windows. No one would have guessed that in four separate houses, plans were being made, casting a pox on Christmas.

Katie was tight-lipped about the goings on at Toll Gate, although she made no secret of her growing bank account. She told her parents Jim just had her doing "stuff," like cleaning the windows and beating some old rugs. It wasn't awful. Still, her mother noticed that Katie came home with dirty fingernails. The place must be a sty.

"What's mileage?" Katie asked her mother, when she came home after the second of her four-hour-long Saturday sessions at Toll Gate. "I don't mean like, how many miles are on the car, I mean what's it worth like to move something around?"

"Why, is he planning on kidnapping you?" Posey asked. Katie was taking Old Jim all too seriously from her perspective. Mileage, indeed.

"Well, he wants me to have some stuff dry-cleaned and gave me the money, but said he'd pay mileage, too, because I have to get you to drive it to the cleaners.

Then Katie hauled a lace tablecloth out of a garbage bag she dragged home across the snow. It was a filigree of fancy handiwork the colour of pale tea.

"This goes underneath," said Katie, pulling out a fine linen cloth that was sturdy, but yellowed at the edges where it had been carefully folded. A swath of napkins followed.

Posey called Farrah Carmichael for an opinion.

"These are serious antiques," Farrah said, with the authority of a woman who can tell the difference between 200 and 220 thread count in a bed sheet with just one touch.

"The linen is definitely Irish, but the lace-work has Bruges written all over it." Although she had never been to the lace capital of Belgium, Farrah prided herself on her pronunciation, squeezing out "Bruges" precisely as though ready to rhyme it with "ooze."

"I would set this with my Polish crystal and the Rosenthal china," said Farrah, fingering the napkins. "But never mind that. We've decided that Ned is going to get an earache in his good ear. That way, I have to stay home with him, because when his good ear goes wonky it makes him dizzy just trying to stand up. Good, eh."

The Fudgers were rumoured to have laid groundwork for a quiet sort of disease, one that would strike suddenly, but disappear for their annual New Year's Eve party. Farrah found out about this in the Town & Country ladies-wear store, where she had spotted Amelia trying on a hot pink down-lined ski suit.

"Now you know she doesn't ski," said Farrah. "She always says she's too brittle to do almost everything. So I asked her what she was doing and she said the suit was her protection for when she swoons after the Christmas skating party and Tom has to take her home with a sudden syndrome of some sort."

"At this stage, I'd settle for haemorrhoids," Posey said glumly. "For Junior, of course, not myself. Except I don't know if a horse's ass can get haemorrhoids. He actually asked me last week if I thought we should take some wine over to Jim's Christmas dinner! Then Katie pops her head up and says, 'It's all taken care of.'"

"Well, at least you'll be eating whatever you're eating off a clean tablecloth," said Farrah, caressing the lacework."Odd, the whole thing is odd."

By the first week of December, the ice had frozen on Northcote Pond. Snow fell in beautiful crystalline blankets, curling across close-cropped lawns and hedge tops.

Wendy Allen and Amelia Fudger ran into Don Welch at the farmers' market on a Saturday morning in the middle of the month. The place was alive with the scent of cedar boughs and cinnamon. Tinny strains from familiar Christmas songs blended with the boot-steps of people bobbing and jostling through the red-bowed aisles filled with crafts and baked goods.

"Old Jim's turkey is a monster bird, at least 28 pounds, I told him today," Don Welch called out from behind the deli counter, where the Welch Farm's free-range turkeys lay in vacuum-sealed rows in front of the smoked turkey parts and the turkey salami. "We're plucking him on the 23rd. You ladies are in for a treat."

Wendy and Amelia nodded in his direction, smiling as they hurried away. In the parking lot they patted the shoulders of their winter parkas as though something dirty had brushed them. Neither of them had revealed their plans to escape from attending the Toll Gate supper to the other, but now they were both committed to the idea.

Their husbands were professionals. Wendy had helped put Lovett Allen through law school by teaching piano lessons from their cramped off-campus apartment. Tom Fudger, a chartered accountant, had plucked Amelia out of the steno pool and made her his wife, much to the dismay of his mother who always thought he could have done better.

"Isn't there some law against telling everyone your business?" Wendy demanded of Lovett, as soon as he came home. "I can't even go shopping without everyone knowing that my Christmas supper is some sort of custom-killed monster ordered up by a geezer who looks like Ichabod Crane."

Lovett gazed out the bay window, sucking on his pipe, watching the snow fall.

"I don't think there's any case law, honey," he said.

Amelia Fudger sulked. She had a terrible feeling that even if she keeled over dead in her pink ski suit at the skating party, somebody would plant her at the Toll Gate table and shove a fork in her hand. As was his custom, Tom steered clear of his wife when she was in one of her moods. He had actually seen Jim outside the farmers' market on his way home. Offered the old boy a ride, but he wouldn't take it.

"Got another stop to make," Jim said. The brown satchel looked fairly heavy to Tom, but he didn't ask any questions.

Two days before Christmas, Katie Purdie announced that she had never seen a turkey that big before. She had stopped at Toll Gate house on her way home from school and she was there when Don Welch delivered the bird.

"Jim's oven is bigger'n ours," she told her mother.

Posey snorted at this piece of trivia, but Junior found it comforting.

"At least there will be enough dark meat to go around," he said.

"Salmonella, you mean," Posey muttered. She would not be touching turkey on Christmas Day, no matter what. Farrah Carmichael had already pre-cooked two Cornish Game Hens that she could just pop in the microwave. Even Old Mother had told Junior that they didn't have to stay after church and lunch with her at the nursing home because the turkey there was bound to be too dry to swallow.

Of course, the twenty-fifth day of December arrived. Presents were opened and hymns were sung. Northcote glistened in the winter sun like a polished ornament. Around two in the afternoon people began filtering into the street, waving their new gloves at each other as they walked down the snow-covered road to the skating pond.

The carollers were already under the gazebo sorting out song sheets. Lovett Allen had been down earlier to check the ice, and gave it a final going-over with the blade attached to his lawn tractor. Then he decided to put the ice to the test. Wendy watched him lace up his skates while she blew her pitch pipe, sounding the highest note she would have to reach in "Hark the Herald Angels Sing."

The Fudgers and the Carmichaels walked down together. Ned wore a new pair of ear muffs, but he knew from watching Farrah's wide mouth and flashing white teeth that she was explaining the provenance of the new pots and pans he had given her. He reached in his pocket and savoured the warmth of the finely etched silver flask full of brandy that she had given him.

"A little something to help you with your wonky ear routine, my darling," Farrah told him, when he unwrapped it. Then she rubbed Ned's cheeks with one of her bath towels and purred something about the joys of Egyptian cotton.

While Farrah was fairly prancing down the road, Amelia Fudger clung to Tom's hand, afraid that she would slip and fall before she had a chance to swoon. Her face was already as pink as her ski suit. Tom wished they had taken the car.

The pond was covered with skaters by the time the Purdies arrived.

Both Posey and Junior were surprised that Katie had allowed herself a special moment with her grandmother before leaving the nursing home. With her own money, Katie had bought her a blue cashmere shawl.

"You look cool, Gran," she said, wrapping the new shawl around Mother Purdie.

But once they got home, prying Katie away from her new computer games had not been easy. When she finally got her skates on, the sun was dodging clouds and the carollers were breathing stiffly as the temperature dropped.

Wendy Allen couldn't hit high C under the circumstances. After two hours, the Northcote singers decided to call it quits

When Lovett saw his wife leaving the gazebo, he knew it was time. When he was almost certain no one was watching him, he skated in a zig-zag and made a sharp right turn. Letting his skates slip out from under, he slid gently to the ice and sat there. Then he reached for his ankle and continued sitting there. Finally, his wife came skidding across the ice to his side. And a few people had noticed he was no longer skating.

Amelia Fudger swooned at exactly four o'clock. There wasn't much of a sound, she was just standing on a snow bank near the footbridge one minute and lying on the ice the next. Tom had gone to get hot chocolate and missed the whole thing when he got caught up in a discussion about tax rebates.

The pond was divided into two crowds. In the centre of the ice, Lovett Allen hunched over his right foot, emitting sporadic groans he hoped sounded convincing. Wendy wrung her hands and worried aloud about how to move him. Had Lovett only decided to fake a broken collar bone he could have at least walked home. He didn't even have enough sense to fall close to the pathway.

"How about the tractor?" said Katie.

Lovett agreed that if someone could drive the lawn tractor to him he could probably manage to drive himself off the ice. Wendy took off his skates and tried wrapping his foot with her new plaid scarf, until Laura Douglas, the school nurse, insisted that packing the injured ankle in snow was the correct procedure. Lovett howled for real, while Katie skated off to find Ned Carmichael who had sold the Allens the tractor in the first place.

At the base of the footbridge snow bank, Amelia lay perfectly still. If she got lucky, her ski suit might be in pristine enough condition for her to return it when this was all over. If not, she thought that she probably looked pretty good, with colour-coordinated lipstick and South Sea Mabe pearl earings.

Someone picked up her wrist and took her pulse with an icy finger. Amelia now stayed still as a pink popsicle. Yes, she was alive. Now where was that husband of hers?

A long minute passed. When Tom finally knelt beside her she could smell hot chocolate when he cupped his hands to her face. Amelia's left eyelid fluttered, but the mascara on her right eye had frozen to her lower lid.

"It's one of her swoons, happens now and then," Tom explained, calmly.

"See, no blood."

He started to lift Amelia's head as proof but voices from the crowd were adamant that she not be moved. No one had seen her fall, there was just a large gouge in the snow bank. Cell phones flipped open like shucked oysters and protective arms pulled Tom away.

"She just swoons and that's usually it," he said pathetically. Amelia heard words like "coma" and "concussion" bandied about.

Katie found Ned and Farrah Carmichael with her parents on the far side of the pond. They hadn't noticed the goings on, but Ned was slumped against Junior's shoulder.

"First really cold weather and his good ear always goes wonky," Farrah kept saying to passers-by. "Makes him lose his balance. Poor baby can hardly stand." Then she took off Ned's ear muffs. "Look, he can't even hear a thing now."

Posey Purdie had heard it all before, but had no idea that Ned could mimic the condition so convincingly.

"Mr. Allen's broken his foot or something and we've got to get Mr. Carmichael to take the tractor out and get him," said Katie. She was so concerned that she skated right into her mother, pushing Posey close enough to Ned for her to catch a strong scent of brandy.

Ned straightened right up.

"What, Lovett's hurt? Where? Get me the keys," he shouted. "I'm on the way, Lovett, hang on." Then he waved his arms at the crowd, flung himself away from Junior and wobbled off in the general direction of the lawn tractor.

A pair of ear muffs were airborne across the ice. Posey shrugged at Farrah. Junior felt them whiz past his shoulder but he was focussed on the crowd gathering at the foot bridge.

"What's going on?" he asked the postmistress, who was already heading home.

"Didn't you know? Amelia Fudger's got a coma or something from falling off the snow bank," she said. "Poor Tom says it happens all the time."

"Oh my gosh," said Katie, skating away, while her father trailed, shuffling across the ice in rubber boots.

Katie had a full news report before her father reached the halfway point.

"She's just lying there all pink and everything with her eyes closed," she told Junior. "And Mr. Fudger says it's not a coma, but it's something else and it's happened before. No one knows why she fell, or if she got pushed."

Junior saw the school nurse in the crowd around Lovett and he headed in that direction. Lovett was sitting upright on the ice with his Wendy's scarf packed full of snow wrapped around his ankle. Someone had stuck a blue mitten over his toes to keep them from freezing.

"Is it bad?" Junior asked Wendy, who had stayed at his side throughout the ordeal.

"Sprained, we think," she said, while wishing to high heaven that Lovett had only gone down closer to the road. They could have been home having hot toddies on the sofa by now.

"You'll be all right, Ned's warming the tractor up now to come and get you," Junior said, leaning into Lovett's ear. "Anyway, there should be an ambulance coming to get Amelia if you need one."

"A what?" cried Lovett.

"An ambulance. I mean she's that out of it, lying over there by the footbridge," Junior said. "She's not in a coma, which is good, but nobody knows if she was pushed or if she just fell. I'm going to have the nurse take a look at her. Okay."

If there was one thing that Lovett Allen could see coming as clearly as a train down a track, it was litigation. The wooden footbridge had needed repairs in the fall, but nobody had gotten around to it. Northcote could be held responsible. Or what if it was a crime scene and people were tramping all over the evidence?

"Gotta get there," he said, grabbing Junior firmly by his knee and reaching out for his hand. His right foot was supposedly sprained, but it was his left foot that gave him the most trouble because it had fallen asleep.

"What do you think you're doing?" Nurse Douglas demanded, as Lovett clung to Junior's shoulders, his right foot firmly planted on the ice and left foot jerking in spasms of pins and needles.

"Call it a miracle. Feels fine now," Lovett called, as he hopped along the ice, braced against Junior, with Wendy following behind, holding his skates and chasing after her scarf as it slowly unwound. By the time Ned caught up to them on the tractor, Lovett was striding forcefully in his wet socks.

Feeling distinctly chilly on the ice, Amelia Fudger hadn't figured on anyone calling an ambulance, but she couldn't just jump to her feet and call it off. She decided to give her head a shake to attract Tom's attention, but he was standing on top of the footbridge looking for lights and listening for sirens.

Instead, the first people to recognize signs of life in Amelia were Farrah and Posey, who had decided they just had to catch Amelia's act.

"She moved, did you see that," Posey noted.

Farrah kneeled beside the body, so close that her long blond hair grazed Amelia's face.

"Come out, come out, wherever you are," Farrah sang, and Amelia's eyes fluttered open.

After being prone for such a long time, Amelia was actually a bit woozy as Farrah and Posey helped her to her feet. The pinkness drained from her cheeks, and she reached out for Tom, who had, seeing her helped up, slid down the snow bank as easily as she had. As they embraced, the chilled hot chocolate Tom was still carrying splashed across the front of the pink ski suit.

"Watch it," Amelia said, jumping back smartly, twisting her shoulders and regaining her posture.

"You're all right, well thank God," croaked Lovett Allen, sliding to a stop and wrapping his arms around them. Hopping from one foot to the other, he grabbed the nearest cell phone and cancelled the ambulance which had yet to arrive.

On the west side of the pond, Ned ran the tractor into a clump of ice. It was still running when Farrah pulled him off.

"I don't wanna hear. I don't wanna hear," he kept saying, while her steady torrent of derision drove him toward the footbridge.

In the near dark of the late afternoon, Katie took her skates off. Most of Northcote had already returned to their hearths. Wood-burning smells filled the air and the word was picking up.

"It's almost time for supper, so I'm going to go straight to the Toll Gate," Katie said. "See you all in an hour."

Posey Purdie had always known it would come to this. Now the others knew it, too. Amelia wanted a nice hot bath. Farrah wanted to shove Ned in a cold shower. Wendy found Lovett's shoes in a corner of the gazebo, and they all started up the hill.

"You sure don't have to skate to have a good time in this town, do you," Junior said. No one responded.

At seven p.m. the doors of four houses reluctantly opened and closed. While they traditionally dressed up for Christmas supper, this time the women didn't bother. Farrah was the only one bearing a gift.

"Chocolates," she sniffed. "Left over from last year's staff party. I hope."

A plain grapevine wreath decorated the Toll Gate house door. Old Jim had made it himself from the wild vines that grew in a tangle on his cedar rail fence. Katie took their coats, while boots were stacked on a raised board to dry in the narrow entrance way.

Wearing a green wool vest with leather buttons over his usual red flannel shirt, Jim shook their chilled hands one by one as they moved into the main room. It was gridded by thick wooden beams that separated it from the dining room and pantry, which were each raised a few steps higher.

"Figure you might want to warm those toes up, Mr. Allen," Old Jim said, guiding the barrister to a well-padded Morris chair beside the fireplace. The planked pine wood floor bore the scars of cinders past. On the other side of the room, there were scattered braided rugs that overlapped each other around a long dining table only partially revealed.

"Lovett, call me Lovett," insisted the weary barrister, who, like everyone else, was still trying to get his bearings. The light was soft, cast from tassel-trimmed spindle lamps and a pair of copper and brass sconces that hung beside a roll-top desk in the front corner.

The Toll Gate house smelled the way Christmases were supposed to smell. There was something of turkey and turnips, mixed with baking buns and boiling potatoes and lemon oil. Posey Purdie picked up the distinct scent of lemon oil from the wainscoting.

She lowered herself carefully into a corner seat on the earth-brown sofa and ran her hand along a log-cabin quilt stitched in kaleidoscope colours before finally settling in.

"It won't bite," Jim said. "How about some grog?"

"Grog" turned out to be hot tea with a hint of honey and a larger hint of rum. A thin brown cinnamon stir stick stood out of the lip of each mug. Ned smiled and turned his good ear to the crackle of the cherry logs in the stone fireplace, while Farrah shoved her chocolate box on the end pine table, where she thought it might blend in with the stack of *National Geographics*.

Conversation picked up when Jim called out from the kitchen that he had seen some of the commotion on the pond, but Katie had told him it looked worse than it was.

Amelia started on about how she still felt woozy and Tom gave her a warning look. Posey's chin slipped into her other chin disapprovingly.

"Can't do too much damage at a skating party," Junior piped up. "You ever been to one, Jim?"

"He watches," answered Katie, hopping up the steps and heading for the kitchen like she owned the place.

"Seen 'em all, only got close once," Jim said, coming into view beside the largest beam, where he wiped his hands on a woman's half apron decorated with candy canes. Wendy Lovett recognized it from one of the stalls at the farmers' market.

"One I remember best, most of you wouldn't because you came on later. It was when young Purdie fell through the ice and they had to use a hockey stick to pull him out," Jim said, feeling Posey's eyes intent on him. "Remember that Junior? I helped your mother carry you home, never saw her so worried then or since. Now that was excitement."

Junior was speechless. Crazy old Jim was going on about his private shame, in front of everyone.

"So that's why you never skate," said Farrah. "Ned can't skate because of the ear-balance thing, but if I ever fell through ice I would never go near it again."

Junior's only memory of that day was the paralyzing terror and holding his breath even after he came up for air. He had never thought about how he got home that day, but even as a young woman, Mother Emma Purdie could never have carried a half-frozen seven-year-old up the Northcote hill by herself.

"I guess I owe you a big debt of gratitude," Junior said, toasting Jim with a mug of steaming grog that Katie had refilled.

"Thank your mother, she's the one who called me out to help. She should be here soon, anyway."

Jim went back to the kitchen and there was a clatter of pans. Lovett looked at Junior and Posey shrugged for both of them . . . as though they had a collective mind, the women all rose at the same time to see if they could help in the kitchen.

Katie was putting the dessert forks at the top of each place setting when the women stormed the doorway to the kitchen. Farrah Carmichael had to catch her breath. The table was set with Polish crystal and Rosenthal china, not her pattern but if she thought for a moment she was sure she could name it.

"Nice, eh," said Katie. "Jim had it shipped home for his mother after the war. Only two teacups broke."

"What a lovely tablecloth," Farrah called out. "Belgian lace, is it?"

"Don't know about that," Jim said, running a basting brush over the nut-brown turkey he had pulled from the oven for the others to inspect. "It was a gift from some Dutch people I met when we liberated one of those Holland towns."

Farrah had a lot of questions about the silver candle-sticks on the table, but before she could ask, there was a knocking. It was Don Welch dropping off Mother Purdie.

Jim went to greet them and he invited Don to share a cup of grog.

"Can't," he said, "big snow coming and I'm wanted at home. But I do want to see the bird." Brushing his boots off, Don walked through the crowd to the kitchen, nodding as he went.

Amelia and Wendy stood back to give the turkey grower a good view.

"Yessir, when it comes to growing a turkey, I'm a real pro. Ya done good on him, Jim." Then he left as smoothly as he entered.

Mother Purdie had dressed for Christmas supper. Wrapped over her cranberry wool dress she wore the blue shawl. Junior offered his mother his seat on the sofa and she settled back comfortably.

"Just tea for me is fine," she told Katie. "The grog is my old recipe, but I think I'm just too old for that now."

There was an air of discomfort in the Toll Gate house. In the kitchen, the women marvelled at the level of organization — the carving set honed and ready, gravy boats lined up, buns in the warming oven with the vegetables and potatoes draining over the sink, ready to be mashed.

"Is it time to pick the salad yet?" Katie asked.

"You do it," said Jim. "I've got mashing to tend to."

"Two at a time if you want to see," Katie told the room. "It's growing in the basement and things are kind of crowded down there."

"This must be the swamp-dirt part," Farrah said.

Lovett Allen was first in line.

"He couldn't use dirt, too much disease," Katie explained, opening a door that stood near the fireplace beside one of the small square windows that looked out over the snow-covered garden.

"It's all grown hydroponically. Careful, Mr. Allen, the ceiling's kind of low as people were shorter in the old days."

In the middle of the room above a floor that was definitely dirt, a system of white fluorescent lights was suspended over a table covered with greenery.

"I planted the red leaf lettuce, and we already had one harvest," said Katie, pulling tender leaves one by one from one of the trays. "We have three kinds of lettuce, and parsley and the usual stuff. The cucumbers take a lot of space, so there are only two plants."

People were still moving up and down the stairs long after Katie completed her harvest and returned with a colander filled with young greens.

"Let me see," said Mother Purdie. "Old Jim said he'd do it and I guess he did, just like in the magazine."

"You knew about this?" asked Posey with amazement.

"Oh yes, Jim's been talking about growing a winter supper for a long time. Just didn't want me to tell you about it until he had it all figured out."

"Then you two see each other?" Her daughter-in-law's eyes were as wide as saucers.

"He comes every Saturday, just like you, only later in the day," Mother Purdie replied matter-of-factly, scooting Katie off to the kitchen.

When dinner was called, everyone took their places at the name cards that Jim had whittled into business-card-sized slivers of wood and coloured with ink.

"He's a bloody old man Martha Stewart," Farrah said, under her breath. She was seated at the far end of the table, on Ned's good ear side, but Jim heard her.

"Oh, Martha doesn't know everything," he said. *"The Joy of Cooking* has been like a Bible to me, one of the old editions that they have in the library. That and Emma, here." Jim nodded toward Mother Purdie.

Posey Purdie was busting to know what those two had in common and why she was even at the table. Her neck twitched when she got like that and she looked a bit like a chunky, restless chicken. Junior knew the signs.

"So what's this about, Jim," he said, when the separate platters piled with white and dark meat had arrived.

"Not yet. First say Grace," said Jim, and heads were bowed while he said something about fine food and fine women and Christmas. Katie poured the wine. Lovett Allen sniffed, sipped and nodded his approval.

Buns passed. Jim baked them himself. He hadn't grown the wheat but after all those years at the mill, he knew what good flour was when he saw it. The yams and potatoes had been harvested from his garden, as had the turnips and carrots.

Posey Purdie liked the carrots, until she saw some small, dark oblong flecks in the orange. She almost dropped her fork, thinking they might be mouse droppings.

"Caraway seeds," said Jim, reading her mood. "You harvest them, dry them and roast them a bit. Most herbs, you want the young leaves, but I like the caraway seeds."

The meal was a marvel to all concerned. Mrs. Purdie said it was the best turkey she'd ever eaten, and the biggest she'd ever seen in a roast pan. Jim glowed.

"And I'm afraid it's my last turkey at the Toll Gate," he said with a sigh, while the women removed the plates.

Before the salad was served (quite properly *after* the main course, as Farrah Carmichael observed), Jim put an old Edith Piaf record on what was probably the last turntable in existence in Northcote.

"Not Christmassy, tired of that stuff," he said. With candles it was perfect.

"See, I'm moving," said Jim, "and that's why I wanted you all here. To tell you and to give you all something.

"I'm old as dirt and I can't run the place the way I used to. So I'm goin' to the nursing home. Got the room next to Emma's reserved." He nodded again toward Mother Purdie. She smiled and Junior took note.

"Thing is the Toll Gate house is history. You folks all live in old houses in town, so you know what I mean. The Toll Gate is the second-oldest building in Northcote, after the front part of the church.

"So what I propose is to give the Toll Gate house to Northcote. Lock, stock, and barrel. Get Lovett to draw up the paper work, Tom to handle the books and Ned to organize whatever fixing-up needs to be done to make it whatever you want. I figure the women can sort that out because they've got the sense for that sort of thing."

Then he left the table and retrieved a square metal box from underneath the sideboard, sliding it across the floor on a scatter rug and hoisting it to the table.

"Found this inside the old cistern down near the raspberry patch, must have been 20 years ago. It's the old toll box, and it's chock full of coins. Mother always told me it was around the house somewhere. Should have gone to the town a long time ago, but my father's father hid it for safe-keeping during one of those rebellions they used to have, and then he got himself shot.

"With a musket, right?" said Katie.

"That's what I was told," smiled Jim.

He opened the latches on the box and turned the contents toward the table. Coins rattled forward, odd-sized and tarnished grey.

"They're not much to look at now, but I sent a handful to a coin specialist and they clean up nice."

Jim pulled a small wad of plastic-covered coins from the pocket of his vest.

"These five here came back with a value of about $1,000 for the lot. Different prices for each one and all kinds of reasons, including how many curls you can count on Queen Victoria's head.

"I don't know what the whole lot of them is worth, but it should be enough to pay the taxes for a few years and give the thing a start.

"All I ask is that I can putter around in the garden. Don't matter to me if the kids cut across anymore. Just so long as it stays and doesn't become some sort of stacked-up subdivision. So that's the thing of it, why I wanted you here." Jim paused and looked at Mother Purdie. "If it's all right with Junior and his Missus, Mother Purdie and me are fixing to get married in the Spring. Miss Katie's already agreed to help me grow the supper, for that one too."

Jim sat down and patted Emma's hand.

Dessert was a huge trifle served from a cut-glass bowl. Old coins passed from hand to hand. Lovett and Tom were talking about trusts. Jim brought out a bottle of brandy that he said was half as old as dirt. Ned wandered around knocking on the old wooden beams. By the fireplace, three generations of Purdies poured over a scrapbook of newspaper clippings Jim had kept ever since the war. Posey orchestrated the clean-up crew in the kitchen, where the women were already arguing about the historic site versus daycare centre.

When they left the Toll Gate house that night, the Northcote Eight, and even Katie, were slow walking up the hill.

"And all this time, I thought Old Jim was crazy," Junior allowed pensively, between puffs on his pipe. Posey Purdie just shook her head and stamped her feet. No one else said a word.

SMOKE GETS IN YOUR EYES

On Christmas Eve, I would desperately like to order in Chinese food the way my parents used to do when I was a kid. But you cannot do that in the country, so I get out the wonton wrappers and soy sauce and try for a reasonable facsimile. It is a tradition, although one year it nearly went by the wayside. That year I was lucky to have a household.

On a cold and clear night a few weeks before Christmas, the house almost burned down. It was one of those crisp, starry December nights without any wind to blow the snow. Chores were done and dinner was waiting to be made.

Old brick houses hold a lot of heat, and I plunked a few pieces of cedar beneath a maple log to rekindle the fire in the wood stove. There was time, it seemed, for me to write a long overdue letter to a friend before I started peeling potatoes.

I headed upstairs to the "room of my own" where the computer hums and the books overflow in piles. Pictures on the wall range from old jazz musicians to navigational charts of bodies of waters that I am unlikely to ever navigate, but would like to. By the fifth step, I knew there was trouble. Farming develops an uncanny sense of smell — a nose tuned to sensibilities of cured hay, or the sickly smell that can come from either end of an animal that is not feeling right.

I smelled smoke, but did not see it, until I opened the closed door of the guest bedroom. It billowed out at me in the darkened hallway, an acrid sheet that hurt my eyes and sent the smoke alarm into a hyper-wail.

Peering into the room, I could not see anything ablaze, only yellowish smoke. In a gesture of self-preservation that was almost primeval, I grabbed the brand new, two-piece dress I had laid out on the guest bed in preparation for the annual meeting of the Proton Township Federation of Agriculture where I was scheduled to speak the next evening. Then I slammed the door shut and ran down the stairs.

I have played out this drill in my mind before, but I had no idea how effective it would be. By the placement of the smoke, the only conclusion was "chimney fire," a fact that I calmly announced to the Moose.

He placed the emergency call, while I sealed the wood stove, to avoid feeding oxygen into the chimney. Suddenly, I was able to assemble the boots, scarves and gloves that I never seem able to find otherwise. We clambered into them to get a look at what was going on outside the house.

The century-old chimney pokes out of the second-storey roof, above the guest bedroom. Big red embers and flames were shooting out of it. I turned on the Christmas lights that circle a cedar tree on that side of the house, and we watched the sparks landing and dying on a cover of ice and snow. The residual of a blizzard I had cursed a few days before was protecting the roof over my head.

The smoke had not spread, so I ran upstairs on a mission that I knew would have to be fast. Memories are scattered all over the house, but I keep the photo albums in one big drawer of the hall cupboard. I had never realized how many there were or how much each one meant until I started tossing them into a laundry hamper.

Then I scurried downstairs, knowing I could not return. When I passed the guest room door, smoke was seeping from the bottom. I stuffed a pair of long johns under it to stem the tide. The back of the door was cool. A good sign I thought, as I visualized the room — the apple doll scrunched on the night table and the pine armoire stacked with summer clothes. Against the north wall lay the spool bed on which so many friends say they got their best night's sleep. At the end of it was the quilt with twelve ladies holding parasols that my Grandmother made out of scraps and pieces of clothes I wore when I was a little girl.

The Moose was looking worried when I came down with my booty of memories. Everything seemed to be moving in slow motion, except the crackle and snapping sounds in the chimney. We scooped the usual clutter from the hallway into the hamper to clear the path for the firemen and put the ungainly haul in the back of the truck for safekeeping.

Animals sense when something is up. The sheep and horses had left the barn and gathered at the fenceline to quietly observe the odd activity. Even Diva Dog accepted her truck-seat assignment with unusual dignity.

In short shrift, an emergency van and two fire trucks were in the lane, along with my neighbour, Joy, and her daughters. When anything with a siren blaring roars down a country road, you can bet everyone pays attention. Joy heard the commotion and went outside to see what was happening. Sure enough, above the tall trees that surround my place, she could see black smoke covering the stars.

While the firemen went about the business of spreading tarpaulins around the wood stove and investigating the upstairs nightmare, Joy, Angie, Amy and I shuffled boxes of files and computer disks outside. Moose disconnected the "brain" of his computer and ferried it to safety.

Upstairs, in the room next to the fire site, sat my own computer and its precious, helpless brain where my own manuscripts and mangled thoughts awaited possible incineration. I tried not to think about that.

Outside, the firemen were going swiftly about their business. Ladders helped them scale the roof, but the blessed protective blanket of snow and ice did not make getting to the top of the chimney easy. When I saw them unravelling the water hose and adjusting gauges on the pump truck, a wave of horror hit me. For the first time, I noticed that some of the men were wearing what looked like oxygen masks as they entered the house. This was not a movie, the danger was real.

In the kitchen, where there was surprisingly little smoke, I recognized Len, the man who runs the feed mill at the local Co-Op store. He was spreading a huge tarp over the cluttered kitchen table.

"Anything else we should cover, Marsha?" he asked.

In my heightened state, I noticed two things — one was the operative word "cover," and the other was the easy, soothing way that he said my name. These were not unknown firemen. Underneath their masks and black and yellow suits — these were my neighbours, people whom I had seen cheering the home team at the hockey arena and people whose houses, farms and children I knew by sight.

When you are facing the potential loss of all of your "stuff," identifying one thing as "special" is hard, but I asked Len if it would be possible to throw something over the old wooden cabinet in the kitchen corner. It conjured visions of the day we discovered it in the dusty corner of an old curiosity shop. Then there was the struggle to get it through the front door and the joyful decision to leave it as we found it, with the colourful green and orange paint that its Ukrainian pioneer builders had given it.

While Len pondered the logistics, I started stuffing knick-knacks and old salt and pepper shakers from the shelves into my purse for safekeeping. When I found myself carefully charting a course across the kitchen floor carrying a martini glass that holds a collection of hand-blown glass swizzle sticks bought at an auction years ago, I knew I was losing my composure.

Apparently, at that very surreal moment the chimney fire bowed to the assorted flame retardants and suffocation efforts of the heroes upstairs. Amy whispered in my ear that she heard one of the firemen say he did not think they would need water. An hour later, it was over. Len and the men were cautious; they checked the attic and the roof many times before they were satisfied that every last ember was dead and cold. It was quite impressive, and the impossible task of conveying thanks to them left me tongue-tied.

While standing numbly next to the spotlight that was trained on the fireman who was poking around the top of the chimney for a last look, I saw a charred lump in the snow. Ringed in soot was a lady holding a parasol — my Grandmother's quilt.

"Sorry about that," said one of the firefighters, whom I finally recognized as the new neighbour who bought a farm two concessions away last summer.

"We had to use it to smother the smoke in the beginning or it would have been a lot worse."

"Never mind," I told him, feeling guilty that sentiment for a blanket could congeal in my mind when he and his mates had risked life and limb to save the roof over my head.

Besides, I have always known that Grandmother's quilt was very special, almost magical in some way. Now it had helped save my house. She would have liked that.

In the aftermath of the fire, that particular Christmas kind of got lost. The insurance adjuster, that faceless name that goes with the premium, turned out to be a very nice man named John. Throughout the festive season, a chaos of cheerful workers — dry-wallers, painters, carpenters and cleaners — streamed into the house. Smoke does an amazing amount of damage, but they managed to clear the air and I no longer felt as though I was living inside a barbecue. Ultimately, the house will be better — and safer — for all of their efforts.

Before I warmed up the wok on that Christmas Eve, I was still putting the final trim on the Christmas tree. A bit late, perhaps, but every ornament and every strand of tinsel seemed vividly alive. When I made my final visit to the barn at midnight, I searched the stars for Santa's sleigh, so that I could send him on his way. My chimney had had quite enough visitors that year. The fact that it was still standing was enough of a gift for me.

WHEN SLEIGH BELLS RING

In rural communities, if a town is large enough to have a Main Street, you can bet that it has a Santa Claus parade. This tradition usually involves giant transport trailer trucks, fire engines, police cars with intrusive siren and tractors trimmed with Christmas lights. Drum majorettes strut and men in skirts play Christmas carols on sheep bladders. The grand finale is St. Nick himself, and the whole thing ends in a rage of shopping that warms the hearts of the members of the local Chamber of Commerce.

But in one southwestern Ontario village, there is a distinctly different parade. No lights, no sirens, no fossil fuel fumes, no commercials, and nowhere much to shop afterward.

Instead, Holstein, Ontario, 100 km north-west of Toronto, hosts a non-mechanized Santa Claus parade featuring the clip clop of homemade, horse-drawn floats and cutters, and the vocal charms of local choirs. There are no razzle-dazzle bands, but a gaggle of children plays "Joy to the

World" and other seasonal favourites on multi-coloured plastic kazoos.

The whole parade lasts less than an hour. At the end, free hot dogs are served at the pavilion in the village park where a child-oriented Snofest features such activities as wreath tossing and photo sessions with Santa.

When sleigh bells ring in Holstein everybody listens. Six years ago, when the first old-fashioned Christmas parade marched down the road past the Holstein General Store and the Feed Mill, it was primarily local people who clawed their way through a December fog to watch the horses go by and wave to friends who festooned pony carts and hay wagons with homemade nativity scenes and garland-wrapped trees.

But word has spread about this homespun environmentally friendly parade. For the past couple of Christmases, several thousand visitors have lined along the 1.5 km parade route. And for many urbanites who come from Kitchener, Guelph, Collingwood and, yes, even Toronto, it is quite overwhelming.

It is not uncommon to see tears well up in middle-aged eyes.

Last year's parade featured nearly 50 animal-powered entries, including two teams of miniature horses, one donkey, two cows and an unidentified number of dogs wearing reindeer ears.

There is nothing overtly pretentious about the parade — cedar bows on wagons are often affixed with duct tape — but the sentiment is sincere, genuine and infectious.

"People pass each other on the sidewalk saying 'Merry Christmas,' and everybody is smiling or singing," marvelled University of Guelph professor Nancy Ellwand.

A second-time visitor, Ellwand's three children were so captivated that they wanted to be a part of the parade. Kazoo Band organizer Dinah Christie happily accommodated their mother's request.

"There's a lot of leeway in this parade," says actor/singer Christie, who has a farm nestled in the rolling hills surrounding the village. "Besides, you don't have to know much about music to play the kazoo — as Bacall said to Bogart: 'You just put your lips together and blow.'"

Seventy-year-old Lyle Rawn has been in the parade from the beginning along with his grey Percherons, Bud and Duke. He prepares the horses by taking them for long sleigh rides across the fields of the family farm on the outskirts of the village.

The day before the parade, he brings "the boys" into his heated shed and washes their white manes and tails until they gleam.

"I don't have fancy show harnesses, but I like them to look good," says Rawn, who is by no means the oldest driver in the parade. His 76-year-old cousin, Russell, brings a team of chestnut and cream Belgian horses.

The hooves of the big draft horses are the size of pie plates, and they clomp along the snow-covered route guided by seasoned drivers who like nothing better than to show off their gentle giants. There is even an eight-horse mounted choir, whose songs are interspersed with the occasional whinny.

While it looks simple, assembling a non-mechanized parade has its own peculiar problems and rules. Although

Holstein is home to Baxter, a fifteen-year-old Bactrium camel owned by the area's Member of Parliament Murray Calder, Baxter is banned from the parade.

"Horses go wild at the smell and sight of a camel," explains Parade Marshall Dennis Boychuk.

Starting in the spring, Boychuk begins making casual rounds of interested parade participants, checking out training programs, harnesses and "overall character."

By parade day, he knows every driver and horse by name from Linda Raeburn's shaggy Shetland pony Dazzle to Allan Horsburgh's prize-winning grey and black Percherons, Dick and Jed. In between there are elegant Arabians, high-stepping Morgan horses and unknown quantities such as Squiggly, a nine-month-old, sleigh-pulling calf.

"Once we even had a lady walking a lamb," laughs Boychuk, who sets the order of the parade according to the temperament of the animals and their handlers' skill. Santa's sleigh always comes last, pulled by a reliable team of bays named Bob and Reuben.

The whole extravaganza costs less than $1,500 to produce, with horse owners providing their fancy-dressed rigs at their own expense and the local Boy Scouts stuffing goody bags for the kids.

"Everyone pitches in and it seems to bring out the best in people," admits organizer Erika Matheson, who taps volunteer resources from nearly all of the 117 families in the village.

"It's special all right," confides Lyle Rawn. "And you know why? I think it's because the horses like the parade as much as the people."

CHRISTMAS ANGELS

From where I sit, it looks like a white Christmas and I could not be happier. All of the hustle and bustle and shopping and tree trimming are done. In the country, we tend to get everything done one shopping day before Christmas Eve, because you never know when a blizzard is going to sock you in and close the roads.

The farm really does look like Christmas. At this time of year, I know once and for all why I painted the barns red and green. Even the sheep are decorated with shades of red and green across their rumps.

While it may look as though they have been designer imprinted for the season, the fact is that the red and green marks simply indicate that they have been bred by the ram. He sports a red crayon on his breeding harness chest plate that rubs off on each ewe as she is bred. Halfway through the breeding cycle, I change the colour to green.

The sheep look quite jolly actually. Of course, the horses are now wearing red and green halters. After chasing the biggest goose around the manure pile several times, the cat now sports a red collar, complete with jingle bells.

Who knows, maybe this sentimental penchant for dressing up animals at Christmas has something to do with a childhood spent in suburban Scarborough, where my parents foisted red ribbons on the cats and dogs and goldfish bowls at Christmas. It just makes me laugh.

While I was doing the last minute shopping for cranberries and whipping cream and cognac, I added extra carrots and apples to my shopping cart. On Christmas Eve, I will chop them up and toss them with pails of oats mixed with warm molasses. Around midnight, I will head out to the barn.

The animals will no doubt be sleeping when I tune the barn radio into Christmas carols. They won't understand why I'm waking them up, or why they have been roused for such a feast. Once they have eaten, they will settle back down and let me wander through the crowd, petting their noses, while the horses nuzzle me with frosty breath.

I will lean on the manger, jingle my sheep bells and let the emotion of the season wash over me in this most private of settings. Animals do not care if you get tears in your eyes, they nuzzle you anyway.

I will think about my family and Christmases past. I will think about the Christmas my dad and I built a model Brontosaurus, and I will think about the Christmas I had cancer.

I will think about all of the kids I have seen at Christmas and I will think about my long-departed grandparents who left me their memories and their recipes.

It is funny the things the mind flashes on. The baby lambs in the spring bouncing around like silly putty animals. The sweet corn from the garden. The goose hatching a dozen fuzzy goslings. The puppy trying to make friends with the barn cats. The horse trying to make friends with a skunk.

I will recall the sunny day we spent baling hay. I will think about the laughing and forget about the sore back as I celebrate the rewards of all the work that translates into the security and tranquillity of a warm barn on Christmas Eve.

I will think about an old lady I know who is missing her family from her nursing home bed, and my friends whose baby died, and the family I know who are losing their farm. I will let myself weep for them and ask, as they ask, Why? And I will think about how blessed and lucky I am.

It is not a maudlin ritual, just one that seems to happen every year. Once I have had it all out with myself, and everyone who needs patting is patted, I will close the barn door. On Christmas Eve the barn radio plays carols all night, and hang the hydro bill.

As I walk back to the house, with the carols softly ringing and the smell of the wood-burning stove inviting me to join my mate beside the Christmas tree for a cup of eggnog before Santa comes, I will find an untrod spot in the snow.

Then I will lie down in my snowsuit and do what I have done ever since I can remember on Christmas Eve. I will wave my arms and legs and make an angel in the snow.

Merry Christmas.

THE PUMP HOUSE WARS

As I grabbed my pick axe and handsaw and went out into a blizzard to do my chores, I realized that maybe farming in winter does mean I am a few pickles short of a jar.

While city folks battle brown-grey slush in the downtown streets, I often find that just getting to the barn means leaping through thigh-high snowdrifts.

One energetic, albeit "mature" Scottish shepherd friend has set up a kind of winter hazard fenceline to guide him to and from his barn in blinding snow. He spaces the poles at intervals and each one is decorated with orange reflecting tape. If he takes three snowshoe steps without seeing a pole, he knows he's off track. The man is positively canny.

I try not to tread off the beaten track myself when snow is swirling. I have heard too many tales about pioneer days and even more recent times when a simple amble up an icy, snowed-in laneway led to disaster.

There are some chores that simply cannot wait for the weather to break — feeding and watering livestock, for example. Unfortunately, ice often freezes the edges of the big round bales of hay that are intended to allow the sheep to feed freely and provide some convenience for me.

This leaves me in the inconvenient position of having to bash the frozen bale with my pick axe and rip away the outer core of hay with my trusty hacksaw. Sometimes it gets pretty frustrating. As soon as I have axed and sawed a bale open, the eager sheep descend. Making a quick exit comes close to scaling a Matterhorn of snow and wool.

Just when I manage to get everyone fed, the water pump generally freezes. At this point I have been known to pull my snow-covered toque over my face in the hope that what is obviously a bad dream will soon be over.

This year, the annual water freeze-up came after the chores and after supper. I discovered it as I prepared for a long hot soaking of tired muscles before bed. Oops, no water.

I have learned to keep a few gallons of water in the basement for just such occasions. While they boil on the stove, I clamber into my damp snowsuit and assemble assorted flashlights for the dreaded trip to the pump house, 150 long yards across a snow-drifted wilderness.

The pump house is a quaint little barn-shaped structure perched over a well and the pump is six feet down in a styrofoam-lined hole. Every winter I promise to install a staircase, but every spring I forget about it. An old crate is my only step into the pump hole.

After years of experience, I know that the trouble generally lies in a little rubber hose called the venturi tube, which must be massaged with hot water. It usually takes a few jugs before the pump clicks in, by which time a damp snowsuit can start to seize up. Getting out of the pump hole in a frozen snowsuit is an almost arthritic exercise.

Then there is a mad dash back to the house to make sure that the water is flowing. Air gets trapped in the line and it takes a few spurts and burps for it to work its way through to the taps. When the water begins to flow freely, the sight and the sound are mesmerizing. It's cheap entertainment, and it fills my heart with gladness.

After one particularly gruelling pump house war, a girlfriend from the big city called me as I was thawing out by the fire. The poor darling had endured a dreadful day in the city streets and the road salt had fairly ruined a fine new pair of suede boots.

"I had to call you, because I just know that you are out there in the country having a great time, with your feet up by the fire and those darling dogs curled up beside you," she said. "I wish I could be there."

"Absolutely right," I told her. "There's no life like it." Then one of the big furry dogs shook wet snow all over me.

ALL SKUNK'S EVE

When I was a kid, my parents would get dressed up on New Year's Eve and go to a big party somewhere that kids could not go to. I'd stay home with the babysitter and my little brother and sister and I would try to stay awake until midnight, when Guy Lombardo and His Royal Canadian orchestra would play "Auld Lang Syne" from some glittering ballroom in New York City. I would always imagine that my parents were dancing at Mr. Lombardo's party, and that someday I would do the same thing.

In my dreams. But New Year's Eve on the farm has its own peculiar delights. I've had lambs born on New Year's Eves in the middle of blizzards, and one year the hydro went out for three hours, so instead of raucous music blaring, we greeted the New Year to the crackle of an ancient transistor radio and blew our little whistles by candlelight.

And then there was the New Year's I remember only as "The Eve of the Skunk."

It happened not too many years ago. I was getting ready to visit neighbours three farms away to celebrate with their family — maybe play a few hands of cards and tell a few tall tales. Nothing splashy. Nothing that needed a party dress or a fancy hairdo, but I do try to make it a rule to wear high heels on New Year's Eve, just so that I don't get out of practice. Also, I find that if you wear high heels on New Year's Eve, you can rely on gravity to tell you when you've tippled too much because you start to wobble in those dam things.

I was just set to leave, when I decided to let the dogs out for their constitutional. After five minutes, they had not returned. After 15, I knew something was amiss.

When I finally heard the familiar scratch at the door, one whiff told me they had found a skunk.

The larger, furrier dog had somehow managed to evade the black-striped beast, but my little dog — my house puppy, my wrinkled black Chinese Shar-Pei, Diva, who loves to lick my face and leap all over me — was suffering from a direct hit.

I slammed the door, whipped off my high heels and called the neighbours to explain I would be a tad late. No need to mention the skunk-sprayed dog.

Big Stella the Akita could have easily spent the night in the barn. In fact she often chooses to stay with her sheep. But the victim in this case was short-haired and spoiled rotten. Even closing the barn door in the face of the darling Diva dog is enough to set her into a baleful mourn.

When you greet a dog that is covered in skunk juice, the first issue of concern becomes containment, because nothing rubs off a dog easier than the fragrant oil of skunk. I quickly ran to the bottom drawer of a cupboard that holds a cluster of old clothing that's too badly damaged to donate to anyone.

Suitably attired, I dug the dog crate out of the basement rubble and lured the stinking Diva into it with a lamb-burger meatball that was supposed to have been part of my New Year's buffet contribution.

Diva did not take kindly to this entrapment, but I figured it was a better solution than having to de-skunk my entire household.

When I showed up at the nearest Becker's store looking like yesterday's hobo and buying out the entire stock of six cans of tomato juice, the fresh-faced young woman behind the counter said, "Gee that must be quite a recipe you're making."

A man who was carrying a bag of ice cubes offered his own opinion, saying, "Looks like someone's having a Bloody Mary party tonight."

But behind him there was a woman carrying a jug of eggnog who had "been there, seen it, done it" written on her face — "Skunk" was all she said.

"Dog got it," was my cryptic response. Profound communication is often the most succinct.

Fairly quickly, the other folks in the store caught the downwind scent of me, no doubt the consequence of hustling the dog into its temporary cage. It is amazing how the smell of skunk can permeate an entire Becker's store in the space of two minutes even after a minor contact.

Back home in the mud room, I proceeded to remove anything that I did not want to have ending up smelling of skunk. This included ambient clothes and boots, as well as snowshoes, an ancient toboggan and a misplaced garden rake. I mixed half of my tomato juice with warm water and coaxed the stinking dog into a large plastic tub, while a space heater tried to keep pace with the freezing temperatures outside.

De-skunking is an unsavoury art unto itself. Once the poor dog had abandoned herself to the inevitability of being bathed, I got into the swing of moistening her thoroughly with ladles of warm tomato juice. The theory is that some acid in the tomato juice neutralizes the skunk juice, but that takes time and more than one ladling.

After 10 minutes of ladling, Diva dog decided she'd had just about enough to suit her. She did what dogs will do — braced herself and gave a mighty shake — sending skunk-stink-laden tomato juice all over the mud room — and all over her impatient handler.

Three more tins of tomato juice and a few shakes later, we both repaired to the in-house shower for a well-deserved shampoo and rinse. By 11:30 p.m. we were both blown dry. The faint odour of wet dog, skunk and baby shampoo still clung to the air. Just in case I missed a few spots, I sprayed myself with flowery cologne. Then on went the New Year's Eve clothes and, of course, the high heels.

I arrived at the neighbours' just in time for the final countdown. Then there came a tap on my shoulder.

"Guess there's no point in offering you a Bloody Mary," said a low, familiar male voice.

Sure enough, the man buying ice at the Becker's store turned out to be my neighbour's brother-in-law.

The woman next to him, another vaguely familiar face, offered me a glass of eggnog. Everyone at the party had heard the story about the lady in rags at the Becker's store who was buying gallons of tomato juice because a skunk had sprayed her dog.

Soon people were whacking me on the back so hard that I was tottering on my high heels before I'd even tippled. In the country, everybody has a dog-versus-skunk story to share.

Somewhere, I thought, there is a glittering party happening. Women in long dresses are dancing with elegant men and drinking champagne out of crystal glasses. In my dreams.

AN INVENTORY
OF MIXED BLESSINGS

On a farm, New Year's Day is traditionally Inventory Day, and if you do not start the day with a headache, you are headed for one by the end of it. I have resolved to getting the thing over with, and that is my only New Year's resolution. I like to think that my Uncle Ed, who was a real farmer all his life, would be proud to see me out there taking stock of the stock, counting bales of hay and straw and trying to assess grain tonnage.

The sheep have no idea why I spend a whole day in the barn with them, counting their heads. They do not understand about inventory. They are inventory. And sheep don't make New Year's resolutions. Why would they? They don't even know what year it is.

Ah, but if they could, I can think of a few things I would like them to work on as we coast toward the end of the millennium. For instance, maybe, just maybe, they could develop something approximating table manners instead of behaving like convicts at a prison riot when they see me coming with the grain bucket. And maybe they could pause to chew all of their hay and lick their lips clean before they put their muzzles in the water trough and muddle it with dried grasses that I have to scoop out by hand.

There are so many simple things that I wish they would consider changing. After all these years, you would think that they know that only three sheep at a time fit through the gate that leads to the barnyard, but every time the gate is opened five sheep try to jam through. It is not as though I am opening the door to paradise. Once they get to the other side, they generally all want to go back where they came from.

I know that sheep grow up with the notion that the whole world is their lavatory, but I do wish that they could consider controlling themselves when their wool is being sheared. And I do not understand why they think that they should all feel the call of nature whenever I get out the camera.

At least, sheep are never vicious. Even rams do not mean to flatten you when they decide to butt for no apparent reason. To them it is play, and let the shepherd beware.

But my wild tom turkey, Bourbon, has no excuse for attacking me. I wish he would resolve to stop treating me as a target.

I have known this bird since he was an egg. Bourbon was only a week old when he first pecked me, and he has not stopped trying for all of his four years. I have built him a split-level cage with perches high and low and a view of the fields that is as good as my own. I gave him a hen named Blanche to be his mate and friend. But if I so much as stroll by his pen . . .

When I replenish his feeder, I enter the pen with a garbage can lid to use as a shield. True to his breeding he goes wild — lashing out with wings so strong they can bruise. The pen door may be wide open, but Bourbon will not even try to fly to freedom as long as there is any possibility of putting a dent in me. When I clean his pen, I hustle him outside and he gobbles at the door, waiting to jump back in and attack me. He is too tough an old bird for me to resolve in the roast pan. So I will have to hope that Bourbon's millennial resolution involves turkey-shepherd detente.

You might expect some peace and quiet on a farm, but it does not work that way. I know a certain plumber who would probably like all of my guinea fowl to take a deep, permanent vow of silence.

Anything new or different — from a plumber to a gust of wind —sends guinea fowl into a cacophony of sound. They do not cluck softly like chickens or get it all over with in one great bellowing crow like roosters. Instead guineas have a shrill squawk, dominated by the females cackling, which sounds like a non-stop repetition of the word "buckwheat." Although I begged them to be quiet, those birds "buckwheated" for two solid hours while poor Tom the Plumber wrestled my water pipes into submission. A good plumber is harder to replace than a few guinea fowl.

In my perfectly resolved farm world, geese would not hiss or chase small children. Horses would never swat their tails near burdock bushes. Cats would play with dogs. Cows would resist the temptation of green apples and squirrels would eat the nuts they should have stored for winter instead of raiding the bird feeders.

Imperfection is nothing more than the nature of the beasts. The new year will see a whole new crop of everything on the farm — fresh starts at life and four whole seasons to make this year better than the last. Maybe I will widen the darn barnyard gate so that five sheep can fit through it, since it means so much to them. And maybe while I am taking inventory, I will take some time to count my blessings instead of sheep. That may be the best coping mechanism for a New Year's Day headache.

TRAINING TAFFY LOVELY

I had one of the errant dogs out on a leash the other day in an attempt to update long-forgotten dog obedience lessons. A passing Mennonite family pulled up their buggy to watch our antics from the roadway.

I have been known to pull up my truck to watch a Mennonite barn building or observe them in the fields with their horse-drawn ploughs, so I guess it shouldn't surprise me that they might also take the opportunity to observe the curious ways a former city person has of interpreting rural life.

In fact, I suspect it was the same buggy that paused a few years ago to watch me walking the piglet up and down the lane one frosty day. I hope they think that I have finally come to my senses and decided to train dogs instead of pigs.

The pig in question was only a few months old. A pink little girl pig named Taffy Lovely. She came to live with me to learn proper manners. It was nothing my life experience could have prepared me for.

When I lived in Toronto, the closest I ever managed to come to actual livestock was to observe the occasional chicken that tried to make a desperate escape from the late-lamented Stork's Poultry Market on Queen Street West. My altruistic 80s move to the country changed all that. I figured that I could manage raising a few sheep to break the solitude of a writerly lifestyle. After all, sheep are smaller than cattle, they do not kick or scratch and they only have front teeth on their lower jaw, so they cannot bite. What could be so difficult?

Soon I was adding chickens of my own. But I have always tried to keep the assorted livestock confined to their pastures and barn. This piglet was going to live with me, in my space, in the parlour where the Irish ghost of pioneer Tommy Noonan still holds euchre parties. It was all highly undignified.

Taffy was to become a "star." At least, she was to be used as a promotional pig for an entertainment magazine for swine breeders called *Playboar*, which was intent on entering the U.S. marketplace.

I had known the magazine's publisher, Tom Hagey, for quite some time. I was working as the editor of the "People" section of *Maclean's* magazine, when Hagey wandered into the offices one day wearing a pig nose and demanding to see "someone in authority." I'd just returned from an interview with Engelbert Humperdinck, so I guess the receptionist decided I could handle this guy.

My career has always been guided by the intervention of unique talents, and Hagey proved no exception. After I became the first editor to abandon a national newsmagazine in favour of sheep, *Playboar* invited me to freelance as its resident book reviewer of the Miss Piggy tomes, and as feature satirical writer on subjects such as "Hog Air Ballooning" and "Hogtoberfest."

So when the notion of training a promotional pig occurred, naturally I was called. After all, what does a shepherd have to do in the off-season except train a pig.

Without a bunch of newborn lambs to tend, or crops to harvest or hay to stack, the "off-season" is something I've learned to look forward to. But the challenge of playing Miss Manners to a sow was irresistible.

My pig-training instructions were quite clear. Taffy had to learn to walk gracefully on a leash tethered to a pink body halter. She had to enjoy being petted and respond favourably to having her picture taken. Tricks were not out of the question. I was assured that the generally sociable nature of pigs would see young Taffy Lovely literally begging to sit on my lap and snuggle within a few days. This was not correct information.

The pig was moved into a rubber-matted pen in my parlour. I was assured the intelligence of a pig was such that any piglet could be easily house-broken in several hours.

This was also not correct information.

Taffy confused my lap with a lavatory.

In the space of a very long week, I learned that a lot of things I had been told about pigs were totally untrue. At least, in the case of Taffy Lovely, stereotypes did not apply. She was nobody's Arnold Ziffle.

Taffy did not appreciate her comfy parlour pen. She vigorously applied herself to destroying it and she abused her squeaky toys mercilessly. Her idea of fun was to knock over her water bowl and squeal madly at 2 a.m.

She did not like to eat her pig chow while being held. In the lexicon of *Wayne's World*, she preferred to "hurl chunks." I tried coaxing her into proper etiquette with carrot sticks and slivered apples. Pig that she was, she quickly learned that emitting a deafening scream produced such tidbits to shut her up. In that regard, she was a quick study.

While training a dog involves making it fun for the dog to obey, training a hog as bull-headed as Taffy Lovely turned into a war of wits. Her halter, which was the same variety some parents use to tether agreeable toddlers, sent Taffy into hysterics. Asking her to walk calmly at my side rooted her miniature sow feet firmly to the ground.

After two weeks of trying, I was forced to admit that my best attempts at pig-training were a dismal failure and I had created a monstrous porcine brat.

Taffy was whisked off to complete her training with a "professional."

Within a few weeks, she was virtually performing cartwheels and smiling her pig smile on cue. By the time she arrived by plane for her debut in Chicago, she had flight attendants cuddling her and bringing her apples.

There was a full moon out, and from the sofa I could watch the wild rabbits as they grazed on the fallen sunflower seeds underneath the bird feeder next to the satellite dish. I tuned in *P.M. Magazine* to watch "my pig" on American television.

The cameras were rolling as she emerged from a limousine and toddled elegantly along a red carpet.

A star was born.

Taffy and her publisher were interviewed in their hotel suite. Hagey wore his trademark pig nose and she wore a lavender garter. Taffy oinked contentedly on his lap when the microphones turned her way.

But I knew that pig well enough to see a certain glimmer in her little pig eyes. Sure enough, Taffy still thought a lap was a lavatory.

NO AULD LANG SYNE

So far, after two decades on the farm, excepting matters of life and death, taking down the Christmas tree is the hardest thing I do every year. This follows with some logic, since putting the tree up is one of the hardest things I do at the end of each year.

I'm not saying that this year's tree was necessarily any larger or complex than in any other years. All of the trees that have graced the family room in the old farm house with its 14-foot-high ceiling have been at least a foot taller than the ceiling, causing the star at the top to loop sideways.

Decorating it is a two-day chore, and un-decorating takes an equally protracted time. I take it slowly, one branch at a time.

When it is all done, and the furniture is rearranged, I can truly say that I feel the New Year has arrived.

But this past year there was Wally the clown in a dog suit to contend with and perhaps some of the issues that marked my ill-fated leap from the hay mow.

The holiday season was an endless fascination to His Puppiness, with a seemingly constant stream of new visitors to lick into submission. But it was the Christmas tree that Wally liked the most of all. He would lie underneath it at the base, and stare up its trunk at the sparkling lights and baubles, mesmerized for hours.

When I began chopping the tree down, there was considerable puppy angst.

It would be convenient to be able to remove the Christmas tree neatly in one piece, but with such a large tree it is impossible.

Just getting the tree into the house involves removing windows and the use of pulleys and levers and at least six hands.

Such enthusiasm seldom prevails past the transformation of the turkey carcass into broth, let alone into the early weeks in January.

So I get out my hacksaw and gradually whittle the tree into a singular vertical log, removing light strands and ornaments as I go.

I had the first of the bottom branches removed before young Wally realized what was happening. The boughs were scattered on a white sheet beneath the tree that approximates "snow" and helps keep the fallen needles from clogging the vacuum.

At first he was merely bewildered. Then he began to howl. His face was now a mask of sorrow. If I didn't know better, I would have sworn there were tears beneath the triangles where his eyes live. I opened the window beside the tree and hurriedly shoved the branches outside. Immediately, Wally demanded to be let outside.

As he was bounding through a snow drift, I watched him grab a tinsel-covered branch and drag it steadfastly to a corner of the backyard which he has claimed as his own.

This went on all day long, resulting in a well-worn path speckled with spruce needles. At the end of it there lay a chaos of Christmas tree branches.

In the living room, the trunk of the once bountiful tree was all that remained of Christmas past. Wally whimpered at the base of the ladder when I slipped the star from its lopsided crowning branch. Whined big time when I took what remained of the tree out of the stand and lobbed it javelin-style out the window.

Under normal circumstances the detritus of the stale-dated Christmas tree would be stacked behind the wood pile for future burning or wood chipping. But for now it has new life as the playground for a Snoopy clone.

Wally spends hours rearranging the branches, jumping on them, crawling through them and shaking them vigorously. There is no *auld lang syne* for this tree.

Like the blackened sunflower stalks that still nod heavy-headed in the snow-covered garden, the piecemeal recycling of the old Christmas tree is a small reminder that what goes around, comes around.

Wally doesn't know that yet.

But I can't help thinking there are only 345 days, give or take a week, before we comb the forest for a new tree and rearrange the furniture for another holiday season.

That's how I start the New Year with a definitive, optimistic vision of its end already in sight. Whoever said "familiarity breeds contempt" must never have lived in the country.

THERE'S NO LOON IN MY SOUP

In the city, every kind of food seems to be available all year long. If there is a stalk of asparagus growing somewhere in the world in the middle of darkest January, some clever restaurateur will have it plucked, flown in and served on a big plate with a slice of lemon and a sprig of chervil. Roads can be closed, snow can be piled almost to the tops of telephone poles, but when you wander through an urban supermarket you can find a plump fennel bulb, an eggplant and cobs of sweet corn. But baby beets, bright red peppers, smooth white endive, even radishes that *schmeck* are items that do not turn up at my local produce counter in the middle of winter.

Sometimes it is a challenge trying to find lettuce in flavours other than iceberg.

Sure it is great in the summertime to announce to the world that you are "living out of the garden," but in the winter it is no fun to admit to a steady diet of root vegetables. Forget about chocolate eclairs — in the dark days of February my idea of a treat is pasta dressed with the tomato and basil sauce that I froze in the summer when the tomatoes were red and juicy instead of pink and rock hard.

On mornings when I find that ice rain has coated the tree branches like liquid crystal, I run to the freezer to cherish that last baggie of strawberries picked in July.

If I close my eyes, I can recall a sea of tight-curled fiddleheads growing at the edge of the forest, waving in a spring breeze. And wild leeks. Only in the gloom of winter can one possibly have positive thoughts about those pungent, lingering stink rods.

Call me a masochist, but during the winter-food doldrums my favourite nighttime reading is cookbooks. Oh please, tell me that someday I will make an arugula soufflé. Salsa, I can do that. I waft off to sleep savouring Julia Child's instructions on how to eat an artichoke. In my dreams, Mark Twain holds my hand and reminds me, "When one has tasted watermelon, he knows what the angels eat."

It is an event when something new appears at the produce counter. One week a pile of rock-hard avocados arrived. I could ripen them, I knew I could. *The Joy of Cooking* suggested putting them in a paper bag. Julia said room temperature. Someone else suggested burying them in flour overnight. I had frozen raspberries. I could make avocado with raspberry vinaigrette and crème fraîche! I tried all three ripening techniques and turned up mush.

Then one week came the ultimate food distraction. Neat little packages of bright green zucchinis perched beside cabbages. It is common knowledge that zucchini has virtually no taste. Julia simmers it in vermouth to jump-start some semblance of flavour. Still, if it was sautéed with garlic and onions and sprinkled with Parmesan cheese, it would make a feast.

But not at $3.99 a pound. I checked the label again. I checked the signage. It *was* $3.99 a pound. Zucchini is mostly water, for goodness' sake. I stood in awe, holding two zucchini with a price tag of $4.56.

It was Seniors' Day at the supermarket. The bus was parked outside, and the free coffee was brewing across from the deli counter. An elderly lady next to me was busily squeezing the wax off a turnip.

"The zucchini is $3.99 a pound," I said, still stunned. I showed her the package.

Another couple of oldsters came along and we all joined carts in the worship and wonder of the $3.99 per pound zucchini.

"You can't give them away in the summer," tsskd the lady in a blue coat with a Persian lamb collar.

"Don't even know how to cook 'em," said a sprightly geezer in a lumberjack jacket.

The young fellow who rotates the cucumbers in the produce section came along and we asked him if there had been an error.

"I always spell zucchini wrong," he said and he took away the sign for correction.

By this time, a thousand years' worth of citizens had congregated at the produce counter.

"If we plant the seeds, maybe we could all afford to retire," said one gnomish woman with a perm so tight that it looked like a Chia pet.

We started giggling. Then we were laughing. Someone tried to steady themselves on the grapefruits and the whole lot came tumbling down. By the time the produce manager came back with his revised spelling, the guy in the lumberjack jacket was trying to auction off Brussels sprouts to the highest bidder and the turnip squeezer was juggling woody parsnips and humming "Yes, We Have No Bananas."

Finally, we all went back to shopping. Nobody bought zucchini.

On the way home, I remembered an odd recipe I found in *The Eskimo Cookbook*. Under the heading "Loon Soup" it said simply, "Do not make loon soup. "

Sometimes, even when food is fresh and available, it is just not worth it.

SOLVING A CLEAR AND PRESENT DANGER

Birds and glass are an unnatural combination, but every winter they are bound to meet with disastrous results, usually for the birds. The resident chickadees, blue jays, nuthatches and cardinals consider the bird feeders their personal fast food drive-thru. They know where the outdoors ends and the glass begins on the windows that overlook their feeders. It is the newcomers and migrating flocks touching down for a quick feed who tend to confront glass head-on.

The sound of a bird hitting glass is distinctive — a dull thump rather than a crash. Sometimes the crasher flies off before it can even be located. Other times there is a period of head shaking and a general shutdown of birdlike activity, as though the creature is checking to see if all systems are still a "go."

A barn owl once shot clear through a friend's garage window and it spent the whole day regrouping in an old laundry basket. His Wiseness's only movement was the

rotation of his head to observe his host's every movement. After a day at the recuperation station, he flew away.

Victims of head-on window collisions are not always
so fortunate. With the exception of installing STOP signs
over the exterior of the house, it seemed impossible to
warn the birds without cluttering up the view of them. I
knew that they were not banging into the window because
they wanted to watch television. It was just a matter of
finding some way to warn them that they could understand at a distance.

Oddly, the solution was an owl — a huge, stuffed
horned owl posed in mid-air with its talons in attack mode
and its wings spread. Even birds who pal with owls
would have to find this thing as scary as Jabba the Hut.

A taxidermist who lives in the North had stuffed the
road-killed beauty for practice. Transferring the bird to
me involved letters of permit and all sorts of administrative jumble. In this country, it may be easier to keep grandfather stuffed on the couch collecting pension cheques
than it is to put an accidentally deceased bird of prey in
a window to ward off headaches in juncos.

The owl is perched at the side of one window on top
of a stereo speaker, a stance it would hardly take in real
life. Still, even the sunflower-seed-crazed blue jays kept
their distance until finally it filtered through their bird
brains that the owl was not moving, not going anyone's
way, neither a fellow traveller nor a threat to the niger
seed.

The owl certainly gives newcomers pause. When
migrating flocks come through, the leader is generally
wary enough to scout the zone and spot the owl. Instead

of grazing within its "sight," they choose the feeders at the side of the house, where the windows are smaller and much easier to identify. It is a win-win situation.

The natural habitat of birds does not include plastic gazebos filled with food and rendered lard does not sprout seeds of its own accord. However, in the popular culture of birds, anything containing seeds or suet is as obvious in the landscape as an Inuit *inukshuk* marking a route once travelled. Survival accommodates unnatural combinations.

Come to think of it, I never in my wildest dreams ever imagined that I would be dusting a dead owl in my living room to ward off thumps on the windows.

THE CAT NOT DEAD

Sometimes when I am out in the garden in the summer time, I find that Webster the Cat is lying under a zucchini leaf or curled up in the middle of the parsley.

"Are you dead yet, Cat?" I ask.

And then slowly, remembering the languors of youth, he stretches and gets along. The old cat has no new tricks.

And when I say old, I mean it.

Webster is at least eighteen, twice the years that even a nine-lives cat often averages. In cat years to human years ratio terms, he is Methuselah — well over 120.

While he was once a sleek black kitten, Webster is now about as gnarly a cat as anyone has ever seen.

A fine long tail was reduced to a stump years ago by the fan belt of the truck.

His slender ears bear the ragged edges of his years of confrontations with local tomcats and puppies.

His main frame has been buffeted by rams, kicked by cows, tumbled under horses hooves and grazed by every-thing from Corvettes to manure spreaders.

When he runs, the right side of his body leads and the rest hops after it.

A lump of scar tissue on his belly, where he was once shot clear through by an arrow, has become a sort of talisman that he loves to have rubbed.

When he purrs, his nose scrunches up, revealing fang-like incisors and worn molars. His claws are sharp, but he seldom uses them for defence purposes. When I watch him rolling around on his back in the sun on a pile of warm earth, punching his arthritic legs at the clouds like a geri-atric prize fighter, I wonder where on earth he gets his stamina.

Stretched out flat like a lizard in the middle of the lane way, Webster looks like a stray piece of wood. But when I call out, "Are you dead yet, Cat?" he creaks to life, if only to turn his head and give me a glimpse of a single crooked fang.

There's not much meat left on those bones, yet Webster's tiny belly is like a bottomless pit.

As a young cat, he lived on dry kibble and an abundance of eggs. If he wanted fresh meat, he caught it himself in the form of barn vermin — mice, rats, the occasional chipmunk, even rabbits.

But dry kibble presents a challenge to Webster's aging choppers. So now, his super-deluxe, getting on in age formula, veterinary marked-up kibble is soaked in home-made chicken and lamb broth. I freeze some stock for him every time I make soup.

He gets meaty table scraps and his eggs are scrambled in milk. He loves turkey dressing and peanut butter cookies.

Webster enjoys feasts that could quell a prison riot, but none of it seems to stick to his ribs. After he eats, his stomach is round, but that's as far as it goes. His bony, cow-hocked back legs have trouble keeping up with his pigeon-toed front legs and he moves like a little old man whose pants are falling down.

Last winter, I thought he was a goner for sure.

In the throes of an ice storm that made walking any-where a treachery, Webster disappeared for two days. For all I knew, he could have slid down a rabbit hole. Sending out a search party wasn't practical. Moose was away on business, and it was up to me to hold the fort.

The next day, I found Webster curled on his quilted barn bed, fringed in icicles.

"Are you dead yet, Cat?" I called, fearing the worst.

One scrawny back leg gave a kick and I moved closer to pet him. He lifted his head and I drew my hand back.

Normally, Webster's head is like the size of a mid-season potato, but it had mushroomed to twice its size.

Crested between his ears was a huge boil, an abscess that stretched his skin taut. His amber eyes only half opened and he made a pitiful meow.

It was a Sunday. The roads were closed due to ice. Phone lines were down, hydro often flickered. I set up a heat lamp over Webster and dried him off slowly with the old hair dryer I keep in the barn for use at lambing time. He barely moved.

The storm was in full swing, howling wind and freez-ing rain. I crawled back to the house on all fours in my snowsuit, it was that slippery. Then I pondered what to do.

Seeing the old cat in so much pain was hardly bear-able, but I didn't have it in me to shoot Webster. There had to be another way. I decided to give him an hour to warm up while I formulated a plan.

I knew that if I was similarly afflicted, the doctor would have me on antibiotics. Although I keep injectable antibiotics on the farm for just such extraordinary circum-stances involving the sheep, there didn't seem enough of Webster left to inject.

In the refrigerator, I found half a dozen antibiotic cap-sules left over from one of Moose's long-ago tooth-aches. I scrambled an egg into a tin of tuna and sprinkled a third of a capsule into the mix, topping it with warm milk.

I have always found that if even the sickest animal has the will to eat, there is potential for recovery. My hope was in the Tupperware container that I tucked into my snowsuit for the long crawl back to the barn.

Webster was dry and warm. His favourite rooster had joined him under the heat lamp. I propped the cat up on his elbows and presented "the cure." Sure enough, he lifted his swollen head and lapped up the warm, fishy drug-laced gruel. Then he fell back on the quilt and curled his paws over his face in a deep sleep. Any thought I had about moving him into the house vanished. Webster needed to be in his element, with the smells he knew, and the sounds of the sheep and the storm, and the comfort of his rooster.

I worried that I might have overdosed the cat.

I worried that I might not have given him enough.

Before I went to bed, I crawled out to the barn again, this time through a foot of wet snow. Webster drank his fill of warm medicated milk. Then he dropped back into a deep sleep.

The next morning, the sun shone and the ice-coated landscape sparkled dangerously.

Wally the Wonder Dog shot out the front door. He slid across the lane like a greased medicine ball. When I hunkered down for the ritual barn crawl, Wally tried to hitch a ride on my back and we both splatted on all fours. There is a sense of total unreality that falls over you when both you and your dog are lying on a sheet of ice, looking up at the winter sun.

Wally started licking the chest of my snowsuit. That's when I remembered where I had tucked the Tupperware container with a cat breakfast of beef stew, egg, warm milk and drugs. The crawl back to the house was soggy.

When I finally got into the barn, after reconstituting the cat's food and hacking the ice off the barn door, the sheep shared their greetings. While they baaed, I raced to find Webster, hopefully, not dead yet. And he wasn't.

Again he ate heartily. Before he dropped back to sleep, I held his bloated head and stared into his amber eyes. Webster was still in there.

The storm stopped two days later. Early that morning I prepared a list of supplies I needed in town and contemplated calling the vet about Webster.

When I went to the barn, the sheep were bright with anticipation of spending time outdoors. Webster was gone.

At the back of the shed, I found tiny cat footprints that headed into a field. I imagined him dragging himself out across the snow, like some ancient Eskimo relieving his family of further responsibility.

Then I felt badly because, after all those years, I wanted the responsibility and I felt Webster was cheating me out of seeing him through the final transition.

Well, Webster doesn't disappoint. When I came home from town, he was back under the heat lamp. He jumped to his feet when I came through the door. The lump on his head was substantially gone and he wanted more of my special gruel. Once Webster chowed down, I examined his furry skull and found a festered puncture wound, probably from an encounter with a neighbouring tomcat that had gone badly.

Later, when I held him, bathing the crater in his head and dressing the damaged area, Webbie purred with the vigour of days gone by.

Then he rolled on his quilt, contorting himself into a shape worthy of a yogi.

"You're not dead yet, are you, Cat?" I said, and Webster yawned.

The cat healed nicely. His rooster went back to his roost. In the barnyard, Webster followed me around, picking his way through the snow like a dainty spider.

One of these days, Webster will make transit into the realm of memory. But I wouldn't bet that it will necessarily be any time soon.

In the meantime, if he wants to spend his summer days curled up in the parsley, or underneath the sunflowers where he can watch the blue jays, I say, more power to him.

The amber eye of this barn cat has seen a lot of things, and he's still in there.

MAXIMUM BLUE JAY

Country living is definitely for the birds. And I mean that literally.

I have been feeding the birds for years — starting with one battered bird feeder and expanding to five that vary from rustic barn-style imitations to high-tech, Plexiglass models and homemade suet holders.

The feeders are scattered throughout the bare branches of a huge lilac bush right outside the living room window, and the display of activity is non-stop. There is no set feeding schedule. The birds just come and go from dawn till dusk.

No doubt about it, the birds have figured me for a mark. Every spring I plant rows of sunflowers that grow to great nodding heights. I have yet to harvest any seeds, however, because the birds always beat me to it. Once the sunflowers are plucked, I begin to rely on the feed mill for a variety of seeds, and by mid-winter the birds are generally up to 40 kilograms per month.

Which brings me to my concern about a bird I have come to know as "Maximum Blue Jay."

This bountiful bird lives in the cedar and birch trees near a small marsh. I suspect that the only exercise he takes is the short flight to and from the feeder. Considering his paunch, I am sometimes surprised he can render himself airborne after gorging on sunflower seeds. Once I watched Maxi try to take a brief stopover on the upper branches of a craggy old apple tree, but then the bough bent under his weight, causing great hysteria among the resting sparrows.

None of the other birds are overly plump. The chickadees who play and eat constantly seem to stay roundly sleek and the nuthatches are still trim enough to perch sideways on a branch without falling prey to gravity.

Finches, juncos, wrens, cowbirds and grosbeaks all visit the feeders at various times in their migrations. A variety of woodpeckers cavort on the suet balls. One year a robin startled me in February. It is only Maximum Blue Jay who finds it difficult to take a seat on the sunflower seed feeder and enjoy a mannerly meal. Lately his girth has become such a problem for the bird that he simply pauses to tip sunflower seeds on the ground where he plops down to eat in comfort. Frankly, I think Maxi is becoming an embarrassment even to his brother and sister blue jays.

Since they're relatively large birds and feisty by nature, the jays generally take control of the feeders when they swoop in to feed, relegating the smaller species to eat tiny seeds until their departure. The jays particularly enjoy scattering the more timid cardinals. However, Maximum Blue Jay has a tendency to ignore the other birds and concentrate on eating while they defend the territory.

Regulating feed in farm animals is a relatively simple thing to do. If a few ewes bulk up beyond a reasonable level, I can isolate them and cut back on their grain just enough so that they return to a healthy level of fitness. If I want a good plump chicken, two or three weeks of additional corn works wonders. But there just doesn't seem to be any way to work Weight Watchers on a wild bird that is determined to empty the trough.

Perhaps Maxi is the first wave of a strain of mutant wild birds, the off-spring of generations of feathered friends that have grown accustomed to the comfort of full feeders in winter. If that is indeed the case, it should be no time before my feeders spawn eggplant-sized chickadees and beefsteak buntings. I might have to reinforce the old lilac bush and add platforms to the feeders.

This may be the beginning of a trend. If Maximum Blue Jay claims a mate this spring, it could be the start of something much bigger.

I should notify the feed mill in advance. Ultimately, there may just be an emerging marketplace for sunflower seed "Lite."

IN PRAISE OF
LONG UNDERWEAR

One of the things you don't worry much about on a farm is keeping up with current fashion. A good suit might help when you're making your case to the bank, but it's not going to get you very far in the barn.

Occasionally I will glance in a full-length mirror before heading out to do my chores, and everything I see confirms that the only fashion statement I am making in the dead of winter is keeping warm.

In contemporary terms, you could call it Country Grunge.

It really doesn't matter to the sheep if I look like the Pillsbury Dough Boy in my snowsuit. The chickens don't even blink a baleful eye at my hat with the earflaps and the lopsided toque I wear on top. If I wear mitts of different colours, the horses will not shun me, and my clunky old felt-lined boots may look like something from a construction site tag sale, but they have a lot of sole when it comes to maneuvering on ice.

Of course, when you are working with animals and spending a lot of time living in their barnyard environment, you must resign yourself to the fact that at least your outer layer of clothing is bound to pick up the odours and even the evidence of animals. Somehow there is always one lone chicken roosting in the barn rafters who manages (or maybe plots) a direct plop somewhere on my toque or torso. And sheep anticipating grain are fairly direct about cuddling up to the person holding the bucket.

The horses are the same. They have no compunction about taking a great drink from their water bucket and then turning to wipe their dripping lips on me while I'm combing their tangled manes.

Outerwear takes a beating on the farm, but the backbone of any rural winter wardrobe has got to be underwear. Specifically, long underwear.

When I lived in the city, I did not even think about long johns, but in the country a woman that's without long underwear is nothing more than a popsicle waiting to happen. And until I got to the country I had no idea of the variety of long underwear that is available. I had a cartoon concept of a one-piece sort of uniform with a trap door in the back that never seemed quite practical for the female form.

Today there is state-of-the-art long underwear. Two-piece long underwear, colour co-ordinated long underwear, and long underwear that Madonna might consider if she ever plays Antarctica. There's combed cotton long underwear and pure wool long underwear. Long underwear printed with little snowflakes on it. Long underwear with lace trim. Slithery, silk long underwear and denim checkered long underwear.

You've got medium-weight long underwear for cold days and expedition-weight long underwear for really cold days. On days when it's so cold that one pair of long underwear just won't do, there is puffy down insulated long underwear to layer over top.

You can even find catalogues with huge sections devoted to long underwear. They sell underwear that "wicks" moisture away from your body, and underwear that comes with two layers so you don't have to dress yourself twice.

The most fascinating concept to date is something called the "heat strip body warmer." This appears to consist of some sort of space-age material that you wrap over your naked body, securing it with ties at the waist or wherever else you please. You plug this into a portable battery pack that you wear while the "strip" keeps you as warm as a Montserrat suntan.

Of course, you wear a layer of clothing over the heat strip lest you be mistaken for a crazed nudist, or Madonna playing Antarctica. The advertising says it's a "chill killer," but somehow I'd rather put my trust in long underwear any day — it never needs recharging.

Long underwear is like socks, you can layer them on and layer them off. You can't do that with pantyhose and bustiers. And since only you know what's really underneath, there's something simply sexy about long underwear.

I try to keep that in mind when I look in the mirror.

ALWAYS OVERESTIMATE THE INTELLIGENCE OF SHEEP

When I went to the University of Guelph to study sheep raising, one of the first things the instructor told the class was to always overestimate the intelligence of sheep. He was right.

Today, as I braved a snowstorm to pile forks full of hay into the outdoor feeders, I found one ewe standing quietly inside one of the feeders.

How the sheep got herself in there I do not know. The feeders are four feet tall and meticulously designed to allow only the head of the sheep to enter the feeder. But there she was, and all I had to do was check the tattoo in her ear to confirm that one-year-old Gertrude had reached new heights of ruminant lunacy.

You would think that if she got into a feeder by herself, she ought to be able to get out. Not so.

Gertrude could not budge even when the rest of the flock was being fed grain which generally makes a sheep contort itself into extremely odd postures just for a nibble.

Under normal circumstances, I should have been able to just gently tip the feeder over on its side and send her gamboling off. However, the feeder was lodged in ice.

I would estimate that Gertrude has got about 60 pounds on me, but that didn't stop me from leaping into the octagonal feeder and trying to lift her over front feet first. I could get her front legs poised at the edge. But, when it came to hoisting her rump, Gertrude responded by collapsing her hind end like a full sack of wool at my ankles.

I reasoned that she must have bounded up into the feeder with a running start. Getting out would require some form of staircase.

Operating on this theory, I tried to squash a bale of hay into the feeder to give her the height she needed to step to freedom.

Wrong. The bale could not squeeze in beside Gertrude and leave her any space. To complicate matters, the addition of hay to the feeder attracted other sheep who decided they should eat over, around and above the enclosed Gertrude. I managed to rescue the bale of hay, but not my toque, which Gertrude immediately decided to use as a foot warmer.

I tried levering the feeder loose with my trusty crowbar. After 15 minutes of bench-pressing the ice-encrusted feeder full of Gertrude, I felt it shift. Triumphant, I raised the crowbar above my head and let out a whoop to no one in particular.

This attracted the notice of the old ram, who has — for all intents and purposes — been fairly passive. But there's always a first time.

Out of the corner of my eye, I saw him charging. I had just enough time to dive un-toqued head first into the feeder with Gertrude. When you find yourself trapped in a hay feeder with a belligerent ram circling you and an immovable ewe standing with one foot in your hat and the other on your foot, the only thing to do is scream internally. No point in exciting the situation more than it already is. Once the ram lost interest, I literally crept out of the feeder and sidestepped my way to the closest fence.

It was time to involve technology.

I pulled up the truck, turned the lights on and cranked up a rowdy Hank Williams Jr. tape. The impact of this was enough to cause even the ram to back off as I leapt over the fence with a hook and a logging chain to tie onto the Gertrude-bound feeder. Scrambling back over the fence, I tied the chain to the bumper and put all four wheels into a slow reverse.

Through the flying snow I watched the feeder shift and, ever so gently, tip over despite Gertrude's attempts to counterbalance it.

So there was the feeder, tipped on its side. Such is the intelligence level of sheep that, instead of backing out to freedom, Gertrude was joined in the sideways feeder by another sheep with an identical I.Q. After a few blasts on the truck horn, they finally wandered out together.

As I disassembled my chains and fished my cap out of the feeder, I really had to wonder whether the intelligence of the shepherd is something that should not also be overestimated.

DEEP DITCH BAMBI

There is a sign on the roadway warning, "This Road Is Used By Horse-Drawn Buggies."

That is a courtesy to the Mennonite community, who travel the route regularly to get to town. The problem is that it also attracts warm-weather tourists who sometimes tour the road trying to get a look at the "buggy people." It can be kind of embarrassing for all concerned.

One sign we could use on the road is a warning that the entire route is a deer crossing in winter.

At dawn and dusk, the deer are on the move. I know that they have a path through the wildest part of my forest. It comes out near the mailbox. I have watched them pause there, before they fade back into the forest like grey-brown ghosts.

Sometimes I will be out walking with the dog and she will get a whiff of them and take off on a tear. Not to worry, in snow she is not even fast enough to catch a three-legged groundhog. Often, there is no warning at all. A rustle through the trees is followed by the twang of a fence wire as the deer bound over it. I like knowing that the deer are out there. The problem is they do not know how to cross a road, or when.

Almost every week, the local newspaper reports on some sort of confrontation between a deer and a vehicle. Like rabbits, deer will freeze when they are caught in headlights. On slick roads, a sudden stop can become a doughnut that leads straight into the ditch.

If the deer runs off before this happens, the ditch is still a danger. Where one white-tail crosses, more are sure to follow. Many times, I have watched one, two, three cross safely well in advance of an oncoming car, only to have a fourth scared young doe leap out of the ditch at the last minute, raising everyone's blood pressure.

In blinding snow, the phenomenon becomes particularly heart-stopping. I was rounding the corner on the final few hundred feet of a messy drive home, when I checked the passenger window and saw the haunting figure of a big buck barrelling in my direction to avoid a snowmobile that was closing in on him.

Velvet nose, frightened eyes, a swirl of antlers and snowflakes and he was gone. I cannot say which of us was more shaken by the experience. Windshields and antlers can be a nasty combination.

I guess driving a horse and buggy might give me more time to watch for the warning signs of wildlife at the road's edge. Certainly, if I tried to make the trip to town on a throbbing snowmobile, I would be hard-pressed to see anything except the occasional backside of a deer. There must be an in-between ground that we can all live with so that Bambi does not become a road warrior, or a road kill.

Deep in the forest, there is a spot where I know that deer gather. It is called "yarding up," and you can tell that they have been there by the flattened snow, the tracks and the droppings.

I can understand why they like the spot. The place is hard to find, but it is sheltered. When the sun filters down, the dapple of light creates all sorts of shadows to hide in.

I do not want to alter the course of nature, but I also have no desire to collide with it. So, I put salt licks in the deer yard. That way, the deer do not have to scavenge for whatever tasty minerals might be lurking in the sand that is occasionally laid on the roadway. Deer prefer the small, sweeter white licks that feedstores sell for bunnies. Some stores even have elaborate apple-flavoured concoctions for deer. With great difficulty, the Moose and I managed to roll a big bale of hay close to the path that the deer take to the yard, but far out of sight.

I never expect the deer to stay there all winter without moving, and I never let down my guard when I am driving. Occasionally, I find some roadside evidence of a path that they frequent. When I hear a giant tree creak in the forest, I imagine some buck is rubbing against it. At night, I search the fenceline for the glow of their emerald eyes in the barnyard lights.

When spring comes, and the tourists start stalking the Mennonites in their buggies, the deer will have vanished from the roadways. They will become grazing silhouettes on the fringe of the forest — almost imperceptible, almost back to the wilderness.

EVERYBODY GETS THE FEVER

Around the middle of winter, the fever generally strikes. Cabin fever that is.

I don't recall it happening when I lived in the city, where I could call a taxi to take me to the airport on a moment's notice, or stroll into a cinema and have an instant choice of movie gratification, or dial a pizza when the cupboard was bare.

Life is different in the country, even when you've got your fax and your modem working, and all the folks on the Home Shopping Network want to be your friend.

There are days when the roads are quite simply closed. Days when the only external sounds you hear are the cackles of blue jays, the thunder of faraway snowmobiles, and the insistent baaing, mooing, neighing and crowing of livestock waiting to be fed.

There is splendour in such isolation, but too much of anything can make anyone go a bit loopy.

Even my stoic Mennonite neighbours get a feeling of cabin fever.

The other day I was driving along a snow-covered road when I noticed some strange tracks at the roadside. I discovered the contraption responsible for them was a horse-drawn buggy with a difference. A tow rope was rigged behind the buggy and the Mennonites were taking turns "skiing" from the back on a piece of cardboard!

It can strike anywhere, any time. So when I find myself lugging frozen logs from the wood pile and stripping off layers of snow-wet barn clothes while a blizzard rages outside, it does not surprise me to find my thoughts drifting into the unlikely realm of what sort of evening gown I would wear to the opera.

Wondering whether the Home Shopping Network sells Vanna White endorsed tiaras is a sure sign of the onset of cabin fever.

However, most of my symptoms manifest themselves physically.

One year I got out the stepladder and tried to clean the exterior windows in mid-winter.

Another year I bought some cement and tried sculpting a birdbath in the basement.

Last year I attempted to install new chicken wire around the old coop during a snowstorm.

This year the indicators have been more subtle, but the diagnosis is definitive.

For example, I have accumulated six tins of anchovies in the pantry. I believe I must have been dreaming about summer days when the romaine is at its sweetest and a Caesar salad is called for. Or perhaps I am subconsciously stockpiling in the event of an invasion by a desalinated foreign power.

I do not even like anchovies.

I have the mail delivery timed to within five minutes, and I read every speck of it thoroughly, including the pale ink on the back of my bank statements and all flyers. On clear days I have contemplated driving 30 miles to buy a laundry hamper on sale.

I have ransacked the tour package catalogue rack at the local travel agency, and devoted myself to analyzing destinations, prices, likelihood of tornadoes and vaccination requirements. I am not going anywhere.

I seriously thought about ordering a pair of pink pedal pushers from the Home Shopping Network. And I have considered calling one of those 900 numbers to find out what any person could possibly say that would be worth five dollars per minute. In lieu of that, I painted my toenails shocking red.

These things, plus finding myself wandering through the barnyard gyrating wildly to old Rolling Stones tunes, led me to confirm a cabin fever diagnosis.

In my case, the cure is multi-faceted. One of these days I will leap on the bus and head for Toronto, which we up-country types call "the Big Smoke."

I will go to a hair stylist for a spruce up and catch up on what is "hip" by observing the shampoo person's fashion statement. I will buy some naughty underwear and try on hats. I will have lunch with my urban girlfriends — which will confirm for me that I could never go back to a desk job or apply that much makeup daily ever again.

On the home front, one of my favourite remedies is to take a course. So far, I have studied marine navigation, firearm safety and the art of deboning a turkey. This year I think it will be fly-fishing. The mail is a cure in itself.

I have a drawer full of seed catalogues that started arriving before Christmas. Plans must be made and orders placed. Soon packets of giant pumpkin seeds and variegated French green beans and exotically named Chinese vegetables will arrive.

I have already set up my potting bench and gathered the old pots and trays. In a couple of weeks every window ledge will be sprouting with something and the smell of earth and growing things will make any ice storm bearable.

I don't know if city folks contract cabin fever, or if it is possible in the midst of all those buildings to notice that sundown is taking longer to come every day.

I guess cabin fever can strike anywhere.

This year my remedy for anyone who finds themselves stockpiling anchovies for no apparent reason and wearing red toenail polish with no place to go is fairly simple.

First, order a seed catalogue. Then keep your eye open for sales on hip waders and oil your fishing reel.

Get a haircut and gyrate wildly to the Rolling Stones or whatever moves you while wearing spicy underclothes and a new hat.

It works every time for me.

SPRING WILL BE SPRUNG

When it is time for winter to be over, I do not need a groundhog to give me a date. Every living thing seems to have an opinion.

I was at the Holstein Feed Mill the other day. It is as much a place about "what's going on?" as "what are you going to feed the pigs?" One of the senior farmers was holding court next to a pile of blue salt licks that lined the wall and made a perfect jumping ground for half a dozen calico kittens.

"March is going to be a cold one," he announced.

I shivered in my toque.

"But in April we'll all be wearing shorts," he said, confidently, digging his hands deep in his pockets and lowering his chin to his collar.

Good news at last. I had visions of greening fields and planting early radishes, peas, onions and carrots. I rushed home and started the tomatoes in a flat beside the sunniest window in the house.

Animals tell you when the season is going to turn. My gaggle of geese is never about to keep quiet when they feel a change coming on. They are out there falling in love left, right and centre. It is a hissing and honking ritual that hardly smacks of the poetry of love, but the ganders are gradually staking their claim to the females. One old layer is already gathering materials for her nest.

As the days get longer, the chickens start laying eggs. Nothing organized, mind you. Every once in a while I will pull a bale of hay from the top of the pile and an egg will drop. Sometimes it's a freshly laid egg, so I scramble to catch whatever I can before it scrambles itself.

I might get a touch of cabin fever waiting for the weather to break, but so does the livestock.

I once had a Hereford cow named Hazel who gave birth to her calf in a snowbank in the middle of winter. A month later, she took off over the fields with the little guy at her heels and ended up camping out beside a dairy barn.

"I think she needs the bull," said the Mennonite man who found her.

That is a sure sign of spring.

When old Lady the horse gets bored, I take her out for a walk to the end of the lane. Then her daughter Karma wants the same change of scenery. Both of them greet me each day like anxious puppies waiting to see what new "activity" I have planned for them. If they are lucky enough to be at the bottom of the lane when the snowplough goes by, it makes their day.

Once the ice melts, I can take them on trail rides. It will not be long, because when I groom them, handfuls of their shaggy winter coats come out in the brushing, but I am still wearing long johns.

In the meantime, I can get a head start on renovating a little pasture where a few ancient apple trees still provide a bounty of fruit. It is a hilly and bumpy plot of ground, too rough for regular ploughing. So, I go out and toss clover seed on the snow, in the hopes that a spring thaw will take the seed down into the earth and add a touch of goodness for the sheep to chew on in the fall.

"Frost seeding," they call it at the feed mill. It is hard to believe that such tiny seeds can survive in such miserably cold weather, but doing it makes me feel better. And "I'm Looking Over a Four-Leaf Clover" sounds great on the old kazoo.

When March comes in like a lion and goes out like a lamb, it means I am headed straight into an April that is filled with lambs. The sheep grow round and full with a bounty of babies. Through it all, there is a delightful calming that comes over them, balancing the constant honking antics of the hormone-crazed geese and the anxious prancing of the horses.

I can accept that to every season there is a time and a purpose. But just in case the farmer at the feed mill is right, I have been nosing through the summer clothes. When the warm day dawns that I can wear shorts again, I will be ready.

MAPLE MEMORIES

Once there was a four-storey-tall maple tree in the centre of my pasture on a high knoll overlooking the barnyard.

It was a straight and majestic tree. In the summertime the sheep would cluster at its giant base. Cows and horses would rub against its rough bark. In the spring huge flocks of crows gathered in its branches. In the fall flocks of Canada geese swept over the tops of its branches so closely that the beating of their wings would cause its gold and red leaves to flutter to the ground. In the winter its stark outline stood against the backdrop of snow, and occasionally I would find it coated in ice, glistening in the morning sun.

Two years ago the tree was struck by lightning during a brutal storm. It was night and I was alone with the dogs. The thunder clapped so loudly that the windows rattled. Forks of lightning streaked the sky. Outside, the yard was lit up like a movie set. When I saw a fork hit the ground in my garden less than 100 feet from my kitchen table, I put on my rubber boots.

Grandmother once told me she was peeling potatoes during a lightning storm when a bolt landed outside her window and shot through the wall of the farmhouse and right across the floor to where she was standing. Lucky for her, she had just come in from the garden as the storm began and was still wearing her rubber boots. Science may disprove it, but she always claimed those rubber boots saved her life — and I always feel better if I can ride out a storm in my faithful Wellingtons.

At the peak of the storm, the hydro went out. While I was tripping over the dogs in the dark looking for matches to light the candles, a huge flash illuminated the barnyard.

I just caught a glimpse of the lightning as it was zapping the old maple tree. The light was unearthly — shades of purple and blue against silvery-green leaves. The ground seemed to quiver, and along with the constant thunder I could hear a great moaning creak coming from the tree. In the morning I discovered that the lightning had hit the tree at its crown.

All summer long the tree kept all its leaves. In the autumn the leaves turned to burnished gold and only in the winter did the damage become truly apparent. Stripped of its leaves, the lightning-cracked branches were easy to see — hanging awkwardly amid the sturdy limbs.

That spring a few leaves unfurled on one side of the tree, but the rest was bare. I knew in my heart of hearts that the tree was slowly dying. A dead tree can be a dangerous thing, unstable on the ground and disquieting to all who view it. So I called John the Tree Cutter.

John emerged from his truck with a chainsaw that would have been the envy of old Leatherface, the antihero of the *Texas Chainsaw Massacre*. Two men anchored a rope while John sawed into the base of the big tree, taking out wedges of wood carefully to ensure that it would fall without damaging fences or lives. At one point the chainsaw was silenced when a change in the wind rocked the tree backward and it sank on the saw. The men were greatly concerned about recovering their chainsaw, but I saw it as a sign of lingering character from the tree. It would not go down easy and it would go down at its own speed.

I watched the tree finally fall. I cannot remember the sound. Men were running. Suddenly there seemed to be a gaping space in the sky. John the Tree Cutter carved the tree into firewood, but I saved a big slab of it to use as a garden stool.

It hurts me to see the stump in the pasture. On summer nights the sheep still crowd around it to sleep and the lambs use it as a jumping platform in the moonlight. The horses have transferred their affections to a younger maple which I had not paid much attention to before, but it seems to be a tree with potential.

This winter, I am bidding my final farewell to the grand old maple tree. When I look for a huge and heavy hunk of wood to keep me warm all night long, I turn to the place in the woodpile where I shed a few tears while stacking its fresh-cut limbs.

The wood is dry now. Cracks splinter the great rings where sap once flowed. At night, I fill the woodstove with maple and sleep in comfort. In the morning, all that is left are embers.

It takes more years than I have left in this life to grow a four-storey maple tree, but it takes only a quick month of winter chill to reduce such singular beauty to ashes. I think that in the spring I will go back into the woods and find a suitable sapling to plant beside the weathered stump. The knoll deserves another fine tree, and perhaps one day the tree that I plant will bring as much pleasure to those who view its grandeur as my departed maple gave to me.